The Perfectly Competitive Market

The Perfectly Competitive Market:

A Pinnacle in the Development of the Laws of Classical Economics

By

Igor Golod

Translated by Yuri Lukyanov

Cambridge Scholars Publishing

The Perfectly Competitive Market:
A Pinnacle in the Development of the Laws of Classical Economics

By Igor Golod

This book first published 2021

Cambridge Scholars Publishing

Lady Stephenson Library, Newcastle upon Tyne, NE6 2PA, UK

British Library Cataloguing in Publication Data
A catalogue record for this book is available from the British Library

ISBN (10): 1-5275-6949-7
ISBN (13): 978-1-5275-6949-2

TABLE OF CONTENTS

It deserves to be remarked, perhaps, that it is in the progressive state, while the society is advancing to the further acquisition, rather than when it has acquired its full complement of riches, that the condition of the labouring poor, of the great body of the people, seems to be the happiest and the most comfortable. It is hard in the stationary, and miserable in the declining state. The progressive state is, in reality, the cheerful and the hearty state to all the different orders of the society; the stationary is dull; the declining melancholy.

–Adam Smith[1]

[1] Adam Smith. *An Inquiry into the Nature and Causes of the Wealth of Nation.* Book I. Chapter VIII.

INTRODUCTION

The year 2007 marked the beginning of a world economic crisis that we are still be recovering from. The financial system of modern capitalism not only failed to prevent this crisis but also caused it to explode dramatically.

The goal of this work is to design a new financial system that is fundamentally different from the existing one. It is a financial system of a new formation that we call a Perfectly Competitive Market, or PCM. I would like to note that from a theoretical viewpoint this design is *the only possible option*, despite the abundance of theoretical and practical approaches to economics.

One fundamentally, though not the only, important feature of the new system is a separation of the legacy combined credit and payment system into two parts: provision of credit and processing of payments. In this book, we introduce our new financial system in the following order: Chapter 1 focuses on the national payment system and issuance of money, Chapter 2 describes changes in the credit system, Chapter 3 shows how national monetary systems can be linked and Chapter 4 contains some additional considerations for PCM.

Our proposed transition from the traditional three-level, heterogeneous credit and payment system (central bank ↔ other banks ↔ market participants) to our new, robust two-level system (central bank ↔ all market participants) can be difficult to understand. This is not because our new system is complex, but rather because of the convoluted nature of the existing system where many details appear to be totally different from how they really are. These details may look different depending on your chosen viewpoint, bringing to life certain all-encompassing categories, like "money stock", that contain some very diverse components.

Most people don't understand even some of the basic elements of the existing financial system. To appreciate the simplicity of our new proposed system, and to show that no critical functions are being sacrificed in the transition to it, we will have to take an exploratory walk up and down the legacy financial system.

Among byzantine labyrinths and curved mirrors of the legacy financial system, some people are making serious money. Given my own entrepreneurial past, making money doesn't concern me anymore. However, the money made by exploiting certain features of the legacy financial system adds the burden of extra costs to the "real" (non-financial) sector[2] of entire national economies, which is a serious issue. Furthermore, the legacy system contributes to moral decay in society by questioning things like elementary frugality on our planet with its limited natural resources, efficiency of private property institutions and even the creative nature of our civilisation.

In the course of our exploratory walk, our fundamental concepts about the existing financial system, and the economy in general, may not completely agree with the reader's view (possibly due to my atypical background for a theoretical economics author). Having spent my economic "childhood" studying at Moscow State University, I jumped into my economic "youth" by becoming one of modern Russia's first entrepreneurs back in 1989. Given that in the subsequent 14 years I "grew up" to manage a few firms that were quite noticeable in their respective sectors, the nuances of marketing, procurement, finance and other kinds of hands-on economic activity have indeed become part of my identity.

[2] Firms engaged in producing goods and services are hereafter referred to as "firms". We may also call them *microeconomy* with a degree of rigor being lost, as the "firms" definition is wider than "microeconomy" – see *Glossary*. We won't need either *microeconomy* or *macroeconomy* to define any scientific disciplines, as we only use the term "theoretical economics". In the existing model of the economy, the "real" sector does not include firms operating in the financial sector, taking into account that the latter has expanded out of all proportion. Financial firms will still exist under our PCM model, but the scope of their operations will be much more limited. We can say that financial firms will just be a thin layer between commercial banks and the "real" sector of the economy. Currently, the best way to present them is by pooling them along with commercial banks into the broad financial sector, as they are actively working with credit instruments and securities. Here, it is useful to draw a parallel with state-owned firms. When we discuss firms' activities in a market economy, by default we are making generalised theoretical statements assuming these firms compete under natural selection principles. But we know that right between the state and the "real" sector, there exist state-owned firms where the rules may differ. If state-owned firms are disproportionately dominating under socialism and financial firms are a juggernaut of capitalism, both become mere thin layers between private firms in the "real" sector, and state and commercial banks, respectively.

In lieu of using the frequently abused term "experience", I will try to illustrate what I am saying using a certain "database" (in this context meaning all the data and knowledge of an individual person rather than a reference to rows of data stored in a computer). A popular saying attributed to Archimedes is: "Give me a place to stand on and I will move the Earth." I would argue that science could use a more fitting maxim: "Give me a database and I will explain everything." However, the means for obtaining this "database" fundamentally differs between natural and social sciences. In the former, the database is often assembled in a laboratory setting by using instruments to measure and collect primary experimental data, both inside the laboratory and outside in the world. The better the laboratory is equipped, the more comprehensive and precise is the database, and potentially the more qualified are the research scientists. Conversely, if your laboratory and university run on a shoestring budget, you are unlikely to make progress or produce talented scientists. Let us also point out that the data used in natural sciences can be easily structured and formalised. This in turn opens up two fundamental options. First, one can gather, store and transmit data. Second, one can use formal mathematical methods to analyse the data – it would be impossible to imagine modern theoretical physics without the extensive use of advanced mathematics.

In social sciences, or at least in important fields such as political science and economics, we have a different situation. Here, primary experimental data is represented by people's actions and their consequences, while academic institutions often find themselves isolated from the data. This data can only be collected in person and "in the field", and it may be subsequently transformed inside an observer's brain into a complex array of conditioned reflexes (later we'll show that the said database-building transformation is not guaranteed by fulfilment of these two conditions). The simplest practical corollary of this feature characteristic of social science institutions is that an advanced education in political science or economics may not be required to achieve the highest degree of qualification. That is, to become a professional politician or entrepreneur, it is not necessary to have a synonymous education. On the other hand, no matter how much you invest in social science laboratories, the chances of producing a future Vladimir Putin or Bill Gates will not materially increase.

A person's actions and an observer's (or rather, a participant's, as distinct from natural sciences) conditioned reflexes cannot be formalised, making the collection of primary data (or actions) and transmission of a participant's conditioned reflexes resulting from these actions nearly impossible. Advanced mathematical methods, with a few rare exceptions, are also not applicable to the field of theoretical economics. Later in this book we will show how these methods can be selectively applied to a socialist economy.

Let's revisit our earlier postulate of "Give me a database …" which is nothing but a buzz phrase; nobody can know everything and even a researcher armed with this "database" is not guaranteed to draw correct conclusions from the data. First, our researcher should use his built-in biological "computer" to run clustering and regression algorithms in order to sift through massive amounts of primary experimental data, identifying key factors influencing the process, and then establishing a cause-and-effect relationship between certain data elements. In reality, researchers do not have a complete database of this sort (while you are reading this sentence, there are millions of economic events happening in the world). They are forced to use data with varying levels of quality and confidence. In this case, the researcher's qualification becomes very important.

People start leaning towards certain professions while still in primary school. Given the rigorous requirements for future scientists, they must continuously meet ever-increasing specific qualifications. To be able to work with the primary economic database, economy practitioners also need to have certain qualifications. However, their analytical brain activity is often accompanied by processing hard-to-formalise data obtained using their five senses, which is something computers still cannot do.

You might have asked yourself at least once why, in some firms, the people who appear to be intellectually gifted are working for nondescript owners. A younger employee might argue that "Everything has been divided, so I put up with this." I would say that this situation is realistic, but the answer is stereotypical. In the 1990s, we observed the division of labour happening quite naturally in nascent Russian businesses. Leadership roles were assumed by people meeting the "entrepreneurial" qualifications, i.e. capable of processing primary economic data to make correct decisions. This selection of entrepreneurs has not disappeared, but now it happens much more slowly and is hindered by the dominance of large firms in the current economic formation (we are going to address this extensively further below).

We are not talking about some "all-seeing eye" of fairness, which would reward every new entrepreneur according to their talents, but rather we observe that, as a rule, successful entrepreneurs do meet the above "entrepreneurial" qualifications. People sometimes exaggerate the importance of exclusive information used by top managers to make business decisions. In reality, there are individuals around the boss who have complete or nearly complete information, or else the firm would be grossly mismanaged. However, it should also not be taken for granted that these informed professionals will make timely and correct business decisions, given the variety of input factors and the potentially high cost of mistakes. We should note that stereotypes often accompany bad decisions, including "do nothing" scenarios, as comparable business situations are generalised and nuances are ignored. Having incomplete information often precedes this pattern.

In a practical economy, numerical information (including prices) is not only mandatory but also the most important component of the seemingly verbal process of formulating and sharing business information. Managers' qualifications are tested by their accurate "digitising" and evaluation of input information to make correct decisions. In a nutshell, a managing owner's database is formed in the following order: processing of primary (not obvious) data about people and their actions → forming a more precise database (all learned reflexes) → price management → refining the database which consists of learned reflexes. If prices are managed with a positive bottom line, our market participant is confirmed to have a certain understanding of the structural links between the primary database components in a chosen economic activity sector. Profit (or loss) is the ultimate litmus test to distinguish "I understand this" from "I am watching this."

Now, we may draw a simple but initially not so obvious logical conclusion: our "database" will display the best precision when it is formed in the heads of entrepreneurs. Any learned reflexes formed in the economy, while being directly connected to the gains and losses of market participants, are necessarily based on the outcomes of numerous events and *decisions* made primarily by the active owners. It works in the following order: events and decisions → business gains and losses = entrepreneur's income → learned reflexes are formed without any distortions.

Coffee break: you might have heard funny stories about how "New Russians" loved to buy the most expensive things available. There is a psychological underpinning for this behaviour. There is not only a desire to stand out ("conspicuous consumption" a.k.a. the Veblen effect), but also a learned reflex of price management. Entrepreneurs working with consumer goods know well enough that setting prices incorrectly is akin to throwing money away. Yes, some people may be willing to pay higher initial prices, but if buyers learn that quality does not correspond to a high price, they will develop an adverse reaction, so that even a subsequent price lowering might be interpreted as a sign of weakness. In the end, simple arithmetic calculations show that it would be more profitable to set lower prices from day one. Thus, faced with new and unfamiliar goods, entrepreneurs (especially new rich ones) may believe that sellers who set the prices think the same way. Indeed, prices for mass consumer goods follow this logic, whereas peddlers of luxury goods are very happy to attract such consumers. The sellers guess this psychological twist, perhaps intuitively. Although the Veblen effect is stronger, these nuances exist as well. We may add that when dealing with goods that they know inside and out, these same heroes of funny stories would often demonstrate their nearly flawless understanding of how things work.

Summarising the above, we can say that observation, participation and price management represent different levels of primary database qualification, because they assume different skill levels required to understand the data hierarchy and cause-and-effect relationships. This generalisation is by no means complete as "databases" can be vastly different. For example, a database formed while managing a restaurant will differ from a database formed while managing a conglomerate. A database formed while managing a commercial bank may help develop analytical rather than theoretical skills.

Having no access to a primary "database", theoretical economists usually work with existing theories, statistical data and observations. It is a certain "view from above", while this book is largely a "view from below" driven by primary and fundamental data. Thus, do not be surprised if some of the material contradicts your familiar narratives. This may be due to either error on my part or your false stereotypes. One way or another, in this book I promise to tell you something new (including comments on some well-known economic theories). Regardless of your own views, it will just be a different perspective.

Along our little journey you may encounter certain inconveniencies. It is impossible to cover every level of both the old and new systems at once, and likewise it is impossible to stay on one side and completely ignore the other. Even for the simplest element of a financial system, explaining the finest theoretical points will demand tracking of interactions arising in several diverse aspects. In any economic system that we set out to either describe or mention, there is a myriad of dependencies that is difficult to describe, just as with an analogy of light bulbs being turned on sequentially. A set of theoretical generalisations does not easily match an actual flow structure, even if the latter is simplified to a rough draft. Therefore, to preserve consistency in our narrative while keeping it true to the actual economy, we will use footnotes extensively (and the text in footnotes is often no less important than the main contents).

This abundance of footnotes is a known drawback. However, if I (and not some other author who might be more skilled in structuring the information) were to give up on footnotes, the text of this essay would be harder to understand. This book also offers a collection of applied essays (Chapter 4), Conclusion and a glossary of terms. A lot of seemingly odd and insignificant content will be better understood once you've read the whole book. These reservations are even more appropriate given that we not only construct separate national financial systems, but also link them together in the framework of a global financial system in Chapter 3. However, that is not all. We will see that changing the current system to a new one is consistent with the development of economic laws of our civilisation. The new system we'll design in its basic features will not be capitalism in its (yet another) modification,[3] nor will it be a socialist or a communist formation, but a more perfect, market-based formation.

Therefore, different from most other market economy studies, explicitly or implicitly aiming to modernise capitalism, our intentions towards capitalism are purely diagnostic ones. We focus on discovering fundamental costs of modern capitalism while presenting a new formation that by design would be free from these costs. This study will require using a somewhat unusual methodology. To a large extent it involves not the categories themselves, but firstly, interpretations of these categories, and secondly, a hierarchy of these categories. To put it simply, we place different accents on a generally traditional system of categories. Even simpler, we use common bricks to build a seemingly unusual home that would be much more durable and cheaper to operate compared to our current one. Our key secret to achieve this goal is not to rearrange the bricks but – continuing

[3] This statement, as I saw from early reader feedback, will leave little impression on some people with leftist beliefs as their principal ideas are wrapped around the form of ownership, whether private or social. Correspondingly, they will simply perceive our new proposed formation as yet another modification of capitalism. From a motivational point of view, I don't care what it will be called, though it is important to move to a more modern design of the economy. Strictly speaking, this will be a new formation indeed, as I will try to show in this book.

the construction analogy – to make good use of scientific and technical progress.

The term "formation" was introduced to theoretical economics by Karl Marx. Besides this fact and besides using some formation names originating from Marx's socio-economic theories, this book has no meaningful intersections with Marxism. However, it is worth mentioning materialism as a methodology that I support, not in the philosophical sense of the word but literally. From my point of view, Marx's materialism was a temporary stage in the materialistic perfecting of theoretical economics and philosophy. In the 18th and 19th centuries, the scientists' fight with the religious interpretation of the structure of the world led them to radical demonstrations of a person's independence from the church. As often happens with radical changes, economic theories took a turn in the other direction. In lieu of God, man was endowed with mystical powers to create some speculative "value", allegedly hidden in the product itself and thus distinct from the product's price, which is also routinely called "value", with the key difference that price is visually represented by a certain monetary equivalent. Belief in the existence of some "flowing clots" or "abstract human labour" seems to be essentially close to religion. No wonder that in all 14 years of my entrepreneurial "lab research" I have not seen anything like this. This study is based on the realities of the world around us, on materialist categories.

As it can offend the ear to juxtapose "matter", objectively existing and "categories" (see *Glossary*), subjectively represented by man, I will explain the materialism of the category I understand as the *veracity of human perception* (either sensual or numeric). To paraphrase, you and I can have different opinions about a chair I am pointing at – Is it good or bad? Do we need it or not? – but we still agree that it is a chair. This definition is insufficient to explain "everything" in the universe. However, it should be enough to deal with economic realities linked to decisions being made by one exact biological species, *Homo sapiens sapiens* (hereafter referred to as *Homo sapiens*), on planet Earth. At least from the dawn of human civilisation to our present day, materialism in this narrow sense is a prerequisite to enter the real economic world.

This definition of categories' materialism makes the use of reflections and representations as basic categories impossible. Ideas do matter, and humans not only can but must think in order to increase their share of material wealth. Thoughts themselves originate from very material brain activities. However, before they manifest themselves in a material form adequately perceived by other people, thoughts can only be a bridge to the economy. For example, while intellectual property is not yet embodied in a patent registration, book publication or in another materialistic event obvious to a bystander, the fruits of thought will not become part of the economy or part of actual events.

Not everyone is likely to completely share my view on the "materialistic" criteria with this very succinct description, so let me point out that I am simply describing the boundaries within which our study will unfold. All *basic* categories in it are materialistic exactly in this mundane sense. They represent material objects and numbers, whose objectivity should not be doubted, even if the reader does not agree with our reasoning about the cause-and-effect relationships among these categories. Below, we will lay out some basic categories of our study, with very minimal explanation at this stage. In this introduction, we are going to elaborate on only one category, namely "property". When saying "property" without any explicit decoding, we assume one of the following two fundamental meanings of it.

***First** fundamental postulate: property is something that belongs to people* (in the form of private or collective property). To set the proper tone, let us reiterate it as follows: property is something that belongs to *Homo sapiens*, a biological species dominating planet Earth. Everything that is used in our economy belongs to the human population. This biological emphasis is strong. If we apply the "right of ownership" concept with a legal tone, it may feel like there is a certain higher authority that confirms the rights of *Home sapiens* for planet Earth or at least for its biosphere. In fact, humans have received this property due to natural selection and if we try to find any "right" here, it would be the "right of might", which thus deviates from the legal sense. We can add that the stated tie to biology is not in the way of our study as it does not impose obligations on it, unlike mathematics or jurisprudence. We use biological references mainly to point at an "umbilical cord", so later we'll talk in detail about biology as a fundamental science for theoretical economics in such a fundamental thesis as "*Psychology and rationality in theoretical economics ...*".

Now that we have introduced the "property" category with a biological emphasis, it is fitting to introduce "the right of ownership" with a clear legal emphasis: inside the population of winners, relations between the owners need to be regulated. However, there are some nuances here. There are relations between nations and within the nations. In politics, especially in international relations, the right of might often dominates the rights of owners and the winners write their own laws. As human civilisation develops, this situation evolves, but violence still takes place when certain people do not recognise the rights of ownership of others. Two main manifestations of such violence are warfare and criminal offences. Let's leave these to political and legal scholars and return to our description of ownership as it applies to the economy, given that the above paragraph has simplified our task of formulating the next important statement.

***Second** fundamental postulate: in the economy, owners recognise the rights of other owners*. The author is not to be considered naïve – respect for rights to property in the economy can depend on the level of civilisation development. However, this respect for owner rights in the economy at practically any given moment has been much higher compared to the respect for these rights in politics, to say nothing about criminal offences. There is a simple but very important biological explanation for this phenomenon. Species other than humans might also have "economies" as they produce (mainly harvest but sometimes also process) certain products, at times even using a simple means of production. However, humans became smart enough at a particular stage of development to not just steal or confiscate another family's property but, recognising the rights to property of others, to exchange it for something they already have.

A macroeconomy, being a set of exchanges or deals, is a "temple" of theoretical economics in our framework that we'll explain shortly after decoding the four basic types of property. We put "temple" in quotes simply because we won't need to use any mysterious substances to explain "value" creation in a microeconomy. Instead, we use good old price, which is easy to understand and calculate.

Let's list the primary, fundamental categories of our study (here, "primary" does not have any special methodological meaning; we are just saying that some of these categories break down into other fundamental categories): **property, exchange (deal), property increment, property alienation, price, managing owner, physical turnover in monetary terms, credit turnover, costs, cost regulators**[4] **of managing owner** and **profit**.

---

[4] The existing model of the world economy is tied to *bureaucratic* regulators (both national and supranational). The latter (especially the central banks) play a key role in managing the modern financial system. In our new formation, *market* regulators

"Property" contains four basic elements: **goods, people, land** and **money**. "Goods" are commonly referred to as **commodities** in deals. For ease of understanding of the text by English-speaking readers, I use the term "goods" routinely, unless minor loss of rigor is crucial here.[5] "Money", in turn, breaks down into **money as credit** and **money as payment**.

We consider **bilateral (purchase and sale)** and **unilateral (lease)** basic exchanges (deals). We'll use symbols "↔" for bilateral and "←" for unilateral property alienation. The arrow shows the direction of property alienation between managing owners. When crossed with basic ownership types (C for commodities, P for people, L for land, M_C for money as credit, M for money as a means of payment), we get the following four basic deals:

Purchase and sale[6]: C ↔ M

Lease: P ← M, L ← M, M_C ← M

In all three basic lease deals, only M (money as a means of payment[7]) is being alienated. M serves as the price of leasing people, land and "money

---

will play this key role. You will see that we use this "influential" term without any exaggeration.

[5] The term "commodity" in English has been traditionally associated with raw materials and exchange trading. This is different, for instance, from Russian, where it applies to all kinds of goods.

[6] Including purchase and sale of services (lease of goods). See also "*FAQ: Services ...*" in Chapter 4. Absent any special disclaimers, whenever we discuss turnover under the term "commodities", we mean "commodities and services" (similarly, under the term "goods", we mean "goods and services").

[7] Here, we have to at least mention some important links that would require more detailed discussion in a theoretical textbook. Without losing sight of the goals of our study, here is my digest. The "goods" category is fundamentally characterised by the presence of usage wear. Goods are made for purposeful destruction (wear), which is consumption – be it personal or production. Thus, property alienation, one form of which is wear, is baked into the natural essence of goods from the outset. For the owner of goods, this alienation happens regardless of whether goods are consumed for personal or production use, and regardless of how and whether the owner accounts for wear (for example, by calculating depreciation). This alienation, a natural essential characteristic of goods, is organically shown in price categories. For example, we can preserve the goods to make physical deterioration negligible, but we'll inevitably incur extra preservation and storage costs. Generally speaking, all four basic types of property are susceptible to diminished functionality after being employed by the managers: goods and money (paper currency in this case) wear out, while people and land simply get tired. However,

as credit" in these deals, also known as wages, rent and interest, respectively. These are **basic cost types** for a managing owner and can be treated almost as **basic cost regulators**, but in a strict sense, these are the *rates* of wages, rent and interest. This difference is most conspicuous in credit deals[8] whereas in the two other lease deals it is less visible. Thus, examples of basic cost regulators proper are **the price of hiring a worker for a unit of time** (further referred to as **"wages"**[9]), **the price to lease a**

---

three out of four – people, land and money (in our study we call these *resources*, separating this term from the well-known expression "natural resources" that I find difficult to explain, even if by default it is most often used in the same sense as "goods") – are able to restore their functionality without direct involvement of firms and their associated costs (firms are not indispensable to sustain life on planet Earth). In this exact context – from the manager's viewpoint – we are talking about resources not susceptible to wear in a *microeconomy*, and so we carry this thread over to a *macroeconomy*. This macroeconomic sustainability of resources is organically reflected in lease deals with unilateral property alienation (where only money as a means of payment is being alienated), which are basic deals in resource turnover. As for wear and tear of goods, including fixed assets, it is non-discretionary, and no manager would avoid incurring maintenance and replacement costs. That's why purchase and sale deals, characterised by their two-way property alienation, are more suitable for goods circulation, including the lease of goods described as services. ***We'll wrap up this purely theoretical footnote with a general methodological observation***. Notice the logic that we first used when talking about firms: all reasoning was from a managing owner's ("the person who pays for everything") viewpoint. This logic forms the backbone theory of our "view from below" approach that we mentioned earlier as one of the characteristics of our study. Among other things, it will allow us to recognise certain false stereotypes (usually related to bringing the reasoning over to a macroeconomy) and avoid a good deal of pointless narrative.

[8] When one pays $100 a year to obtain a loan of $1,000, this 10 per cent is called "interest" in everyday jargon. Strictly speaking, interest is actually $100, while 10 per cent is the credit price of the currency unit (in this deal) or an interest rate. Let's rejoice that the last and most important term is equally understood in theory and practice (we will not focus on the tricks of bankers who tend to interpret freely the accrual and payment of interest at what seems to be clearly marked as an *annual rate*).

[9] Unless noted otherwise, all variations of prices in this text are so-called "nominal", i.e. usual everyday market prices that we'll refer to as "final" prices as opposed to "real" ones. As far as I see it, the prices that are typically called "nominal" are in fact real ones; as real as the amount of property used by managers in an actual deal. On the other hand, so-called "real" prices may be best described as derived ones. So, in order not to confuse the reader, I will not use this terminology at all, but in some complex cases I will say, for example, "the price of [something] expressed in [something else] (goods, money, foreign currency)".

unit of land for a unit of time (further referred to as **"rent"**[10]) and **the price of borrowing a currency unit for a unit of time** (further referred to as **"interest rate"**). The fourth basic regulator is a kind of "money as a means of payment" in the one and only deal where money in a sense can be the price of itself, namely **the price of a national currency unit expressed in a foreign currency** (further referred to as **"cross-price"**). If you have paid attention, the last basic regulator is not related to lease deals but is a specific case of the purchase and sale deal (international currency exchange), where foreign currency plays the role of specific commodities. This should not offend the ear if we assume that within a national economy there cannot exist money and some "other money". Only one thing can be designated as money. This theoretical postulate would need to be stretched to apply to capitalism, but in our new formation it gains visual rigor.

Negative profit (or loss) is yet another basic category that is a variation of profit and serves as the **final cost regulator of a managing owner**. Negative profit can complicate, and in extreme cases (one time or cumulatively) stop altogether, the managing owner's activities at the helm

---

Sometimes, this price is a form of derived price: for example, a payment was processed using the national currency but recalculated into a foreign currency for comparison. These are rare and exceptional cases, and it will be clear from the context whenever we are using a derived price. In general, I make infrequent use of derived prices, typically called "real" prices, and I am not going to argue that their use can be fully justified, especially for analytics.

[10] In our text, the term "rent" is used in its simplest meaning, as the rent paid for land use. To my mind, both differential rent I and II seem to be speculative categories, brought to life by attempts to construct the tower of economic laws around "value", "utility" and the like. From my point of view, these categories are speculative since they do not manifest themselves naturally in practical economic life. One way or another, we won't need to use these categories in our study, as we'll rely on the naturally precise categories. It must be clear to all that the price of a land parcel with an oil deposit underneath will be higher than the price of the same parcel with a gravel deposit, and that the price of a gold jar will exceed the price of a bread loaf. And if in some exceptional cases the reverse is true, we'll accept this as a reality which is indeed a deal; an actual exchange that takes place as a result of mutual consent between owners. We will be building our study based on facts, primarily reflected in final prices. In this case, the price of land is reflected in rent as the price of leasing the land. Also, rent is not always charged as an easy-to-understand time rate. As in the case of mining, it can be calculated depending on the amount of goods extracted from the land (alternatively upon the sale of them in the form of commodities). This feature is not unique to rent alone, as wages can also be hourly or piecework.

of the firm, as these are not effective from a market viewpoint. This final cost regulator is the "fifth element" having a direct impact, a net sum of all other basic cost regulators. If other cost regulators are formed in particular deals (for instance, the interest rate in money loans and wages in a labour hiring), the negative profit is formed as the bottom line of all preceding deals. As a rule, revenue (and thus forming the final profit) takes place in purchase and sale deals for non-banking firms and in credit deals for commercial banks. However, costs are directly impacted by many other diverse deals.

You might have paid attention to one common feature that unites all our cost regulators: they are all expressed in terms of money and on all occasions, money is used as a means of payment. Therefore, all of them are either market-driven prices as basic cost regulators, or an aggregated total sum as a final cost regulator obtained by using simple arithmetic operations. This observation will help us further refine the scope of this study, e.g. to exclude barter deals where no money is used at all. These deals certainly make their own economic sense as all the people, including entrepreneurs, do exchange mutual services. Our main reason to narrow the scope this way does not stem from neglecting barter but rather from the inability to apply scientific methods to it. Without money involved, we don't have a common measure to evaluate the barter.

You won't find any sophisticated mathematics in this book. Apart from simple arithmetic operations used by market participants to account for their business processes, and a technological "black box" of production where mathematics is used by engineers, more complex mathematical models are always fraught with varying degrees of conditionality and assumptions that formulas or graphs represent actual, real life processes. Not everyone will agree with this emphasised disinterest in mathematics, especially given its universal use in theoretical studies of recent decades. One way or another, we will only be using precise equations, specific economic equivalencies produced in the millions by everyday economic activities. These are understood as deals in which managing owners[11] evaluate different kinds of property and equate them by agreement. In my mind, there are no other theoretically important precise equations in

[11] If the term "managing owner" triggers questions, please look it up in the *Glossary*. And if upon taking a glance at the longest and most boring definition in the history of theoretical economics you conclude that it is not that critically important, this will also be a good choice. In short: as a rule, we assume "entrepreneur" whenever we use the term "managing owner" in this text, but generally speaking, it is every one of us.

economics that would compare different kinds of property, or functions describing precise proportions between them. Engineering, logistics and accounting calculations have important practical (applied) meanings, but not theoretical ones. With that said, for our precise reasoning, we'll use ***a set of deals where prices expressed in money are forming***.

As previously mentioned, we will call this set of deals a ***macroeconomy***. We will use this term only to describe a significant sector of a national economy. This definition is narrower compared to the commonly accepted understanding: "an object being researched by macroeconomics" (in both plain and scientific lingo, it is often also called "macroeconomics"). Meanwhile, the traditional term "macroeconomics" in its alternative meaning of "an object to study" looks more like what we call in this text a "national economy". As the latter is naturally the main subject of our theoretical study and given that the essence of theoretical postulates is formed in a macroeconomy (let me remind you that in our study this is defined as a set of exchanges), the difference between the traditional definition of this term and ours is not crucial. But it does exist, of course.

Besides macroeconomy, a national economy contains some other fundamentally important sectors, including the following "reproductive" blocks. There is a microeconomy proper (goods and services), households (people) and a government in a broad sense, including the central bank (money). The fourth basic type of property – land – unfortunately does not reproduce. Unlike relatively static reproductive blocks, a macroeconomy appears to be a set of operations (processes) which maintain economic connections between blocks as well as within them.

To get a better visual understanding of a macroeconomy, let's portray a deal as the movement of money accompanied by (a) the movement of property that is changing hands in exchange for this money and (b) the mutual exchange of relevant information. Movement of non-cash money here is facilitated by commercial banks.[12] As for the movement of property

[12] Here, we are talking about the existing formation, but in the first paragraph of Chapter 1 we are going to find out how it will be set up in the next formation. All the while, commercial banks will remain macroeconomic enterprises. We may also note here that since non-cash deals and the next formation are often mentioned in the same context, the evolution of money under the PCM will sooner or later cause cash to disappear. This will not make it easier to collect taxes – in this book you will not encounter this reasoning. In fact, a higher tax collection rate may actually put the shackles on national economic development. This is not good or evil per se and nobody questions the need to collect taxes; this is just the way it works in a

and information, these are largely performed by third parties specialising in transportation, logistics and communications. [13] Note that money transfer can take place entirely within a firm. Likewise, transportation, storage and communications may sometimes be classified as internal firm operations. No deals take place in this case and all these events fall within the scope of a microeconomy.

That is, the indication that – from an in-kind point of view – reproductive blocks can be thought of as static property sets and a macroeconomy can be represented as a set of operations needs to be accompanied (as often happens in economics, especially when using in-kind categories) with a "generally" disclaimer. There are commercial banks, with all the property they own, that do not fit our definition of a macroeconomy but in fact they are clearly macroeconomic enterprises (one might be tempted to place commercial banks into some reproductive block labelled "money" but later we'll explain our reasons for not doing this). There are also certain operations that look macroeconomic but cannot be properly classified as such. That's why the best possible definition of a macroeconomy is as follows: a set of deals where prices in monetary terms are formed.

The most diligent study of a macroeconomy in a sole historical epoch will not lead to the discovery of a system of fundamental economic laws. It takes less effort and ensures more precision to compare the present day macroeconomy to one of the past. The kinds of deals and prices, as well as basic property types, have been changing (functionally or materially) significantly as human civilisation developed, driven by scientific and technological progress. By the way, modern economists enjoy an undoubted advantage over the great theoreticians of the past. None of those at the peak of their intellectual maturity had comparable opportunities to obtain and analyse current economic data, nor did they know what real economic life would look like at the turn of the millennium, nor imagine what technological achievements directly impacting economic development would be available.

---

market economy and the way it will work under the PCM, hence it cannot be a theoretical argument. Leaving details aside for now, we can say that the PCM payment system will work like a Swiss clock when no cash is used but incur additional costs whenever cash is in play.

[13] We can add that in our study, "infrastructure" is understood by default as specific technical assets, including buildings and means of communication designed to carry out the three said functions, without any connection to specific deals and sectors of the national economy. This is just a term we define and there is no special place for infrastructure in this study.

Studying how basic categories and links between them evolved over time allows us not only to refine the principles of changes of an economic epoch (formation) but also to make an educated guess about the look and feel of the next formation. Here, I will get to the point and set out the general scheme of historical-economic logic that, in my opinion, forms the cornerstone of the dialectical unity of our civilisation's economic development.

In the most stringent way, economic formations are defined using the concept of freeing cost regulators, which are superimposed on the evolution of the physical form of money. This classification is easier to understand once we pre-examine the historical metamorphosis of the basic types of property. Basic resources – people (P), land (L) and money as credit (M_C) – are gradually used less and less by managing owners in the outright private property mode.[14] Until they are barred (i.e. until certain resources are classified as non-reproducible within a microeconomy by law), corresponding economic formations are called slave-owning (P), landowning (L) and capitalist (M_C), respectively. Conversely, commodities

[14] The discussions we have later in the main text fit well for people and money as credit. Land, however, may pose additional questions and hence the first phrase in this paragraph. Nevertheless, our reasoning is rigorous enough to cite that (and this is a subtle moment) the usefulness of the right to private property is most precisely manifested in the reproducibility of this type of property inside a microeconomy, i.e. by managing owners. For example, the children of slaves belonged to slave owners, while goods producers could extend credit under capitalism. *However, land is not reproducible in principle, so the rule of reproducibility (or non-reproducibility) inside a microeconomy shows precisely, and without any ambiguity* (so this is not a stretch and to agree with it someone would not need to show compassion to the author), *why our reasoning does not quite fit in the case of land.* Before we continue on to basic cost regulators, the principle of usefulness of the right to private land will have to be only generally understood. But the non-reproducibility of land is such a powerful input factor that we won't be able to avoid reservations while talking about basic cost regulators. In this book, you will encounter a few subtle moments requiring more attention, but the non-reproducibility of land is not simply a subtle moment in the relationship between the author and the reader – it is built into the foundation of our economy. There is always "something wrong" with land; for instance, agriculture may not quite fit into the principles of economic management or into theoretical generalisations, requiring a special approach in terms of laws and categories. One can abstract from this inconvenience and many do just that (with the understanding that in theoretical economics it is easier to do than in practical management), and this study is hardly an exception. However, we made a point to indicate the root cause of problems: ***the non-reproducibility of land***.

(C) are used (as they can be reproduced in a microeconomy) by managing owners in the outright private property mode. When this practice was questioned and barred, socialism was born. The essence of basic resources' metamorphosis is even easier to understand if we note that resources are gradually (step by step) shedding their commodity component. During the last few thousand years, when it made sense to talk about the economy, people always remained people in their physical form but, for economic purposes, slaves were essentially a commodity and human surrogates. Thus, a purchase and sale deal P↔M was often used in lieu of a basic lease deal P←M (despite the fact that C↔M is a basic purchase and sale deal). As for the M_C part, under capitalism the use of commodity and money surrogates (in general, securities; in this case, securities with a credit component, as we are talking about money as credit) has gradually grown to a disproportionate size, even for capitalism adherents.

This simplified understanding, described in the previous paragraph, does not include socialism, indirectly suggesting its optional nature for Mediterranean civilisation, whose development (at least from a mere economics viewpoint) eventually came to determine the course of global economic development. For now, staying within the scope of this simplified understanding in order to more easily classify formations, let's write down in one column our four basic economic deals:

$$\mathbf{C \leftrightarrow M,}$$
$$\mathbf{P \leftarrow M,}$$
$$\mathbf{L \leftarrow M,}$$
$$\mathbf{M_C \leftarrow M.}$$

On the left side, we have all the resources getting rid of their commodity component over the course of economic evolution as well as the commodities themselves. On the right side, there is only money. In the scope of this study, we will use the definition of money as valuable numbers used as a means of circulation (details are in Chapter 1). Over the course of evolution, money gradually shed its goods form (this form is increasingly less dominant than the numerical essence of money – it is impacting the value of money less and less) in this simplest physical understanding: gold (metal) money → paper money → digital records (non-cash money).

There is one subtle moment that illustrates the difference between commodities and goods: while analysing metamorphoses on the left side of deals, we noted a "commodity essence", but in the preceding paragraph we spoke about a "goods form" of money. In the first case, the physical form of these property types is not essential. More important is the level of rights on this property bestowed on managing owners by law (full rights or limited rights). In the case of full rights, this property gets its "commodity essence" that under our PCM model, the supreme formation, will be reserved (within a single national economy) exclusively for commodities proper. Conversely, change in the physical form of money is deterministic when we observe its metamorphoses. As the physical form does not depend on the type of deal (remember that a good becomes a commodity only in a deal), it would be more accurate to talk about the "goods form".

The emergence of money as numbers blatantly demonstrates the transition of people from the very first and longest formation (traditionally called primitive) to economic formations proper, and for Mediterranean civilisations this would be the slave-owning formation. It is clear that the latter (slave-owning) formation is called this particular name not because there was no slave ownership in the former (primitive) one. It is less obvious that while using livestock, seashells and other goods as equivalent exchange media was undoubtedly a necessary step towards using money, the very first real money was metal. Even when this money had no minted denominations, comparing the weight of homogeneous coins made economic measuring much easier and facilitated the work of the basic cost regulators.

The evolution of money also played a major role in the emergence of two intermediate formations (the fifth and the sixth): paper capitalism[15] and

[15] Present-day capitalism is based on the centralised credit issuance of money, where the gold standard has been abandoned in favour of reserve currencies domination. This domination led to the emergence of two cardinally different (which is important from a theoretical point of view) groups of countries: "normal", or peripheral, countries and the issuers of global currencies (now mainly US dollars and euros). We will also call these groups "near-classical" and "wonderland" respectively, paying tribute to the classical economy. We will also briefly call the existing formation "paper capitalism", as the alternative label "credit issuance capitalism" sounds awkward: both capitalist formations are founded on the credit issuance of money. In general, as we'll try to show later, the *theoretical essence of capitalism* is the nearly unlimited use of diverse *credit* operations, and commodity and credit surrogates, while the credit issuance of money is only part of the system. The first systematic description of paper capitalism was attempted by Keynes. The classical "gold" capitalism of Adam Smith was transformed into this new formation without any pronounced, sudden jump. To me, these two economists, along with Marx (socialism), have made the

socialism, respectively. While the emergence of socialism is best described by the abandonment of the final cost regulator (negative profit), the evolution of money should be exclusively[16] credited for turning "gold" capitalism into paper capitalism. The latter itself is an intermediate formation, due to the intermediate nature of paper money in the transitional process from gold to non-cash money. The simplest historic timeline shows the transitional nature of paper formations: compared to the length of dominance of the gold (metal) standard and the length of dominance of the future non-cash standard, paper capitalism has a very limited life span.[17] It would seem to be a tiny twist in history, especially

---

most significant contributions to theoretical economics. However, Adam Smith was a true pioneer of regarding theoretical economics as a science and it was he who introduced the "invisible hand" metaphor. We keep that in mind while building our logic upon its quite visible parts (namely, basic and final cost regulators). With all that, Adam Smith and, for instance, François Quesnay, who along with other physiocrats called for *laissez-faire* ("leave alone") policies, stressed the need for society to encourage the personal initiative of entrepreneurs. This emphasis was quite necessary in times when administrative pressure on the economy on behalf of the aristocracy was not at all lightweight. Now, when capitalism is so powerful, a focus on basic and final cost regulators would be more precise and more fitting, to bring up not only the society but also entrepreneurs by using stringent discipline. The goal is to create and maintain a highly competitive economic environment, which in turn would bring us closer to achieving the ultimate goal: *having minimal costs* when producing goods destined for consumption by *Homo sapiens*.

[16] If the word "exclusively" leaves the reader with an impression of a stretch (traditionally, any narrative on the history of capitalism points to some impressive technological achievements), let me clarify that we are comparing the influence of the evolution of money to other categories of *theoretical* economics. This is my instant technical disclaimer (I have to make it, though it may not help much). We will go over the details in Chapter 2 ("*Insert: Rough History*") and I hope this will be interesting. However, this will cause an increase in "dimensions" of the views on the economy (it can be viewed from different angles and none of these are false), which appears to be unnecessary in anticipation of Chapter 1, full of theoretical details on the movement of money.

[17] To be more specific, I put the beginning of paper capitalism in 1913, the year the Federal Reserve System was created in the US. It would be impossible to fully justify the use of this or some other date, while there were earlier precedents of centralised paper money issuing (in France or Britain). However, the centralised paper money issuance by one leading national economy in the 20th century triggered this chain of events (the law of 1913 → stock market crash of the 1920s → Great Depression → transformation of the US dollar into a global currency → abandonment of ties between the US dollar and gold) and gradually separated the new emerging formation from gold capitalism, where paper money typically

when paper capitalism did not reveal itself until the 1930s and the dollar was tied to gold until 1971. But when nascent paper capitalism triggered the crisis of 1929, the whole system of gold capitalism's rules and logical ties that had formed in both theoretical and practical minds suddenly stopped working as expected. All the mirages and other specifics of a modern financial system that we discuss in this book are manifestations of this paper capitalism, and are very different compared to its older brother, gold capitalism.

Having paid attention to the physical evolution of money, let's return to the regulators (basic and final) that exert considerable influence on the transition from one formation to another. This is even more relevant for our study as the freeing of the last two cost regulators forms the essential part of the forthcoming transition to the next formation.

Once again, let's write down in one column our four basic economic deals, but this time adding the names of the three prototypes of basic cost regulators (functional names of money as a means of payment) next to the corresponding lease deal:

C ↔ M;
P ← M, wages;
L ← M, rent;
M_C ← M, interest.

Functional varieties of money as a means of payment in lease deals (wages, rent and interest) have always or nearly always existed, but for each one of these there was (or will be) a historical period when its importance as a basic cost regulator was critically important. Deal C↔M gives us the remaining basic cost regulator, or cross-price (the unique nature and the theoretical tie mechanism to the C↔M deal was explained earlier). The deal C↔M also has the last say when a final cost regulator (negative profit) is being formed at firms.

In the previous book[18], we dwelled extensively on the basic features of several formations and I faced the need to cover these features in more depth, given the abundant variety of historical material. This meant an

served only as a proxy for gold circulation. By the early 20th century, the US was quickly becoming a new ideological leader of the world economy.

[18] Голод, Игорь. Новая финансовая система. – Москва: Экономика, 2012. – 237 с. [Golod, Igor The New Financial System – Moscow, Economica, 2012. – 237 p.]

extra year or so of work and it substantially increased the text volume, inevitably distracting us from the main goal: a theoretical justification for the transition from the existing formation to the next one. Therefore, in this book, only the Introduction will contain this material. Here, I will point out an important change in the understanding of the landowning formation that, following Marx's paradigm, I used to associate with feudalism. However, I did not see the need to *substantially* correct the concept after analysing the critique of the previous book.

So, the following sequential application of cost regulators paired with the material metamorphoses of money gives us the following classification of economic[19] formations[20]:

> Primitive-communal → (*emergence of money*) → slave-owning → (*wages*) → landowning (wider than "feudalism") → (*rent*) → classical (gold) capitalism.

So far, we've singled out only the first four formations. Let's put in a disclaimer that any schematic depiction of our civilisation's development should not be initially thought of as a certain set of building blocks laid in

---

[19] There is no compelling reason to add "socio-" in front of every "economic formation".

[20] You won't see any mention of Asiatic-specific formations (a.k.a. "Asiatic mode of production"). This is not because they did not or do not exist, but because it adds nothing to understand the laws of classical economy and further complicates the situation. (For instance, what is the present formation in China – socialist, capitalist or some separate "neo-Chinese"?) The reason is that in these formation varieties the political component plays an oversized role, where "vertical" political management permeates all authority layers. Power centralisation has long been vitally important for Asian nations; the physical geography of Eurasia may be the main reason. It is easy to see that in Western Europe, the Gulf Stream allowed for agriculture for economic development while the seas, mountains and forests assured natural protection from horse-mounted Asian invaders who mainly raised livestock. However, this priority of the "vertical" can bend – and for a long time, simply be suppressed – forming the "horizontal" ties between owners that are mandatory for a market economy. I would add that the undoubted similarity between power "verticals" under socialism and under the "Asiatic mode of production" does not make the former a variation of the latter. Socialism as a standalone economic formation can be traced against the fabric of the historical development of *all* countries. It is a different story that the prominent geopolitical status and certain economic achievements of the USSR were, to a great extent, caused by socialism's fit (as of early and the middle of the last century) with Russia's nature as both a European and an Asian country.

a straight line and this study is no exception. Our brief enumeration of the main stages of economic development does not mean, for example, that there were no wages and salaries in the slave-owning epoch, or that slavery did not exist in the primitive-communal system. We'll make this clearer later.

To begin with, we'll note that formations differ more from each other than the planets of the solar system, though we certainly do not draw any parallels between formations and planets. One outstanding formation (say, Jupiter) is the landowning one. This stems from the non-reproducibility of land that has been influencing the economy all throughout economic history. We have already discussed that and we'll talk more about it in the main text. However, some questions can already be answered by looking at the following chart where we picture the landowning formation in the relatively modest way in which it takes place in the historical sequence of formations:

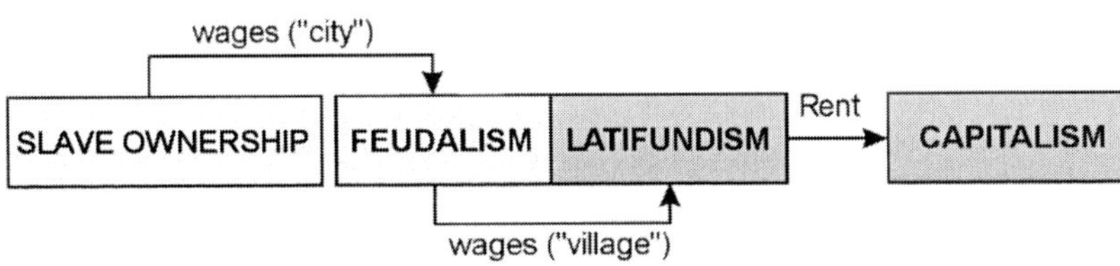

Fig. i-1

You may have noticed that the beginning of the landowning formation rectangle is painted in the colour of slave ownership but the remainder has the "capitalism" colour, where the abolishment of personal dependency of peasants together with the final liberation of wages made working hands available for the development of capitalism (and also facilitated the purchase and sale of land). Still, the outsized economic (and legal) influence of major landowners (aristocracy, landlords, etc.) does not allow us to detect the beginning of capitalism as a predominant formation. Let's emphasise that the actual event was the liberation of wages as a result of slavery abandonment, and not the transition to the landowning formation because of this liberation as one might think. The spread of wage labour practices was quite slow. In the "village", it took longer as the private ownership of land by landlords was accompanied by a lack of personal freedom (in fact, enslavement) of peasants. The latter did not have an opportunity to earn additional income, given the dominance of agriculture in the economy. In the "city", the transition was slow due to the insufficient development of natural sciences. Accordingly, the industry, which would require a rapid concentration of workers, was also undeveloped and did not adequately stimulate the emancipation of peasants.

Of course, history is not limited to these four formations and right about that time there were two other independent formations emerging:

→ (*paper money*) → paper capitalism;
→ (*paper money; abandonment of the final cost regulator*) → socialism.

This feeling of parallel development, in addition to historical simultaneity, is associated with the rejection of the gold standard and a complete transition to paper money. However, this parallel is quirky; imagine two "sworn brothers" each limping on different legs. The footnote attached to this statement[21] clarifies the remark about the "curved mirror" parallelism of these two formations but *not their essence*.

---

[21] In general, a methodical redistribution of property to favour investment over consumption began following the first 10–15 chaotic years of Soviet rule. In other words, the redistribution favoured microeconomy at the expense of households (i.e. the non-market lowering of costs in the national economy). This is a very important management feature of the socialist national economy and is rooted in centralised planning. Due to the iron-fisted use of this feature by Joseph Stalin when he was at the helm, the country achieved certain and in case of the World War II, crucial success. Such redistribution would be impossible to carry out based on the gold standard. If gold falls into people's hands, it cannot be redistributed unless the state keeps practising direct expropriation of property like it did in the early years of Soviet rule. Gold had, has and will have value in the foreseeable future, unlike paper money (on the internal market) which was easy to manipulate by totalitarian rulers. Figuratively speaking, under socialism, in its fast growth phase, it did not matter what people of all ranks earned as their earnings could be thrown into the furnace of economic modernisation. It was not that this manipulation was taking place primarily by tweaking the value of paper money but it was an essential component. Of course, this economy was bent, but the monetary system, for instance, created by the communist regime did not have, and will not have, competition for its low maintenance costs. As I see it, an economist leaning towards any ideology should still recognise this. Even the monetary system of our proposed PCM will cost more to the nation and a comparison with the existing monetary system does not even make sense. There is no system where costs spiral out of control and, after rejecting the paper capitalism, there will not be one either.
Under paper capitalism, past earnings enjoy a disproportionately prominent place. There is a vast system of financial markets where "money makes money". At some point, the priority of consumption over saving (households over the microeconomy) becomes completely shameful and the economy gets into yet another crisis over

The transfer to the seventh economic formation that we provisionally call the PCM[22] requires the third and fourth basic cost regulators, interest rate and cross-prices, to be entirely market driven. Mere numbers will become

---

the painful shedding of excessive costs. (We are talking about the crisis proper, as there are the pre-crisis and post-crisis phases when, conversely, stimulation of consumption is warranted). They say that man (i.e. the household) is in the centre of the modern economy. This is partially true, if we compare it to socialism, but not entirely. To be precise, this is a man from the "golden billion".

[22] If we look at the current situation in theoretical economics, a PCM is an example of a name lacking a theory. Instead, there is a set of jerky and somewhat idealistic assumptions:

- An infinite number of equally valuable sellers and buyers;
- Uniformity and divisibility of goods sold;
- An absence of barriers to enter or exit a market;
- The high mobility of production factors;
- Equal and complete access to information by all market participants.

The new financial system that we are modelling in this study is the skeleton of a PCM. Clearly, the name is not "prescribed from above" but rather provisional (that's why the working title of this book, "The Perfectly Competitive Market", has morphed into simply "The Market"). It might be more precise to formulate it, for example, this way: the most competitive market model among the feasible ones. This realistic "to the bone" character of our new system is its mandatory condition. It is definitely more complex than the aforementioned traditional suggestions that we are not going to use in our study, although at times there will be visible common points. We won't be adding anything extra to the product of theoretical logic. For instance, if the term "perfect competition" makes you think that all the international trade restrictions will be lifted under the new formation, it may not necessarily be the case. At any rate, the standardising of customs tariffs under the new formation does not somehow stem from the theoretical logic of our study. I picked this example from the listed traditional PCM suggestions as, for me personally, moving in this direction seems to be quite probable, due to the simple thought that if costs decrease in the world economy as a whole, then each single country should benefit from it. Moreover, this consideration appears to be logical either with a simplified approach (tariffs are costs), or with a slightly deeper analysis, conducted by Adam Smith in his famous work (Book IV, Chapter 2, which has a telling title, *Of Restraints upon the Importation from Foreign Countries of such Goods as can be Produced at Home*). With a plausible disclaimer that Smith was writing not so much about the costs but rather about the "sum total of industry", let's paraphrase the gist of the convincing part of his argumentation in the way that with import restrictions in place (it may be prudent to point out the retaliatory measures here), the share of artificially stimulated production of goods will increase, pushing average world costs higher. Here, let me reiterate the statement about "moving in this direction", as the theoretical logic of our study has no obvious corollary of the immediate standardising of customs tariffs in a single country after its transition to a PCM.

the dominant form of money. While the last money metamorphosis has a pronounced evolutionary character, and the process has already started, the transition to full market functionality of interest rates (Chapters 1 and 2) and cross-prices (Chapter 3) will require radical, revolutionary changes.

In the theoretical toolset used for modelling the financial system of a PCM, there will be little specialised terminology and we will try to minimise the introduction of new terms. However, some habitual terms and processes will not receive so many habitual definitions. A system of definitions used by one or another theoretical economist largely reflects their historical localisation. Often, they are tied to a particular formation and inadvertently lose precision once that formation changes. All our basic definitions are tied to a PCM. In my mind, only by having this tie to the seventh formation, where all basic economic laws will reach their apogee after many centuries of maturing, can we reach the desired accuracy of definitions and terminology.

Definitions that work at all times are infrequent. Such is the definition of price, which is a fundamental definition in economic science for me. Having noted its pivotal character, we won't talk much about it but we'll encounter direct references to the definition of price when we construct money issuance under the new financial system.

In general, the proposed theoretical construct shares certain common features with all other known theories but differs from them in several principal moments. Despite my adherence to the principles of defining formations pioneered by Marx, I am a liberal economist (advocating a self-regulating market economy). As for a view from the outside, I guess those who read my work tend to classify it as a variation of neoclassical theory. With all due respect for these views, it may or may not be true.

Briefly deviating from the theoretical identification of this study, I would note that neoclassical theory is not really a "theory" at all. Unlike well-known theories of Karl Marx and John M. Keynes, which despite all their gaffes were marked not only by their integrity but also by cutting windows into the real economic world at the level of describing the principles behind entire formations, neoclassical theory appears to be more of a cosy virtual warehouse strictly intended for internal use. Once the place of this warehouse was occupied by the initial Theory (by Adam Smith describing "classical" – or in our parlance, gold – capitalism), the assumptions of it were gradually clarified and added. The neoclassical theory is convenient to teach students and gain recognition by the scientific community. One can "dig" into it for needed parts among the wrecked mechanisms of yore and notions about economic fundamentals of variable credibility. However, due to its fragmented nature, the neoclassical theory by itself cannot offer anything to "outsiders".

Classification of this study will be further complicated, as we have already stated, by the difference between some PCM-specific definitions and those tied to the existing formation. The reader's perception can be further confused by a combination of seemingly incompatible things. Many people who lived in the 20th century have bits and pieces of the contrast between socialism and capitalism etched in their minds. Our new financial system will be rigorous and laconic, earning a solid second place after socialism from that point of view. As for market self-regulation, it will achieve previously impossible heights in the new formation.

If someone thought that the author, with all his love for the market economy, was just sitting and thinking while constructing his new system, "And here we'll go against our own convictions by adding a pinch of state regulation in the name of higher goals …", this is definitely not the case. The entire proposed PCM model is built on the foundation of **price definition** and the visible (easy to formalise) portion of the "invisible hand of the market", i.e. cost regulators[23] (with our attention focused on the four basic ones). The latter are based on the four defined basic types of property: **commodities (goods), people, land,** and **money**. It is impossible to knock down our model without denying the words highlighted in bold type in this paragraph – there is room for unlimited additions and clarifications, but the model will stand, immune to crucial changes. I hope that upon a closer look (and with a degree of forgiveness for the fact that I skipped a specialised education inside academic institutions causing the structure of this work to not be perfectly balanced) you will notice how the methodological toolset covers and ties together all the important parts of the economic system.

For our designed model of a self-regulating economy (the PCM model), we use the names "rigorous classical economy" or simply "classical economy", which in particular allows us to set it apart from any neoclassical models and at the same time shows its ties to the theory developed by Adam Smith (even though this puts it somewhat closer to

---

[23] In a market economy, prices (for example, these same cost regulators) result from the interaction between supply and demand. Meanwhile, "supply" and "demand" are impossible to formalise. We'll address them further in this study.

the neoclassical theory). That being said, under a "classical economy" we assume in this book a competitive market of managing owners that is self-regulated to the greatest extent possible and not a detailed following of the classical theory founded by Smith (see "classical economy" in the *Glossary*). Simply put, a classical economy is the economy itself and not the process of studying it. Nevertheless, I think that the principles describing how this economy is organised can be distinguished only by using a certain, more modern methodology that is different from the one used by Adam Smith[24] over two centuries ago.

I am using the non-rigorous expression "laws of classical economy" when talking about the basic (theoretical) relationships inside the practical economy, of which a classical economy is the most developed form. Since this book is a sort of presentation of the classical economic model, I have chosen this form for the brief naming of these laws. I also believe that in an economy (any national economy of any formation) there are and there will be certain *uniform* governing laws (or some bent versions of the laws stemming from applying them ahead of time, by mistake or not to a proper extent). I am not sure that it can be proven flawlessly, given the unpredictable nature of human behaviour and some mentality differences between nations, but I have yet to see any direct indications of a flaw in this statement. This uniformity of economic laws is best seen from "above" (the chain of formations) and "below" (fundamental principles of *Homo sapiens*' behaviour which will be described further in our "*Psychology and rationality ...*" thesis). As for the "middle" part, I could not commit myself to a detailed review of all formations, to say nothing about all national economies, but as you will see, some particular features of paper capitalism are easier to explain from the viewpoint of the PCM.

Let me finish the Introduction by pointing out a few key moments of this study in comparison with a summary of key milestones in the development of theoretical economics since the time of Adam Smith. Our comparison is not strict and its sole purpose is to facilitate a mutual understanding with the reader.

The fathers of classical economics, who arranged scattered observations of earlier economists into a system and thus founded economics as a science,

[24] Thinking about any possible subtitles of theoretical works that would only employ some basic categories most frequently used by their authors, the famous *Inquiry into The Nature and Causes of The Wealth of Nations* by Adam Smith would be something like *The Labour and The Capital*, while this book would be subtitled *The Costs*.

put an important emphasis on the producer *costs* and *microeconomy* in general, coining a fundamental hypothesis about the creation of "value" that ostensibly takes place inside the microeconomy.

Marx was one of the most consistent followers of detailed microeconomic research in the middle of the 19th century. He offered further dissection of "value", supposedly formed by actual production costs (hired labour expenses), against the background of the carefully arranged "iconostasis" which classified the means of production. If I managed to offend the reader by using the term "iconostasis" here, I can easily bring my apologies to the memory of the great German theorist. Let me clarify that it stems not from a lack of my respect to Marx, but from what happened later: the studying of the works of only one, undoubtedly genius, economist by an entire national cohort of economists for decades makes one think of some religious associations. Generally, a certain theoretical narrative about the means of production is useful in teaching future economists and not only to make them familiar with the basics of accounting. However, it is much less useful in trying to find the theoretical essence and can lead to the inference of some erroneous relationship.

Marx's theory played a substantial role in the history of both theoretical economics and human civilisation, but the development of mainstream economics took another direction. Emphasis on the priority of costs caused a natural protest due to the simple reason that besides producers there are also consumers and besides supply there is also demand. This brought to life the utility theory, which made an attempt to measure, and even sort out, buyers' motives in deals.

The most unpleasant outcome of microeconomy studies in the 19th century was not even "value"; something that is not taken seriously by modern economic scientists. Rather, these studies gave birth to "marginal quantities", with the most recognisable among them being "marginal cost" and "marginal utility". Alfred Marshall used his "equilibrium price" to tie these two into a well-known trio that struck a temporary truce between the adherents of the supply theory and the demand theory in their versions at the time. This construct is remarkable for the fact that all three of its components are contrived, as none of them can be distinguished in the real economy.[25] Subsequently, these components followed different life paths. Many have doubted the validity of marginal utility from the outset (for no

[25] Such constructs, where one fantasy relies on another, are remarkably virulent. Let's remember the tie between "value" and "abstract human labour".

obvious units of measure) and the equilibrium price is used primarily by analytics (for instance, for technical analysis of the stock market), but the marginal cost, unfortunately, took a sizeable foothold in theoretical studies. They are used to create mathematical models and entire theories, like Ronald Coase's transaction costs theory. The latter by themselves cast serious doubts about their ability to reflect real economic processes. Later in this book we'll devote some time to transaction and marginal costs to better understand why we do not use them.

In the 20th century, theoretical economists, with Keynes being the most prominent of them, started prioritising studying "aggregate demand"[26] and here the important part was shifting twice compared to the traditional classical school: from supply to demand and from microeconomy to macroeconomy (to the level of national economy). This accent is present in modern day theories as well, given that the current model of the world economy (paper capitalism) makes it very natural at first glance. However, we'll see later that Keynes's theory may trigger some fundamental questions.

As for the costs proper, microeconomic costs are still in the limelight to a large extent, thanks to the influence of neoclassical theory, which traditionally (albeit with some modifications after Keynes's theory emerged) pays attention to the production of goods as a crucial factor driving the supply. The notorious marginal cost is also playing a role here.

---

[26] The term "aggregate demand" is not used in our study. Generally, demand is a process in which people with money "in their pocket" are sizing up the price for something they want to buy. The importance of this category as one of two primary components of the "invisible hand of the market" cannot be overestimated. However, being merely a set of considerations, "demand" cannot be a basic category and this may have triggered a "clever" category of "aggregate demand". At the level of definition, it still shows some conservative proximity to the traditional immeasurable demand, simply pointing to its certain parts. However, these parts are treated as expenses, i.e. the actual outcome of deals that is turning this "aggregate demand" into an aggregated statistical number regardless of its definition. This number is quite materialistic, but this whole story about using a live category in a statistical portrait with under-the-cover substitution of "demand" looks doubtful to me. First, I prefer to use "demand" in its primal meaning; second, I am trying to use it only when necessary to avoid ambiguous situations. In this book, the term "demand" is most often used in two cases: while talking about demand's priority over supply in a microeconomy and while discussing other economic theories, mainly by Keynes.

Now, it is very easy to explain the key points of this study: instead of following the diagonal line of "microeconomic costs – macroeconomic demand", I put emphasis on a different one: "microeconomic demand – macroeconomic costs". I admit to finding this out for myself towards the end of working on this book,[27] i.e. 14 years after I had traded my career as an entrepreneur to that of a theoretical economist, when I faced the problem of visualising my theoretical views.

So, the first moment in our study of the market economy is the priority of sales over production and, correspondingly, the priority of demand over supply inside a firm (inside a microeconomy). This moment should be easier to understand by post-Soviet economists, as we have witnessed a radical shift in priority once the economy shifted from production-dominated socialism to a market economy. Despite the relatively modest place of these discussions in the text, understanding this simple moment will guard us from trivial mistakes (for instance, a modern manager ostensibly makes decisions based on some "marginal cost") and will make us feel more confident while thinking about processes taking place in real firms.

The second moment has a cardinal theoretical meaning: at the level of the national economy, costs are fundamentally more important than demand. This is impossible to observe at the micro level and cannot always be seen while analysing a single national economy under a single formation. There are various formations and diverse national economies. If we are talking about present times, the macroeconomic priority of costs over demand will be the last thing on your mind when discussing the modern US economy. Indeed, Keynes's theory, despite its questionable nature, is still applicable to the American economy.

The macroeconomic priority of costs is easier to see when analysing the world economy as a whole. Worldwide economic crises are especially illustrative, as attempts to explain the root causes and work out anti-crisis measures without taking this priority into account will cause inevitable mistakes. As for finding out the essence of formation changes, including ideas about what the next formation will look like, it is impossible without taking this priority of costs. Note that we are talking about the ***theoretical priority of costs in the national economy as a whole***[28] and not only about

[27] This is actually my third book (the first one was published in 2007 and the second one in 2012), but since I just keep refining the same text, it makes little sense to read the first two editions if you are reading this one.

[28] We'll be talking about it in detail at the beginning of Chapter 2.

cost priority over demand that is matched with costs to provide a better visual link for theoretical thought development. Earlier in this Introduction, we have already seen the categories succinctly reflecting this priority: ***basic cost regulators***. This priority is best illustrated while discussing the principles of formation changes and informally we focus on them when calling these regulators a visible part of the "invisible hand of the market".

The structure of this study is a little unfamiliar. At the beginning of each of the three chapters (beginning at the second part of Chapter 2), we put a brief description of yet another component of the PCM financial system, followed by clarifications, comparisons and justifications. We begin with the payment system.

CHAPTER 1.

PAYMENT SYSTEM

Imagine there are no traditional plastic bank cards with imprinted names of a payment system (like Visa or MasterCard), nor the name of the commercial bank that issued the card. In the whole country "N" (inside its customs borders) there is only one legally accepted card type with the imprint "Central Bank N".[29] The payment system is owned by the central bank, which maintains payment accounts for all economic agents, including individuals and corporations (as well as commercial banks) without discrimination.

Someone would smell "socialism" in this picture, but by the same measure an automated phone exchange would be considered "socialist" once it had replaced scores of human operators of yore, switching phone lines by hand. In our case, we are merely lowering deal costs using modern computer technologies. Servicing payments is an exclusively technical operation, since computers and standardised automated teller machines do not decide how much is being paid and to whom, or how much cash is being withdrawn.

Let's remember how modern commercial bank (debit) cards work. When we use our card at a store to buy something, we authorise our commercial bank (which we trust with our money) to transfer some of our funds to the store. Anybody who has ever used regular wire transfers without cards involved may have heard the familiar expression "… once the money comes in", and knows that there is always a time lag between the time money is sent and the time it is received. That's why a plastic card may seem to be some magic instrument, as it takes only a few seconds to pay for our purchases at the store. In fact, the store has not received any

---

[29] This is simplified for easier understanding. For example, foreign tourists will still use their cards issued by their nation's central bank but the funds they use to pay with their card at the moment will still be located at the Central Bank N. See Chapter 3 for details.

payment, only a confirmation that it will be paid. In our example, the only agent experiencing actual property alienation is the store. The goods have left, but the money has not been received yet.

When paying with a bank card, money is following the usual (bank transfer) path, which is further convoluted by the abundance of small payments and the variety of payment systems.[30] Money from the buyer's bank should go to the seller's bank and this chain may include more than just these two banks. Also, the buyer's bank does not rush to pay immediately upon receipt of payment instructions from the buyer. As we said, it just sends a confirmation down the bank communication chain that the buyer is solvent. At the end of the day, the bank balances out all the payments pending with other banks, as bank clients pay and receive payments. The net sum of the payments is used to settle payments between the commercial banks.

In our unified payment system everything will be simpler, cheaper[31] and faster: essentially, all agents in the national economy, including foreign

[30] In the main body of this text we will not cover some payment systems that became popular at the turn of the century using open access networks (with minor loss of rigor we'll call these SEPs, for "systems for electronic payments"). The main reason for SEPs' popularity was insufficient security when using regular bank cards online. In recent years, most security concerns have been resolved and the use of this kind of "electronic money" went down. Thus, SEPs do not signal a renaissance of "private currency", as adherents of certain right-wing economic theories may hope, together with founders of even more extravagant systems like Bitcoin, who pocket the issuance premium with nary a curtsy. Interest in cryptocurrency offerings seems to be in the rush stage and it is important not to remain among the unlucky cryptocurrency owners when it all ends. History repeats itself, but every new asset bubble appears to be something never seen before. At one point, people collected seashells "produced" by the sea in limited quantities. There is no shortage of internet articles explaining why "crypto shells" are worse than money, but this does not deter the enthusiasts blinded by the unusual idea, technologically advanced implementation and, most importantly, a chance to make money.

[31] We can see it using the same example of a purchase made in a store using a bank card. Somebody has to pay the commercial banks and the payment system for facilitating this transaction, and that "somebody" is the store. Suppose that the store pays a 2 per cent fee for the transaction (this and subsequent numbers are realistic). In this case, the buyer's bank (the one issuing the card) gets around 1 per cent, the merchant's bank gets some 0.8 per cent and 0.2 per cent goes to the payment system for processing this transaction (directly or by using a third party). Once our new payment system matures (it may be hard to foresee all costs and ways to compensate them at the outset), I see no reason for the store (and

tourists, will be clients of one giant "bank" with corresponding unification of all operational protocols. Nothing, in principle, prevents the store from having money deposited in its bank account at the time of purchase,[32] Here, we use "in principle" as its literal meaning and not as an introductory phrase. Let us illustrate it by asking a simple question: Why won't commercial banks pay sellers right away? A standard answer, "Because banks make money by holding on to cash even for short periods of time", is partially acceptable but the deeper reason is different: if commercial banks were to have instant settlement, many of them could face a shortage of cash and at least some parts of the financial system would experience a liquidity crisis at the moments of peak transaction load. Our new payment system would be genuinely free of this problem (we'll have substantially more money in it), otherwise the very first paragraph in this chapter would seem naïve. Later, we'll go over the reasons for differences in payment settlement speeds. Meanwhile, let's elaborate on one important moment.

We know from theoretical economics that "money is a measure of value". Even when being aware of the artificial nature of the "value" category, this phrase seems to make sense. However, the initial tie to "value" gives this phrase a fundamental meaning, which, if left unnoticed, will keep it meaningful even in a "world without value". The problem with the phrase is not that it is wrong in principle after certain efforts to clarify it, but that it does not reflect the essential meaning of money.

Can you give just one example from a practical economy where money is not reflected in numbers? It is obvious that money serves as a natural unit of measurement in the economy, both at individual transaction and aggregated levels. From the outset, money is a number of a special nature, otherwise we wouldn't need it in any formation except the most primitive one. That is why we explicitly tied the scope of our study to money in the introduction of this book. However, money is more than "economic kilos", as kilograms are indeed units of measurement and nothing else.

---

indirectly, the buyer) to pay more than 0.2 per cent in this example. Note that both the manufacturing of the payment card and the installation of the card reader equipment at the store are separate charges.

32 This crucial acceleration of payments will be important for retail trade modernisation in the new formation, naturally stemming from the transition to the new financial system. We'll go over the essence and advantages of this modernisation in the Chapter 2 thesis titled "*Trade credit ...*".

Money is a *self-contained* form of property used as a *means of circulation* (we'll be using this broader term without vesting it with fundamental differences to the commonly used one, *medium of exchange*).

We have not yet considered theoretical categories that describe the circulation of money, but from our payment system example we may notice that a difference in the quantity of little "working wagons" (means of circulation) used – which the new payment system will have more of can seriously impact the economic system, notably without a concurrent increase in consumption. This crucial difference in the amount of "working money" is spreading not only over the payment system but also over the whole national economy, and it is directly tied to the origins of economic crises.

Technology-driven simplification that makes payments cheaper and faster is an important side effect of forming the new payment system. However, our main goal is a fundamental transformation that we have started by *distilling the payment component from the mixed credit and payment system*.

The following thesis that we use to more closely explore the world of money will be relatively brief but it will also be one of the most complex to understand due to the abundance of terminology clarifications.

Money and money stock. Deposit multiplier.

Currently, only commercial banks[33] have accounts at the central bank (they are called *correspondent accounts*). The sum of (a) all money in these accounts and (b) all paper money outside the central bank forms the "monetary" component[34] of the monetary base. If we could just say "And

[33] There are some insignificant exceptions from a theoretical point of view, namely the accounts of non-credit institutions in the central bank. In the existing classification, they may be counted as a part of the money stock and not as the monetary base, which makes some sense. We are leaving these out entirely while discussing the existing system. In the new system, these accounts will also be at the central bank and will undoubtedly be classified as a part of the monetary base.

[34] More precisely, (a) + (b) is money, as the remaining parts of the monetary base (broadly defined) are either represented by securities or essentially taken out of circulation, being required reserves or commercial banks' deposits in the central bank. From a viewpoint of being present or absent in the economy, required reserves and deposits of commercial banks in the central bank are no different

further, all the money in the correspondent accounts at the central bank are broken down to smaller sums in their clients' accounts", then our new model would merely be a technological improvement. However, we cannot say so. In the existing credit and payment system, the sum of banks' liabilities, reflected in smaller client accounts,[35] is many times exceeding the sum in their correspondent accounts at the central bank. (We'll call these funds in the correspondent accounts, reflected in banks' assets, non-cash money).

In our new system, a substantial portion of this non-cash "money stock",[36] i.e. banks' liabilities reflected in their clients' current accounts, will simply

---

from freshly minted banknotes stored in the central bank's vault, which are intended for the gradual replacement of worn-out paper banknotes. Everyone might agree that if money is not in circulation, it is not considered money from an economic point of view, though it can be counted as money to balance the bank's books. Also, our new system does not need required reserves. It does not envision banks keeping deposits in the central bank either. One way or another, by default, money in this book is understood exactly as (a) + (b), without any quotes or disclaimers. There is no money of different "power"; it is either money or not.

[35] Here, one might want to say: "The sum of money in these accounts ...". However, this is not money but banks' liabilities to their depositors. Were it indeed money, the problem of commercial banks going bankrupt would barely exist. The main problem of the "money stock" category lies in the incorrect mix-up of money and liabilities, to say nothing about securities that are sometimes also classified as "money stock". The name of the term itself is not perfect either: the "money" adjective may contribute to a distorted perception.

[36] In the existing system, "money stock" includes cash in circulation and the non-cash part of liabilities in the client accounts owed by the commercial bank to the depositors. Let's clarify that this non-cash "money stock" includes only relations between the middle level (commercial banks) and the bottom level (individuals and non-credit institutions). Banks' liabilities to other commercial banks and the top level (central bank) are not counted as part of the "money stock". Besides, the definition only talks about national currency. Foreign currency and, as we have already noted, securities (in a broad sense, including derivatives) are also counted in some extended definitions of "money stock". We'll talk separately about securities and foreign currency, while using this definition of "money stock" in the existing system to retain the transparency of reasoning applicable to both systems. As a whole, it is close to the M3 money aggregate, which along with cash and cheques treated as cash includes these three basic types of deposits: two well-defined ones (time and demand deposits) and various mixes of the first two. For simplification, we'll call them all *deposit accounts* to indicate that they represent banks' liabilities to bottom-level clients. Given that in our new system the non-cash "money stock" will consist only of time deposit liabilities, this simplified picture won't hurt in principle.

"disappear".[37] Of course, the accounts themselves will not disappear but a portion of that "money stock" will disappear. All these accounts will be reflected in the monetary base, which becomes much larger[38] and more detailed under the new system. Former bank clients will have actual funds and not liabilities in these accounts. The only remaining banks' liabilities will be the accounts reflecting certificates of deposits as credit deals in the scope of primary lending,[39] where commercial banks act as clients and borrow money for a set term from creditors (account holders), paying interest without any collateral required.

All these changes will impact the size of the bank multiplier, which we'll also call the deposit multiplier. This name better reflects its essence, helping in particular to dismiss other incorrect names – sometimes it is called "credit multiplier" which is not precise from an arithmetic point of view, or "money multiplier" which contradicts our strict definition of money.[40]

Once the credit system and the payment system are separated, the deposit multiplier shrinks. In principle, it can be even less than one. This is not difficult to see, even if we take it in its traditional form (the ratio of money stock over monetary base). It is even easier if we take a simple and visual proportion (do not count cash and securities). We leave the sum of all bank liabilities to their clients (all client deposit accounts) in the numerator and put all non-cash money (the sum of money in current client accounts at the

---

[37] Some savings accounts will likely be converted into time deposits with the clients' consent. Here, we are referring to the strategic outcome.

[38] More details on this are in the last chapter, "*FAQ: The shrinking of money stock and the interest rate.*"

[39] We'll be using this simple term instead of "funding".

[40] Money, as defined in the following thesis, has to circulate in the entire national economy. In the existing financial system, a non-classical mix-up of the credit and payment systems is causing the existence of money and "money". In our PCM model there is only one kind of money. From a theoretical point of view, it is better to define money early and rigorously, based on classical economic definitions, which is the same as the economy of the PCM. Otherwise, we'll be confused by stereotypes. A strict definition of money makes it easier to classify any type of "money". We'll see the difference between "credit money" and "clearing money", as well as between "low-powered money" of gold capitalism and "low-powered money" of paper capitalism. Correspondingly, we'll be able to better trace the origins of costs specific to paper capitalism – costs which our PCM will not incur. At the same time, to provide a better understanding of some features of paper capitalism it will be warranted to pile up all the definitions. In this case, we'll be using the term "broad money".

central bank) in the denominator. This method preserves the essence of the deposit multiplier and it is good because it is straightforward (it does not depend on the definitions of money stock or monetary base). Our new system will have a greatly reduced deposit multiplier as some money from the numerator is now in the denominator. In the new system, commercial banks will not facilitate client payments (and correspondingly, won`t touch their current accounts). Looking a bit ahead, note that once a commercial bank issues a loan, the money is immediately transferred from the creditor's account at the central bank to the borrower's account (this is related to the process of inflating the multiplier under the existing system).

As a terminology corollary, note that in the new financial system the terms "money stock" and "monetary base" are unlikely to be used, albeit for different reasons. "Money stock" will lose its sense as an entire category, as it will not just "shrink" but will cease, in its specific meaning, to be anything meaningful for the money circulation process. As for the "monetary base", its importance as a category will increase but the name will become dated, as under the existing system it reflects the foundation over which a banking system builds up "money".

The levels of payment system. Definition of money. Property alienation as a bridge to price definition.

We have easily turned the three-level payment system (central bank – commercial banks – other market participants) into a two-level one (central bank – market participants). Before people invented computers, such a system was unlikely to have been implemented or it would have turned out to be prohibitively expensive given the scale and speed of the modern economy. It is easier to see the connection between powerful computing systems and money if we use the following *definition for money*: **it is nothing but valuable numbers**[41] **used in a national economy**[42] **as a means of circulation**. This value was historically attained by different means – for instance, by using some valuable monetary objects. Since the transition from cattle or seashells to metals (money

[41] Positive rational numbers with a scale of two in the decimal system. If a commercial bank provides overdraft services, its client's account may occasionally show negative numbers. This may seem as money expressed in negative numbers, but it is just a record of a credit liability related to "money stock" but not to money in a strict sense. In the payment system of our PCM, this will become obvious.

[42] The indication of the national economy ties this definition to the PCM. Generally, we would be talking about a certain territory.

proper), whatever objects were used money was tightly associated with numbers – when coins had no numbers stamped on them, people accounted for the weight of metal to settle deals. Today, with traditional money objects disappearing, these numbers, accounted for by the central bank, are increasingly acting as money proper ("non-cash" money). If we rely on this definition, it is obvious that "good old money" does not indeed turn into something entirely new as the role of traditional money objects diminishes. Moreover, money is evolving towards its final numeric form by shedding its commodity origins, as if this final form has been programmed by the laws of classical economy. The invention of computers has dramatically increased the speed of numeric information processing, enabling us to make revolutionary changes in the financial system. These changes, as viewed from our definition of money, have a solid economic foundation and it is only computers that have made them possible.

The theoretical significance of the changes described above is that we begin to separate the credit and payment systems. We'll continue to do this in Chapter 2. When a financial system is understood primarily as a credit and payment system, this may have a deeper meaning than the first impression suggests. This stems from the dual nature of money in deals: *money as paymen*t and *money as credit*. Only the separation of money functions in deals gives us the required degree of rigor (as prices are formed only in deals), while money in deals is always used in this dual manner. As payment, money is alienated "for good" and as credit, it is alienated "for a time", being loaned. By the way, this simple classification of whether we have property alienation or not in a deal will be enough to work out a definition of price later.

The secondary nature of the deposit multiplier. The fundamental nature of the primary lending rate.

Once we have the credit and payment systems separated, the secondary nature of the deposit multiplier becomes obvious – it now looks a bit like the quotient derived from dividing cucumbers by tomatoes. It is hard to say what other useful meaning we can extract from dividing all credit system liabilities by all the money in the payment system when these two systems do not intersect more than any other parts of the economy that are linked to money, one way or another. In the existing formation where the payment system is governed by credit institutions (commercial banks), the significance of the credit multiplier is undoubtedly higher, though not as fundamental as it may seem. This is akin to measuring the angle of trees being bent by the wind while studying the wind itself – young kids may believe that wind is caused by the swaying trees. Nevertheless, no one questions the importance of having an instrument to measure wind speed. Ditto for the credit multiplier, which in the existing system serves as an important gauge for processes inside the credit and payment system. Note that "an instrument to measure …" and "factors influencing the process" are indeed two different things.

Let's talk briefly about the root causes of the "wind", which we will revisit periodically in this book. In the existing system, non-cash money, loaned as credit, still remains in the bank system. Money will remain there even if the borrower does not loan it further but instead pays for some goods or services. Therefore, with one or another correction dependent primarily on the required reserve ratio, commercial banks loan this money again. This credit cycle leaves a footprint in the form of growing deposits, which is measured by the deposit multiplier. Correspondingly, the deposit multiplier nudges a researcher in the following direction of logic reasoning: the more loans, the more deposits (banks' liabilities to their clients). That's why the deposit multiplier is also called a credit multiplier (which will be shown later as not quite precise).

However, the essence of bank lending is more accurately described when reverse causation is used: before a commercial bank can lend any money, it should have it. Likely, the bank will borrow it. Here, the primary lending rate is the most useful numeric indicator used in our study of the "wind" root causes. Primary lending is best understood as commercial banks borrowing money. However, under the existing credit and payment system it is better to discuss primary lending in a "broad sense", as not all the money (subsequently used by commercial banks for lending) is documented as loans. Simply put, commercial banks enjoy the free use of money in the payment system since they service it. Thus, their effective rate is close to zero per cent, save certain inevitable costs. Besides using demand deposits, this lowering of the primary lending rate on the market is also caused by using savings deposits, which typically pay modest interest.[43]

---

[43] In the existing system, primary lending in a broad sense also includes loans made by the central bank (our new system will not have these and we'll discuss the new credit system in detail in Chapter 2). These loans also contribute to the lowering of the primary lending rate and with an active monetary policy, this contribution plays a decisive role (with a disclaimer that not all central banks can afford a sharp lowering of the rate). In a broad sense, primary lending also includes

The multiplication of credit deals as a consequence of credit and payment systems mix-up.

We'll call this credit cycle in the system where commercial banks facilitate payments for all other market participants the *multiplication of credit deals*. A few words about the purity of terminology are appropriate here. It is more precise to say "deposit multiplier" (and not "credit multiplier") and "multiplication of credit deals" (and not "multiplication of credits or credit"). Why "deposit"? Because we have the sum of all deposits, not the total money loaned, in the numerator. Deposits and money loaned are not the same thing, they are not equal and they are reflected on different sides of the bank balance sheet. Why "multiplication of credit deals"? Because credit, like payment, is money – either money as credit or money as payment. It is important that they are handed over differently, but they are both money all the same, without an inscription classifying it as credit or otherwise.[44]

While "credit multiplier" and "multiplication of credit" are mere inaccuracies that you can brush off, saying "money multiplier" is a mistake. It is part of the more common misconception that commercial banks allegedly create money by lending it. Those prone to this misconception do not pay proper attention to the fact that they confuse banks' liabilities with money ("reserves"), which is reflected as banks' assets.

---

foreign bank loans, which we will not have in the new system. These loans also contribute to lowering of the primary lending rate and this is especially visible in cases where loans are made by foreign commercial banks from countries that issue global currencies. Note also that unlike the current case of "funding", we will not treat domestic interbank loans as primary lending (but at the same time we will keep them in our new system). These loans have their special purpose – by "plugging the holes" they form their own market-based interest rate, which is different from both the market interest rate (when commercial banks lend money to other market participants) and from the primary lending rate (when commercial banks borrow money from other market participants). In further discussions, we will not pay attention to this specific rate.

[44] When trying to work out definitions, it is best to avoid some hard-to-define meanings of the term "credit" as a certain relationship. What we really need from this relationship is present in the "credit deal" category.

A game showing that commercial banks do not really create money when lending. The importance of centralised money issuance.

For those who doubt the word "allegedly" used above, I recommend playing this simple game with your friends: half of you will play as commercial banks and the other half as clients. Take 100 roubles and give (loan) it to the first bank (ignore interest for simplicity). The first bank loans 100 roubles to a client who then puts that same loan into the second bank, etc. All game participants write down two things: who owes them money (assets) and whom they owe money to (liabilities). It is easy to notice that banks' liabilities (in this case it is just a reflection of client deposits, the same as the non-cash portion of the notorious money stock) are indeed growing, but the initial 100 roubles have not changed. The situation will also not change if cheques are used instead of cash in this circulation; there will just be more writing involved. Have yet another person play the role of central bank – as soon as the first commercial bank gets 100 roubles in deposits, it transfers it to the central bank, which subsequently just keeps track of the money switching between commercial banks. With a degree of fantasy involved, a commercial bank can issue unlimited credits by simply opening a new client account regardless of the amount on this bank's correspondent account at the central bank. However, the central bank should not allow the borrower to transfer this funny "money" into another commercial bank or get cash, provided it does not agree to refinance that creditor bank. Refinancing is indeed the mechanism used by the central bank (or the government in a broad sense) to create money, though the initial impression suggests that money is created by the creditor bank. The latter will run into problems if the credit operation is not confirmed by the central bank money issuance.

Before money issuance was centralised by the government (the most prominent example being the creation of the US Federal Reserve System in 1913), banks did create money by lending. Bank bills issued as loans then served as surrogate money. The law creating the US Federal Reserve is often mentioned by popular publications in a negative tone along with the general bad impression of bankers, but nonetheless abolition of private paper money and the transition to centralised domestic money was indeed an important step forward in the economic development of our civilisation. *The fight against deflationary crises* and *the accumulation of issuance income by the government* mark two crucial moments for this progressive move. Further, we'll address these fundamental problems of the classical economy mechanism (connected between themselves and its other parts) in more detail and with more rigor. Now, let's point out the principal development stages of these problems under capitalism, paying attention as to why a totally new financial architecture is required to resolve them. For a better understanding of the connections, I will use some figurative comparisons.

Enter deflationary crises, issuance income and the direct issuance of money. The credit issuance of money as the first stage of reverse issuance of money.

The most obvious reason for the law creating the Federal Reserve was to fight against the 19th-century deflationary crises, the frequency of which was directly correlated with the frequency of money-issuing banks' failures. After the centralised money issuance centre had been created in the US, crises indeed happened less often, but the euphoria of the 1920s ended with the 1929 crisis, which was followed by the Great Depression. The centralised production of money lowered the economy's dependence on a single bank failure by raising liquidity[45] (and most importantly, reliability as a liquidity component) of paper money. However, a higher liquidity of paper money caused a higher liquidity of securities as commodity and money surrogates: the more reliable the currency in which a security is denominated, the more liquid is the security itself. The modern securities market is only growing, having gained sizeable weight following yet another even higher stage in money liquidity (its second component is transportability, as here we are talking about non-cash money) and correspondingly, in various "financial instruments" as a result of computer technology development.

The stock market serves as a good illustration of the difference between a liberal and a "liberal" economy. It appears to be quite "liberal", seemingly based on the institution of private property it got connected to money at the national central bank by using the banking system (and largely subordinated it). We are talking primarily about the central banks issuing

[45] We'll understand liquidity as reliability + transportability. The higher these components, the higher the liquidity, and vice versa. "Liquidity" is not a basic category and our definition is not a strict, theoretical one. Someone may offer different terms or additions, but here these two components give the most concise definition possible. Also, note that under liquidity we understand only the property's characteristic and not the property itself (I have often heard finance professionals calling money "liquidity" as well).

the most liquid money, namely the global currencies. Money flows have been "charmed" with the remarkable liquidity of surrogate assets, far exceeding the liquidity of any physical firm's assets and traditional bank loans. By feeding off these money flows, the stock market is forcing the real economy to give up a significant portion of the pie to cover consumption by masterminds and participants of the stock market. These extra costs put a burden on the real economy and may ultimately contribute to an overproduction crisis (or in this case, a deflationary crisis). Along the way, credit chains are lengthening and wind up in a Gordian knot, impossible to untie in times of crisis except through massive bankruptcies and the demise of inflated assets. As a result of the transition to the monetary system of the Perfectly Competitive Market, we are going to treat the stock market as a genie, by putting it back into the bottle[46] with help from our trusted Guards (also known as cost regulators). Having achieved the utmost liquidity of money, we can stop using money surrogates not only without any noticeable loss of efficiency in goods production but also with obvious efficiency gains. Here, the centralised production of money in a national economy becomes a mandatory attribute of the high liquidity of money.

The causes of deflationary crises are not limited to the stock market. To get rid of these crises, as we'll see in Chapter 2, we'll need to give up the credit issuance of money in favour of direct issuance, where money will be issued not as credit but as payment (we have undertaken the main step already, by separating the credit and payment systems).

Before we start talking about the direct issuance of money, we'll need to clarify the term "credit issuance of money", which will be a fundamental clarifying point. Presently, this term is used to describe lending in general by the central bank and other commercial banks alike. However, as we saw in the example given in our preceding thesis and as we will see later, lending by the commercial banks does not directly increase the amount of money in the economy. It does, however, increase the sum of liabilities ("money stock"). Therefore, while describing the existing system, we'll be using the term "credit issuance of money" only for the direct issuance of money through lending by the central bank. While diving into the nuances of bank lending in the combined credit and payment system, we'll be using terms such as "credit deal multiplication", "lengthening of credit chains" and "production of additional broad money".

---

[46] Of course, we won't limit ourselves to this declarative paragraph. In Chapter 2, several theses will be devoted to the securities critique.

We have already pointed out that the participation of the state in a broad sense (read "central bank") in credit operations makes the market character of the national interest rate quite conditional, especially when one takes into account the key importance of the rates set by the central bank. We will see more clearly a direct connection between the credit issuance of money and deflationary crises. However important the credit issuance of money today, it is not the centre of the universe. But the regular issuance of money is generally as essential for the economy as, for example, water or sunlight is for plants.

Let's imagine that participants of the fantasy-genre club gathering had their dream come true when they got magically teleported to some wonderful uninhabited land. Let's assume that, after a period of communal economy, a small spot with a market economy and money circulation forms. From this very general picture, it is clear that in several decades, once both the new settlement and its economy expands, this closed economy will have much more money (recalculated to the initial purchasing power) in circulation. To serve this new economy, more "working wagons" (means of circulation) will be required. However, since money does not grow on trees, it will need to be gradually added to the economy.

Few would deny the need for regular money issuance, but the following questions would pop up right away: "How much?" and "How to?" Judging by the first question, it may seem that money issuance under a PCM is described by an adherent of the quantity theory of money. At the end of this book, there is a thesis titled "*FAQ: The quantity theory of money (and monetarism as its extension)*" that shows some fundamental differences between this study and the quantity theory of money. As for the second question, one might notice a distant semblance with Keynes's ideas as the direct issuance of money amounts to government expenditure, which Keynes paid much attention to and which we'll revisit in Chapter 2. Now, we need to introduce the term describing a "reverse issuance of money", but first let's make four technical observations.

First, no matter what money issuance is called (direct or reverse), in both cases money is "printed" by the state following the orders of the central bank (which determines the issuance of money volume in both cases).

Second, unlike the existing order of things with banknotes bearing the inscription "Bank of Russia Note", under the new formation the inscription will be something like "Monetary Unit of Russian Federation" with the understanding that those monetary units do not belong to the central bank any more. With a credit issuance of money, money production is built using the bank balance sheet principle: when the broad government (central bank) is issuing money, this is duly reflected on the central bank's balance sheet. With a direct issuance of money, new money *from the bank balance sheet perspective* comes seemingly from nowhere – it is just a national economy's issuance income received by the state.

Third, one more distinction will be that while under the present system the same agency (the central bank) determines the volume of new money and disposes of it, the government will dispose of all new money under our PCM.

Fourth, the nature of money issuance (direct or reverse) is determined by the method used to introduce new money into the market sector of the economy. The features reflected in the first three observations are important but only *preparatory*. Looking a bit ahead, note that this meaning applies also to money issuance calculations under a PCM: all transfers taking place before new money enters into the market sector of the economy (e.g. state employees' wages, the financing of state-owned firms) will be just preparatory transfers within the state system.

Thus, the money issuance used under our PCM is called the direct issuance of money in this book. It takes its meaning from the nature of new money flow, which enters private businesses as money received from buyers (households and state-owned enterprises engaged in infrastructure development) and enters commercial banks as money received from depositor clients, usually households. In other words, money enters "from below". We'll call the existing order (central bank → commercial banks → firms and households) and the reverse, as money entering "from above".

The direct issuance of money enters the market sector of the economy "from below" and without using credit liabilities. It is a natural fit for an economic system where markets determine interest rates. Keynes offered to implement a similar method (technically, it was not money issuance) to President Franklin D. Roosevelt in the 1930s. We'll talk about it in detail in Chapter 2.

The reverse issuance of money enters the market sector of the economy "from above" starting with the first phase – credit issuance of money by the central bank and marked by the aberration of the primary lending rate (the central bank rate), which is formed by administrative methods. Under this aberration, we can no longer talk about market-determined lending rates. Therefore, we incur some unpleasant consequences that were partially discussed earlier and will be studied later. What's important is that reverse issuance of money enters the national economy "from above". The direction of money flow itself foreshadows an overproduction crisis, as we'll show in Chapter 2.

New money issued by the central bank via credit issuance of money gets into the existing credit–payment system and is mixed with the rest of the payment system money that commercial banks use for lending. This "new in a broad sense" money (including new money proper, issued by the central bank as well as the payment system money that commercial banks use for lending, lengthening the credit chains and creating that notorious "credit money") enters private firms "from above" in the course of the second stage of the reverse issuance of money.

The direct issuance of money makes forming viable market-driven lending rates possible, in particular helping the economy get rid of deflationary crises and, in the long term, clearing the path to creating a self-regulating classical economy. However, this issuance of money should be well calculated – we need to know exactly how much money needs to be added to the economy. Otherwise, we'll get a bureaucracy-regulated issuance of money with inevitable inflation bouts and corresponding administrative stop-and-go policies.

When we resolve the problem of money issuance calculation (by using price definition), the only drawback left will be that state expenses are allocated using bureaucratic procedures. This unpleasant moment exists today, but under the new system, the volume of state expenses will increase due to the absence of the credit issuance of money and a larger monetary base. In countries with high levels of state accountability, such increases in government expenses should not cause major problems, especially given that the direct issuance of money allows for lower taxes – in other words, we leave some of the money inside the market sector and lower the budget expenses accordingly. In countries with high levels of corruption (like in today's Russia), the effect of transitioning to the new formation will be less pronounced.

Before we finish up this current thesis-preview, let's touch upon the categories of "issuance income" and "seigniorage". One obvious difference between the two is that the seigniorage benefit stems from the difference between the nominal value of currency and the value of various currency materials, whereas the issuance income benefit translates to the *additional* money issued into circulation. Under the gold standard, the former is clearly more important than the latter (with high prices for precious metals behind it) and as soon as coins are replaced by paper and non-cash settlements, the issuance income clearly becomes more important (from seemingly nowhere, you get money that does not require any metal to produce it).

Seigniorage is a milestone of money evolution, which lost its importance when gold capitalism was succeeded by paper capitalism. The monetary system of paper capitalism appears to be an intermediate phase, meaning the replacement of seigniorage by issuance income too late to tally the amount of seigniorage but too early to count the amount of issuance income, despite transition to centrally managed domestic money (or, at any rate, I do not know how to do it correctly, given the coexistence of the credit issuance of money and securities).

There is one more crucial defect of the existing system that gets in the way of not counting the issuance income and its correct collection, and therefore it deserves a separate mention. We are talking about atomising a large portion of the issuance income inside the national banking system. In the new system, we need to resolve this issue by commandeering this share of issuance income from commercial banks for the benefit of the state. Besides lowering ordinary taxes, this will allow us to increase the amount of "working money" in the economy. In theory, we have already stripped commercial banks of these privileges by taking the servicing of payments out of commercial banks, but we have not applied this viewpoint to our analysis yet. Let's do it now.

A continuation of the game, and less obvious examples of how commercial banks create money in payments and not in lending. Physical turnover.

Besides everything else, the misconception about commercial banks allegedly creating money by lending masks the way commercial banks really create money under the existing three-level system. It turns out that lending itself does not play a major role here, and the crux of the problem lies not so much in the bankers' "greed"[47] but in the diminished issuance

[47] This appeasing clause does not apply to monopoly banks such as the giant Sberbank in Russia. This thesis in particular explains why this bank once

income, which in turn slows down the natural growth of a monetary base. Correspondingly, the national economy will be more prone to inflation (if the natural growth of a monetary base is limited, a desire to increase "monetisation of the economy" comes more often) and at any rate this particular national economy will develop slower, lagging behind its competitors.

Let's assume that in our game (the version with the central bank participating, i.e. non-cash money deals) we run another 100 roubles. Let's also assume that we have doubled the number of bank clients who processed this additional money flow regardless of the first round. Now, each commercial bank has two clients and each client has a deposit of 100 roubles. Let's take one commercial bank that has no money in the central bank. If one client of this bank buys certain commodities C from the other client of the same bank and pays with money M (for instance, 30 roubles), we'll get the usual legitimate purchase and sale deal C↔M where the commercial bank settles the payment by subtracting 30 roubles from the first client's deposit and adds this amount to the second client's deposit. The fact that the commercial bank has no money (disregarding cash, let's remember that this commercial bank has no money in the corresponding account at the central bank that is reflected as assets on its balance sheet) does not affect the deal at all.

So, is money stock the same as money after all? No, it is not. We can prove this by looking at a case where both clients come to claim their deposits from the commercial bank. The latter won't be able to give them cash or transfer their funds to another commercial bank, making it impossible to treat the 100 roubles partially used for settlement as full-bodied money or, strictly speaking, money at all. This is simply one of the mirages of the existing three-level credit and payment system, where every commercial bank can play the role of a "local" central bank,[48] making inside settlements. It is clear that in our new two-level payment system, this mirage is not possible in principle, as the system is too simple for it.

Our new system is also free from other less obvious mirages of the existing system. For example, two commercial banks open correspondent accounts with each other. When payers (clients) at one bank are more active, this bank has to transfer money to its correspondent account at the

---

announced that it was ready to lend at rates well below those of the country's Central Bank.

[48] Ditto for other clearing firms and organisations, including the systems for electronic payments.

other bank using the usual central bank route. However, there is a subtle moment involved: the net amount to settle between these two commercial banks can be relatively small, while payers' activity is indeed very high.

Here's a simple example. In our game, let a client of bank A pay 70 roubles to a client of bank B, while another client of bank B pays 50 roubles to another client of bank A at around the same time. Banks have no compelling need to transfer 70 and 50 roubles to each other – bank A would simply transfer 20 roubles to the correspondent account of bank B at the central bank and thus the latter will settle only 20 roubles in payments. In our new system, the central bank will settle the full 70 + 50 = 120 roubles in payments, which will be a complete (or at any rate a much more realistic) reflection of deals that happen in the real economy.

Why are these mirages and that "good old clearing" so bad that the author is scaring you with economic backwardness? You can hurt your eyes scrutinising the existing bank clearing system in search of answers but conclude with merely a shrug. The key to understanding is to compare it with a system from which mirages have been eliminated. Only with this comparison can we realise the limits of our perception of these mirages as something that goes without saying and does not require changes. By giving the production of "working money" to commercial banks, we lower the issuance income and therefore we cannot use it as explained above, for example, to lower taxes.

Note that there is no magic here: from the viewpoint of the lower level (physical persons and firms), the amount of money used in the economy does not change immediately after transitioning to the new system. The fact that in the existing system only part of this money represents full-bodied national roubles, while the balance is made of "roubles" issued by commercial banks in the process of clearing, does not impact the lower level and it will not be felt immediately after transitioning when all money will become wholesome national currency.

One might also ask the question: By using an analogy with the laws of conservation of energy or matter, does the private sector (commercial banks) somehow compensate this shortage of issuance income by settling payments without the state's involvement? And would we lose something by giving up bank clearing? It turns out there is nothing to lose, only to gain (and by a lot), by applying the same general principle that once made human telephone operators obsolete: moving non-cash money (just numbers) with the help of computers ("inside the computer") does not incur massive costs. The private sector could save costs if money was physically massive and hard to move. Producing the "clearing money" represents the fee (a part of it) charged by commercial banks to facilitate payments in the combined credit and payment system. The national economy's costs to maintain the payment system after transitioning to the PCM will obviously decrease, enabling the new financial system to collect higher issuance income without sacrificing anything.

A fragment of technological evolution is very visible here (like replacing candles with light bulbs, for example), but the difficulty is that this particular fragment can be executed without creating imbalances only in the formational (revolutionary) transition as part of other changes in the financial system. Some of these changes are tied to using new technologies created with the help of natural sciences too and some are purely economic reforms. The good news is that <u>all</u> these changes and reforms (that is, each one taken separately) increase the efficiency of both the national and world economies. We'll address the relationship between technological evolution and revolutionary transitions from one formation to another in detail at the beginning of Chapter 2 within the scope of our main discussion about costs.

Thus, we have designed a low maintenance, unified payment system that looks something like a giant computer. Along with making payments cheaper, we make them run faster. Both improvements have been quite a visible quantum leap. We have also attained the highest degree of procedure standardisation, making regular control over the fees easier in principle. All these improvements did not just fall from the sky. We have taken this operation from a group of people (commercial banks) who used to make money on it and trust it to a computer. By doing this, we reacted to the evolution of money, which culminated in numeric information by shedding its commodity shell. This information is the highest form of asset liquidity (in this case, we are talking about transportability as one of the liquidity components) and the use of computers for its processing is very appropriate. We can say figuratively that money's transition to its ultimate form gives back to us a portion of its "power" that was previously wasted on circulation costs.

The category of "physical turnover expressed in monetary terms" (or simply "physical turnover", as we won't introduce another similar sounding category into this text) gives us an important pivot point. In other words, it is the sum of all purchase and sale deals of property. This category once included the purchase and sale of people. Under the PCM, it will mostly appear as the turnover of commodities and services, or to simplify, commodity turnover (expressed in monetary terms). However, due to the non-reproducibility of land, there is an additional group of deals *related* to land turnover (these are commonly called land purchase and sale deals, but strictly speaking, they serve as a proxy for the purchase and sale of R_{PL} – rights of primary lease). With the transition from capitalism to the PCM, these deals will not undergo any crucial changes. In general, any examples proving the importance of the "physical turnover" category will be discussed using commodity turnover, but as land-related deals are also present, we need to use the overarching category of "physical turnover".

The need for such an overarching category is even more obvious while talking about paper capitalism, as its economic system is prone to an excessive use of surrogates (securities as commodity and money surrogates). Here, using the term "physical" requires a certain effort, but at their core the associated deals are still purchase and sale[49] ones.

We'll be making good use of this seemingly modest category ("physical turnover") in our theoretical analysis, but it comes in most handy for understanding the principles of calculating issuance income. Even school kids know that the economy needs "enough money" to function. Add too much of it and you'll have inflation; add too little and you'll have deflation.[50] Let's begin by stating that tying money issuance to GDP growth will cause deflation (though in rare cases, it may cause inflation). As we know, GDP is calculated based on "value added".[51]

---

[49] The vague character of surrogates compels us to put a disclaimer upon disclaimer: in reality, it is impossible to account for securities turnover based on physical turnover. We'll talk about this in Chapter 2.

[50] Here, we are talking about issuance-related inflation and deflation, meaning that money has lost part of its value (inflation) or gained it (deflation) due to the quantitative misalignment between money issuance and the amount of money required by the economy. We'll be refining the definitions of inflation and deflation as needed. However, for simplicity, it makes sense to treat inflation not as the higher price for goods, but as the lower price (depreciation) of money, simply because not only goods are exchanged for money. So, this will be our ongoing definition of inflation and deflation, here and elsewhere.

[51] In this expression, the word "value" is really used in a sense of "price", namely as "final price". I regard the GDP indicator to be a secondary one, although not because it is not realistic. What is not realistic is the mythical "value" that mysterious clot of some substance which, by the assumption of the founding fathers of the classical school, is hidden in the product itself. Here, the term

Important examples demonstrating the fundamental nature of physical turnover expressed in monetary terms.

Main example:

Let a firm based in A sell some commodities C_0 to a firm based in B, and subsequently, the firm based in B processes C_0 into commodities C_1 and sells them to the end consumer based in C. This one sentence represents the whole example (we'll only be adding two payments made for C_0 and C_1). It does not matter whether these firms are in different cities, whether they purchased additional goods or services for processing C_0 into C_1, or whether C_1 was sold to the end consumer.

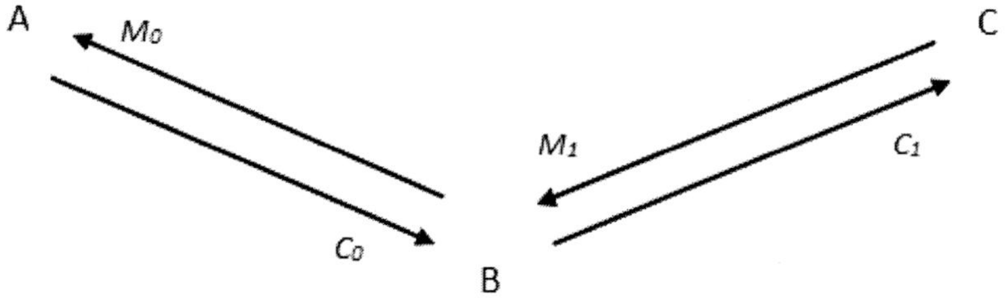

Fig. 1-1

Thus, we have two purchase and sale deals: $C_0 \leftrightarrow M_0$ and $C_1 \leftrightarrow M_1$ (see Fig. 1-1). To illustrate this, imagine a freight train carrying C_0 from A to B and at the same time a certain container M_0 (money, means of payment) is shipped by rail in the opposite direction, i.e. from B to A. Likewise, after processing C_0, a freight train goes from B to C carrying commodities C_1, while the M_1 container goes in the opposite direction. Note that to produce end consumer commodities C_1 we need $(M_0 + M_1)$[52] of money and this

"value" has an everyday but realistic meaning of "price", regardless of what initial sense was once assigned to it by those who coined the term "value added".

[52] We need to insert a disclaimer here that in its pure form this is true for the PCM. In the existing model, payment deferments (or trade credits) are commonplace: there is no payment M_0 for C_0 until M_1 payment takes place (until the final consumer pays). Therefore, the first firm lacking the M_0 cash, is forced to borrow funds, and the money for this borrowing should be available in the economy. For this example, the situation with the amount of money does not *crucially* change, though an exact match may not happen. Once we expand the example to include the sources of money for commercial banks (the lengthening of credit chains), the situation with the amount of money does change a lot – under paper capitalism, the

sum is important, unlike the value added. This is the essence of this example. Likewise, this sum is important to calculate the additional amount of money required to serve the growing commodity turnover.

For a quantitative illustration, let's say M_0 = 100 roubles and M_1 = 200 roubles. Further, let's say M_0 is entirely value added, as C_0 is natural raw material or an imported ingredient. In this case, the total value added in our example will be equal to M_1 = 200 roubles, and the sum ($M_0 + M_1$), also called physical turnover, expressed in monetary terms will be 300 roubles (100 + 200). Assume the demand has doubled for these commodities, and now instead of one unit of C_0 and one of C_1, we have two units of each. In this new period, M_0 is 200 roubles; M_1 has also doubled and now equals 400 roubles. Though the value added in our example (which is equal to M_1, as a little bit of GDP) increased only by 200 roubles, the turnover sum ($M_0 + M_1$), which is now equal to 600 roubles, grew by 300 roubles. This happened for the simple reason that M_0's increase by 100 roubles contributed to M_1's increase without any rise in value added.

It turns out the author was retelling, using his own words, a well-known problem of "double counting", which the GDP indicator is designed to remediate. However, it was worth it, because here the *theoretically* less important GDP indicator is going against the fundamentally important indicator of physical turnover. If one needs to understand, *for analytics of management purposes*, how much has been produced in goods and services ready for either final or industrial consumption or export, the GDP indicator is indispensable. Still, money and goods are two different kinds of property. Money is "working" as a means of payment. It will accompany deals along the reproduction path up until final consumption as many times as needed. Whether it accompanies the sales of raw materials to make a chair or the sale of the chair itself, it will still be just money. Used properly and without haste, commodity turnover expressed in monetary terms (which we'll generally call physical turnover expressed in monetary terms) is one of the keys allowing us to unlock many mysteries in the economic mechanisms.

---

amount of money is less but it turns over faster. We have already discussed it, and in Chapter 2 we'll address the consequences of the ubiquitous trade credits practice. Our attention to these and other elements of "credit pollution" of the paper capitalism economy that results in extra costs, monopolization processes, and overproduction crisis phenomena, will occupy a significant part of this study.

Additional example:

Before we transition to these mechanisms, let's offer a disclaimer: strictly speaking, mandatory deflation does not stem from tying money issuance to the GDP growth in our example above. If we compare the relative increases, both the value added (200 versus 400) and physical turnover (300 versus 600) have doubled. It may seem this disclaimer proves the logical merit of tying money issuance to GDP growth, but let's not draw quick conclusions here. Let's assume that the increase in demand that caused doubling of value added has been caused by deeper manufacturing processes, and a new firm B_1 has plugged itself in between buying goods from B for 150 * 2 = 300 roubles and selling the final product to the end consumer for 200 * 2 = 400 roubles. Value added has still doubled from the first period, but physical turnover has tripled (900 versus 300). This would require issuing more money compared with the amount "hinted" by GDP growth.

Conversely, if a firm disappears from the chain (for example, as a result of acquisition), then the *relative* increase in physical turnover (and respectively, justified money issuance) will be less than the relative growth of value added.

In other words, the strength of ties between GDP growth and money issuance is not fundamental. This is not the sole, and certainly not the most important, corollary from our additional example. Very soon we'll see how money "loves" well-developed manufacturing. After that, we'll see its "distaste" for large firms (and once more, for the large commercial banks that we have already discussed), and later, how our examples relate to the "Dutch disease", and near the end of Chapter 1, how physical turnover is linked to global currencies.

We won't need this additional example in our next thesis, as relationships uncovered in the main example should be enough to demonstrate what I consider to be the main definition, i.e. ***the definition of a price.***[53]

[53] The central bank specialists in China and other countries, who are trying to implement central bank digital currency (CBDC) payment systems, seem to not understand how important this definition is. I assume that they are unaware of this definition, because it is unlikely that they have read my book published in Russian (Голод, Игорь. Новая финансовая система. – Москва: Экономика, 2012. – 237 с. [Golod, Igor. The New Financial System – Moscow, Economica, 2012. – 237 p.]), where the principles of such a system are described. Otherwise, these

Money alienation (payment) as a moment when property price is formed. Forming the price of money in a credit deal. Definition of price. Link between money issuance and price of money.

First, let's clarify one important moment that frequently evades understanding. It was already present in the example with two trains but without due focus. We are talking about the money "container" M that is going in the opposite direction to commodities C in the process of exchange. Everyone well understands that in this purchase and sale deal, M is the price of C, but it often gets forgotten that, in turn, C is the price of M. One owner has voluntarily given up property C in exchange for property M, and C has been alienated for good. The other owner has voluntarily given up property M in exchange for property C, also with alienation. In a classical economy, a purchase and sale deal is prominently featured among other deals, and the forming of the price of money constitutes one of its most remarkable features.

We often give the following reasoning: "It does not matter what the producer of goods was hoping for or how much money and effort he spent to produce his goods, but it is important how much money he will get from buyers in the market. This will determine the true price for the goods." In other words, views of sellers or buyers, economists and people in general about what the price would be are not important here. The only important thing is the quantitatively determined fact of voluntary property alienation by the buyers.

Generally, voluntary alienation of one's property is very important. The entire economy is built on the desire to preserve and increase one's property. Thousands and thousands of years of natural selection took care

---

specialists would find that without the use of price definition, a CBDC payment system (which in fact is an empirically discovered piece of the financial system of the future, as described in this book) will never be able to be fully functional. If you find it difficult to understand the essence of CBDC (or more precisely, the essence of the corresponding element of the future PCM payment system) from recent open media publications, please refer to the first paragraph of the current chapter. If you still find something incomprehensible about CBDC, it is not crucially important, since these publications merely reflect the arduous attempts to integrate CBDCs into the current financial system. We certainly do not question the professional qualifications of the Chinese Central Bank employees. The problem is that organically (i.e. theoretically) these two systems cannot coexist. There can be only one or the other.

of distilling the simple truth: without property, you or your progeny may perish, "cutting" your genetic line short. We all happen to be descendants of those people (and earlier, primates) who were concerned with the survival of their children. In my view, this happens naturally: a coincidence between the price forming for some property A (not necessarily goods, nor necessarily in a sale, but it can be in a lease) and the opposing voluntary alienation of property B (which therefore is the price of property A). At the same time, property A is not always alienated in the exchange process: if alienation does happen, the price of B is formed (which is A); without alienation (the case of leasing A), the price of B is not formed. To ease your possible confusion of A and B, let me remind you that in our scope of study, B is always money as a means of payment.

What we say about the true price of producer goods, we can also apply to the money in the C↔M deal: the true price of money in this deal is the goods that the buyer receives as a result of an exchange. The reasoning behind economic growth, followed by increased money turnover in a country N and thus creating an expanded money issuance mandate for its national monetary authorities (and they better do it on time to avoid deflation [54]), is only correct when the money turnover increase is accompanied by a higher price for this country's money (the price of *all* money, while deflation is the price increase of *one* monetary unit). Money turnover in a real economy has many facets – there are some deals where the price of money is formed but also others where it is not.

One example of a deal where the price is not formed is a hiring deal. Sure, the price of hired labour, called wages (more precisely, the price of leasing a human), is formed. However, the price of money (the price of wages in this case) does not get formed. For example, if hired workers sat idle all day long, by the entrepreneur's fault, then they would still get their contractual wages, although possibly less than they expected. Meanwhile, the entrepreneur won't get anything in exchange for his money. Of course, this conspicuous idle time is rather an exception. But at any rate, from the entrepreneur's perspective, the money he pays to the hired workers are costs and nothing else. This is valid not only from the entrepreneur's

[54] We'll discuss why deflation is bad in Chapters 2 and 3. Some conservative members of the Austrian School should be our prime audience for this. "Austrians" are compelled to defend deflation, as otherwise it is impossible to justify the gold standard, which inevitably leads to deflation, but without which, in their opinion, it is not possible to cure the ills of the existing financial system. You'll have a chance to learn how our new financial system solves all these problems without a rollback to the "golden caves" of economic history.

perspective but also from the whole national economy's perspective (the lower price of hired labour compared with more developed nations is the main factor contributing to the economic miracle in China). Only purchase and sale deals will show how justifiable are the costs incurred in producing goods and services. If this were not the case and the price of money was formed in hiring deals, one could simply print money and pay it out in wages regardless of the ultimate results of the work.[55] In real life, meaning the place where laws of classical economy operate without major disclaimers, unnecessary costs are filtered out by the "invisible hand of the market" (at least to the extent to which it is possible in a given economic system).

Using symbols to depict property alienation, the formula showing how the price of hired labour is formed (and the price of money is not formed) can be written in this compact way: P←M. This formula applies to a hiring deal, where P is people and M is money as a means of payment, and the deal itself is classified as a lease deal, i.e. money is the only property being alienated. In basic lease deals, which differ from purchase and sale deals, generally only the price of the leased property is formed. If we agree that **only alienation of property from one of the deal participants makes this property the price of the other participant's property in the same deal,**[56] then besides purchase and sale deals there is one more basic deal where the price of money is formed. We are talking about a credit deal, $M_C \leftarrow M$, where M_C is money as credit and M is money as a means of payment. Here, like in any other lease deal, the price of leased property is formed and it equals M. In a hiring deal this price is traditionally called "wages", in a land lease deal it is called "rent" and in a credit deal it is called "interest". Correspondingly, if we are talking ***about money issuance, the amount of money in circulation needs to be growing in proportion to the growth of not only physical turnover (adjusted for inflation or deflation) but also credit turnover***.[57] At the same time, we

[55] To a degree, it was happening in the former USSR (the closed economy effect) and has been partially happening in the US, starting in mid-20th century (the issuer of a global currency effect). These disparate examples have one technical aspect in common, namely the absence of currency devaluation. While cases of a closed economy are of little interest for our study, we'll devote much attention to the features and consequences of the issuance of global currencies.

[56] One exception to this definition of price in bold type would be a gift deal.

[57] *(You may want to either skip or glance over this hard-to-digest technical footnote, at least until the sentence where "money velocity" is highlighted).* **To calculate the portion of money issuance stemming from growth of the credit turnover, we need to increase the sum of M_C in proportion to the growth of**

have no need to separate these two – as we said earlier, there is no inscription classifying money as credit or otherwise. By the way, mandatory accounting for credit turnover allows us to confidently say that tying money issuance to GDP will cause deflation in most cases.

---

the sum of M, national interest, i.e. aggregate interest payments (total amount of M does not include the returning money that was lent earlier as Mc, so it is markedly less that Mc). **This calculated growth of Mc in absolute numbers will be the portion of money issuance that we are looking for**. Here, a mechanical analogy with C↔M may potentially cause two problems. First, there is our subconscious attention to how the growth of "M" behaves, as only money as a means of payment constitutes a common element in these deals. However, the growth of "M" in a purchase and sale deal makes up the portion of money issuance that we are looking for, whereas in a credit deal it makes up an increase within a given time frame that we account for in order to calculate the money issuance required for growing Mc. Second, it pays to note that while the C↔M deal is a double-sided equation (however weird this may sound to mathematicians), Mc←M is a single-sided one in terms of property alienation. Correspondingly, in a purchase and sale deal, increases in C and M will match in both absolute and relative numbers. More precisely, they would match in absolute numbers if they were measured in the same units. They do not – and moreover, commodities do not – have unified units of measurement. Taking advantage of the double-sided equation, we simply disregard this and calculate the absolute increase of physical turnover in the national economy using money as the measurement, which after adjustment for inflation (or deflation) will give us the required money issuance volume. In a credit deal, we have identical units of measurement at both sides but only relative increases will be matching. Based on this increase, coupled with a known increase in national interest in absolute numbers, we can calculate the required absolute increase of Mc. For simplicity, we have ignored **money velocity**, i.e. all our calculations are valid within one money cycle. Accounting for the money velocity ratio is not a problem – if, for a given period of time, the ratio is equal to or less than 1, all the money issuance volume calculations above are valid, and if it exceeds 1, the money issuance volume should be divided by that ratio. It is more important to state that in our new system, money velocity will decrease significantly due to an expanded monetary base and the absence of a lowered interest rate for primary lending – simply put, commercial banks will lose the opportunity to initiate and extend their "endless" credit chains using some "free" money. In a strict sense, there is a reversed fundamental accent: the high money velocity that we witness in today's US economy is an anomaly from the rigorous classical principles upon which our new system is built.

Physical turnover and manufacturing.

We'll be talking about credit deals in detail in Chapter 2. Meanwhile, let's revisit physical turnover expressed in monetary terms and try to look upon some familiar things from a different perspective. For example, everyone is familiar with some kind of understanding (though under paper capitalism, it may not be so obvious, taking into account fundamental differences between countries issuing global currencies and ordinary countries with near-classical economies) that the degree of development of the manufacturing industry is quite indicative in a discussion about the development of a given national economy. There are economists sharing this understanding and those who are not, citing increases in the services sector [58] despite the dramatic rise of China's power in the shortest historical time possible. However, there is simple arithmetic (which, by the way, combines goods and those services that organically fit into the manufacturing technology chain, e.g. engineering, packaging, design, etc.) – manufacturing enterprises often have a lot of subcontractors and, correspondingly, significant volumes of physical turnover.[59] As shown in the additional example in our thesis "*Important examples ...*" above, this national economy can naturally accommodate more money. Therefore, with an identical increase in GDP, the volume of money issuance will be higher in an economy featuring more developed manufacturing. As a result, this economy will be less vulnerable to issuance inflation even under the existing financial system. In addition, under our PCM financial system, well-developed manufacturing will contribute to a higher issuance income, allowing an increase in state investment (like infrastructure) or deeper tax cuts.

Physical turnover and large integrated firms. More on mirages at large commercial banks as viewed through a physical turnover prism.

Here's another similar example. There is hardly a need to prove that monopolistic firms are harmful for the economy (save for those who make good money inside/on them). However, if we change "monopolistic" to

[58] We'll talk about the well-known concept of "post-industrial society" in Chapter 4, thesis "*FAQ: Services, "post-industrial society", information, opportunity cost.*"
[59] And they will have these significant volumes in the foreseeable future, despite ever-shrinking machinery and production processes due to technological evolution, unless someone finds a "philosopher's stone" to turn one chemical element into another.

"large", this general understanding may take an awkward pause. In Chapter 2, we'll dwell in detail on the cost features of large, integrated firms,[60] but now let's highlight the same arithmetic reasoning. With all else being equal, in an industry consisting mainly of specialised firms (firms of moderate integration or no integration at all), there will be more market deals and, as a result, more physical turnover, compared with the same industry characterised by the significant role of large integrated firms. In this case, an organic increase in both the number of deals and the amount of money in the national economy will surely be an effect of the increase in the number of firms, driven by natural competition and not by administrative restrictions on a firm's size. In other words, an increase in the number of firms should happen in the scope of further division of labour between goods producers (firms), which should be distinguished from the division of labour between workers inside a firm. We'll address this in more detail in the Chapter 2 thesis "*Ronald Coase and transaction costs ...*". There, we'll also see how the insufficient attention that Coase paid to the historical logic of division of labour, originally described by Adam Smith back in the 18th century, caused this well-known American economist to make certain fundamental mistakes.

For the future, let's note that the evolution of division of labour among goods producers has critical importance for the core logic of our study. In the existing system, it is held back by the lack of a comprehensive, market-driven, third basic cost regulator, i.e. an interest rate.

In the meantime, let's point out a simple arithmetic fact that not only large commercial banks with many clients, as we showed in our earlier thesis "*A continuation of the game ...*", but also large integrated firms contribute to lower issuance income in the combined credit and payment system.

Our example with large commercial banks in the thesis "*A continuation of the game ...*" is also easier to understand after we introduce the "physical turnover" category. An increase in commodities C turnover requires

---

[60] In our study, we assume that large integrated firms (here we have to limit ourselves to an assumption due to lack of a strict definition) are either vertically or horizontally integrated, with a degree of integration higher than it would be necessary for purely technical cost optimization reasons. The level of integration in large firms is more influenced by their fight for market share. A firm comprised of one sprawling industrial site (for example, steel works) is not necessarily "large" in this sense, as every industry may have a certain optimal size from a technological viewpoint. As a rule, large integrated firms have significant sales volume and a sizeable workforce, but medium sized businesses can be as excessively integrated.

issuing new "containers" M. In the existing mixed system, these money "containers" are partially issued ("clearing money") by commercial banks whenever they settle payments between the clients of one commercial bank or clients of other commercial banks where they have correspondent accounts set up (this is particularly noticeable when looking at large commercial banks). In the PCM financial system, the required-for-trade "containers" will be issued as usual as real money by the state, which would receive extra issuance income to cover budget expenses. This won't be a one-time increase in the amount of money (both relative and absolute) while transitioning to the new system, but a future repetitive issuance increase in absolute numbers (money). Should we crank up issuance to this extent under the mixed system, high inflation would result.

Further, let's address not speculative but very real inflation. It emerges for the same technical reasons, when money issuance exceeds the numbers necessary to serve the physical turnover that has grown. Namely, the risk of deflation nudges the state to issue more money, but deflation does not disappear. The possibility of having concurrent inflation and deflation can cast doubts, considering their traditional definitions (inflation as price increases for goods; deflation as price decreases). In our study, they are understood as impairment and appreciation of money, respectively, that can happen in relation to *different* types of property. Before we proceed with the detailed analysis of the Dutch disease (and we are talking exactly about it here) and then finish up the talk on physical turnover, we'll clarify our classification of inflation and deflation types.

Inflation and deflation.

We have already mentioned issuance-related inflation. The second type of inflation (depreciation of money relative to goods stemming from high costs of national producers) that we are going to call "inflation resulting from costs", or simply "inflation from costs", is more important to understand given its significance for the new system. We'll use the classical understanding of inflation from costs, i.e. view it as it would happen in the classical economy of a PCM. By doing it this way, we are filtering out the noise arising from the chaotic (market + administrative) regulation in the present financial system, which is also saturated with money surrogates.[61]

---

[61] Let me guess that the last two phrases were read with diminishing attention compared to those at the beginning of the paragraph where a new term was

With inflation from costs, money loses its value not because of technical excess over the required money issuance volume, but because domestically produced goods begin to lose to the international competition both inside the country and outside it due to excessive producer costs. Market demand for the national currency required to purchase domestic goods is going down in this case, while demand for the foreign currency required to purchase imported goods is growing. Accordingly, national currency depreciates. The relative depreciation of the national currency compared with foreign currencies is a key moment here, but the inflation from costs also includes the subsequent relative depreciation of money compared with non-monetary property (for easier understanding of this thesis without missing any important moments, hereafter we'll be talking only about goods and not just any non-monetary property). It is about the national economy experiencing higher prices for exported and imported goods, as well as goods produced with exported or imported components.

Note that while this term sounds close to traditional "cost-push inflation", they are not identical. The term "cost-push inflation" is traditionally used in conjunction with the equally traditional definition of inflation, viewed as an increase in the prices of goods.

The term "inflation" originated precisely as a characteristic of the increase in the prices of goods expressed in money (as the term itself suggests) – this type of increase is the most obvious to an observer. However, we have noted that in purchase and sale deals C↔M, M is the price of C while C is the price of M. Accordingly, in technical terms, an increase in the price of goods is simultaneously the depreciation of money, so a qualified researcher only has to choose which one is more convenient to study. The tie between "inflation" and "deflation" to money is more robust compared with their ties to goods, as money is as homogeneous as numbers, while at the opposite ends of deals it encounters endless kinds of property.

---

introduced. That's why I am stressing that due to the particular nature of the existing financial system, money transfers and transactions reflected on the capital account (capital and financing operations) have outsized importance. Often, they obscure the international sales of goods, directly or indirectly affecting their nature and volume (this phrase contains a whole world but this is a world of the outgoing formation). Under our PCM, everything will be exactly opposite (simply put, the way it should be). Therefore, here and further in our reasoning, whenever we need to account for international trade we will focus on the characteristics and consequences of moving goods and corresponding payments across national borders.

With this, I am not going to argue the independent meaning of the term "cost-push inflation", at least not the part that describes an increase in the prices of goods and services offered by monopolies; that they are connected as "cost-push inflation" is one of the factors for inflation from costs. However, "cost-push inflation", despite its relevance for national economies with a high influence of monopolies (including outside ones), does not have a theoretical meaning as large as inflation from costs. The category of "cost-push inflation" is largely an analytical (managerial) one, as it depends a lot on the characteristics of a country and the nuances of an industry.

As a rule, the definitions offered in this study simplify the understanding of categories and processes. However, definitions of inflation and deflation as the depreciation and appreciation of money, respectively, can partially complicate this understanding – for example, when talking about inflation we now need to distinguish (where appropriate) between money depreciation relative to non-monetary property and money depreciation relative to foreign currencies. I consider this complexity well justified, as our comprehensive understanding of sophisticated processes will compensate for more complex terminology. At the same time, our understanding of the terms "inflation" and "deflation" will not materially deviate from the traditional understanding.

This is a perfect moment to clarify that this tie to money does not exclusively mean a monetary character of origin, whether inflation or deflation. In the new system, free from many problems including those that economists are trying to solve by applying quantity theories of money,[62] we'll see that the accents are rather opposite. In our new system, inflation from costs, stemming from competition between producers of goods, will have a prominent place among all other kinds of inflation or deflation.

Deflation from costs begins similarly to inflation from costs, such as from an overproduction crisis, i.e. when goods are burdened by excessive costs but a rapid depreciation of money (relative to both foreign currencies and goods) does not take place. Here, we see that the deflation mechanism is more difficult to understand than the currency depreciation mechanism, which lies at the core of inflation from costs. When we talk about currency depreciation, we find ourselves in a comfort zone of a simple quantitative

---

[62] We'll talk about these in detail in Chapter 4, thesis "*FAQ: The quantity theory of money (and monetarism as its extension).*"

change ("now, there is more money than needed"). Conversely, in our talk about deflation we need to take into account, in addition to the same quantitative change (albeit with a negative sign: "now, there is less money than needed"), the influence of a "second component". This can be either gold (under the "gold" capitalism), which is preventing money from depreciating under the gold standard, or global currencies (under the paper capitalism) that have assumed the operational functions of gold as an international means of payment.

Accounting for the influence of gold money on the quantitative mechanism of deflation does not bring about more complexity (as the amount of monetary gold in the world economy is quite stable). We could describe a version of deflation under the gold standard with just one sentence, using an example of the processes unfolding in the US in the 19th century: when trust in paper money (the notes issued by some commercial banks) was falling abruptly, it was practically not accepted and resulted in a physical shortage of money (more detail in Chapter 3, thesis "*Deflation from costs*"). The substitution of gold with global currencies complicated the deflation mechanism, up to the point where it went beyond the domain of theoretical economics, as the latter lacks the appropriate instruments. (Dollars and euros are just money as well, issued by somebody, and the role of gold is performed not only by these currencies but also by government bonds denominated in these currencies.) This is not the only complex moment of the financial system under the current formation, but the sharp increase in complexity of the deflation mechanism may well be the main reason for analytics implicitly replacing theory, even in theoretical writings starting in the middle of the last century. Note also that despite the transition of the operational functions of gold to global currencies, gold itself did not "disappear". We are going to address this increase in complexity among other things later (Chapter 3, "*Gold under paper capitalism*").

Under modern capitalism, deflation from costs (in its pure form) happens in countries issuing global currencies while inflation from costs happens in ordinary, peripheral nations. Due to economic globalisation, it is hard to say whether these kinds of relative money depreciation and appreciation accumulate only in their countries of origin. This potent and convoluted combination of inflation and deflation is intrinsic to cyclical deflationary crises. Characteristically, the mix will vary substantially at different crisis phases, as seen in the crisis that started in the first decade of the 21st century.

The degree of resistance to the depreciation of the national currency serves as a crucial separation line drawn between the centres of origin of inflation and deflation from costs, as well as between the "ordinary" and the "wonderland" parts of the modern world economy in general. Hyper-stability of global currencies coupled with their oversized clout over the world economy makes it easy to identify "wonderland" as the breeding ground of prolonged deflation crises spreading over the world economy. By the same token, low stability of peripheral currencies makes it easy to identify the place where inflation crises originate, touching a limited number of nations and ending relatively quickly (except in cases where these crises stem from a worldwide deflationary crisis).

Besides particular characteristics that depend on the economic development phase (boom, recession, one or another crisis phase), national currency type (world, intermediate, ordinary)[63] and national characteristics (for example, industrial specialisation or import preferences), certain key characteristics of capitalist formations contribute to the variety of inflation and deflation patterns. Here, we are talking about the differences in behaviour between "high power" and "low power" money, as well as about the considerable manual intervention of the broad government in credit and monetary systems. These characteristics, which differ depending on whether we are dealing with a gold or paper version of capitalism, have an especially strong influence over manifestations of inflation and deflation at a time of crisis. Had we tasked ourselves with healing capitalism, looking at these in detail would be interesting. However, we do not face such a task (it would be impossible in principle and, besides, our PCM model which we can transition to after just a few years of preparation is substantially better). Under the advanced PCM, there will remain mainly inflation from costs and its probable consequence, issuance inflation.[64]

---

[63] For example, US dollar, Swiss franc, Russian rouble.

[64] We should distinguish between issuance income and inflation tax *under the new formation*. Unlike the relative ease in calculating differences between issuance income and seigniorage, the difference between issuance income and inflation tax is obscured by the fact that both are new money. Also, note that under capitalism, this distinction is extremely difficult to draw on a technical level (without vague arguments about the rich and the poor). Thus, under a PCM, the money issuance equal to the issuance income won't lead to either depreciation or appreciation of money. The inflation tax, also present in the new system (as dictated and limited by the time of gross deterioration of the payments balance), is equal to the volume of excessive money issuance, i.e. the amount of money issued over the issuance

We'll be sure to keep pointing out manifestations of inflation and deflation in the modern economy, because they are closely tied to the costs created by the financial system of paper capitalism. There are two very important ones from a theoretical point of view. First, there is one kind of issuance inflation influencing the world economy as a whole; it is the depreciation of global currencies (and eventually all others) relative to gold and other strategic goods, as well as land. This kind of issuance inflation originated in the "wonderland" part of the world following the creation of the euro as the second fully fledged global currency. We'll address this in Chapter 3.[65] Conversely, the second kind is typical for peripheral countries with an oversized share of raw material exports in the modern world economy. Here, we are talking about a variant of stagflation known as the "Dutch disease".

Physical turnover and the Dutch disease.

Let's talk a bit about the Dutch disease, which is a special kind of deflation (or inflation, depending on one's point of view). I would prefer to call this odd mix of inflation and deflation[66] "stagflation" (generally, without tying it to a pronounced case of Dutch disease). The existing definition of stagflation (stagnation + inflation) is not an obvious error but

---

income. Correspondingly, money issuance can exceed the issuance income once the inflation tax appears. As a rule, with normal economic development, the volume of money issuance will be equal to the issuance income (unless part of the issuance income is spent to lower ordinary taxes and in this case money issuance will be less than issuance income). Let's repeat that with a PCM we'll be able to draw the distinction. Before a PCM is enacted, the difference between the issuance income and the inflation tax is hard to trace. That's why the credit character of a central bank money issuance is justified under capitalism: absent a better mechanism, the amount of money in the economy is determined, *to the extent it is possible*, by market participants' demand for an administratively managed credit supply.

[65] At this point, note that gold could not stay away from participating in the world liquidity championship, which the present-day world financial system ironically resembles. From the beginning of the 21st century, paper capitalism has been going out of equilibrium enough to cause a partial return of the gold standard. Demand for gold began to rapidly grow before 2007, the starting year of the world economic crisis.

[66] As we have noted earlier, one can see this mix only upon tying the definitions of inflation and deflation to money. If one remains within the framework of tying them to goods, there is no escape from the thought that a mix of inflation and deflation (concurrently) may not even happen.

it is destined to be vague. It either combines a loosely defined process (stagnation) with precise calculation (money depreciation), or it mixes up "cucumbers and tomatoes" while trying to decipher "stagnation" using the unemployment level or low GDP growth. If we define stagflation as inflation (in this case, money depreciation compared with non-monetary property) *without sufficient money depreciation* against foreign currencies, this definition will remain in the arithmetic domain with money prices.

The absence of due currency depreciation adequately explains both low economic growth and high unemployment, which are typical with deflation. While inflation is easy to observe, as it is expressed in absolute numbers, the appreciation of money against foreign currencies (revaluation) may not even happen, at least against all or the majority of currencies. Insufficient currency depreciation leads to the same processes as deflation in general. In these cases, I will sometimes use the imprecise term "heavy" (for example, a heavy rouble), to imply that the inflated price of a unit of a currency compared with foreign currencies "exerts pressure" on the competitiveness of national firms.

The Dutch disease originates in countries exporting goods. It is easier to understand why this mix of deflation and inflation hits exporters once we remember that the price of money is formed in a purchase and sale deal. Excluding countries blessed with their own global currencies, export deals of other countries are generally denominated in a foreign currency. Hence, the price of the foreign currency paid for the exported goods is formed in lieu of the price of the exporter's domestic currency. As a result, if exported goods are sold using US dollars (further referred to as "dollars"), this may serve as a reason for an issuance of dollars to facilitate the physical turnover of world trade expressed in dollars. However, this does not serve as a reason for issuance of national currency (via purchasing dollars by a central bank). It seems to be natural to issue, for example, roubles upon having received dollars. By doing this, we lighten the rouble but promote inflation, as this issuance is not backed up by physical turnover expressed in monetary terms.[67]

---

[67] Our main example (the thesis "*Important examples ...*") will radically shrink: producer A extracted raw materials and exported it. (In real life, A would surely make payments for equipment and spares, but we can leave these out for a better understanding of the essential theory.) As exports increase, value added (and correspondingly GDP) also goes up, but physical turnover *expressed in monetary terms* is missing altogether, either before or after an increase in exports. Foreign currency is not money within a national economy. Under our new formation, we

An increase in physical turnover expressed in monetary terms can serve as a partial reason in our case for issuance to only facilitate deals *between subcontractors*, i.e. some intermediate deals helping to prepare the export deal inside the national economy. Here, we revisit the particular features of the extraction and manufacturing industries. It takes fewer intermediate deals to produce a tank car full of crude oil compared with an automobile, even if their prices are comparable. Therefore, an economy that is heavy on the extraction side can "digest" less money than an economy with developed manufacturing. For this reason, the Dutch disease is much more painful in countries exporting mainly raw materials compared with those exporting mainly manufactured goods.

There exists an argument about the real reason for the Dutch disease being frequent and substantial price increases for raw materials, with the prices for manufactured goods not catching up. This objection warrants some additional, albeit not entirely new, clarifications. Indeed, it would be hard to imagine, at the system level, a sharp increase in prices for automobiles that would be comparable to oil and gas price hikes, but it is conceivable to have an increase in manufactured goods exports leading, *at the level of the entire national economy*, to an impressive influx of foreign currency. This increase has been demonstrated, for instance, by various Asian countries. Nevertheless, the Dutch disease in these countries has been moderate, despite causing headaches to their national financial authorities.

The primary task facing these authorities is to keep in check the appreciation of the national currency. Since the state cannot simply seize the foreign currency from exporters if they opt to keep this currency inside the country, it must issue money to meet the increased demand on behalf of foreign currency owners. The easiest way is to exchange this new money for foreign currency directly with exporters, so they can pass it on down the chain. However, these chains vary in length between countries exporting raw materials and countries exporting manufactured goods. That's why the former are facing inflation notably higher than the latter, making the former seek to decrease money issuance. However, a decrease in money issuance leads to the strengthening of a national currency – there is no perfect solution and manoeuvring between Scylla and Charybdis cannot be avoided.

---

won't have a reason to doubt this, but under the existing system, foreign currency cannot serve as comprehensive money for the primary reason that we cannot issue it at will. The use of foreign currency in a national economy is an example of using a money surrogate.

Having touched upon the topic of inflation and deflation, let's return to physical turnover. With a comparable GDP level, manufacturing requires a more advanced division of labour between producers of goods and, as a result, more "working money" to facilitate this than raw materials extraction. When new money is injected into the economy of a raw-material-exporting country, it contributes to the overheating of consumer demand as there is no corresponding production demand for this money. Even if one tries to create this demand, it takes time, while the economy needs new money right away. Therefore, inflation is quick to follow. There would be a similar picture in manufacturing nations if more time were required to create the production demand, as money is no magic bean sprouting new production facilities and equipment overnight. However, due to the high number of deals, i.e. high physical turnover in such an economy, new money immediately ends up in some "prepared cells". Though manufacturing nations also face the risk of overheating (stagflation in this case), it is spread over a long time before actually happening.

All this reasoning in the background of simple calculations shows once again that with the same magnitude of GDP growth, physical turnover may grow at a totally different pace, both in absolute figures (money) and relatively (per cent). There is no theoretical problem here, as unlike the GDP indicator, physical turnover volume has significance in determining the amount of money required in the economy.

As we have already mentioned, after the previous book was published, it turned out this important fact caused doubts and therefore we are revisiting the subject.

Once more on the relationship between physical turnover and GDP as partial proof of the price definition.

Goods production expressed in money can be roughly represented (for example, over a geo map) by a three-dimensional graph, where work and components are being added at each node. (The aforementioned are goods by themselves, but we won't be depicting these as separate graphs, only noting the price increase of the initial goods.) The graph continues all the way until the purchase of goods by the final consumer. To visualise it, the graph will consist of vertical segments for price increases and horizontal segments depicting the physical movement of goods on the geo map. The

GDP indicator ("value added") reflects precisely this picture and its total sum is equal to the graph projection P_3 on the vertical axis (Fig. 1-2).[68]

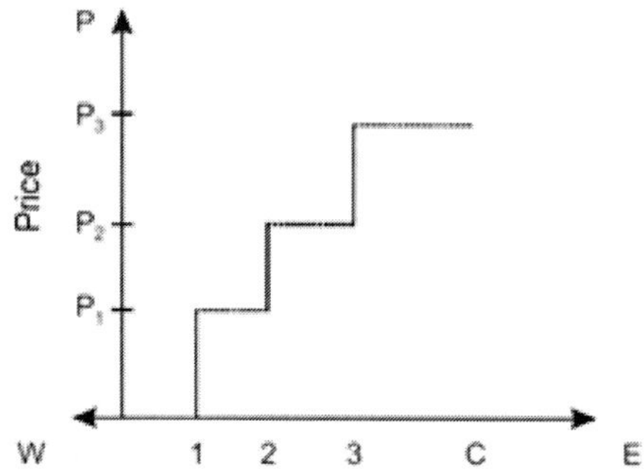

Fig. 1-2

Value added accounts only for the part of money that reflects the price difference between a purchase and sale by the same firm; for example, $P_2 - P_1$. The total value added in the production of goods will be equal to one, the final projection of the graph onto the vertical axis, which is equal to all value added by all firms. However, money has to serve not only one projection (even the final one) but also the whole turnover. That's why to account for monetary circulation we need to "grow a leg" for each firm adding value (Fig. 1-3), i.e. extend the projection showing the magnitude of value added by each firm to show the whole payment received by that firm, as each subsequent firm pays to the preceding one the full price and not merely the price increase.

In particular, it means that not only the accumulated value added but also *the growth* of value added during an intermediate deal (in our case, $P_2 - P_1$) will *repeat* at every subsequent deal in the chain, and thus inflate the increase in physical turnover compared with GDP growth. So, once the economy is growing compared with the previous period, we need to issue additional money according to the sum of all extended projections, and not

---

68 Here, P_1, P_2 and P_3 are prices paid for intermediate goods by firms located at 1, 2 and 3. The final consumer is represented by C. We have simplified the geo map to a one-dimensional west–east axis and goods in our illustration are always moved eastward. In a real-life situation, goods can move in any direction, including turning back westward.

just according to the growth of the final product, i.e. in accordance with growth in physical turnover and not in GDP[69] (Fig. 1-3).

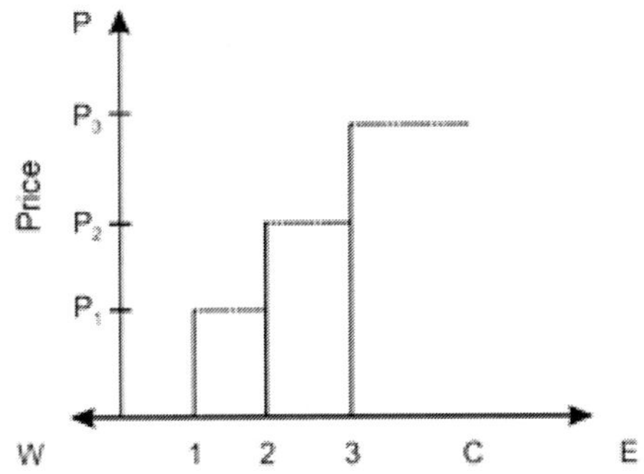

Fig. 1-3

Note that considering completed deals (physical turnover includes only deals that are completed and paid for), the subsequent breakdown of turnover components doesn't really matter – it can be labour, parts, materials or something else. Despite all the complexity of monetary circulation, we should not overly mystify the mechanical "movement of money containers". There are two important moments: first, whether *the price of money* is formed in a deal; second, *what kind of money* is used in a deal. As we saw while discussing the Dutch disease, it could well be foreign currency and not the national one. And as we noted in the thesis "*A continuation of the game ...*", it could be a bank liability record, which is also not a national currency (differing from the central bank's liabilities).

The reason for mirages originating from clearing lies in the combined system. Until we separate the credit and payment systems thereby eliminating bank clearing, at least within the framework of our model, we

[69] We have left out all mention of credit operations. In brief, the situation is as follows: a) the introduction of monetary credit into the process does not change anything at all, and b) the introduction of trade credit into the process does not change anything *major* (just as before, the amount of money depends on physical turnover and does not depend on GDP), but it lowers the amount of money required, including *arithmetically* bringing its required additional supply closer to the relative GDP growth indicators. That is, with more widespread trade credit, there is less money in the economy, and less money we can and must issue. We'll talk about trade credits in separate detailed discussions (Chapters 2 and 4).

will not be able to visualise how harmful this clearing was. The reason for Dutch disease is located someplace else, where national monetary systems are being stitched together. If under our new classical system all countries are equal in a monetary sense, now they are divided by type of national currency into two main groups: elite countries issuing global currencies (dollars and euros) and peripheral ("ordinary") countries with currencies circulating within their national economies.[70] These countries do interact on the world market, but their interaction is not organic, as we saw while discussing causes of the Dutch disease.

There may seem to be a way to avoid catching that same Dutch disease, as we are dealing with an ultramodern market economy boasting a mind-boggling array of financial instruments. However, the cure is not possible in principle, as goods are sold using either national or extra-national (world) currencies. Though the economy of neither peripheral nor elite countries is classical, the former has preserved some general classical features (we will call it near-classical). Conversely, some important economic elements of countries issuing global currencies have been bent to the extent of turning the classical principles upside down, so we will call this type of economy "wonderland".

For the ordinary countries, export development, frugality in government spending in order to keep the budget balanced and, correspondingly, attention to the level of national debt and money issuance controls are vitally important. Otherwise, depreciation – that main instrument of inflation from costs – will have a free reign, causing the destruction of the financial sector under the existing system. In these countries, living standards largely depend on the international competitiveness of domestic goods. So, consumer demand is a double-edged sword, as it also includes demand for imported goods. Hence, an increase in private spending cannot serve as a viable economic growth engine, at least in the long term.

For the countries issuing global currencies, both imports exceeding exports and government budget deficits are quite usual phenomena (this fully characterises the US, but it is less pronounced in the euro area due to its

[70] There are some countries with developed economies whose currencies (we'll call them intermediate) display features of both main groups to an extent (e.g. yen, Swiss franc and others). These countries and their currencies play a visible role in the world economy, and any economic analysts and theoreticians studying options for preserving capitalism should account for their influence. However, we'll abstract from them to point out the fundamental differences between regular and "wonderland" economies.

multinational character, as well as the less important role of the euro compared with the US dollar). Increases in public and private spending stimulate both the national and world economies, as consumption in elite countries is a mandatory element of the world economic engine. Living standards in these countries depend the most on the export competitiveness of their national currency and not on the export competitiveness of their national goods. Because global currencies have high (unnaturally high, non-classically high) resilience, classical inflation from costs cannot serve as an instrument regulating national costs in the countries issuing global currencies, despite chronic budget deficits and enormous public debt.

As for the classical deflation from costs, we have observed it while looking at Greece's anguish from late 2009: the prolonged deflationary lowering of costs with the euro remaining resilient. However, it is a rare sighting of a well-recognisable, "self-contained" deflation under the global financial system of modern paper capitalism. Fairly recently, we have observed central banks of some European nations practising an unusual thing, namely dropping their deposit rates to below zero,[71] to stave off appreciating their intermediate currencies (against foreign currencies) due to money inflows from the euro area. Their fears were triggered by energetic actions by the European Central Bank, which was worried about deflation in the euro area. To counter deflation, central banks in developed nations also use negative interest rates, which, unlike the aforementioned negative savings rates of a prohibitive nature, play the role of a "carrot" for borrowers and are aimed at encouraging inflation.

From a theoretical perspective, interactions between two different subsystems (near-classical peripheral and "wonderland") are more important than interactions within nations issuing global currencies, or interactions between these issuers and countries with intermediate currencies. These interactions share the common characteristic of turning deflation into inflation, as costs for countries exporting *currencies* are decreasing not within these countries, but within countries exporting *goods*, by the way of inflation from costs. We'll discuss this in detail in other theses.

---

[71] From a PCM monetary system perspective, an offer to pay merely for storing numbers on computer hard drives is ludicrous. It is also curious that the bill holders are asked to pay for their storage by the issuer himself (central banks insist on the bill nature of money under paper capitalism, even though it is not quite the case today – we'll touch upon this towards the end of this book, thesis "*FAQ: The old central bank versus new central bank ...*").

Physical turnover expressed in monetary terms and global currencies. Credit and physical turnover as a basis for the existence of global currencies.

Here is the last example in this series about physical turnover expressed in monetary terms and the price of money. We have touched upon this topic while talking about the Dutch disease – why is the US able to issue so many dollars? The only rationale for global currencies is their use to facilitate the world trade of goods (purchase and sale deals) and international lending (credit deals). The price of money used in these deals is formed during the deals. Therefore, an increase in dollar-facilitated credit and physical turnover (including securities and derivatives turnover) in the world economy requires more dollars issued by the US central bank (Federal Reserve) to service this increase. Thus, our inferences here are not materially different from those we used when discussing the required money issuance calculations based on physical and credit turnover within a national economy.

As a result, the US, which does not inject these dollars into the world economy "for free", can afford (before the dollars hit international circulation) elevated consumption of its citizens (including covering their expenses like healthcare), as well as elevated capital expenditure; for example, in infrastructure, science and defence. Once we started talking about it, the translation of issuance income into elevated consumption happened using the following main channels, which will be mentioned later in our study with additional clarifications:

- The issuance of government securities used by the state to cover a budget deficit.
- High government expenses and investment that would be possible even without the first point above, thanks to economic growth in the US.
- The issuance of corporate securities that have a higher value compared with securities issued in other countries, especially to those denominated in ordinary currencies.
- Consumer lending at low rates.
- Lending to national firms at low rates. This point is only partially independent as a channel (profits and wages paid by firms). It is also included in the second and the third points.

Attempts to explain GDP and consumption levels in the US by internal factors ("Americans work more and better") are not correct. From a classical, i.e. self-regulating, economy's perspective, it is hard to imagine national economic growth amidst a budget deficit and current account deficit. With the systematic character of these factors, growth would simply be impossible. A chronic combination of trade and budget deficits resulting from spiralling consumption would cause an immediate cut in extra consumption through depreciation and, consequently, an immediate drop in GDP with comparable prices. Here, expenses that would be regarded as excessive from a classical point of view, do not adversely impact GDP, but rather serve as an organic part of economic growth and justification for further money issuance. This non-classical metamorphosis of "negative" into a "positive", accumulated over a long time, is only possible when some "second economy" exists beyond this given national economy.[72] In this case for the US, the use of the dollar as a global currency is the "second economy" that gives the currency its super-resiliency and *in turn* causes the wide use of the dollar as a reserve currency.

US government borrowing plays a significant role in channelling new dollars into federal spending. The role of a global currency issuer is also the role of the most prominent consumer in the world economy, which is reflected in chronic trade and budget deficits. As a result, the US government is forced to borrow dollars, partially in the open market and partially from the Federal Reserve through token participation in the open market. Market participants, being aware of – or at least observant of – the dollar's super-resiliency, are willing to lend money. Investors are unlikely to believe in the US's ability to pay back all its creditors at some moment without dollar devaluation. Still, they keep lending since magically reliable and growing assets in the economy do not exist in principle. Nobody is likely to reprimand an official or an investment manager for buying top-rated securities either.

The issuance of US Treasuries has displayed a clear Ponzi scheme characteristic, which is best felt by understanding the fact that the US Federal Reserve does not hold all these securities. For the sake of accuracy, let's note that part of the US government's debt does not have economic but rather legal or historical roots. If the new dollars, required to

---

[72] The term "second economy" is traditionally used to depict foreign firms sending profits to residents of another country. However, profits from foreign firms are too insignificant to explain the viability of such enormous skews in the US economy.

facilitate growing international economic relations, initially belonged not to the Federal Reserve (central bank)[73] but to the US government, which would be more accurate from an economic perspective (this is approximately how it will be set up in the new financial system), some part of this debt would not even exist, as is the case with any other country under capitalism.

US government debt is represented by securities, known as US Treasuries. Securities, in the form of commodity and money surrogates,[74] significantly contribute to the complexity of the modern capitalist economy. In this case, as with other commodities, their circulation framed as purchase and sale deals (the commodity component of securities and derivatives is most visible on the secondary market) requires more dollars, as the price of money is formed in purchase and sale deals. In the short term, US Treasuries, like any other dollar-denominated security, are a factor of dollar price (aggregate price of all dollars) strengthening – they contribute to increasing physical turnover, allowing in turn for the secured issuance of dollars. On the other hand, Treasuries in their monetary components are obligations to return borrowed money with accrued interest and if creditors simultaneously flood the market with these securities, they will fall by themselves, taking the dollar with them. This would not be a massively dangerous situation if credit liabilities were documented as credit. However, they take the shape of securities with free market circulation. Thus, in the long term, dollar-denominated securities contribute to the

[73] As soon as the central bank issues new money, it is instantly reflected in the bank's liabilities, which may cause doubts regarding the initial owner of this new money. Here, it would be more important to reflect deals ("deal" and "bank balance" are categories of different weight) serving as money issuance channels – lending the new money and using it to buy high-liquidity assets (foreign currency or securities). These deals can be carried out only by the initial owner of the new money.

[74] The commodity component of these surrogates is not difficult to understand as, like commodities, securities are exchanged for money in purchase and sale deals. This footnote clarifies the money component, driven by the extremely high liquidity of securities that does not characterise any other basic property type except for money. In deals, money can be used either as payment or as credit. This is also reflected in securities. For example, travellers' cheques represent a mix of commodities and money as payment, while bonds mix together commodities and money as credit. These are the most obvious examples, but there may be other types as well. For example, Sberbank deposit certificates paying a small amount of interest, which were actively used in Russia in the 1990s due to the cash deficit, were a mix of all three. It is a simple example, but it is substantially more difficult to single out all three components in stocks (though we'll be doing this in Chapter 2).

weakening of the dollar price. When the dollar ceases to be a global currency, a decrease in the US Treasuries' reliability will drop the dollar more than it would without these securities.

This conclusion is valid for other dollar-denominated securities, albeit to a lesser extent. The *reliability* of a denominating currency is an important factor in demand for securities and other financial products. For example, even if things are going well at a Russian firm itself, under the threat of the rouble's devaluation some market participants might seek to get rid of the firm's securities so as not to lose part of their property in terms of global currencies. These fears are built into the demand for securities from the onset. Correspondingly, the super-resiliency of the dollar as a global currency contributes to the advanced market growth of dollar-denominated securities. The great number of deals happening in this market also leads to the increased issuance of dollars required to facilitate these deals. When the dollar ceases to be a global currency, this may trigger a flight from not only Treasuries but also all dollar-denominated securities.

Creditors put up with the gigantic debts of the US government only because the dollar is a global currency. The logical reasoning goes as follows: dollars (along with euros) are prime currencies facilitating international trade and international credit. Therefore, dollar- and euro-denominated securities are the leaders (it is easy to see it looking at the reserves of central banks). If someone tries to do the opposite by issuing an excessive number of government bonds and aiming to make a national currency "just like the dollar", that said currency will turn into dust.

Since we are talking about both physical turnover and credit turnover, let's mention one important corollary, namely low interest rates in the US. Generally, lending incorporates the possibility of currency depreciation relative to foreign currencies into the interest rate. If someone is lending roubles at 5 per cent a year and the rouble loses to the dollar more than that in a year, this creditor would not add to their property but actually lose some of it. Therefore, by taking the non-classical, super-resiliency of the dollar as a global currency, one can obtain properly secured loans in dollars at low rates in the US and in Europe.

One possible question is what is more important for the status of a global currency – facilitating trade or facilitating credit? Under the existing financial system where everybody lends money to everyone, it does not seem to be simple. Nevertheless, if the question is rewritten slightly differently as "what is more important for the economy?", then trade begs for priority. Our PCM financial system stresses this priority well, as we'll see in more detail in this study. To cut our wait short, let's get familiar with the definition of economy.

Definition of economy. Labour. Preview of Chapter 2.

An economy is the reproduction of *consumable property* that is sufficient for the expanded reproduction of *the human population*. This definition gravitates towards biology and towards the development of a biological species, *Homo sapiens*. For example, if we take an anthill, there is a different system of reproduction of consumable "property". Biology and theoretical economics are different basic sciences,[75] but running some fundamental concepts through a biology sieve (at least at an early stage) helps to get rid of exaggerations that arise from mixing up theoretical economics with other sciences and disciplines.

Traditionally, a desire "to explain everything" has been associated with philosophy that sometimes had, and still has, an oversized influence over theoretical economics. For example, Marxists put heavy emphasis on "society" as something unique to people to distinguish an economy from the mere battle for subsistence food and "human labour". As for "society", the simple example of an anthill shows that this is not correct, as ants (and other species) are way more "societal" in their "labour" than people. As for human labour, here's a little joke: "I have delivered the firewood!" shouts the courier when driving his cargo into the yard. "*Look at him – **he** has delivered*," the horse thought. I guess one can make up a similar story about how an apple tree comments on the gardener's effort to produce an apple without the tree's help, or how an adherent of the labour theory of value tries to plough a vegetable garden on Neptune. Of course, human labour plays a major role, but to consider it the primary source of everything is just pride. The latter word is mainly used (and often appropriately) by priests. However, in my mind the source of this pride hides precisely in theology: "God created man in his own image."

[75] This is stated with an unequivocal understanding that humanitarian sciences, including theoretical economics, cannot contradict natural sciences, i.e. natural sciences are primary to humanitarian ones. I cannot recall any humanitarian science not having biology as at least one of its primary sources. With all that said, it does not pay to look for substantial intersections of our study with those versions of theoretical economics that emphasise the use of apparatus and patterns of natural sciences. This is a bit too much.

Materialistic philosophers who challenged idealistic religious beliefs went too far by putting man in God's place.

The reality is such that *Homo sapiens* is the ruling biological species. The claims on the material wealth of the planet by the human population (obtained by physical confrontation with the other species inhabiting Earth) were substituted with claims to be creating some "value" by the economists of the 18th and 19th centuries. They also suggested the existence of the category of "abstract human labour", which creates this "value" in their mind. So, one "creates" another but this cannot be verified, since neither really exists.

> Back in the Introduction, you may have noticed that "labour"[76] is absent from our basic categories. Labour is impossible to define, as there are no units of measurement. If a person found a raw diamond in the jungle or that same person spent months working the field, both are labour. However, in what units intrinsic to *labour itself* do we measure and compare these two? This situation is exaggerated, but we can make up many more plausible cases with the same rhetorical question at the end.
>
> But this is not all about the units of measurement, it turns out. Suppose our farmer found one more diamond, then his villagers found more and then finally many farmers abandoned their fields to focus on finding diamonds. If someone prefers the examples of gold, ginseng or giant crabs, it does not change the gist. What's important is that man's decisions to conduct economic activities are guided not by labour but by what can be obtained in exchange – how much can be added to the property given the exchange, or simply put, how much money can be earned. This guidance also works in a more prosaic search for work, given that the man is *able* to perform the work. Even if our farmer learns one day that salaries for bank managers are really good in a nearby city, this is unlikely to change his life. That's why we used diamonds in our example, as gathering them does not require highly specialised, professional skills.

[76] The word "labour" can have two different meanings in English: (a) a process carried out by a person; and (b) people who carry out a process. In theoretical texts, this ambiguity needs to be resolved. Therefore, everywhere in this study, please understand "labour" only as a "process" (as in Russian).

> The importance of work, as opposed to the pursuit of easy money, is part of society's morale, backed by a legal system that often reserves severe punishment for illegal property gains. Respect for work is instilled by family, school and church from childhood, with the reason being not the work itself but the understanding by adults that there won't be enough diamonds for everyone and that an expectation of easy money can make a young person's life broken and purposeless. From a dry cause-and-effect perspective, however, property gains are a true priority. When a young person grows up being grateful to his parents for a good upbringing, *under the market economy*[77] he or she is motivated by the desire to make money.

The economy of *Homo sapiens* is distinguished from the systems of reproduction of consumable property of other species on this planet by ***using exchange***.[78] At some point in evolution, we had enough brainpower

---

[77] As almost always when talking about the economy, here we assume "generally". In some sectors of the market economy there might be contradicting cases. And if we are not talking about a market economy, there are a growing number of cases where this property gain priority does not work directly. For example, in my conversations with physicists in Dubna (a scientific research centre in Russia) about the "brain drain" phenomenon, I heard each time that the main motivation for young, promising scientists to leave the country was not their material compensation but their desire to conduct experiments on modern equipment located at the leading Western research facilities. This exodus of smart youth starts when they are still in college, once having an adequate experimental base becomes more relevant.

[78] There is a conspiracy version that during the early stages of our civilisation's development (before capitalism) there was practically no exchange, so the economists just made it up "to please the market theories" (conceivably, merchants were also invented). However, absent some number of exchanges, there would not be money either (of which many specimens await visitors in archaeological museums). As one may guess, money did not appear overnight but as a result of very long reflections on how to facilitate exchange. Generally, downplaying the role of exchange fits well with *theoretical exaggeration of the "social" factor in discussions about property or labour*. It can be a consequence of an ideological approach, when an author is extending some familiar ideas on the organisation of society in general or some group of people within it. Exchanges then become a "nuisance", inadvertently focusing attention on property and property owners. A technical error is also possible, when insufficient attention to exchanges leads to the aforementioned exaggeration. Exchanges straighten one's logic: vague discussions largely give way to the analysis of *the property* movement between the people making *these* deals.

to voluntarily alienate some property in exchange for something else, and not merely destroy another tribe in a fight for food or try to steal something from those people; we learned to give something in order to get something. At the same time, the instinct of property preservation and increment is intrinsic to people as well as to all inhabitants of the planet. An act of voluntary alienation of one man's property in exchange for somebody else's naturally lead to ***division of labour***,[79] without which the development of means of production would have never attained its present-day level.

Consumable property includes commodities (more precisely, goods that we call "commodities" in deals). Humans, just like other life forms, are a delicate species and won't necessarily consume whatever is available. To survive and raise children, a human should receive consumable property unconditionally, because consumption is a targeted destruction of property, even if it happens with a varied degree of frugality depending on the goods. That's why a purchase and sale deal in its basic "commodity" form ($C \leftrightarrow M$) is more important than any other deal, including basic lease deals ($P \leftarrow M$, $L \leftarrow M$, $M_C \leftarrow M$) as well as other purchase and sale deals (including the purchase and sale of securities as commodity and money surrogates).

Therefore, returning to the subject of global currencies, the dollar's dominance is built primarily on the fact that by using dollars, we can (and do) purchase any goods produced on this planet, and this has been going on for over half a century. In Chapter 3, we'll learn how to make national currencies equal – in theory, it is not complicated.

In the next chapter, we'll finish the separation of credit and payment systems, and prove that the lesser importance of credit deals compared with goods purchase and sale deals is far from shifting the former to the theoretical vassals of the latter. This is akin to comparing the height of two skyscrapers while standing on the ground next to them. Our analysis of the subtle moments of the interest rate's influence over production may pose a challenge – this is likely to be the most difficult part of a modern economy and this difficulty primarily has a psychological nature. We'll closely see how liberalism really contradicts "liberalism". We'll need to choose between, on one hand, our advancement to free market institutions, which includes:

---

[79] Like an exchange, the division of labour can also "get in the way" if researchers exaggerate the "social" factor while talking about property or labour. We'll have to address this in Chapter 2 in greater detail, considering the views of Ronald Coase on forming costs within a firm (company) and forming of the firms proper.

- Liberation of the "invisible hand of the market" (i.e. from obsolete elements of capitalism that impede the forming of basic market regulators).
- Less of a role for the state.
- Increasing the number of goods producers and stepping up competition between them.
- Consequently, increased efficiency in producing goods and services in a self-regulating economy.

And, on the other hand, there is the no-brainer principle of "let everyone make money the way they want", which leads to a totally different outcome.

CHAPTER 2.

COSTS AND INTEREST RATE

Systemic costs. Labour productivity. Revolutionary (formation change) and evolutionary (technological progress) cost reduction.

In our science,[80] all basic elements (except for price definition) have been known since the days of yore – we have all the essential parts present, albeit mixed up with non-essential ones and even some we better get rid of. Given this cornucopia of parts, accents play a major role. In our blueprint, there are two methodological accents:

- Costs formation.
- Movement of property (first and foremost, money).

The combination of these two quite different methodological accents can be viewed as inconsistent. Without pretending to give strict definitions, let's clarify that both accents are united by the "invisible hand of the market". According to our study, market cost regulators make up its formalisable, measurable (in this sense, "visible") part, while supply and demand, as symbols of market movement, form its non-formalisable (in this sense, fundamentally invisible) part.

In the first chapter, we have addressed the movement of property more than once. One can say that technically we continue to extend the idea outlined by Marx (with the original circular flow model offered by François Quesnay). However, Marx's circular flow was "getting its

[80] As in Chapter 1, the first thesis may be the most difficult to understand. While in Chapter 1 the complexity was caused by multiple refinements of monetary terms, here we suddenly find ourselves on the "high seas" of theory. It won't be easy to concentrate, as sometimes it will seem that we are talking about everything at once. Going forward, we'll focus on specific themes for a more comfortable understanding.

power" from the microeconomy, where a hired worker, per Marx, endowed goods with this power ("value"). We cannot use this analysis of property movement in general, due to its overt descent into the microeconomy, and especially due to the mysterious character of "value". Keynes expanded the use of macroeconomic movement of money, which stemmed from his keen attention to *macroeconomic* demand, especially to the demand curve (function) itself. Our own position regarding the possibility of formalising demand was briefly stated in the previous paragraph. Differences in the approach to studying demand resulted in dissimilar methodological accents for "charting" the movement of money. While Keynes focused on *psychological* nuances of market participants, we concentrate on prices (as basic cost regulators).

The accent on how costs are formed is a conceptual characteristic of our study. Note that together with a focus on building a self-regulating market model, it puts this study in the classical branch of theoretical economics. Thus, as opposed to the great architects like Marx and Keynes, we are simply modernising "the house that Smith built". With all that said, our final conclusions are noticeably different from those of Adam Smith, as well as from those of Marx and Keynes (to the extent that our Perfectly Competitive Market is different from classical capitalism, socialism and paper capitalism, respectively).

The theme of costs is not just a complicated topic but a *very* complicated one that has been studied from the very beginning of theoretical economics. Over time and up to the present day, these studies have, on one hand, moved our discipline forward, and on the other, tangled it with inferences having little to do with the real economy. Gradually, we'll take a walk along all the "levels" where costs are formed. We'll wrap up our targeted conversation with a critique of marginal cost at the end of the book. Let's begin with *systemic costs*, as they are *the most difficult* to understand.

"Systemic costs" is yet another name for macroeconomic or national costs, the latter meaning costs specific to the national economy. We recognise that there is room for discussions about the best-fitting term, but there would be no crucial consequence to these discussions as we do not distinguish any other kind of costs generalised to this degree.

The complexity is clearly visible as there does not seem to be a way to measure systemic costs. There is one more important kind of costs that is impossible to calculate precisely, namely coordination costs. However, these can be relatively easy to illustrate using the example of a given firm's activities. We don't have such an opportunity when clarifying the essence of systemic costs – as macroeconomic costs, they are unevenly spread around a national economy. If, when talking about microeconomic costs, we assume by default an average total (unit) cost, this clarification would not advance our understanding as it is more important to point out their location and the reasons for their forming. We'll clarify this terminological complexity using the example of this study, in which we are mainly trying to remodel the existing financial system by finding out ways to lower its carrying costs for the national economy (for example, how will payment system costs decrease after transitioning from a heterogeneous three-level system to a separated, two-level system). Here, the real economy is the most important part of the national economy (see the definition of economy) and ***lowering costs of goods production is its ultimate goal***, even if on the surface goods production and the real economy itself seem to be detached from mainstream events. Correspondingly, if we wanted to create some indicator for general average systemic costs, we would put absolute costs incurred by the financial system (or a certain element of it) into the numerator of this hypothetical fraction, while the denominator would look quite improbable. Using an analogy with microeconomic unit cost, it would need to be the sum of the physical quantity of all microeconomic output.

In brief, systemic costs are hard to trace because they accumulate while basic cost regulators are *idle*, and the consequences are not spread evenly. Understanding is further complicated by systemic costs in a national economy becoming obvious mainly after the fact, i.e. after basic cost regulators kick in and systemic costs decrease. Here, the idle state of basic cost regulators can be either *temporary* (see some examples in the next paragraph) or have a prolonged character stemming from fundamental drawbacks of a given formation. Speaking about formations, now – when the PCM exists only on paper – the systemic costs of paper capitalism can be shown only through theoretical calculations.

Only the immediate decrease of systemic costs through a depreciation of money relative to foreign currencies is relatively easy to understand. This simplicity is explained, first, by a decrease in only one price (the price of money expressed in terms of foreign currencies, i.e. the cross-price which is one of four basic cost regulators) and, second, by the monopoly of the government ("wide government") on money production, which makes the effect of this money price decrease uniform and instantly applies it to the whole national economy. If the time has come for basic cost regulators to work but there is no currency depreciation, this triggers a slow "manual sunset" represented by scattered deflationary processes for decreasing systemic costs at firms and commercial banks, which may take years to significantly decrease production volume and salaries. Despite the vast difference between these two scenarios of systemic costs decrease, accumulated while basic cost regulators have been idle, the definitive element in both cases is the price of money expressed in terms of foreign currencies. The final state is also identical: a decrease in excessive consumption which happens mainly due to lower wages, the only difference being that with a currency depreciation scenario, wages (expressed in foreign currency terms) are lowered automatically.[81] We will follow tradition (established when the Marxist theory originated) and call the economic crisis, two varieties of which we have just generally described, an overproduction crisis (although our reasoning laid out above suggests they may also be called an overconsumption crisis). The term "overproduction" describes only the initial phase of a crisis, and even when we focus just on this phase, overproduction is rather an external manifestation of basic economic motivating factors, which we are going to discuss towards the middle of this chapter.

Let's make a couple of digressions.

> First, the importance of wages allows us to see better why the labour productivity indicator is useless here, although the scope of the national economy begs to use it. This indicator is a variation of the GDP indicator (GDP per working person), i.e. it is calculated based on *purchase and sale deals*. This is valid for both absolute GDP figures (GDP proper) and for its derivatives, like labour

[81] Under the currency depreciation scenario, the cross-price unconditionally impacts one more basic cost regulator, namely rent. However, the impact of a rent decrease on the decrease of *consumption* of people working in the *market sector* of the economy is significantly smaller and can be disregarded. First, its scale is different compared with wages; second, a decrease in rent payments lowers a firm's costs but does not decrease the consumption of people working there (the only obvious thing is a decrease in income from the subleasing of land, including cases where it happens using a proxy of real estate built on a given plot). As for rent-related taxes collected by the state and subsequently distributed among entities financed exclusively by state appropriations, their decrease does lower consumption of those working in these entities (albeit to a lesser extent than their wages decrease). Also, this additional decrease in consumption usually does not happen unconditionally but manifests itself later as a tangle of various processes that are not the subject of our study.

productivity. Meanwhile, wages, like most other basic regulators, is a price indicator based on *lease deals*. The "costs" category is a suitable "omnivore" here, meaning that costs can be accounted for in both types of deals (regardless, again, of whether we are talking about absolute or relative costs).

Discussions about decreasing costs are psychologically complex, as we are talking (bottom line) about decreasing consumption by people. Of course, it is more agreeable to talk not about decreasing consumption, even when in this case it is about excessive consumption, but about growth in labour productivity. This is probably why, in economic literature, the theoretical importance of this indicator is often overstated. In a practical economy, its importance is low.[82] For example, an average consumer definitively does not care that labour productivity in the US is substantially higher compared with the Philippines when deciding between a \$3.50 t-shirt made of decent cotton fabric in the Philippines, and a \$35 t-shirt made in the US (coincidentally, these t-shirts coexist in my wardrobe, so don't rush to any important conclusions merely by juxtaposing these two prices). It is common knowledge that the might of the Chinese economy has been driven not by high labour productivity but by low costs. Starting in the 1990s, labour productivity has been growing rapidly, but the sequence of factors for Chinese economic growth is still as follows: first, low labour costs as the primary contributor, then increased labour productivity resulting from the high competitiveness of Chinese businesses and corresponding GDP growth. Upon a *closer* look at the modern US economy, one can see that accents have shifted. Nowadays, its might is driven not by advanced technological capacity, as was traditionally the case since the era of gold capitalism, but by the

[82] The business use of labour productivity numbers is supplementary, even if it is often calculated internally by accountants (for example, in manufacturing). These calculations make sense *for decision-making* only with a constant production base (for example, it may be used to compare the efficiency of different workers). When it gets down to complex decisions involving the possible deployment or upgrade of equipment, reliance on labour productivity indicators may result in gross miscalculations, in cases when it contradicts the indicator of average total *cost*. If the reasoning for this strong statement is not clear from looking at the labour productivity indicator itself, we can suggest a small arithmetic exercise for turning the fraction upside down. The resulting indicator is labour intensity (personnel expenses to make one item of your product), which is the inverse of labour productivity. It is easy to see that it describes only partial costs.

leadership of the American financial system under paper capitalism. This results in higher GDP and, accordingly, higher labour productivity as a quotient from dividing the GDP by the number of workers.

In Russian economic literature, the excessive attention to labour productivity is largely a legacy of a socialist past. The importance of labour productivity was exaggerated, with the expectation that an emphasis on producing the means of production would automatically lead to success. It did not happen, but the high costs of "developed socialism" required a complete rebuilding of the economy ("*perestroika*"). In this century, there have already been many discussions around the optimal use of petrodollars piled up at Russia's Central Bank and one popular (and still lurking, considering the highly étatist Russian economy) thought was to use them to build modern factories. The problem is that the factories would likely not work with the desired efficiency and for the same reason; first, manage your costs and then the rest. It is not enough to buy and install new equipment. As a minimum, production costs of the new manufacturing output should be low enough for it to be competitive. This will be easier to understand if our reasoning is not clouded by "productive forces", "labour productivity" or some other grand term. Imagine a firm as a producer of goods, which, thanks to the division of labour, is able to run many concurrent operations, paying for everything with its own funds. An answer to the question of whether a worker or a shiny new machine is more efficient in performing some operation largely depends on the price (cost) of the operation, but I have not heard any entrepreneur prioritise the labour productivity indicator in this situation. Nobody is eager to produce a warehouse full of goods that is decomposing due to high costs.

Labour productivity is an important overall indicator and it may have high value, for example, for the professors trying to visually demonstrate the pace of economic development of our civilisation or of single countries. As soon as we narrow the scope to explain specific mechanisms, its practical value goes down markedly, indicating the crude nature of this indicator or at least the fact that it is not remotely as flexible as costs, permeating all levels of the national economy.

Let's summarise. Despite its loud bang, labour productivity is just a variation of GDP. GDP itself is a "scoreboard indicator" and nobody is trying to belittle its importance. However, it is fair to have strong doubts about whether it would serve as a pathway to knowing the subtleties of "the game".

Second, in order not to burden our text with complex constructs, let's give it an artificial terminology compression: we won't include systemic costs forming due to a *temporary* idle state of basic cost regulators, or in other words, those decreasing through currency depreciation and deflation (we could name them, for example, *crisis costs*, though it is not very important due to our terminology compression). Under systemic costs, we'll assume only the ***formational*** ones, i.e. those requiring the transition to a more advanced formation. This terminology compression won't be the only one, but the second one won't be artificial as we are going to separate *theoretical* systemic costs (that have been, and will be, included in our discussion) and *management* systemic costs (that we'll simply point out).

Prior to these two digressions, we devoted a paragraph to reflect, in general terms, the essence of a crisis cost reduction through currency depreciation and deflation, despite crises traditionally being a complex topic. It was relatively easy to accomplish, since we did not go outside the scope of *price categories*. As for the decrease of systemic costs, it is impossible to carry out *without changing the physical character of work*. Earlier in Chapter 1, we saw how the transition from a three-level payment system to a two-level one changes the functions of the central bank and commercial banks and, accordingly, the nature of work there.[83] In this chapter, we'll see how other transformations will require changes in the physical nature of work in the microeconomy, though transformation of the financial system is still the pivotal point.

As the above reference to some "physical character of work" can be difficult to understand, let's explain it in detail. Inside of a market economy we get used to being "embraced by the invisible hand of the market" and don't always pay attention to the fact that our moves are reactions to the prices being formed. This happens all the time, but in the case where we lease ourselves out to managing owners (a "gentler" commonly used phrasing would be "lease out our labour power"), it is harder to notice, as we are getting only the echoes of decisions made by

[83] Use of the term "work" in this case is a mere indication that, as a rule, some crucial changes will be required in the way people and machines work.

"the bosses" that result either in firm-wide changes to work or in changes to the work that we perform (either at this same firm or at another). Once systemic changes take place, such as currency depreciation or deflation, changes in the work performed become more noticeable.

In order to attain lower systemic costs (and return to the "embraced by price categories" at a different, higher level thereafter), one needs to do the exact opposite: we, the people, should help the "invisible hand" (i.e. the laws of classical economy) by changing the physical character of work in selected areas of the national economy, causing a noticeable "*perestroika*"[84] (change) in the way price categories interact.

Changing the physical character of work crucially complicates the task (as well as the demonstration) of reducing macroeconomic costs because, unlike microeconomic costs, they do not have a single defined *centre* of accounting and management. The absence of this centre (attention!) is no less a crucial complication than changing the physical character of work. However, once we can line up a macroeconomic chain of price categories in which one basic cost regulator transfers (or does not transfer, *for one or another* reason) its reaction to some economic events to its peer, the absence of this centre is not conspicuous. On the other hand, even with such an obvious impact of the physical character of work on firms (in general, a firm's activities consist of physical elements that exist in harmony with the *natural laws* of the universe), the presence of a single centre of accounting and management (personified by a managing owner) allows a "bypass" of the physical factor while talking about the carrying costs, all without thinking much about it (i.e. reducing costs to price categories that are organically included in the macroeconomy).

In the case of systemic costs, we get a strong impression of being left out on the "high seas".

There is another important consequence of a missing single centre of cost accounting and cost management that makes lowering systemic costs an extremely burdensome process, both for understanding and carrying it out in the real economy. A targeted change of the physical character of work is always accompanied by a *temporary upswing of carrying costs*, due to both implementing machinery and the low efficiency of workers during their learning process (this is especially valid for coordination of their actions).

[84] Although this term is squarely associated with Russia's transition from socialism to a market economy, its use is appropriate for any case of formation changes.

As you may have guessed from our mention of firms, pointing out the "physical factor" does not identify systemic costs. Cost reduction stemming from changes in the physical character of work can be classified approximately in the following ways:

- The kind that *can be* regulated by natural market forces at firms and commercial banks). We'll be calling this a technological cost reduction and the process itself will be called a technological *evolution.*
- The kind that can only be regulated by the state, but not requiring changes to the physical character of work at firms and commercial banks. We'll be calling these *management* systemic costs, as their reduction results from tactical actions undertaken by the government. These actions may lead to profound shifts in political power configurations, but they do not crucially change the actions of firms and commercial banks.
- The kind that can only be carried out by the state, involving radical changes to the physical character of work at firms and commercial banks. This one requires a *revolutionary*[85] change to the economy's legal framework. We'll be calling these theoretical systemic costs, or simply systemic costs.

Out of these three outlined types of cost reduction linked to changes to the physical character of work, we are understandably most interested in the first and third ones. Only analytical types can dig into the details of management costs (these are not strictly tied to the changes to the physical character of work), while theoretical economics lacks the instruments to analyse the algorithms of tactical interactions between administrative forces and the market.

Technological evolution: the big movement. Neoclassical and Keynesian mathematical economic models. The priority of demand in a microeconomy.

In our last thesis, we mentioned the analysis of property movement as one of the two (along with cost analysis) most important methodological

[85] This radical change of the economic model should not be confused with a political revolution, inevitably starting with government overthrow. The political forces destined to make the required economic changes can get to the helm this way as well, but at any rate, an economic revolution can only be efficiently carried out from "above", i.e. by the state.

accents of our design. As for the demonstration of property movement in general, we have already used this technique in examples big and small, starting with discussions about the multiplier and a mixed credit and payment system. The most challenging, from this perspective, was our analysis of physical turnover, as we had to superimpose the movement of money on the movement of goods. At the same time, we have mostly used, and are going to use, demonstrations of the movement of money, or as it was called in the title of this thesis, the big movement. Rather than money, goods slated for consumption by *Homo sapiens* constitute the most important type of property, which is duly reflected in the definition of economy. However, one important accent related to understanding the material essence of goods will be made on their location in firms, as the ultimate reason for goods to be in the economy is the gradual *transformation* of raw materials and component parts into property suitable for final consumption. As a rule, this transformation happens in firms. If we also add transportation, where the focus is on preventing any transformations in the process (with certain exceptions), we'll get a general (maybe the most general possible) understanding about "goods in the economy". As for money, it is a fundamentally non-transformable type of property that exists mainly *to move* incessantly as a means of circulation.

Every theoretical economist analysing money flows understands the importance of reflecting a practical economy, including entrepreneurial activities, in their constructs. However, here it is easy to get caught in the production trap (or socialism trap), as can be seen in the neoclassical, mathematical economic models. Let's put a disclaimer that you can view these models in textbooks with any desired degree of detail, while we just point out their main drawbacks.

As envisaged by researchers, these models must represent (or at least reflect) the movement of property. However, they are essentially a set of static pictures. Even a million of these pictures would be a better fit for statistics. As a result, they have more analytical value rather than theoretical.[86]

For example, if we digress from mathematics in favour of essential economics, we can see that the image of a managing owner dividing

---

[86] If the Cobb–Douglas production function reflects the traditional neoclassical focus on production, the Solow model includes some pictures from outside of the "black box" of the economy, such as consumption level and saving rate. The latter model is a mathematical economic representation of the synthesis between neoclassical and Keynesian currents in theoretical economics.

expenses into "labour and capital" forms the base of the neoclassical production function. Considering its focus on productive forces, the neoclassical production function assumes "labour" and "capital" to be physical categories first and foremost. However, if we take their monetary representations, both wages and capital expenditures, *from the perspective of a managing owner* (and remember, that's the person breaking down expenses into "labour" and "capital"), they are nothing else but costs that need to be minimised. Besides, *from that perspective*, the neoclassical focus on output (production volume, i.e. supply volume) looks unnatural. In a market economy, a single firm can increase production usually without particular problems through increasing "productive forces", but later it may face a problem with sales (demand) and things will not turn out so rosy. The focus on output (supply) is valid in discussions about the whole *national economy*, but using a picture of a single firm operating in mathematical models (here, we are talking about a competition-based market economy, i.e. an economy with a pronounced impact of negative profit as the final cost regulator for managers) *under conditions of demand priority* is far-fetched.

Here's the reason: we cannot formalise demand in a market economy. Market demand cannot be formalised at all and we'll be talking about it further (for instance, in the theses with Keynes's theory critique). The most obvious impossibility is demand formalising *in a single firm*, as *decisions by the buyers of our goods are exogenous*, i.e. buyers do not report to us. Figuratively speaking, when neoclassical models link firms' output to national economy output, it is not so much trying to make "trousers out of shorts", but rather trying to make a suit out of shoes.

Here's the opposite example: under socialism, the link between the "downstairs" output and the "upstairs" output was quite natural (including two-way versions), since both the national economy and socialist enterprises were oriented by centralised government planning towards maximising the supply of goods, and thus naturally enabling demand formalisation. We remember that the administrative regulation of prices, including a possibility to *fix* them, greatly facilitated this formalisation. By the way, the need for economic mathematicians in the Soviet Union was obvious. Their slow but sure departure from the stage upon transition to the market economy was equally obvious, albeit with an opposite, sad undertone. To avoid a feeling of excessive unfairness, note that now, when computerisation of the economy is in full swing, the need for mathematicians is hard to overestimate. Still, it is important to understand that we are talking about applied research only, regardless of how well deserved and often globally recognised some of this research is. The good news is that applied researchers' pay is often much better compared with those doing theoretical studies.

It is possible that our argument, considering that we knocked out the bottom of some well-known models, seems too simple. We can respond to this with the unsophisticated remark that an attempt to explain "everything" (production, demand, economic growth and much more, depending on the model) using a couple of formulas is a far more simple-minded attempt to "hit a home run". But let's also try to reason that the fine line between true and false can simply be overlooked in this case; for instance, if a researcher never had a laboratory (i.e. a firm). If they had one, however, and lived the results of their experiments, it would be easy to defend one's position: demand priority for a single firm (i.e. priority of exogenous decisions that are immune to formalisation) is impossible to disprove.

Technological evolution: movement of investment money. Savings and money stock. Remarks on Keynes's theory (savings and stimulation of consumption).

The money allocated by a managing owner to develop "capital" (if we are talking about modern theories, for example, in terms used by Paul Samuelson and William Nordhaus[87]), i.e. the money paid by entrepreneurs for means of production, fits the description *only* in the context of this scenario *in a given firm*. Money, as we know, belongs to people and not to machines, and therefore this money is further distributed in the firm that sold machines to our entrepreneur and is used to pay various expenses. One can suggest that, in the end, all the money that was paid for means of production goes to consumption via chains (cycles) of various lengths and with some time lag.

> Once we mention time lag, we assume the emergence of savings. Attention to the latter is often hyperbolised, with the term itself bestowed with a false fundamental nature. We'll be fair to note that the situation is objectively convoluted by the complexity of the paper capitalism model, though with an artificial contribution by Keynes due to his theory's accent on macroeconomic demand. With a strictly classical economy (in the next two paragraphs we'll

[87] Samuelson and Nordhaus, 2010, pp. 107-118.

get teleported to the PCM), it is easier to understand what is meant by a "one or another" time lag.

Let's consider savings. If we don't inflate the meaning of this term in the name of a "higher goal", then it is simply as it sounds: the money paid by a firm to workers that is kept by households either in their accounts at the unified payment system or (similarly to paper capitalism) somewhere in a drawer. This money is mostly spent on consumption until the next pay cheque. Accumulation of some of this money (the "under the mattress" part) has always happened and will always happen. At some moment, these accumulated funds are either spent on more expensive goods and services, or further saved for a rainy day. Note that under our PCM, the amount of "stashed" money will increase, as taking the payment system out of the commercial banks' purview will shift the money associated with this system out of it. This won't be a theoretical issue (in principle), as there will be considerably more money in general, but right after the transition it may cause a temporary upswing in interest rates,[88] since commercial banks won't be able to use spare cash for lending. A sensitive attitude towards "under the mattress" savings under paper capitalism stems from the mix of credit and payment systems, when *there is not enough money in the economy*, since privately accumulated cash limits the commercial banks' ability to use spare cash for both lending and covering the clearing settlements for their depositors. I cannot see any other fundamental explanation or reason for creating a whole theory around "savings". We won't be able to formulate the root cause until we suggest a possibility of separating the credit system from the payment system.

We need to mention a few words about the money being returned to the microeconomy: it happens in one of two ways. First, money flows back into the microeconomy via primary lending deals with commercial banks, triggering the forming of the market interest rate. Savings do participate in forming this interest rate as well, but they are hardly more than a connecting word – it is clear that one has to save something before passing it on. Second, money flows back via direct investment – we are talking about sending money into a new or an already existing business (i.e. buying a share of a

---

[88] See also Chapter 4, thesis "*FAQ: The shrinking of money stock and the interest rate.*"

business or making additional investment in it). Upon returning to the microeconomy, money goes through the usual cycle, gradually leaving firms to be spent on human consumption.

The picture is way more complicated once we return to the present time when savings, though not deserving the heavenly category status bestowed upon them by Keynes, indeed occupy a more important place. We won't harbour your intrigue and point out the stumbling block right away – it is securities (with a credit component). However, it is easy to get lost in a tangle of various subtle moments, so let's break it down into the following five moments:

Moment #1 is *methodological* – unveiling the theoretical character of these subtle moments without *relying on the strictly classical PCM framework* is very difficult. There are no surprises here. Often, cracking the problems formulated by past generations is easier from a modern knowledge perspective. Knowing how it happens under a PCM, it is easy to see the most logical way to study the "savings" category under paper capitalism (*if there is a desire to do so*, as it is not quite necessary) – one needs to observe how the strict classical framework changes once securities are introduced. If we pretend that we don't know about the PCM model, it is practically impossible to study "savings" correctly ***without separating money into 'money as payment' and 'money as credit'*** and with a subsequent analysis of money movement at each incarnation of it, like we did in Chapter 1 (and continue to do so in this one). "To completely separate" and "to assume the difference from the context" are not identical, and so in the latter case, in my opinion, it is hard to avoid some crucial mistakes.

Moment #2, or the main objective reason for raising the status of savings under paper capitalism: *the existence of a securities market* leads to the partial replacement of classical deals (purchase and sale, as well as credit ones) by surrogate deals bearing the features of both classical deal types, often in a byzantine way. These surrogate deals, in turn, give birth to surrogate assets (securities as a mix of commodities and money) that also play the role of savings used in the movement of investments. As a result, plenty of various surrogates displace classical clear boundaries between households, the real economy and commercial banks.

Moment #3, or the artificial reason for a hyperbolised status of savings under paper capitalism: *a theory by Keynes*. As he suggests, saving is one of the cornerstones, while the propensity to save together with expectations of market participants explains a lot, if not everything. Here, we may remember "fundamental psychological law" or "paradox of thrift", but the gist of it all is that market participants either send or don't allocate their savings for consumption or investment. This is (with the subsequent conclusion that government investment is necessary to stimulate consumption and increase employment) the main idea of Keynes, which was largely inspired by the great British economist's reflections about getting out of the Great Depression. The main unpleasant theoretical effect was that by actively advocating demand, Keynes was *in fact* trying to formalise it by breaking it down into components.[89] The resulting convoluted system of marginal and "psychological" categories is accompanied by very plausible *analytical*[90] reflections, but it leads to forming a "dead zone" in theoretical economics. Its sad influence on the progress of theoretical economics is akin to the influence of the logical reasoning sequence "abstract human labour → value → surplus value" by another great economist, Marx. Taking into account the authority of both, one can forever circle inside the "dead zones" they created, but it is better not to get into that at all.

Moment #4, as an afterword for Moments #2 and #3: if we set a goal to show correctly all the interactions demonstrating the elevated status of savings in the paper capitalism model (and we

---

[89] Formally, Keynes used a calculated indicator, a sum of consumer and investment expenses, with the disclaimer that expenses were "expected". We'll be talking shortly about attempts to "materialise" supply and demand.

[90] Often, analytics try to beef up their argumentation by referencing some "theory", meaning well-known cause-and-effect relationships from economics (and not necessarily theoretical) textbooks or well-known publications. Even though analytical literature may indeed be based on theoretical relationships, in general analytics is as different from theoretical economics as jazz is from classical music. Unlike theoretical economics, the goal of analytics is to explain what happened (or what is going to happen) "here and now", irrespective of the scope of the events, from a single firm to the world economy. Everything goes – theory, periodic publications, statistics (from multi-year to one-time precedents), geopolitics, events personification (analysis of decision makers' characteristics), manipulations with technical analysis's "flasks", mere intuition and, sure enough, the insider advantage. With all this variety, it is not difficult to see a priority of analysis of "broad government" decisions in general and of financial authorities in particular.

don't set such a goal), neither our schema of splitting the funds invested in the equipment purchase nor Keynes's theory are suitable. Our schema is highly specialised, while Keynes's theory simply does not see some of the interactions, at least with enough clarity. The following simple observations appear to be obvious: savings in global currencies are more resilient, and the speculative market allows savings to grow without application of any skills in the real economy or banking. This growth is even easier if securities are denominated in global currencies and even better if one has an opportunity to borrow global currencies at "domestic" (low) interest rates. The last phrase alone is a clue to the fact that the credit issuance system is a valuable addition to the securities market and to global currencies. Thus, the elevated status of savings in the present economic model is a consequence of its core characteristics, and so there is no need to "rewrite the book" choosing savings as a starting point.

Moment #5: *if readers forget about "savings", their understanding of money movement in the real economy under the existing formation will only improve.* Despite the turbulence happening under paper capitalism in the classical flow chart showing money movement for the funds invested in equipment, we'll still consider it to be the fundamental chart, since purchase and sale deals with equipment suppliers, coupled with hiring deals, describe it well. These deals (save for leasing, which we have not discussed yet) practically all happen in a classical style. As for credit deals, they mainly (and in cases of small and medium businesses, almost universally) take place without the use of securities or the participation of "the broad government". Besides, as we have seen in Chapter 1, the money reflected in depositors' accounts under the existing system is not sitting somewhere in bank vaults, but simply represents the commercial banks' liabilities, making these savings "virtual" ones.

There is a classical schema of splitting the funds invested in equipment purchase, which is still doing a fairly good job describing the gist of the events but there are some objective and artificial circumstances distorting this gist. There is another important moment helping to further understand the origins of that hyperbolised theoretical role of "savings". Despite its "invisibility", it is hard to call it simply a "moment", due to the real importance of the category. We are talking about one of the two main components of the market's "invisible hand", about *supply*, and to be precise, about the supply of money.

In modern economic literature, whenever talking about the money supply, they usually mean "money stock", i.e. the sum of cash, bank liabilities and certain types of securities.[91] Note that two of these components, which actually are not money, are also used in lieu of money. Add that these components are easy to calculate at the national economy level, and this term may seem to be a lucky combination of pleasant and useful things, helping to create some mathematical economic models in statistics and analytics.

Money stock is an important aggregated indicator, but with all its importance it is just a statistical indicator that doesn't reflect the essence of demand and supply, nor the volume or direction of the suggested property movement.[92]

As we have just mentioned "property movement", let's make an important terminological clarification: the demand for some goods (to buy them) is essentially the same as the supply of money *for these purchases.*[93]

---

[91] There is also a narrower view on money supply, which limits its scope to the credit market (within the current financial system, the market for relevant securities is also included). It is difficult to understand that such a fundamental category as supply (in our case, money supply) has been possible to "materialise", but for some reason it applies only to loans and does not directly apply to goods. When there is not any special money stock intended only for loans (since money does not have an inscription whether it is credit or not), we will proceed from a more general view. By and large, this is not important, since in any case the definition that "materialises" the category "supply" is a fiction *from a theoretical point of view*, as we'll try to show further in the current text box.

[92] No doubt that analytic types not only have the right but they also *have* to use any accessible data to accomplish their complex assignments, especially given that theoretical economics as a rule does not offer any instruments for solving current problems. However, the lack of required instruments does not allow us to classify all the data used by analytics as theoretical. Their incursions into "the theory" (usually through the use of complex terminology, which may be unconsciously perceived as the "right of passage") contribute to bending the fundamental essence of things.

[93] (1) The situation with basic lease deals is not materially different, but we better avoid mixing up the explanations. Otherwise, we may start triggering various "paradoxes". For example, somebody may offer the following argument (*if this is hard to absorb on the fly, it does not make sense to read in detail, as this logic*

For example, if I want to own a spacious six-bedroom flat in a prestigious quarter of Moscow, this does not construe demand, because like most other people I don't have enough money, whereas the sum of savings owned by these people is *by far* exceeding the sum of the supply prices[94] of these high-end flats.

---

plays no role in our study): as demand for goods is growing, the demand for money as an asset, according to Keynes, is decreasing. Thus, money supply should also decrease, although your author seems to be arguing for the opposite. However, you may have guessed that unlike in our phrase, the types and *timing* of these deals are mixed up here. (2) This simple phrase with the footnote link attached also serves as a demonstration of the difference between analytics and theoretical economics in the way each one uses the terms "demand" and "supply". In the way we used the term "supply of money", it is practically not used in analytics (or, as in the counterargument above, it can prompt reflections on a certain chain of events that may occur *after* the relationships described in our phrase). It is not used for two main reasons: first, it cannot be calculated, and second, few participants in the speculative market are interested in what is happening, for example, at the tomato market in the city of N (at the same time, it is difficult to find any more *theoretically* important component of the supply of money than the one determining daily life of all businesses in the world).

[94] *(Let's clarify that wherever we mention "supply" in this book, it is meant to be a part of that same "supply and demand" pair for the theoretical studies, without taking into account (as this was not our invention) any nuances of using the term "supply" in the English language practical economy.)* We assume the simplest interpretation of supply price, i.e. something that a buyer can see (on a price tag, in a price list, in a publication, etc.) or hear. On one hand, we will not use the terms "offer price" or "asking price", rejecting any attempts to mix up theory with sending instructions to computers in the process of exchange trading. On the other hand, in economic writings, "supply price" is often meant to be the minimal price acceptable to the seller. I am not sure where to obtain this information ("What's the lowest price you would take?" one asks, with the subsequent reply of "How much, when and where will you pick it up?" – this conversation between the same people, but a week earlier or a week later, may result in different outcomes) and, frankly speaking, I don't see any theoretical necessity for this doubtful precision. However, the origins of this approach are clear. It is plausible that if in a certain mathematical formula (for example, designed for recalculating a supply volume) there is a variable called "supply price", the author of this formula may want to clarify it. However, the reflection of objective processes in a *market* economy is not the same as an attempt of mathematically minded people to explain to each other how these processes work. Even if a researcher does not try to convince anyone that the minimum *supply* price exists in the real world, a deeper problem is that use of a "typical" or any other supply price (as one of the basic categories) in a far-reaching theoretical reasoning will not result in correct conclusions. In my entrepreneurial past, I personally handled price forming on goods worth hundreds of millions of dollars and I could speak volumes on the nuances of supply prices.

Sometimes in these cases, demand is qualified by adding the word "solvent" in front of it. This is not a mistake, but in general, it is a tautology. At the same time, people who have enough money to buy such a flat may not be interested in purchasing it for some reason and thus they do not affect demand either.

I am not sure if you are with me on this, but in most cases it is more convenient to discuss the supply of money (as it is closer to the movement of property) in the same market segment where purchase and sale, or leasing, deals of non-monetary property take place, rather than to discuss demand for the same property in the segment.[95] We'll continue our reasoning with this equivalent in mind.

Let me hypothesise that the key reason for the doubtful balancing of "money supply" and "money stock" is the positive relationship between an increase in the total amount of money (in this case, money stock) in the economy and an increase in the total amount of purchases. Thus, this amount of money is named "money supply" and it has stemmed from an ever-present desire to formalise everything. The result is an awkward substitution of theoretical relationships with a juxtaposition of analytical pictures. Instead of having identical "live" categories (demand for purchase/lease of some non-monetary property and supply of money for purchase/lease of the same property), a pair of categories, the similarity between which is hard to imagine, snuck into theoretical economics independently: "demand" (in the case of purchases, represented by "aggregate demand") and "money supply" (represented by "money stock").

In addition to our example of an expensive flat, let's give another, similarly unsophisticated one. On a given day at a farmers' market, we cannot precisely determine the supply of money (demand) *here and now* – even the buyers, taken one by one, do not know it (and even those who think they do are likely to end up spending a

---

However, I see no theoretical sense in doing this. Therefore, to avoid turning our discussion into a pub conversation, let's raise the bar and leave the supply price alone as we don't need it. We'll be talking shortly about one major problem provoking theoretical errors, namely "the magic of supply and demand".

[95] This simple algorithm does not apply to credit deals, i.e. where money is exchanged for money ($M_C \leftarrow M$), but it does work for purchase and sale deals where money is exchanged for foreign currency.

different sum). So, the only credible result that we can obtain would be an *estimate of demand changes*, compared with previous days, by the sellers (all entrepreneurs do this) provided that they are suddenly willing to share their unsophisticated trade secrets.

It is easy to see why it is not possible to calculate the real supply of money in the market – it consists of multiple threads of *anticipated* money movement from a large number of buyers to a large number of sellers. It is easy to understand why the ideas to tally up demand and supply are gravitating towards the "macro level" – national economy is, on one hand, a sufficiently isolated economic unit, and on the other, a generalising one. Therefore, a general interpretation can be as follows: regardless of anticipated routes, all these threads at the end are tied up on both ends to a pair of vertically mounted posts. One post represents all the buyers' money and the other one represents all their purchases. A natural hypothesis would be that the higher the first post is, the higher the second one will be. So, there is a temptation (backed up by "theoretical" labels on the posts – there is hardly anything more fundamental than demand and supply, since we somehow "managed" to depict both numerically) to not only explain the height of the second post by the height of the first one, but also increase the amount of money to stimulate economic growth. Attention: in this subtle, single-move chess combination, what can possibly stand in the way of growth of the second post? Eureka, it's savings!

Such an interpretation of the economic mechanism is not a reflection of a particular theory, but its presence can be felt in Keynes's theory as well as in neoclassical writings (for example, in the monetarist school). Despite its shallow reflection of economic relationships and flaky terminology, this rather analytical schema has an important advantage: it contains a link to real-life events.

Conversely, the traditional theoretical approach should be called "the magic of demand and supply", as it relies on the ***meticulous but futile study of demand and supply curves***[96] ***in an attempt to***

[96] For instance, Keynes, in his *The General Theory of Employment, Interest and Money*, was making an accent on demand: "The value of D at the point of the aggregate demand function, where it is intersected by the aggregate supply function, will be called the effective demand. Since this is the substance of the General Theory of Employment, which it will be our object to expound, the

get to the moment of truth, namely the point of intersection of their respective curves (the deal where price is formed). How does one transition from these "curves" that exist only in researchers' imaginations, to something *palpably* simple without mixing them up? For example, Keynes put in a disclaimer that the point of intersection ("effective demand") represents *expected* expenses. There is no mix up, but we are not getting to the actual occurred deal where the price is being formed. The absence of a "click" symbolising our transition from an imaginary economy to the real one is lost in subsequent calculations, disclaimers, functions and, most notably, digressions towards psychology. Here, Keynes likely believed that the line separating intentions from actions could be crossed over and we gradually begin to find ourselves in a world of statistics, known to mimic events that really took place.

One of the most famous attempts to "tame the wild mustangs" in the name of theory advancement is linked, as we have mentioned in the Introduction, to Alfred Marshall: at the point of intersection of the curves lies some equilibrium price, flanked by marginal cost on the side of the supply curve and by marginal utility on the side of the demand curve. It is quite possible that unconsciously we can rely on the knowledge that mathematical functions, having marginal values, never actually attain some target point while approaching it. One way or another, they have been mining this niche to the present day, without entirely throwing out even marginal utility, despite its obviously contrived nature. As we have said already, the significance of marginal cost is contrived as well, though it is not obvious (Chapter 4, "*Appendix: Marginal cost ...*"), while the equilibrium price is nothing but an attempt on the part of "value" disguised as "legitimate" to remain in *theoretical* economics (analytical types are gladly using the equilibrium price, but since analytics is not my job, I am not going to judge them).

In this study, many of the drawbacks of our "posts and threads" analytical schema (described above) are explained to some extent, but these explanations are scattered due to our method chosen to describe the interaction of basic categories. For example, we'll soon see in this thesis how the schema of stimulating "aggregate demand" in a classical or near-classical national economy can be

succeeding chapters will be largely occupied with examining the various factors upon which these two functions depend" (Keynes, 2018, p. 23).

> thrown away due to the presence of imports. We won't perform a comprehensive analysis of this schema and indeed we are not going to enter the "world of magic" at the level of basic categories. ***There are deals and there are prices. Their classification assumes the priority of prices reflecting the cost formation.***

As we have digressed to savings and supply of money, let's go back to the thought that money paid for capital goods ultimately ends up as consumption (by way of staged separation into basic cost types). Mathematically, key features (in the scope of money movement as payment) of this idea, even though it was not a pivotal one, have been reflected by the American economist Wassily Leontief in his input–output model. The latter was created – from the movement of property perspective – to estimate the volume of consumption of basic goods (for example, metals) by various economic sectors.

Using a simple three-dimensional representation for the movement of investment money, it is easy to see the exaggerated nature of fears that would result from introducing new machinery. On one hand, this would occur in storefronts stuffed with goods and, on the other, in crowds of poor consumers staring at them. Even if something like this were to happen (the economy is full of surprises), it would be an abnormal situation. The *normal* situation is that introducing new machinery leads not only to an increase in labour productivity, but also to an increase in average consumption, despite the fact that some workers lose their jobs. We can simply disregard this temporary job loss, as technological evolution takes place gradually. To be more precise, if the machines are reproduced at a pace exceeding the population growth rate (to simplify, this can be thought of as introducing certain "machinery units" with the population unchanged), it will result in an increase in average consumption.

The events are logically aligned as follows: new machines are bought with accumulated savings by entrepreneurs who count on having a demand for their products. That is, the anticipated consumption level is high enough for such purchases (if someone is buying equipment, they need it). Also, it does not matter that the capital spending on new machines is not recouped by the entrepreneur right away, since the money was directed to increase consumption at the moment of the equipment purchase, as can be easily seen from the input–output model.

That paragraph was easy to understand, wasn't it? By asking this rhetorical question, let's note how simple the *normal* process of distribution of additional consumption looks in a classical economy. Our shaded text boxes above are important and rather complex. However, in the scope of this thesis, they serve as logic steps to the last paragraph.

You may have noticed that the logic looks like this: consumption → investment → consumption. The first arrow means that if the consumption level is high enough (as a rule, it corresponds to increasing consumption), the market will duly react by increasing investment. The second arrow reflects our main line of reasoning from the beginning of this thesis, namely how additional investment leads to an increase in the average consumption level. Importantly, if we choose investments to be the driver, we'll be putting the cart before the horse. This will lead to distortions in both the national economy and in theoretical logic. By the way, Keynes made this exact error, as mentioned in the first shaded text box.[97]

Going back to consumption, let's mention a few moments not to lose the main thread. When speaking about Keynes's theory, it always pays to remember that he worked on the foundations of it during a very distinct historical period, namely the deflationary crisis in the 1930s, which was the most pronounced in the particular country (the US). One should also realise (like Keynes did to some extent) that *generally* an attempt to grow a sustainable national economy through a regular stimulation of consumption leads to higher costs, compared with a natural course of events.

From a technical perspective, a decrease in consumer demand in the national economy signals that consumers are not willing to buy goods from producers at current prices. Generally, this process does not construe a certain impaired moment of fundamental economic laws, on which a war needs to be declared, running a risk of a distorted self-regulation mechanism. ***It is part of the natural mechanism of rational resource consumption.*** Thus, the technical manifestation (goods' prices are too high) is based on a fundamental gist – production costs are too high.

Correspondingly, under the natural course of events a decrease in consumer demand will lead to a decrease in producer costs, leading eventually to goods' prices decreasing without major damage to the goods' reproduction in the microeconomy (so it is still profitable for firms). As

[97] We'll be talking about it in the thesis "*The partial direct issuance of money in the economic policy of F. D. Roosevelt ...*" because our main reason for the critique of certain theoretical views, besides the critique in the selected Chapter 4 theses, is to give a clearer picture in the corresponding passages of our main text.

we are talking about the national economy and not about its single sectors, and we are assuming the systemic character of this situation, this means currency depreciation, deflation or a combination of the two,[98] and nothing else beyond these two mechanisms.[99] Seemingly an easy way out, an artificial or non-market stimulation of consumption is almost invariably connected to a non-market increase in the amount of money held by consumers, and thus prevents a price decrease[100] (except for lowering

---

[98] Here, a simple enumeration is enough. Further in our study, we'll see that currency depreciation has been, and will remain (in the scope of a PCM), the most organic method to lower costs in a national economy. As for deflation, it will remain as an essential feature of both gold and paper capitalisms. One difficult moment is that deflation manifests itself differently under these two models of capitalism; another is that under the present model, deflation (intrinsic to the countries issuing global currencies) happens concurrently with currency depreciation, which is intrinsic to regular countries and is often hard to see.

[99] The chances are, many would wonder why sometimes, that when consumers do not have sufficient funds for buying, lower costs are required at firms, where such a significant expense as wages directly impacts consumer demand. There is a simple clue to this: as a result of currency depreciation, the national economy will be getting money from abroad and sending less money in return. There is a more complex clue as well: deflation, which in the end resolves the situation by lowering wages without an inflow of money, makes workers less picky with their consumption and their *choice of employment*. Both processes can be represented as consumption gradually stepping down, though under the currency depreciation scenario, due to the inflow of money, one step is sufficient for all, and under the deflation scenario there are many steps, originating chaotically. There is also our PCM model, where currency depreciation (with some technical caveats) and the absence of deflation (at the system level) will be accompanied by the appearance of a true *market* interest rate. Currency depreciation leads to a serious shock in the national economy and were it the only lever to lower the costs of national firms, this economy would be quite rigid. Chapter 2 is meant to demonstrate how the market interest rate, elevated to the rank of basic cost regulator, helps to either avoid or mitigate the aftermath of the shock. This process can also be represented as costs gradually stepping down, albeit a selective one. Additionally, it can be represented as some barely audible chords, not interrupting the main musical theme, unlike hitting hard on all the keys with currency depreciation or a prolonged cacophony with deflation. This is approximately how a *really* liberal economy should "sound".

[100] For a better understanding of the terms "artificial" and "non-market" used here, we can recall some material devoted to physical turnover. Under a natural course of events, the state adds money into the national economy as the latter grows (first and foremost, in connection to physical turnover growth). The artificial stimulation of consumption switches the cause and effect: the state adds money to trigger the physical turnover growth.

taxes on firms, which promotes product price reduction since producers keep more money to themselves, but this cannot be done over and over). This increase slows down the required cost reduction and may sometimes reverse it.

Here, we can observe a simple relationship, helping us to understand that we did not really escape currency depreciation but only exacerbated its scope: the state cannot stimulate consumer demand outside its national economy, but the stimulation of consumption also attracts foreign firms, directly or through importers. Considering that national firms are burdened with high costs and are therefore less competitive, consumption grows faster than the production of domestic goods. The payment balance deteriorates, bringing about the need for a national currency's depreciation, which is necessary to lower costs and the respective restoration of competitiveness among national firms. The scale of this depreciation will be directly related to the size of consumer demand stimulation.

This would generally happen now, and not only under the PCM scenario, in most peripheral countries, had they decided to experiment with "stimulating domestic demand", albeit on a much smaller scale than it is done by the US. We regard this simple chain of events as a fundamental one. The model that is developed based on Keynes's investment multiplier works in an isolated case, which occurs when the national currency *does not depreciate*. This type of national economy is usually considered to be a closed one. Even at the simple common-sense level, for example, looking at the globalisation of the modern world economy, Keynes's investment multiplier model clearly cannot be fundamental. To grasp at straws, a variable of net exports has been introduced into modern Keynesian models. However, one more snapshot does not change the essence – the Keynesian theory, with a certain degree of precision, reflects processes solely inside the national economy where the national currency does not depreciate for some reason.

We are not saying that Keynes was fundamentally wrong in his recommendations to President Franklin D. Roosevelt. By virtue of their practical orientation, these recipes were a unique case in the history of relationships between theory and practice. But, first of all, Keynes did not give a correct theoretical justification for his recipes.

To some degree, the theory was tailored to suit the result. In our thesis "*The partial direct issuance of money in the economic policy of F. D. Roosevelt ...*", we'll see that the fundamental technological underpinning of these recipes is related to particular features of reproducing new money under paper capitalism, i.e. the recipes worked but the disease they cured was hidden deeper than Keynes believed. If we use our terminology, Keynes in fact suggested to introduce elements of direct issuance of money. However, these elements alone are insufficient to build a fundamental model of the economy.

Second, these recommendations are valid only for paper capitalism. Third, without serious disclaimers, they are valid only for those national economies under paper capitalism where the national currency, being also a global currency, *does not depreciate at all* (compared with other currencies, minus the impact of the exchange rate fluctuations against other global currencies) or *does not depreciate to the proper extent.*

These particular features are much easier to understand if we realise that the world economy under paper capitalism assumes the existence of two complementary types of national economies that are different from a *theoretical* standpoint (we call these "wonderland" and "near-classical" countries). It so happened that Keynes did not witness this stage of paper capitalism's development.

Reduction of systemic costs.

Let's make an unexpected move and tell a tale about a magic planet, where besides the usually expected dragons we also get familiar with the mundane things of magic life, "little flying wagons" (money) and "lamps" (securities). The reason why the author decided to try himself at fiction will become clear a bit later.

Imagine that on one planet some part of the economy worked exclusively for feeding and caring for the dragons. The people were not scared of the dragons, as the only dragon that looked mighty and scary was the Chief Dragon, but rather they appreciated the value brought by these creatures. Of course, some appreciated the dragons more and some less, but nobody saw a way to live without them. As we all know, dragons are magic creatures and ours were no exception. The point is, the whole planet was covered in picturesque mountains. It was beautiful but it was hard to travel across the country, and travel between the countries was not possible at all. The dragons were skilled in making magic little wagons (as light as a feather and nearly invisible) that solved this problem – if you paid for goods using these little wagons, then your cargo and little wagons magically traded places. The Chief Dragon made particularly good wagons and these were used for trade between the planet's nations. The dragons not only made the wagons, but also tried to place them in certain places, lending or selling them, for example, to the people they considered the most useful for economic development based on the sound reasoning that those people had previously shown their willingness and ability to contribute. Occasionally, the dragons did not do something right and the economy slumped, but some learned people always had a logical explanation for it.

Oh, there were also some magic lamps, which were believed to show the way for these little wagons. And if they did not show the way, then they would simply attract wagons. The lamps were made not only by the dragons, but also by some rich people who surely benefited from lamp making – they became even richer, especially when they designed new kinds of lamps. And once something attracted the wagons, it also attracted people (even if they did not quite understand how this draconian carousel really worked).

One day, the people noticed that in each country the dragons preferred to live near a couple of ancient, half-built guard Towers, and that they demonstrated that they did not want to make any changes. In fact, there were four of these Towers, but the dragons were totally oblivious to the other two sky-scraping Towers. The curious people hired engineers who designed the required mechanisms and began to finish up the construction of the Towers. Then, people had an epiphany about the magic abilities of the dragons and fired them all. From that point forward, people could do anything themselves, helped by the Towers' magic power – the inhabitants of the planet had enough common sense to understand that all the talk about taming the magic dragons was nothing but a tall tale.

Unexpectedly, the people who were making food and other goods for the dragons lost their businesses. They had no buyers for their products, as the people who were engaged in the old dragon craft could perform it much more cheaply. So, for their meagre income, they could not buy everything that the dragons used to consume. The people who used to supply the "dragon feeders" in the past and those who had supplied them in turn also suffered, albeit to a lesser extent. Besides, once the Towers were finished, the dragons lost their magic spell and turned into the remarkably industrious people. Some of these people kept servicing the little wagons, but some had to be retrained to make products. This was undoubtedly good for the planet, but it was not quite fitting at that particular moment, as the products were not selling well even without their contribution.

The situation was tough, so many people became nostalgic for the old draconian times. However, it turned out that the planet itself was the chief magician and it rewarded the people by making the little wagons made by them even more functional than those previously made by the dragons. There were many more of those man-made little wagons and they were distributed where they were most needed. The guarding Towers watched impassively to make sure that neither rank nor past services impacted this distribution (they watched as close as possible, of course, but the planet's magic was stronger than the dragons). Also, the countries had no more need for those high maintenance magic lamps. Therefore, sometime after the initial hurdles, the planet's economy started to grow faster than it ever had done before.

You might have recognised the "dragons" as the financial system of paper capitalism. The Chief Dragon's hideout is determined by the Federal Reserve location. From an economic standpoint, we understand that paper capitalism is a mandatory stage in the development of civilisation and, one way or another, somebody needs to do the job performed by the dragons. However, the financial system of paper capitalism has been increasingly slowing down our civilisation's development and there is no economic reason to put up with this, given that the required technological progress level has already been achieved.

Likely, it was obvious that the guard Towers are actually the basic cost regulators, two of which need to operate at full capacity to allow a transition to the new system. *That is, conceptually our study*[101] *can be described in this extremely simple manner: costs → cost regulators.* This is it, or almost it, as we also need to remember the important role of price definition, which helps to unite and arrange the resulting theoretical model.

The purpose of cost regulators is not to make excessive costs disappear (they have been, and will remain, there forever), but rather to assure that punishment for them is inevitable. A simple and understandable punishment, such as charging the actual excessive costs to the manager's personal property, constitutes the final cost regulator: negative profit. An unconditional responsibility of managing owners, backed up by their property, is possible only in an economy based on private property. We are

---

[101] This is for our study only, not the entire theoretical economics. We'll talk about fundamental theoretical postulates of economics in our thesis "*Psychology and rationality in theoretical economics ...*".

talking about a competitive economy, as negative profit forms as a result of competition. The stronger the competition is, the less chance there is left for excessive costs to remain unnoticed. Monopolisation, as we know, is the opposite of competition.

Therefore, let's formulate it this way: monopolisation always leads to excessive costs. When neither the final cost regulator nor anti-monopoly agencies can handle this, we call these costs systemic. Four basic cost regulators indicate where exactly those systemic costs originate. With their help, we can decipher which basic property type (people, land, money as credit representing basic resources in the national economy, or money as payment when it is used in exchange for foreign currency) is used when apparent or hidden monopolisation takes place. Therefore, in our refined model, all basic cost regulators should counter the resource use of monopolisation to the maximum extent possible. In the most precise way, this can be achieved naturally, when the forming of the basic cost regulators (let's remember that all of them are prices) has a market character.[102] Given that both incomplete basic regulators can be formed under fully fledged market conditions, we'll formulate our ultimate goal as such: fully fledged market forming of basic cost regulators.

Our fairy tale narrative helped us avoid the following *unsolvable problem*: unlike the model itself, the transition to it cannot be *described* theoretically. There will be some temporary drop in consumption, that much can be said with certainty. At the same time, we have enough

---

[102] One of the basic cost regulators, rent, cannot be entirely formed by the market, as land is the only basic resource type that does not reproduce. For example, while talking about the connection of monopolisation with systemic costs earlier, we mentioned anti-monopoly agencies. If, for instance, we assume that all the mines with a non-renewable and clearly limited raw material belong to one or two firms, then cost regulators won't help as much as an antitrust service. Generally, market mechanisms become impaired whenever we deal with clearly limited resources, so antitrust governmental control is inevitable. Thus, that seemingly abandoned landowning formation will be to some extent always present in the economy. The market turnover of land is facilitated not by charging rent (let's remember that in this study, rent means *only* payments for land use) but by the purchase and sale of land. This is not a full purchase and sale deal, but rather a supplementary one – we'll touch upon this later – and strictly speaking, it is not even a deal for the purchase and sale of land. Still, rent remains a basic cost regulator, as it safeguards the economy and society as a whole from a very unpleasant private monopoly on land, while the purchase and sale of land without having rent may easily lead to such a monopoly.

transition-related moments for a separate thesis, found closer to the end of this study.

In our next thesis, though, we'll return to the microeconomy, and consider both forming and reduction of costs. We'll reduce these processes to the division of labour, distinguishing it (1) between firms and (2) inside a firm. Looking at some firms as examples, we'll see how the division of labour (2) inside a firm causes a basic decrease in costs (with cost reduction due to technological evolution being a substantial part of it). Conversely, systemic costs intrinsic to the real economy are formed at the micro level.

Let's clarify one definition and terminology in advance. The term "division of labour" was introduced at the time of the labour theory of value, accompanied by dominance of the "labour" category, stemming from a hypothesis that human labour creates a certain "value". A relatively infant state of engineering achievements contributed to this. When a person takes a hammer, the term "division of labour" is not an eyesore and the hypothesis of "value" creation does not appear contrived. Conversely, when an operator pushes a button to trigger an automated process that creates products worth "a million" and keeps an eye on the process by looking at the gauges, the "value" creation hypothesis requires quite a fantastic picture of moving some "engineering labour clots". A connection of this automated process with division of *human* labour is also murky, as many single operations performed by the machines were never performed by humans. Instead of division of labour (2) inside a firm, we'll be using the term "division of operations inside a firm" (or simply "division of operations"), based on the following definition:

- *Division of labour (2) means improvement of quality*[103] *(speed, power, precision) of single operations*[104] performed either by people or machines.

[103] Here, "efficiency" is often used instead of "quality". This won't be an error, but in this case we'll inadvertently move the division of labour (2) to the domain of price categories (as economic efficiency is tested by the combination of revenue and costs, i.e. in the end, by the profit) and lose some visibility.

[104] With technological progress accelerating, our cherished handcrafted quality will be reduced to artwork by selected artisans (who will be using some good tools, I believe). The high prices of their creations will be based mainly on their psychological, not quality, superiority. If we compare our present time with, say,

With all that, we won't be changing the definition of division of labour (1), as at the heart of this (looking a bit ahead) there are certain humanitarian processes, i.e. features of human labour. We also leave the term "division of labour" unchanged, as a generalised conceptual term for this very important backbone of the *Homo sapiens*' economic civilisation.

A descent to microeconomy is quite a risky undertaking for theoretical economics, as branches of the macroeconomy (exact prices) are lost in the "foggy gorges" of in-kind interactions. The possibility of generalisation of this is severely limited due to the lack of units of measurement. When we can cling to price categories, our task will be much easier. But this will not solve all the problems, so we'll also rely on the historical logic of firms' formations and *well-known* principles of their activities. Our elevated accuracy will help us to not think too much, the way it happened with Ronald Coase. His category of "transaction costs", being basic for the new institutional economics, is an obstacle in the way of our research (and not just ours, as only either Ronald Coase's theory or Adam Smith's division of labour can "survive" in the long term), so we cannot but pay attention to it.

Ronald Coase and transaction costs. Division of labour and coordination of labour.

In Ronald Coase's collection of articles, *The Firm, the Market, and the Law*, the theoretical assumptions clarifying his own understanding of transaction costs are partially scattered around the text and are partially implicit, so one is left guessing about them. This likely happened because, as Coase says early on in the first chapter, "As the argument in these papers is, I believe, simple, so simple indeed as almost to make their propositions fall into the category of truths which can be deemed self-evident ...". We'll start with possibly the most general assumptions:

> "... a firm will tend to expand until the costs of organizing an extra transaction within the firm become equal to the costs of carrying out the same transaction by means of an exchange on the open market or the costs of organizing in another firm." (Coase, 1937, p. 395)

In the same article (p. 394), Ronald Coase states that "... a point must be reached where the costs of organizing an extra transaction within the firm

---

the 19th century, we may conclude that "the future is already here". Food seems to be an exception, however, as its quality deterioration has multiple causes.

are equal to the costs involved in carrying out the transaction in the open market-or to the costs of organizing by another entrepreneur".

Let's interpret it graphically in the following way (Fig. 2-1):

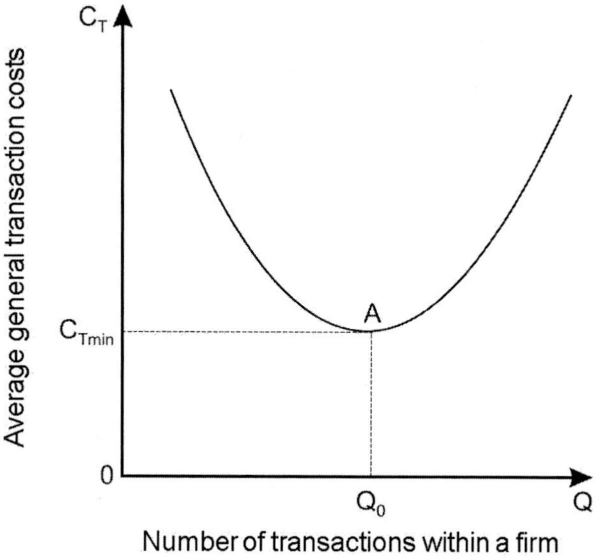

Fig. 2-1. Interpretation of Coase's theory: general transaction costs and optimal firm size

A first close look at the main components of Coase's theory reveals some serious problems. It is impossible to single out either a unit of measure as a "transaction" or a unit measuring "transactions". In no time, we find ourselves in a world of interpretations.[105] Sure, some of the transactions

[105] Marx's reliance on such non-existent categories as "value" and "abstract human labour" did not prevent him from making more or less accurate predictions for the advent of socialism. However, the contrived nature of the fundamental principles of a theory limits its correspondence to real economic processes to some disconnected conclusions. Everything else is shrouded in a veil of interpretations – in the absence of materialistic basic categories, any interpretation goes. As long as theoretical economics exists, there will be some activists who believe that Marx was misunderstood. Still, we should distinguish between errors and irregularities by, for example, Adam Smith, Marx and Keynes, who described the complex systems of selected formations in meticulous detail, and errors made by Coase,

are the deals that can be counted based on the firm's accounting books, but this would be too narrow, as from the viewpoint of John R. Commons, Coase[106] or Oliver E. Williamson. And if we try to describe a complete set of transactions, an "interpretation" chaos will ensue – conceivably, out of the ten adherents of this theory who enter the same firm, you won't find two people who would point to the same set. It would consist of a motley set of actions of people performing their numerous duties along with movement of various types of property. Parts of this set will require their own measurement units, but in general, the task of identifying a common unit of measurement has no solution. For hundreds of years, economists puzzled over sorting out everything that is used in the economy, for example, into various property groups and movement of a property. However, here, some energetic people arrived and mixed everything into a pile before announcing the birth of "transactions". Peeking ahead, we'll say that this was not the only moment of "simplification" of theoretical economics by Coase.

Note that even the use of something as a unit of measurement in a single firm does not guarantee that it can be a theoretically rigorous unit of measure when considering all firms. For example, in firms, payment is often pegged to the number of hours worked, but one hour of ordinary labour (which Keynes suggested considering as a unit of employment) cannot be acceptable. We can define one hour, but we cannot rigorously define "ordinary labour" or "labour" in general. In other firms, we'll always find examples that will impede our attempts to obtain a common classification of labour. Even in the US, easily the most Keynesian national economy in the world, they measure employment by using the number of people or number of job applications submitted by them, but not by the units proposed by Keynes. However, at any rate, Keynes's assumption deserved careful consideration before we rejected it. In the case of transactions, this unit of measurement is practically dead at the first encounter with the economic realities of a medium-sized firm.

Accordingly, the contrived certainty of Coase's cited assumptions is dead too. Let's see what's left. If we remove the "transaction" category that did not pass the simplest resilience test (we will delete it temporarily, since

---

whose study mostly looks like an attempt to find a single silver bullet of "transaction costs".

[106] In his collection of articles *The Firm, the Market, and the Law*, we could not find the definition of what Coase meant by "transaction", so it has to be guessed from the context.

this category is a basic one for Coase's theory and we'll revisit it over and over), then we get that with expanding activities certain costs of the firm first decrease and then increase.[107] Most economists would agree with this brief statement in terms of costs per unit of production and our study is no exception. The difference of opinions begins when economists offer their versions of what cost types decisively affect the behaviour of average cost. From Coase's perspective, the economists underappreciated transaction costs (by the time of his main writings):

> "I have described what I had in mind in the following terms: 'In order to carry out a market transaction it is necessary to discover who it is that one wishes to deal with, to inform people that one wishes to deal and on what terms, to conduct negotiations leading up to a bargain, to draw up the contract, to undertake the inspection need to make sure that the terms of the contract are being observed, and so on.' [See *The Problem of Social Cost*, p. 114.] Dahlman crystallized the concept of transaction costs by describing them as 'search and information costs, bargaining and decision costs, policing and enforcement costs.' [Carl J. Dahlman, *The Problem of Externality*, The Journal of Law and Economics vol 22. no. I (April 1979): 148]." (Coase, 1990, p. 6)

Difficulties in understanding these costs begin with the fact that if we cannot define the transaction set, then we cannot build a bridge from transactions to the definition of transaction costs. Still, a chance to understand the essence of these costs is much better compared with the situation with transactions, as monetary units are used. If, during a conversation about the "transactions", we could not define a standardised unit of measure, then when talking about "transaction costs" we can and should do it, as this is our only chance to stay within generalisations (both scientific ones and those just consistent with common sense).

Whatever name we choose for the costs, they assume accounting for money paid by a firm. There are no costs without payments.

---

[107] A firm's expansion can be measured either as an increase in sales using monetary units (this version is more convenient to analyse labour productivity), or as an increase in the number of employees (this is more fitting for our case when analysing average cost). Such charts will be more meaningful in the scope of a single economic sector having an almost uniform structure of the firms (in general, microeconomic charts are very sensitive to the sector specifics). However, with or without sector specifics in mind, there won't be a need for "transactions", so it would not be easy for Coase to lure the reader into his "transaction costs".

Take depreciation, for example. In *accounting* practice, it is classified as costs, although its economic meaning is not cost but part of gross profit that is equal to the *costs earlier paid* for the equipment. For a managing owner, both the purchase of the machine and the purchase of raw materials or semi-finished products intended for processing on this machine are only temporary investments (i.e. costs) with the intended increase in monetary property. By *conditionally* calculating depreciation as costs according to a *conditional* depreciation schedule, the firm and the state can organise their fiscal relationship which in this case takes into account the *conditional* fact that the machine remains an asset of the firm, which it can, for example, sell or use as collateral. This is often the case, but it may be different – for example, some types of equipment require rigid anchorage using a concrete foundation, so after the final assembly this equipment cannot be sold except for scrap metal, although it has not been used for production yet. On the other hand, some (more gently) used equipment can still be quite a liquid asset after its full accounting depreciation. We may also add that given the conditional nature of depreciation that also manifests itself in a variety of methods, the firm is generally interested in accelerated depreciation, to correspondingly decrease or postpone its tax liability.

Damage, for example, also cannot be counted as costs, but as an estimate of losses, some of which may be irrecoverable and some as an estimate of *possible future costs* that materialise once the firm starts paying, for example, for the restoration of a building that was damaged due to a natural disaster. The following example demonstrates that the cost estimates and costs proper are two different things. If damage was suffered by the firm as a result of someone's actions and a court decision regarding those damages was not only satisfied but also executed by the defendant, the firm would not incur losses, including costs, at least as part of previously assessed damage. Sometimes, as a result of a court decision, the injured party earns more than if the disaster had never happened. Thus, costs are a fact as opposed to damage estimates.

The forced use of barter also comes down to receiving money. Generally, barter can substantially litter the theoretical certainty of reasoning without offering any visible benefit. Therefore, we got rid of it, back in the Introduction, while describing the field of our research.

Here, yet another problem arises. In line with our research, we can easily say that all costs are formed in firm's payments,[108] while payments, except for fiscal or other deductions in favour of state agencies, are formed as a result of deals. Once a deal is made and paid for, we can calculate the costs. However, Coase cannot say this without a disclaimer. The reason is that he is using "price mechanism" instead of "deals" and as far as I understood from the context, while including purchase and sale deals into this mechanism, he is not including hiring deals at all or only including them by using some special method. With this approach, costs originating from paying the employees either disappear or end up suspended in a separate realm. We can make an assumption regarding the source of this vagueness: in fact, the *fundamental* conclusion of Coase's theory is the statement that costs of a company (firm) are reduced when it is formed, because the company's employees reduce *their* costs when combining work in the company compared with the costs they incur when they perform individual work. I do not exclude the scenario where the reader goes over the previous sentence several times without quite understanding why this inference is a blunder. Therefore, later we'll talk about this fundamental inference separately. In the meantime, do not let yourself get confused and remember the common fact that the costs of hiring are *definitely* the costs incurred by firms and are also formed in payments made by firms in the hiring deals.

Now, we can take our next step inside Coase's theory and this step is named "intra-firm transaction costs".

The curve in Fig. 2-1 consists of, according to Coase's theory interpretations, the downward curve of external transaction costs and the upward branch of intra-firm transaction costs. There are also terms like "marginal intra-firm transaction costs" and "marginal external transaction costs". Unfortunately, I won't be able to explain concisely what these are. You would agree that if you had serious doubts about the existence of magical creatures that inhabit forests, lakes and mountains, it would be even more difficult to describe in detail what would happen if they got together one day. Whenever you want, you can read about "marginal costs" that doesn't exist in a real firm in the Appendix ("Marginal cost …"). As for transaction costs, we are still trying to refine these, despite the new obstacles in the way. At times, I feel that I am finally beginning to

[108] The concept of "opportunity cost" contradicts this statement. To minimise digressions, we'll talk about it in Chapter 4, which is dedicated to such discussions, thesis "*FAQ: Services, "post-industrial society", information, opportunity cost.*"

grasp the meaning of intra-firm costs, but then some "naive" questions arise and chase this sentiment away.

As far as I understood the logic offered, intra-firm costs arise when our internal departments take on the work performed earlier for our firm by other firms. For example, let's take a simple trading firm. If earlier we had an agreement with an outside firm to provide secure storage for our goods, now we lease or purchase a warehouse and hire additional workers, both for the warehouse and for the office (for instance, accountants). Besides, we buy forklifts and computers, and perform all loading, storage and supervisory operations ourselves. Let's also assume that if earlier the buyers were driving their lorries in for pickup, now we have purchased our own fleet and hired the drivers, and we do not only load the goods but also deliver them to the stores.

First of all, let's stress that after this expansion, our firm's costs are still measured *in money* (our total payments) and not, say, in kilometres of cargo movement, or in additional sweat or nerves strained due to the increased complexity of managing it all. Simply put, our payments have been partially redistributed from purchase and sale deals to hiring deals (chiefly, wages for new hires), and some new purchase and sale deals.

Now, there is a question: Exactly which costs in our example are intra-firm ones? Are they just the costs incurred by the new department's operations? However, we deliberately picked a trading firm for this example. It is common knowledge that the firm may start with one or two people, so in time all, or almost all, its costs will be intra-firm. This reasoning is true in principle for any other type of business, including manufacturing, but more disclaimers would be required, creating the impression that we are talking for the sake of talking here.

Perhaps a radical simplification of the situation would help us – by treating payments for hiring deals as intra-firm costs, and payments for purchase and sale deals as external costs. However, it is unlikely that this is what was meant – why fuss with some "transactions" and the convoluted renaming of regular deals? Maybe just to make it sound more impressive? Also, if you go back to our example with expanding the firm by setting up its own transport and warehousing operations, it is easy to see that to make our new departments work, we make good use of purchase and sale deals. This applies to both relatively rare purchases of capital goods (lorries, forklifts, computers) and to more frequent purchases of various kinds of consumables (petrol, spare parts, containers).

Perhaps it will be easier for us if we remember that we are talking not just about intra-firm costs, but also about intra-firm transaction costs. On the contrary, it will be not just harder but also totally confusing. As you can guess from the above quotations, Coase ties external transaction costs to the preparation and control of interactions with the outside world, i.e. transactions within the "price mechanism" (purchase and sale deals). Let's look at our example: the seemingly routine transportation, loading and unloading operations performed by many firms. But if you observe the activities of workers in the sales department, then sooner or later you'll see how much attention, on average, both buyers and sellers pay to these (and not only these) operations, as they know from experience that the devil is in the detail. The real economy is not like trading securities, where all transportation, loading and unloading operations may well be reduced to a mouse click. So, our example, where we were seemingly talking about intra-firm costs, is suddenly turned into one with dominating external transaction costs. When talking about almost any department of a firm we begin to deal with, this domination has a simple explanation: unlike in socialist enterprises for which it was important to increase the volume of production, in firms operating under market conditions the priority of sales over production permeates all activities of the firm.

Thus, in the two paragraphs preceding the one above, intra-firm costs sought to fill the entire cost space of a firm. Now, we experience the same effect when we talk about external transaction costs.

Where do all these difficulties come from? In this particular investigation of Coase's theory, the primary reason is the introduction of the term "transaction". It is further complicated by the fact that Coase does not give a straight definition of a transaction in the article collection that we analyse, so we are left only guessing about it from his narrative about the external and intra-firm transaction costs. If we turn to the ideas of John R. Commons, who introduced the notion of transaction, we'll see that he pointed to deals and management acts (bargaining, managerial and rationing transactions) as the main types of transactions. The mere superimposing of his assumptions onto those of Coase leaves a large field for creativity. Other less visible distortions of real-life situations inside firms are then easier to pile on, once readers believe in the term "transaction".

An attempt to line up an elaborate system of categories inside a microeconomy and not in a macroeconomy, i.e. away from the only true equations (price-forming equations) that exist in the economy and form solely in deals, is a methodological error. You may have noticed how assumptions of the transaction costs theory that we analyse periodically gravitate towards simplification, i.e. an analysis of the deals. With all that, we cannot say that the original chart with the interpretation of Coase's theory seems to be improbable. On the contrary, it reflects a process inside a firm that most economists are likely to agree with. However, the hopes for a correct detailing of this process turned out to be overly optimistic and the toolset contrived.

Our assumptions regarding the existence of certain costs in a *microeconomy* should not be, at the least, refuted by real-life situations inside firms. Neither marginal nor transaction costs (intra-firm or external) pass the test of a simple walkthrough inside an ordinary firm. To be precise, marginal cost is totally absent in a real firm, while intra-firm (or external) transaction costs will seek to fill the entire cost space of the firm, unless we tie these to the deals. Still, this tie to the deals radically simplifies the picture, lifting the need for transactions and the related inferences altogether. Note that we are really talking about the simplest walkthrough examples involving such "categories" as "loading and unloading operations", "lorries", and something else similarly obvious and easy to observe.

As a corollary, having learned something from the experience of wandering inside the theories of transaction and marginal costs without a rigid safety tie to deals, let's suppose that the accentuation of certain costs should be fairly simple, in any case, without introducing a complex system of additional categories meant to "deepen" our understanding.

The accentuation of these simple-to-understand costs would be a challenging task for a young person who just started to learn the basics of economics. However, it wouldn't be difficult for a professional economist, given that Adam Smith described the main process a long time ago. We are talking about the *division of labour (2)* (further referred to as division of operations) that determines the downward section of the standard chart of average cost. As for the upward section of the costs curve, it is quite possible that someone mentioned it somewhere, although personally I have not encountered this term in other studies. If the "division of labour" exists, coining the term "coordination of labour" does not seem to be an arduous task.

Before we start digging into details, let me note that we'll be returning periodically to the critique of Coase's interpretation of the standard chart of average cost, which he believed demonstrated the interaction between intra-firm and external costs. We'll try to show, first, that on the upward section, it is better to use a more general type of costs. We call these *labour coordination costs* or simply *coordination costs*. Coase calls the increase of these costs "diminishing returns to management". In literature, one can also encounter "diseconomies of scale" and other terms.

Second, we'll see that if we follow Coase's reasoning, the downward section of the costs curve can be observed in a very limited number of small firms that have not had crucial importance for economic civilisation. Strictly speaking, after we show that Coase's inferences are incorrect for the downward section, there remains only one essential assumption of the transaction costs theory (as it applies to firms), namely an increase in certain costs as the firm expands. We attribute it to the manifestation of the increase in more general costs, related to the coordination of labour.

For the downward section, it would be correct to analyse the impact of the division of operations, which is the ancestor of any type of cost reduction. If it is not clear at first glance what the division of operations has to do with cost reduction, recall the field of Coase's research, as it is so important that it is even reflected in the title of his seminal work, *The Nature of the Firm*. This field is the forming of a company (firm). "But perhaps the most important adaptation to the existence of transaction costs is the emergence of the firm" (Coase, 1990, p. 7). It is not quite clear how not to pay due attention to the division of operations when working on this study topic. So, let's try to explain the moments overlooked or not considered important by Coase.

A division of labour began to take shape naturally, predating the economic epoch of mankind's development. We are talking about the division of labour (1) between detached producers of goods. The exchanges of products they owned (obtained, among other ways, by hunting, fishing, gathering and animal taming) became forerunners of the economic civilisation. Later, after the transition to agriculture, there was a gradual development of the division of operations "within a producer of goods", i.e. inside the production process.[109] The primitive technological principle

[109] It may not pay to place the division of operations too close to modern formations, following Marx who believed that specialisation of certain work functions was a characteristic of wage labour and hence of capitalism. Logically and historically, the division of operations is not tied to wage labour – one can teach either a slave or a hired worker to perform individual functions. This is confirmed by examples of the division of operations in manufacturing (artisan)

of a "jack of all trades" was replaced by production that was divided (and is still being divided) into several stages, each with its specialised workers (and later, machines). This has been leading to a substantial cost reduction – not any special reduction, but a very common one. We'll call this a *basic* or *technological* cost reduction, thanks to the division of operations inside a firm.

As already noted, a division of operations involves technological evolution in the economy. Machines gradually perform increasingly complex separate operations and, accordingly, increasing the technological complexity of firms requires an ever-deepening specialisation of people's labour. So, basic cost reduction includes reducing costs due to technological evolution, which we talked about at the beginning of the second chapter. Let's also pay attention to the simple fact that the division of operations and the corresponding basic cost reduction concerns not only manual labour but also work by lawyers, economists, salespeople, marketers, etc., including the firm's managers. In this case, there are no special workers towering above the grey mass, as a division of operations concerns everyone including intellectuals. For instance, there are six laboratories at the Joint Institute for Nuclear Research in Dubna, Russia. Each laboratory has several research groups. Often, a nuclear physicist from one group simply cannot understand the details of what a fellow nuclear physicist from another group is working on. The times when a mathematician performed chemical experiments in between studying planets with a telescope, all the while making scientific discoveries in all these fields, are long gone. *Meanwhile, the ever-deepening specialisation in learning about our world creates a foundation for deeper specialisation in the production of goods and services*. When talking about learning, we mean not only the fundamental research but also the research activities at laboratories, design departments and workshops of firms. According to our ever-expanding knowledge of the world, nowadays the division of operations often starts with multi-year training in the basics of the future profession. Following this, a budding specialist needs to hone their skills in the process of work and this may take a good chunk of their lifetime. Only because of this, we trust our lives and health to others' trades daily, often without even thinking about it. Only because of this, billions of people can coexist on the planet without killing each other and every living thing in pursuit of food. And in the end, only a community of professionals is capable of making life, a unique phenomenon that

---

shops of ancient Rome. However, a decisive acceleration of division of operations with the advent of capitalism is beyond doubt.

originated on our planet, less vulnerable, including to the people themselves.

Nevertheless, let's imagine that one person is performing all the functions at a modern firm – purchasing, transporting, operating all machinery, maintaining the equipment, selling the products, etc. That person (or a dozen, or a hundred, or a thousand of these jacks of all trades, if someone combines them in a firm without proper division of operations) won't be able to perform all this work well consistently and will spend an inordinately long time fulfilling orders. The same logic applies to bargaining, due diligence, and other functions related to the preparation and fulfilment of contracts. The amount of work will stay the same, either in a real firm or in the imaginary one we have just offered for comparison. One still needs to purchase and sell, bargain with trade partners, litigate, etc. The difference is that our jack of all trades would perform these functions, like any others, worse than a specialist, leading to the plain, basic increase in costs.

The division of operations inside a firm has the other shadowed side as well – using specialists for performing different functions leads to the increase in costs of coordination for their activity. It is easiest to coordinate everything in one head, as the human brain is still an unsurpassed engine for information processing. Although visibly inferior to computers in processing numeric information, our brain is capable of processing data from our senses. Remarkably, our brain coordinates all this information, including simple numeric calculations, often without "our participation" in the process (intuition, common sense). Working with numbers is very important for an entrepreneur, but as we mentioned, for the most part it does not require knowledge beyond arithmetic, otherwise only mathematicians would make entrepreneurs.

It is common to have certain misunderstandings among people, so as soon as the word *firm* is mentioned, the very next words should be *planning* and *discipline*, in order to achieve the coordination of work by different people. With the expansion of the firm, this coordination becomes inevitably more complex, which is reflected in growing labour coordination costs.

A manager's brain cannot then digest all the information fast enough. This information becomes more truncated – gradually managers begin to receive it only in abstract form from other managers or computers, having no opportunity to "look, touch and smell". They largely *lose the advantage of our brain* over computers in the ability to process informal information obtained through the senses.

Along the way, information received from other people becomes less than adequate. A variant of a well-known joke goes that there are truth, lies and statistics: for statistics can show the same situation from different perspectives depending on the scruples or goals of the researcher, and you can carve out different subsets from one large data set. This is true not only in science but also in everyday management, considering that there is no single all-encompassing and universally accessible data set suitable for all goods, with all the technological nuances, in all regions and always. Inadequate information can stem from either a bona fide lack of understanding at the primary source (managers and ordinary workers), or the desire to conceal one's own missteps. Often, it remains a perennial mystery to the person who must make decisions or could make timely decisions based on this information, had they known the situation better.

Two examples illustrating coordination costs.

For anyone who in the course of their career has never actively participated in managing large integrated firms (or simply large groups of people with complex hierarchies and territorial disparity), it may be hard to understand the labour coordination costs that we are talking about here. There may not be many opportunities to observe these costs from the outside, given that managers themselves cannot fully discern the coordination costs, or else they would try to trim them without delay. A full understanding of the problem is further obscured by the fact that, at any moment, there are some industry-specific technological features requiring a degree of integration. Besides, once large firms command a sizeable market share, they begin to justify their high level of coordination costs (for themselves, but not for the national economy as a whole).

For an outside observer, a good opportunity to see that coordination costs do exist could be a management change in an unprofitable large integrated business. The chances are that nine out of ten new – but experienced – managers would recommend the owners to make drastic reductions, ranging from firing individuals to closing entire divisions. Even those observers who do not have management experience but got used to trusting the stock market reports would agree that the secondary market, as a rule, positively treats these cost-cutting measures. Does it mean that all these new managers are more qualified than their predecessors? Not necessarily, as there is no magic agency one can contact to procure a new manager who never fails so the owner is guaranteed to enjoy life afterwards. It frequently happens that dismissed managers, especially the repetitive failures, leave this high orbit for good, but in general the number of highly qualified managers in every industry is limited, and some may find success in another firm after being fired. The high qualification may stem from both victories and defeats.

If you paid attention, often in these cases new management is sourced externally, though from the outside it seems like a paradox. As we found out, a new manager's qualifications generally don't have to be higher than the old manager's, or at least not radically higher, but their knowledge of the firm is almost certainly inferior. However, the new manager has that "fresh look". It sounds glamorous, but essentially, the main advantage of a fresh look is its natural limitation and, I would add, robotic nature. The new managers are not yet overwhelmed by stereotypes, and have no emotional ties with the workers, the owners, the consequences of their past decisions (they simply do not exist yet), or the firm's premises and equipment. Whether some workers are nice, how they rationalised making bad decisions, what good they did for the firm or for the owner personally – all these are not relevant at that moment. The new manager may naturally concentrate solely on the numbers and on the task: to make the firm profitable again. Without optimising the management process in the bloated firm, the new manager won't be able to accomplish the task (of course, unless the manager brings along some genius engineers, but alas, they do not invent the iPads of the world daily). Any planned cost reduction should not be limited to the technology alone. Even if the new managers have engineering knowledge, they simply cannot know all the fine details of the technological processes in a large firm. You can be sure they won't pursue cost-cutting by taking out a stopwatch for manually timing worker performance (sure, in management there is always room for occasional shows that may not make much sense but stay remembered). Let's not forget that with its current losses, the firm's finances are quite limited to afford new equipment. Let's note that we mentioned this just in case, as many beginner entrepreneurs seem to have learned at school that new machines help fix everything. In reality, spending money on modernising without due process and moderation can sink even a previously successful business.

With all that, regardless of the industry, it is not hard to predict the actions of that "new broom". Even if the person has never heard about coordination costs, he or she would press for greater management transparency, rotating or firing single "generals and officers" as well as pruning (selling or liquidating) entire vertical and horizontal management structures with their corresponding divisions. Here, we could say "money-losing divisions" without drawing the ire, but it would be more accurate to call them "excessive". Coordination costs always accumulate with more complex management, even when direct efficiency calculations do not portray a particular business area as "not so bad that it cannot be fixed".

The most difficult task facing the newly hired manager may well be severing the emotional ties of the owner, in case the latter is still to some extent in control. Hence, the best time to do it is when the owner (and the workers, by the way) are still under the spell of the natural, "messianic" magic of the new manager. Later, when it is "suddenly" revealed that the new manager is just a human being with certain weak points, it will be more difficult to accomplish. As someone who has experienced both sides of this situation, I can describe the most characteristic moment of this confrontation. I will note first that in this situation the owner (I do not mean a scattered, collective "owner", but a very specific person) should not be perceived necessarily as a retrograde individual needing to be educated on the intricacies of business by a smarter person, who by fate does not happen to be the owner but a hired manager. In most cases, a self-made owner understands the business better, but his or her brain, like a computer that has not been rebooted in a long time, is stuffed with bits and pieces of various "programmes" and information arrays in contrast with the new manager who has been just "rebooted". The owner could well manage to sort out these intricacies were it not for the "main instinct": the drive to increment property. Often, the new manager's proposals reveal the truth that to save the firm, the dream about rapid enrichment will have to be abandoned and the wagons circled, postponing – possibly for a long time – that brilliant plan for attack. Since the proposals of the new manager are almost invariably a screenplay version of the phrase "you can't make an omelette without breaking eggs" (i.e. coordination costs are rarely removed in an "elegant" way), the instinct may lead the owner to believe that "the baby is being thrown out with the bathwater". This can really happen in some cases, but more often it is fraught with further losses. In any case, in the described scenario the elevated coordination costs will remain in the firm and in the national economy as a whole. Finally, let me note that a managing owner who has bought an unprofitable business does not really need to justify this decision to anyone.

Another example of coordination costs forming due to the expansion of a firm is likely the most obvious among those I have encountered. Many companies periodically face a shortage of available transportation at some peak time (e.g. seasonal fishing campaigns or other seasonal work), as the demand for transportation greatly increases up to the point of having no spare capacity available. Therefore, the firms that are prone to these shortages often set up their own fleets. As a result, some of them, especially those with seasonal fluctuations in the technological process, may not only experience increased management complexity but also find themselves branching out into an entirely new business. Often, there is still a shortage of transportation at peak times, but at other times there is a challenge of finding enough orders to mitigate the consequences of the fleet sitting idle. It turns out that competing with professional transportation businesses is not easy. Of course, there may be some obvious planning miscalculations, but we should say that these are quite expected once the firm has embarked on the path of planning "the whole world economy", which is represented at the micro level by adding new functional or regional areas to the firm. We considered a simple example (the idling of lorries or freight vessels), but even if the firm's operations are not seasonal and planning blunders can be avoided, the market lives by ebb and flow, sometimes inconspicuously. The more the above-mentioned functional areas are in the firm (ranging from accounting to purchase and sale agents), the more imaginary "battles" a firm may lose due to the gap between the optimal and actual department size at that moment. During yet another attempt to cut costs, a popular phrase is often "Yes, right now this division (department, worker) brings about losses, but we have a strategic need for it." Worse, losing these micro "battles" bears the subtle character of a chain reaction. Even if a division is well balanced and headed by an able manager, the imbalances in the work of connected functional areas will inevitably (unlike in cases where these areas are autonomous firms) complicate that manager's life and result in higher costs.

Ronald Coase and transaction costs; division of labour and coordination of labour (continued).

The increase in coordination costs is not confined to the management layer alone, as it touches all functional areas of a firm – production, transport, warehousing and so on. Likewise, the division of operations is not limited only to the blue-collar workers and the coordination of labour is not an exclusive white-collar domain. That is, transaction costs (if we try to estimate them) do increase at some point with a firm's expansion. However, this increase stems from the growth of more general labour coordination costs.

Improvements in the division of operations do partially lower labour coordination costs in the scope of technological evolution. The most visible example would be the development of communications and information processing capabilities, enabling a widening of horizons of effective management. However, it is easy to get caught in the non-linear effect trap. I managed firms at a time of expedited development of the communications infrastructure and noticed that the seemingly easy expansion of business helped by the rapid evolution of phone and computer communications was often accompanied by an avalanche-like flow of information. The complexity of processing this information is growing out of step with increases in production. Once you face the non-linear effect be ready for some unpleasant consequences. Even if one's corporate information processing system is set up proactively and is ready to handle the ever-increasing flow of information, which *does not often happen*, the most important aspect is the people who input information and act upon it. Such unpleasant effects are less likely to happen in firms where expansion is not accompanied by extending product lines or an affiliate network, but the effects can become catastrophic if extending the product lines or the network is accompanied by entering new industries and regions with populations having a different mental organisation, especially abroad.

A practical economy can largely self-address the problem of increased labour coordination costs, mainly through the evolutionary deepening of the division of labour (1) between the firms – for example, the division of labour (1) at the dawn of capitalism was far below its level under modern capitalism. We can draw a non-rigorous but telling comparison between the levels of the division of labour (1) in firms in the mid-1990s in Russia immediately after its transition to capitalism and today's firms, a mere quarter of a century later. The pioneering post-Soviet entrepreneurs engaged in "everything" similar to the businessmen of 200 or 300 years prior to our time. By the way, this is similar to the scientists of yore.

One important consequence of the transition from one formation to another is the deepening of the division of labour (1) between firms, which lowers systemic costs to an extent unattainable solely by their evolutionary decrease. However, this deepening will apply to all industries only after a transition to the PCM. There are two reasons for it.

First, even if each new formation lowers systemic costs, we can assertively talk about the deepening of the division of labour (1) between firms in only those transitions that free up basic cost regulators, i.e. when the de-monopolisation of the use of some kind of basic resources takes place.

There have been two of these transitions – one from the slave-owning formation (people) and the other from the landowning formation (land).

Second, the kind of resources being de-monopolised will determine the sectors that experience a deepening of the division of labour (1) between firms. The de-monopolisation of land created prerequisites for a gradual deepening of the division of labour (1) between *agricultural* firms.[110] Even with agriculture being the dominant sector, the industrial revolution was a pivotal moment at the time. As for the industrial development, the reverse process of a firm's consolidation became a key characteristic of the division of labour (1), while in the division of operations there was a deepening by leaps. It was the development of basic science that prepared the subsequent industrial revolution, with an engineering vision and innovations leading the way. At the same time, the inflow of the freed and/or broke peasants into the cities created a natural base for the industrial revolution.

Yet another key scientific achievement – the invention of computers – paved the way for the next formational transition. Looking at the specific basic cost regulators that are going to be freed up with this planned transition, we see that these regulators are not tied to any particular physical kind of property but they are tied to money instead. The use of money in the economy is universal and, unlike any physical basic type of property, money is used in each of the basic deals. Therefore, we can hypothesise that this time, the deepening of the division of labour (1) between firms will be gradual but visible in all industries, including manufacturing.

Having finished the outline of the impact of division of labour and coordination of labour on costs, let's see how Coase disregarded both historical and economic reasoning when he came up with his explanation of why costs decrease when firms are formed. Generally, we could call a truce by pointing out the incorrect term "transaction" with subsequent

---

[110] As we have already discussed, the *non-reproducibility of land* blunts the mechanism of classical economic laws at a fundamental level. For example, the "fight" for land hinders its market turnover, while rent can be regulated solely by administrative means. Therefore, with active land use (primarily in agriculture), the economy is heavily dependent on politics, both on the level of development of political institutions and on public administration. If we add that the development of companies in any sector depends on the level of industrial development, it would be hardly possible to talk about any noticeable deepening of the division of labour (1) in agriculture at the times that we are describing.

murky terminology and by asking to drop the use of "marginal cost". That is, on either section of the average cost graph, the division of operations and coordination of labour describe the same processes as transaction costs when the latter is being divided into external and intra-firm costs, albeit using different terminology. But Coase, consciously or not, pursued the bigger goal of using his theory as a replacement for one of the fundamental assumptions by Adam Smith, namely the division of labour. They cannot be simply combined. To further understand the gist of it, let's continue to cite Coase's writings:

> "But perhaps the most important adaptation to the existence of transaction costs is the emergence of the firm. In my article on 'The Nature of the Firm' I argued that, although production could be carried out in a completely decentralized way by means of contracts between individuals, the fact that it costs something to enter into these transactions means that firms will emerge to organize what would otherwise be market transactions ..." (Coase, 1990, p. 7)

> "We may sum up this section of the argument by saying that the operation of a market costs something and by forming an organization and allowing some authority (an 'entrepreneur') to direct the resources, certain marketing costs are saved." (Coase, 1937, p. 392)

As often happens, the error is hiding at the very beginning of the logical reasoning chain: the emergence of the firm. Indeed, firms may emerge as a result of people of different professions cooperating and then electing a leader amongst themselves (often, this person is called the foreman or another synonym for "the first among equals"). This is the way small cooperatives form, be it in construction or agriculture, and both in the history of civilisation and right now, "in the street" there are not too many of these. There are also some caveats that further reduce their small number. As Coase has to trace the reduction of costs, he assumes that members of the firm were carrying out, or could carry out, "market transactions" using a "price mechanism" before joining the firm. Coase believes he has proven it, but in the real world the number of people who can magically turn their narrow speciality professional skills into commodities and services at the purchase and sale market is very small. Here, a lack of money (capital) is not the main reason. For example, I was assembling window frames when I was working at the carpentry plant and this unsophisticated set of operations that I was able to perform could not, by any means, become commodities or services. As a rule, people of most professions can only close hiring deals, but in this case the logical chain of cost reduction disappears as the person who has been hired in the deal does not bear the firm's costs, neither big nor small. Conversely, this person's wages constitute costs for the entrepreneur.

After all the above disclaimers, in a limited number of remaining firms (cooperatives) the reduction of costs happens for people who previously worked independently, since in this case they themselves represent the *centres of costs accounting*. Overwhelmingly, people do not combine their efforts and do not merge into firms, choosing instead to "delegate management functions to the entrepreneur". Like it or not, managing owners either forced people to work as slaves or serfs in the earliest formations, or in the capacity of the entrepreneur proper, hired them as free people to perform certain functions (as an artisan would hire an apprentice). Theoretical economics only emerged thousands of years after the economy did and managing owners, although not the only participants in the process of division of operations in the economy, especially at the early stages of our civilisation, have gradually become its champions (well before Adam Smith described the principles of division of operations). Sure enough, entrepreneurs deploy and promote a division of operations while being driven not by the noble principles of civilisation's progress but by the perspectives of their property incrementing in a competitive environment. However, Coase's possible antipathy towards entrepreneurs / desire to be politically correct should not obscure the bending of truth in his beliefs, which he is trying to introduce to the readers by habitually avoiding exact definitions. Although the situation is simple, either people unite themselves, or someone will unite them.[111] Once an entrepreneur gets people into a firm, he or she becomes the centre of cost accounting, as well as the decision-making centre. Having bought the means of production and paid all other expenses, the entrepreneur spends his or her own money to hire people to perform certain stages in the firm's technological process.

[111] I have always liked the early stage of launching a project – it is awesome to see how a new division or even an entire firm, which up until now existed only in your head, emerges seemingly "from nothing". The most important moment while planning for a new project (likewise, while planning for something in an existing firm) is to have a clear idea of all future key prices. That's why at its early stages, a project looks figuratively as a set of numbers on a map, all the way from buying components to selling the finished product. Once a proforma price chain is put together and broken into stages, an entrepreneur has a better understanding of whether he or she will go with this project, what needs to be done, how much money is required and *what kind of specialists* the firm will need.

Coase shifts the decision-making centre downwards and, as a result, we find ourselves in an imaginary economy where everything is unreal. There, people decide to unite in a firm, agreeing with the managerial functions of the entrepreneur ("allowing some authority (an 'entrepreneur') to direct the resources") and apparently agreeing with this entrepreneur buying the means of production using his or her own money. If a reader or Coase himself have not noticed this initial switch,[112] then further down it is easier to get confused, given that the author is very enthusiastic about his idea, nurtured since his student years. Now, when we are talking about the people united in a firm, we seem to be studying the centre of cost accounting. The obvious inference that we account for the "costs" of those who in a majority of actual firms do not incur any costs and whose wages, on the contrary, are costs incurred by the firm does not stop the author.

If readers somehow skipped over these moments, then with the appearance of "transactions" their heads will be hopelessly stuffed as costs themselves are a very complex topic. This is especially valid, given that costs indeed decrease when a firm is formed (otherwise, why bother creating a firm if this does not decrease costs?). At this stage, a thought may arise: maybe the costs go down simply because the people in the firm (united or being united) are separated by their speciality, allowing them to perform their functions in the optimal way? Even if we talk only about the functions accentuated by Coase, a lawyer and a salesperson are two very different trades. However, the new terminology leads the reader away from simple questions.

In a real firm, everything is exactly the opposite – the entrepreneur bears all the costs. It is easy to piece this puzzle together by simply observing and not making anything up. By hiring workers to perform certain functions in the scope of the division of operations, the producer of goods lowers his or her own costs compared with the jack-of-all-trades scenario. The producers also delegate some of their functions to the hired managers. As soon as this happens, we face labour coordination problems, which is a reverse effect of the division of operations. These problems can be undoubtedly classified as management ones, but they occur throughout the firm. If a firm keeps expanding, then at some point the extra costs incurred

---

[112] I believe that Coase was aware of the weakness of his assumption because, like in the case of the missing definition of "transaction", there is no direct quote. Although everything is clear from the context, the "internal lawyer" in Coase leaves a chance for his followers to say, for example, that the economist "has been misunderstood".

due to inevitable frictions in the coordination of labour will push up the average cost of the firm, while the level of the division of operations may stay limited by the level of technological progress at this point.

This is what the situation with "transaction costs" looks like, as viewed through the lens of the traditional division of operations that was generally described by Adam Smith, who in turn had incorporated earlier observations by other authors. On one hand, instead of coordination costs, Coase introduced a limited and, at the same time, vague group of costs that are called intra-firm transaction costs. On the other hand, Coase transferred the effects of the division of labour among hired workers by the entrepreneur to some self-organised human labour, represented by a hard-to-describe conglomerate of hired workers and individual entrepreneurs. You might have noticed that even without a theoretical flirting with wage labour, as willingly or accidentally does Coase[113] who assigned inordinate influence to the role of labour in the *forming* of a firm, one of the conclusions of our study is that an excessive concentration of property in the hands of single entrepreneurs is harmful (even being non-monopolistic by character). One of the ***most important*** advantages of transition to the

---

[113] This flirting echoes the Marxist emphasis on the social nature of man and the social character of human labour, which is used to accentuate the "natural" character of a socialisation of means of production. Not that someone is against pointing out the importance of social relationships in the economy in general (let's remember the "deal" category), but such a fundamental accent on the "social character" seems to be an excessively rushed train of thought, as it was demonstrated to socialism by the "costs" category. We have already cited an example of ants, with their "economy" being much more socially accented compared to ours. Here, we can add that the competitiveness of the ant or bee "economy" is based on the "division of labour" among the insects. Apparently, since insects do not have a mammal's brain, this "division of labour" became possible only with genetic separation into separate casts inside the anthill or beehive. In general, life is very diverse on this planet and there are more or less social species. A more balanced view of our species might be to think that, thanks to the development of the brain, a man can combine various approaches for his relationships with society. Thus, our brain would not "explode" while trying to apply a single concept to both the importance of unifying (ranging from a firm to a national economy) and to the importance of division, based on the processes of division of labour (1) and (2). By the way, due to the deepening division of operations, a stronger *personal responsibility* for the costs created is more visible. In turn, this is not the reason for the opposite extreme view. The deepening of the division of labour means, among other things, that a man is less distracted from his work by various "chores", as the latter are performed by other members of the society.

PCM will be the lifting of obstacles for a gradual (albeit constant) – following the technological progress – increase in the number of entrepreneurs due to the deepening of the division of labour (1) between the firms with a corresponding decrease in the number of hired workers.

With this, we are going to wrap up our discussion on Coase's ideas.[114] However, before we finish talking about division and coordination of labour, as well as how closely related changes in the behaviour of costs are to the firm's expansion, let me surprise you by interrupting this study to tell the Rough History of what the economy really is. This thesis, with elements of philosophy and fiction, will not only help you wake up but may also allow you to better see the boundaries of theoretical economics.

Rough History.

The economic growth of civilisation, expressed in goods, should be credited to natural sciences (the machines, which so far do not ask for wages, are producing more and more goods), while the main goal for the laws of a classical economy is to make sure that this growth is not wasted (scattered for personal consumption by people due to high costs), since the fact that people command all the money is conducive to it. With natural sciences insufficiently developed, people have been using unpaid labour provided by animals and prior to that, they also used unpaid labour

---

[114] Earthlings have more important problems than minding the interests of entrepreneurs. In these cases, if necessary, the state should adopt binding laws to increase the costs for entrepreneurs for the sake of higher goals. The most important of these goals is to protect life on the planet. In the following thesis, we'll point out one threat to the existence of the *Homo sapiens* species itself. For now, let's note that biologists and other scientists are more likely to agree with establishing, say, an "Earth Ecology Tsar" than buy into the argument that environmental degradation can be stopped in principle with the help of bargaining, as suggested by Coase. Many poor people would tolerate serious environmental damage nearby in exchange for money. Accordingly, there will always be entrepreneurs who are ready to profit from this. It goes without saying that in some cases it would be foolish to pass on the opportunity to bargain for payment arrangements, provided there is a public study or hearing, or if there are simply no alternatives. Even in these individual cases, the negotiated payment arrangements will look more like fines, with the only difference being that they are not court ordered. If the enforcement agencies are not involved, there will be no proper regulation of such an important problem as environmental safety, with all the ensuing consequences. Yes, Coase gives some examples of such arrangements, but these are just isolated examples, nothing more.

provided by other people (slaves). While pointing at the sciences, we understand that this is not so much about the achievements of particular people but rather about the use of the laws of the universe, since the former (the achievements) are a subset of the latter.

By projecting this talk about sciences onto practical economy and losing even more rigor, we can say that engineers (in a broad sense) and entrepreneurs represent natural sciences and the laws of classical economy, respectively. Certainly, entrepreneurs keep an eye on costs only to calculate profits (one should subtract costs from sales). And since they cannot take their wealth into the afterlife, anything that is beyond their personal consumption is left to the subsequent generations (once again, in the form of goods, for example, means of production).

Let's treat this as a brief introduction to the Rough History and proceed with the "elements" we have promised. Please do not try to explain a possible discomfort from extremely opposite perspectives: "here is something that all economists prefer not to mention", or conversely, "here, the author messed something up". We do not denigrate the role of natural sciences, as one can see while reading into the details, and we do not have fundamental errors. The Rough History is named as such because it won't explain anything in the economics domain, as it is being told with a focus on the laws of the universe. An attempt to draw a connection between "exploding stars" and currency depreciation is a prime example of what is not to be achieved. Let's run up the stairs of compressing Everything into the subject of our study, i.e. theoretical economics.

Whatever is at the very bottom can hardly be called a foundation. Rather, this is something that theoretical physicists study – let's not shy away from figurative comparisons – and it looks like a solid chunk of Matter.

Rising above this Matter, we find ourselves at a floor where the Soul appears as a replacement for Roughness (hey, why not build a house ...[115]). To achieve this, let's make a simple imaginary move and reduce Everything to the planet Earth. The laws of the universe determine everything there too, but our planet has its own characteristics, starting with the force of gravity. Most importantly, there exists Life and Death. Of course, the stars also live and die, but these processes are so stretched in time that they almost look accidental. I am not going to argue that the stars light up and go out for a reason, but apart from the history of stars and

[115] This may be clear from the context, but just in case, let me clarify – a house, not a church.

planets, all other cause-and-effect relationships look more like the history of a stray asteroid that may wander the galaxy for a long time before bumping into something. As for Life, the kinds of Matter pertaining to it are programmed for a mandatory and far quicker Death. This predetermines a far more frequent genesis of new and more refined forms of Everything. This is what biology studies, with the best-known story about it told by Charles Darwin. Of course, this biological floor is directly related to our text, but we try to stay neither too high nor too deep and only touch upon what we need.

As specialists in humanities, we target the next floor where Consciousness appears, referring to a human consciousness: other forms of Life may be able to think, although we'll use other terms for their thinking. It is easy to see that our study is far from trying to exaggerate the significance of *Homo sapiens*, taking into account the history of the question (e.g. "value" or "abstract labour"), but there is no alternative. The stars can make beneficial dust, and apes succeeded in making people by trial and error, but both are dumb enough to come up with a microwave oven.

Of course, we do not claim the entire Consciousness floor, limiting ourselves instead to the economy. Moreover, we cut off most of the economic history of humankind, leaving it to the archaeologists: in our Rough History, we should have started to talk about the economic distinguishing of people from other mammals; for example, start with a digging stick and proceed with a detailed study of the growing use of the natural science laws by man. However, this would not give us any of the threads that we are looking for. So, we begin with the moment when man had enough consciousness to give something up in order to receive something in return.[116] And it is likely, though it is not a pivotal point, that here lies the economic divide between *Homo sapiens* and other, now extinct, human species. Let me say it this way, as I am not a specialist, that I have not seen any publications about discovering the evidence of trade, like those found at the Cro-Magnon camps, at other species' camps.

An intention to clarify the proper place for theoretical economics was our initial motive to put together this thesis. I had the impression that in our science, an overly favourable attitude towards the invasion of philosophy, sociology and mathematics peacefully coexisted with a cautious but still

[116] We'll be talking in more detail about the birth of Economy (the foundation of the economic civilisation of *Homo sapiens*, which is accessible for studying) in the thesis "*Psychology and rationality in theoretical economics ...*".

excessively "freeloading" approach to the achievements of the natural sciences. This "respectful colonisation" of the natural sciences domain has had some consequences for the "colonisers", as drawing them into the discussions about means of production from the tools of the primitive man to the "3D printer" (this attention reached its peak in Marxism) contributed to the fact that emphasis on cost regulators was not properly set in theoretical economics.

In this thesis, we wanted to single out from Rough History the only humanitarian science that has a fundamental component. We have accomplished this, but the development of Rough History proper, as well as the place of *Homo sapiens* in it, is unfortunately not clear. It seems that our "floors" may not end here, as representatives of those same natural sciences have made clear that they are going to bolt Consciousness onto the non-living Everything. The key problem is that for the robots enabled with artificial intelligence (AI), the floor of Soul is of no crucial importance. We should not rest comfortably with the mid-20th century's style idea that it would be possible to programme robots "for good" to obey humans or at least to "not harm humans". If the situation is left to chance (like it is happening now), then sooner or later there will be an overly curious "small fry", a misanthrope or just a lunatic, who will lift the restrictions from robots. I don't know how the future generations will be solving this Key Problem (one possibility is creating cyborgs (modifications of people), for whom Life and Death will still be the mandatory elements of the chain). I also don't know how the theoretical foundation of the economy would transform due to changes in the definition of property as a result of the emergence of new (main or additional) masters of the planet, but I think that I know the worst course of action – to sit and wait to see what kind of economy "AI will produce for us". This is not only applicable to economics and let someone else tell these stories while we continue to sort out the model of the most efficient economy for *Homo sapiens*.

Division of labour and coordination of labour (conclusion). Costs and a firm's expansion.

In the first paragraph we'll try to outline the essence of the current part of our study, with the focus on a firm's expansion.

The division of operations is the main (basic, fundamental) process for reducing costs in the economy. Its impact, prominent even amid other fundamental processes, stems from the confluence of our Rough History (which, as we remember, tells us how the development of natural sciences determines economic development) and theoretical economics, i.e. technological opportunities to use machines for performing specialised functions go hand in hand with the sensible treatment of costs by laws of the classical economy. Thanks to this in particular, the division of operations helps firms expand. On the other hand, the deepening of the division of operations makes the coordination of labour more complex and thus hinders this expansion due to an increase in coordination costs. If the decrease in costs due to the deepening of the division of operations has a pronounced technological accent, the increase in costs due to the labour coordination problems has an even more pronounced humanitarian character. Given the industrial diversity, and differences in firms' sizes and the level of their integration, the net effect of these opposing processes can also vary (for example, it may be easier to expand a manufacturing firm as it employs a large number of machines, while some coordination costs for people's actions go away as machines are combined in a rigid technological cycle). However, generally when a firm expands, its average cost first decreases and then starts to increase.

Brevity is fraught with drawbacks; therefore, a reader may have a feeling that pitting the division of operations against labour coordination looks like a confrontation of good and evil, more typical of a religion than science. In reality, coordination costs are neither good nor evil, but an important instrument of the classical economy's laws. Also, in reality, they do not hinder the division of labour but help it – *coordination costs prevent market monopolisation and contribute to the deepening of division of labour (1).*

However, this will be possible as a complete process only under the PCM. As firms expand, they will face growing coordination costs and will cede their market positions to more compact firms. At present, large firms are able to accumulate these costs while preserving their competitiveness (albeit a false one, from the classical economy's perspective). This systemic accumulation of costs undermines the competitiveness (ability) of the national economy. The main reason for this status quo is the insufficient functionality (an insufficient "market" character) of such a basic cost regulator as the interest rate.

We will start talking about the interest rate in detail in the following thesis. In that conversation, we'll proceed from the general theoretical scheme for constructing economic formations. At the end of the current thesis, we simply point out two important technical examples (we'll talk a lot about them later) of how the interest rate under paper capitalism contributes to the expansion of a firm.

Imagine that "someone else" pays all the wages for our firm's employees and therefore we can expand at will. This scenario seems utterly foolish, but if we substitute wages for the interest rate, we'll see that this is typical for retail chains, when suppliers provide them with interest-free trade credit. Now, for the second example, imagine that either we pay wages below the market average or – if something goes wrong – we may not pay at all. Projecting this to the interest rate, this is approximately what it looks like when someone issues securities with a credit component. In the future, we'll be sure to talk about these scenarios of circumventing the interest rate seriously and in detail. They contribute to the excessive expansion of firms and therefore to the implicit or explicit monopolisation of the market, in spite of the counteraction of such a powerful basic cost regulator as wages.

Moving along Chapter 2 (Stage 2).

Let's finish the costs preamble here and transition to the explicit talk about the market interest rate as a basic cost regulator (the first of the two remaining "towers" required for transition to the PCM). We'll begin the next thesis with a brief description of the credit system under the PCM. In fact, we have started building it out from the first paragraph of Chapter 1, given that it would be impossible without splitting the combined credit and payment system. However, we did not accentuate it in Chapter 1, as we had a few side topics to cover first.

In the next stage of Chapter 2 we also won't be able to avoid some eclectic narrative, since we'll be covering the technical descriptions of both old and new credit systems while clarifying our theoretical assumptions. Moreover, at this stage we'll be forced to change perspectives more often than anywhere else in this study. Here, we'll be diving deep into the foundations of the economy and taking long walks inside a regular firm from the real economy to try to see where certain irrationality, intrinsic to the economy, ends and rationality begins. Some of the elements of this irrationality were studied, in particular, by Keynes and attempted to be studied by Coase. We have devoted a lot of time to Coase's theory as it was simply in our way. At this point, we will be revisiting coordination costs without referencing Coase. If Coase's theory is artificial as a whole,

Keynes's theory is marked by localisation (historical, geographical and logical).

Thus, in Chapter 1 we found out that unlike reproducing goods, where it is very important to preserve and, moreover, encourage competition among private producers (this is indeed happening with every new formation, save for socialism), reproducing money is gravitating over time towards a higher centralisation, meaning an ever-increasing role for the state. It became particularly visible after the transition from gold to paper money and it is going to be even more obvious after the payment system is transferred to the central bank. However, the monetary system consists of two fundamental components, namely credit and payment systems. If we want to get an entirely market-driven interest rate, it would require a different approach to the design of the credit system – unlike the case of the payment system, the state itself takes a secondary role. In other words, the independence of interest rates from the state is a mandatory component of the PCM credit system.

Modelling of the new financial system, paragraph two.

In the new system, along with taking the payment system outside of commercial banks, we are going to take the credit system outside of the central bank's auspices (and outside the state in a broad sense). It goes without saying that in the new system, the central bank continues to control the credit activities of commercial banks, but at the same time it (and no other agency, save for the private[117] domestic[118] banks) does not lend money (the issuance income, calculated by the central bank, is credited to the government account as a part of the state budget's revenues). Let's recall the relationship with the payment system – the money borrowed by a commercial bank (like any loans received, they have to be accounted exclusively as savings deposits) is reflected, like it is now, in the commercial bank's account at the central bank provided that the

[117] In the simplest terms, neither the state nor the central bank are among the owners of any commercial bank. Only three types of banks are required under the PCM: credit banks, currency exchange banks (the operations of which we'll discuss in Chapter 3) and commercial banks licensed for both activities. To simplify the text, the term "commercial bank" is used throughout.

[118] This important qualifier also applies to both inter-bank and international loans, including loans issued by supranational agencies like the IMF. That is, the credit border is locked to all, without exception. So, for example, if the supranational agencies want to help someone, they would have to really help (for instance, dispense grants subject to certain conditions) but not lend money.

former does not keep it as cash in the vault. However, whenever the commercial bank lends non-cash funds to someone in turn, in the new system it immediately moves these funds from its account at the central bank to the borrower's account at the same central bank.

Market forming of the domestic interest rate under the new financial system and its distortion under the existing system.

After the aforementioned transformations, we end up with both the entirely market-driven primary lending rate and the national interest rate, all without any increase in bureaucratic supervision and even with much less need for this supervision. It is impossible to achieve a market interest rate without the market-driven primary lending rate. Meanwhile, our main goal – the market interest rate that will safeguard the economy from developing clots of excessive goods and services – will become the most important step in removing cyclical crises from the economy. It is not feasible to get rid of the ebb and flow of economic development, but they will not evolve into a prolonged and painful contraction of the economy, marked with mass layoffs and bankruptcies.

There is no truly market-driven national interest rate under the existing financial system. The central bank largely determines the primary lending rate, which is also influenced by the securities market and cross-border credits. The bank interest rate is also distorted by the same factors, as well as by the presence of the state in the market and even by widespread trade credits, and above all by large retail chains demanding delayed settlement from their suppliers. The bottom line is that "money is making money". The larger that a commercial bank or a firm is, the more ways they have to raise money. As there are multiple channels to obtain financing, under the existing system the price of "leasing the money" is not formed by the commercial banks alone.

This distortion of the interest rate has a dual nature – simply put, the rate can either be higher or lower. We won't consider the case of higher rates, not because this situation doesn't deserve analysis but because it doesn't constitute a fundamental sin of the existing financial system – it is common knowledge that higher costs follow rate increases. The impact of lower rates on costs is not that obvious, as it may seem that the opposite – lower rates lead to lower costs – is true. This is true for a single borrower, but what is good for General Motors or Gazprom is not necessarily good for the entire national economy.

Logical connection between a lower primary lending rate and deflation from costs.

The perennial depression of the market primary lending rate brings to life some deals that would not exist in a true market economy. In this case, the economy is permeated with credit chains. Given the byzantine character of the three-tier credit and payment system, one can say that the same money is wandering around the economy, binding ever more victims with credit obligations.[119] In their defence, the victims themselves understand this only at the time of a deflationary crisis, like in 2007–2009. When many borrowers become insolvent during a crisis, the credit chains cannot unwind with the same ease as they ran throughout the economy during the upswing times. If someone cannot repay a loan, this chain requires refinancing. With many of these situations arising, the entire credit and payment system begins to face a shortage of money. There is a purportedly easy solution: add money to the banking system. OK, let's do just that and demand that commercial banks ramp up their lending to untangle the failing payment chains. However, bankers tend to reduce lending, even when monetary authorities begin to build up the monetary base. That is, the shortage of money in the credit and payment system narrows down to the shortage of money in the commodity sector. This has nothing to do with the commercial banks' pricing policies or excessively high interest rates. Only someone not worrying about a particular commercial bank's finances or rather someone under pressure from financial authorities (that promise, for instance, to cover the losses or threaten to levy fines) would actively lend money to the clients potentially headed for bankruptcy at the height of the crisis, when many assets, offered as collateral, have low liquidity. Neither scenario has anything to do with a "normal" market, but this is what often happens in practice, obscuring the problem of insufficient money although not alleviating the problem as a whole, which thus distorts the "natural" flow of the crisis and delays the recovery.

---

[119] Those notorious credit default swaps and other derivatives are largely examples of this practice, albeit more sophisticated. See, for example, Nouriel Roubini and Stephen Mihm. *Crisis Economics: A Crash Course in the Future of Finance.* Updated ed. Penguin Books, 2011.

Bank bankruptcies in the existing formation and under the Perfectly Competitive Market. Observations on the Great Depression.

So, why do the authorities stuff commercial banks with money in crisis situations? The answer to this largely rhetorical question will give us a chance to evoke some important reasoning. To avoid ambiguity, by default this reasoning should be applied to global currency issuing countries – first of all, the US. Often, it is also valid for peripheral nations but the accents may substantially differ.

First, bank bankruptcies in the combined credit and payment system can drag a sizeable chunk of the payment system along with them. This makes bank bankruptcies very risky in the eyes of monetary authorities, even if everyone in charge at these authorities is "in theory" a champion of unmitigated market competition. Note that in the monetary system of the PCM that we offer, this theory "gap" does not exist – bank bankruptcies will surely be painful for the commercial bank's owners and depositors but without a falling domino effect. The payment system will run independently of commercial banks (with payments settled directly through the monetary base) and there won't be any excessive credit deals, i.e. long chains (or "credit money") in the system. Once both primary and commercial banks' lending happens at market rates, the chains simply will not form. This is even more obvious if you noticed that the primary lending rate under our new system is formed exclusively through term deposits by commercial banks' clients, or "how it should be, not how it turns out".[120]

Second, the authorities do not understand what lever needs to be "pulled" in order to not only get rid of something undesirable but also not break something useful. In general, this childish phrase contains way more sense than it may seem. This has become a routine for government officials under the existing formation – once the basic cost regulators of "the invisible hand" fail, they have to roll up their sleeves. For example, many in the US believed it was necessary to use "Keynesian" recipes to get out of the 2007–2009 crisis (by the way, it did not work to the desired extent – we are going to talk about this later). Actually, taking into account the distribution pattern of the centralised anti-crisis money injections, the

[120] Of course, the current situation has not been a brainchild of some evil thinkers. The mix of credit and payment systems is a mandatory stage in the development of monetary circulation. Before the invention of computers, it was impossible to get around it.

recipes looked more like those advocated by Milton Friedman. He maintained (together with Anna J. Schwartz, in their well-known study *A Monetary History of the United States, 1867–1960*) that the Federal Reserve in the 1930s did not pump enough money into the banking system, which thereby caused the Great Depression to be so grave when it could have been avoided.

Of course, the steps undertaken by the US central bank were unlikely to be flawless, but it would not be fair to draw a popular comparison of these steps with the actions of the same agency at the end of the 20th century, when the Federal Reserve was generously saturating the banking system with dollars and no catastrophe indeed followed. At the end of the century, the US dollar was a full-bodied global currency, more pronounced than in the following years when, under pressure from the euro, it managed to survive the sharp increase in monetary base (at least for the time being). By comparison, in the 1930s the dollar did not have this privileged status and the US economy was largely a near-classical national economy, as witnessed, for example, by its share in world manufacturing output (about twice today's share). Had the Federal Reserve begun to pump the monetary base to the degree that would fully compensate for the increase of banks' liabilities (rally of the 1920s → explosive growth of surrogate assets → increase of credit turnover → lengthening of credit chains), it would have been another story. I don't know if this would have resulted in one of the Argentine saga's episodes, but the story would have been different – with a weaker dollar and higher costs for the domestic companies.

In the actual story that took place, the US managed to preserve the dollar by getting rid of tremendous costs inevitably arising in the economy following the aforementioned boom, through hard deflation. In this story, the Great Depression served as a launch pad for the unstoppable might of the dollar and the US financial system. It is common knowledge that Prohibition was a gross mistake, of course, but let's not focus on it and return to our theoretical logic.

The simplest definition of overproduction. Further discussion on deflation from costs (or how contraction of credit chains leads to having less money in the real economy).

When the manifestations of goods overproduction begin to grow in the economy, it means in the simplest understanding that the goods supply (the sum of supply prices) exceeds the sum of money that buyers are willing to offer for these goods *during a certain period of time*, and that the difference cannot be corrected by lowering the prices of goods to the level of their cost. In other words, the number of firms that do not have enough sales to recoup their costs is growing. The credit chains going through these firms are now harder to resolve and commercial banks begin to face difficulties – once their clients default, banks have trouble returning the money they borrowed. Besides, records of outstanding loans make up a large portion of commercial banks' assets and when the latter shrink due to writing off their doubtful portion, it makes borrowing new money more difficult for the bank. Further, the speculative market (secondary trading of stocks, bonds and derivatives) jumps into the process, where the players are trying to take back some money causing the prices of securities to fall. Removing money from the speculative market does not affect the deflation process by itself, since despite certain collective mystique intrinsic to this market, the money from the majority of deals does not end up in the real economy and therefore does not get extracted from it.[121] However, the sharp decrease in demand for IPOs

---

[121] This is a very simple boundary separating the secondary market for securities and the real economy. For example, when new corporate bonds are issued, the initial proceeds go to the firm. Later, after the bonds get to the secondary market, the money received from sales lives its own life. The real economy gets funding from the financial markets either through loans or through initial public offerings (IPOs). While funds do move from the secondary market for securities into the real economy, it does not have a systemic character. This is a fundamental moment – the secondary market itself exists due to money inflow and it is targeted to stimulate this. We'll be calling the secondary market for securities and derivatives a "speculative market", without separating speculative and investment deals. High liquidity of securities blurs this separation line; therefore, these deals do not substantially differ in their brute-force impact on the mechanisms of classical competition and the forming of systemic costs. All economists admit to varying extents that there is harm brought about by the speculative market, especially in times of ongoing crisis. It is more difficult to understand the harm stemming from the incompatibility of marketable securities with the classical, self-regulating

lowers the amount of that extra funding for the real economy that the goods-producing economy got used to. Lower prices of securities further decrease the assets of firms and commercial banks, often classifying them as non-creditworthy borrowers. Simply put, every creditor in the market wants to have their loans paid back, but few are willing to lend money. In its pure form, this situation may lead to something similar to the 1930s deflation that resulted from costs. Then, a large number of bank clients rushed to withdraw their deposits simultaneously, only to learn that there was no "high-powered" or "low-powered" money (that's how the components of "money stock" are often interpreted), but simply either money or the absence thereof. Subsequently, monetary authorities have gained experience and started to guarantee the deposits of the majority of small bank clients. In a serious crisis, this may help the national economy not much more than a straw mattress would help someone jumping from a skyscraper (just compare the monetary base and the "money stock"). However, these steps by authorities do help alleviate the panic.

All that is described above is known as a contraction of "money supply". Since we are using different terminology, let's call it a contraction of the credit chains that is causing the shortage of money in the goods-producing sector. The cyclical deflationary crises happen mainly because of this critical lengthening and contraction of the credit chains.[122] In this situation, injecting money into the banking system (as Friedman recommended) will help to avoid only bank bankruptcies,[123] with everything else left intact – the money would remain in the banking system, save for some "pinpoint" rescues of large firms, as there are few creditworthy borrowers in the real economy. Moreover, most of the extra money will be channelled to the

---

market economy. Here, we are talking about their complete incompatibility, starting from the IPO stage.

[122] Here, we have some similarities to the ideas by Irving Fisher.

[123] This is very important for the US economy today. Unlike the situation in the first half of the 20th century, when US dominance stemmed from its national manufacturing and it was paramount to pull the real economy out of crisis, the backbone of the modern US economy is represented by its banking system due to many years of the dollar's reign. Hence, it is easy to understand Americans when they inject money into the banking system – anyone else would do the same. Beyond this understanding, this tactic only delays the exit from the world economic crisis, as cost reduction (that begins in the "wonderland" world as deflationary and manifests itself in near-classical economies mainly as currency depreciation) has not yet happened to the full extent. This is yet another systemic dilemma of the existing model of the world economy, which is impossible to solve under it.

speculative market, possibly causing the prices to rise for raw materials and thus increasing the world economy costs. Where money does need to be injected into is the real economy, specifically from the consumer side of it.

The partial direct issuance of money in the economic policy of F. D. Roosevelt during the Great Depression. Notes for John M. Keynes's theory (continued).

A meaningful portion of F. D. Roosevelt's (FDR's) economic policy was aimed at this money injection, both through paying unemployment benefits to some 20 million people and through financing of public works (up to 5 million employed). It was important that upon having received unemployment benefits and having built (not always good quality) highways, people were spending their money on purchases, as the poor did not bother much about savings then.

Further, we'll focus our attention on this, but we also won't forget about FDR's artificial devaluation of the dollar by some 40 per cent, with concurrent growth of the gold reserves through mandatory gold sales. The devaluation boosted the competitiveness of American goods, while the gold reserves safeguarded the dollar against further unpredictable devaluation due to an increase in the amount of money in circulation caused by a generous government spending policy. To my mind, that inventive operation (coupled with other factors including the highly developed US manufacturing at the time, the natural distance of the US from their main competitors and greatly increased protectionism in the world economy in a time of crisis) not only served as an important element of FDR's economic policy, but also paved the way to discovering similarities of this policy to the theoretical interpretation of the events by Keynes *in this so-called "closed" economy*. In a sense (meaning the increased dollar resilience), the operations with gold "closed" the US economy, which shaped US monetary policy for several subsequent decades (the dollar was backed up by solid gold reserves).

We should also point out one important moment that was not directly related to FDR's economic policy (and that was not properly accounted for by Keynes): the costs in the US economy had already been reduced to an acceptable level under deflationary pressure. This happened mainly before the FDR administration and then it was time to jump-start the economy.

You have probably noticed that even up until today, there are some contradicting opinions expressed in the theoretical analyses of the Great Depression. We assume this will continue in the future, as the transition from one formation to another, in this case from gold capitalism to paper capitalism, has no rigorous theoretical description criteria.[124] Simply put, the outcome is not clear at this time – the legacy of the old formation is in a chaotic relationship with elements of the nascent formation, and all this may be accompanied by random and natural events, military cataclysms, or some other events that are hard to classify. The transition period is largely a time for executive decisions. If, by this time, economists have a vague idea that a formation change is taking place and what the future economy will look like, the process seems to be chaotic and all attempts to describe it theoretically will see a slew of variable inferences, with empirical proof for each one.

These considerations are also to be accounted for in the case of Keynes, who assumed a comfortable viewpoint of a closed economy, abstracting from foreign trade. We have already touched upon the drawbacks of Keynes's theory regarding this closed economy case, in our thesis "*Technological evolution: movement of investment money ...*". Using simple reasoning, we saw that his theory had a local character; under an ordinary, open economy, stimulating demand can lead to a surge of imports and to a national currency crash.

In the 1930s, during the acute phase of the transition period when the world economy was leaning towards isolationism and import restrictions, the assumption of a "closed economy" did not create a dissonance as much as it would today. This was even more pronounced, given the natural remoteness of the US from its main foreign competitors, despite FDR's personal adherence to free trade principles that was not shared by Congress nor by the public. The aforementioned gold purchases played a role too, given that it was not a one-time event. By the time World War II started, the US gold reserves already accounted for over half of the world's reserves. Soon, the war isolated the US economy even more and the dollar became a global currency largely thanks to post-war reconstruction in Europe. Only from that moment onwards would it be correct to say that Keynes's theory started to work in practice, although

[124] The post-war US economic boom of the 1920s also was part of the transition period, but then it was difficult to see the new formation arising. Besides, when things go well, there is no urgent need to search for new solutions, unlike during the periods when the economy is deteriorating.

not as a "universal" one. However, the "closed nature" of the economy had nothing to do with it.

The US gold reserves, which had grown to 70 per cent of the world reserves by 1949, helped the dominance of the dollar but since the 1970s, they have not played a leading role. A country where the national currency is a global currency can and even must – as a locomotive of the world economy under paper capitalism – run high public spending with a corresponding budget deficit. With all that, it is impossible and unnecessary for its citizens to buy only domestic goods. The modern US economy cannot be called "closed" (we call it "wonderland"), and key assumptions of Keynes's theory still apply to the US[125] because the dollar is a very resilient global currency despite both budget and payment balance deficits.

Going back to the US economy during the Great Depression, let's see why the Keynesian recipes to stimulate consumer demand were valid, taking into account the resilience of the dollar to a budget deficit and the important fact that deflationary cost reduction had already largely happened. But let's note that we won't be using the expression "stimulation of aggregate demand" that for most people is inextricably associated with Keynes's theory. This is because, first, our study is decisively conservative with regard to interpreting the "supply" and "demand" categories. The second reason is that while Keynes's suggestions to stimulate *consumer* demand are of primary theoretical value, Keynes himself was putting emphasis on stimulating *investment* demand. Due to some technical reasons that we are going to explain below (we'll mark these with an asterisk in the shaded text box below), a recommendation to boost the investment demand under the scenario of a centralised credit issuance of money is akin to a recommendation by Captain Obvious. An overstated satisfaction of investment demand is already built into this system. Strictly speaking, that's why – to maintain

[125] With the exceptions of the US, to a lesser extent the euro area and to some extent the countries with non-world but resilient currencies, the non-classical Keynes's theory does not work. Moreover, it will not work under our rigorous classical system of the PCM, where all national currencies will be equal. Even in the countries we mentioned, it does not always work, or it works with certain clarifying circumstances taken into account. There are certain historical parallels not only between socialism and paper capitalism, but also between their respective theoretical foundations. Both Marx's and Keynes's theories work only under socialism and paper capitalism, respectively, and only with noticeable caveats.

the balance – there is a need to stimulate consumer demand not only in crises but also at other times.

To sum it up, why were Keynes's recipes to stimulate consumer demand so attractive during the Great Depression?

First, money was coming to the firms not "from above" (from the banks) but "from below" (from the customers). Guesswork by bankers (or government officials or buyers of securities) regarding whose goods would sell better is not the same thing as actual "buyers voting with their purses". This difference is more pronounced during the critical points in the development of the capitalist economy – the sooner the market sorts out the inefficient owners, the sooner the crisis ends.

Generally speaking, money entering "from below" (from buyers) is vitally important for the economy, provided its players do not want to start preparing for a new deflationary crisis, having barely caught their breath from the previous one. Under our PCM financial system, this problem is absent in the bud, as we have direct issuance of money with absolutely no credit issuance. Under paper capitalism (namely, in its "wonderland" part, where the situation is nearly the opposite), this problem is always looming. Under the existing formation, "new in a broad sense" money – both really new, recently issued money and the money running in circles thanks to the lengthening of the credit chains – enters the real economy either "from above" (as investment) or as loans. Faced with the need to pay back the money they borrowed, firms use the loan proceeds to turn out new goods and services that they need to sell. However, for this increase of production to happen smoothly without creating any prerequisites for deflation, consumers need to have extra money to spend. Even if the firms spend all their loan proceeds to pay their costs and this money subsequently, directly or indirectly, trickles down to the consumers, the latter would still not have enough to purchase all the output, taking into account an amount of profit expected by the firms. For this reason, we can reasonably expect a pile-up of unsold goods over long periods of time (*).

This "extra money" goes to consumer wallets from several sources (since Keynes's theory is valid for "closed" or "wonderland" national economies and since the development of the US economy falls into both categories, we'll be talking about US dollars):

- A supply of “wide new” dollars that would enter the economy “from above” as credits for investment purposes. With enough of these “wide new” dollars entering the economy, they may compensate for the earlier accumulated deficit in the supply of money from consumers. In other words, an expanded supply of money from consumers in this case coincides with economic expansion, which is actively supported by the central bank, commercial banks and the securities market. All these monetary institutions are either generating these “wide new” dollars or amplifying their generation. However, the longer the expansion, the more severe the problem, and if this is the only method, “the time to gather stones” will turn out to be cruel once the economy cools down.
- The situation (just this situation, regardless of a possible recurrence of it at a higher level) is solved by consumer credit.

At the time of the Great Depression when neither source worked – there was no economic growth, while bankers were hesitant to extend consumer credit with the uncertain future situation – Keynes offered an alternative, third way (though Keynes himself, as we have mentioned, favoured the first one):

- The subject of our current discussion, i.e. the delivery of money to consumers through an increase in government spending. Essentially, it is a variant of partial direct issuance of money conducted by the government, but under the paper capitalism model, it still has the credit issuance administered by the central bank, as its top-level source.

Second, money entered the economy without credit liabilities, i.e. without an obligation to repay, for both firms and consumers. In this context, by consumer liabilities we mean “consumer credit”. It may seem to be a certain universal method to combine credit with adding money to the economy “from below”. Indeed, from the immediate perspective of safeguarding against overproduction it does not matter how consumers received their funds, as either wages or loans. However, we could draw a non-rigorous parallel with US Treasury bonds – when the economy is doing well, they strengthen the dollar, but in the long term they contribute to its future crash and increase its magnitude. Consumer credit is perfectly suited for the tactical task of adding new money “from below”, but it begins to involve households with credit chains. Besides, it allows people to consume something they have not earned yet, which as a result stimulates supply on the part of the firms. All of this contributes to preparing for yet another overproduction crisis and augmenting its scale. Characteristically, the 2007 crisis started from household indebtedness.

For an economy tangled in credit chains, the inflow of money that was not burdened by credit liabilities was a godsend. It was like starting a new life on Monday morning and the inflow of new money "from below" marked the beginning of the Great Depression sunset.[126] Still, some elements of the direct issuance of money are necessary for "closed" and "wonderland" economies during the periods between crises. Repeated recommendations by Keynes to FDR, dated February 1, 1938, confirm that the prominent British economist understood this, but in his theoretical reasoning he put an emphasis on consumer and investor psychological traits. Conversely, our study devotes substantial time to the analysis of technical (rational) particulars of the financial system of paper capitalism.[127]

To summarise, the main achievement of Keynes's *theory* (not to mention his achievements as an outstanding analytical mind) is his suggestion to stimulate consumer demand. In Keynes's time, there were many fewer recorded observations of the monetary system of paper capitalism compared with today, over half a century later. Without pointing out the technical details we mentioned previously (marked with an asterisk above), Keynes guessed the right answer (i.e. give more money to consumers) by relying solely on his high analytical skills. As a theoretical justification, Keynes offered a murky psychological trail, based on employment, "propensity to save/consume", "liquidity preference" and a "fundamental psychological law". Further, he threw in the investment multiplier and actively used numerous "marginal" categories, having introduced some of these himself (the "marginal efficiency of capital"). Given the highly respected figure of Keynes, his extraordinary *analytical*

---

[126] It worked then but it did not work following the onset of the 2007 crisis, despite clear similarities between the policies of Barack Obama and FDR in the way money was being delivered to the poor. As we have pointed out, FDR's policies were preceded by a strong decrease in costs in the US, while in modern times, the authorities opted for an immediate hit. Now it is clear enough, but to many, including myself, this important moment at the beginning of the crisis was hard to understand.

[127] This does not mean that we pay less attention to psychology at the *fundamental* level, as demonstrated in the next thesis. We'll also clarify how psychology and rationality are woven into the single economy's tree.

reflections led to serious problems in *theoretical* economics. This partial logic, taken out of a tangle of relationships, shifted long-term fundamental accents from managing costs in the national economy to monetary policy manipulations, i.e. it bundled analytics and theory together. What was appropriate in Washington in the 1930s (as a certain set of analytical relationships, sometimes correct and sometimes not quite) may be totally inappropriate today – for example, right now in Moscow – neither as an analytical algorithm nor as theoretical logic.

Taking into account the ever-present influence of the last great economist's legacy to our modern way of thinking, it makes sense to spend extra time to sort it out, and even sometimes repeat the main similarities and differences between our study and Keynes's theory. A lot can be seen even from the set of basic categories. For example, we do not use the term "employment", as for all its analytical (managerial) importance and the possibility of the moderate use of it in theoretical economics, it still does not qualify as a *basic theoretical category*. In its direct meaning, employment is a statistical ratio reflecting the level of using just *one* basic type of resource, akin to the share of land used in the economy as a whole or in agriculture in particular. Here, one may have a feeling that the author is targeting some sacred cows. As *Homo sapiens* is the dominant biological species, it is hard to avoid bringing sociology and political science contexts into theoretical economics. In critical situations, managerial decisions will rightfully reflect that people – as the only known intelligent biological species – "are more important than a theory" (in a sense, the Great Depression was one of these critical situations). Still, for example, a human's fall from a height is indistinguishable from any other object's fall, from the perspective of the fundamental laws of physics. Also, from the perspective of biology, a man is not fundamentally different from other mammals. Sure, these analogies are very rough, so therefore returning to theoretical economics, let's point out a well-known hypothesis born in the 18th century about creating "value" in the process of human labour. This was likely the chief misconception in our science and it has been showing up, either directly or indirectly, in later theories. We can surmise that mystical "value" somehow influenced the importance of "employment" in Keynes's theory:

> "It is preferable to regard labour, including, of course, the personal services of the entrepreneur and his assistants, as the sole factor of production, operating in a given environment of technique, natural resources, capital equipment and effective demand. This partly explains why we have been able to take the unit of labour as the sole physical unit which we require in

our economic system, apart from units of money and of time." (Keynes, 2018, p. 188)

We are trying to avoid being dragged into any associated philosophical disputes, but note that both the process and the results of human labour will be different on Earth and on Neptune, due to a difference in costs. The humans have nothing to do with this difference. Moreover, people mainly exist because of planet Earth's particular features. We have argued why "labour" cannot be a correct basic category either, in the last thesis of Chapter 1 ("*Definition of economy. Labour ...*"). We have also explained why Keynes's "unit of labour" is incorrect from a fundamental perspective in the beginning of the thesis devoted to critique Coase's theory ("*Ronald Coase and transaction costs ...*").

Now, let's get into details and compare our paragraph (marked with an asterisk) with the last two sentences in the following fundamental quote from *The General Theory of Employment, Interest, and Money*:

> "The outline of our theory can be expressed as follows. When employment increases, aggregate real income is increased. The psychology of the community is such that when aggregate real income is increased, aggregate consumption is increased, but not by so much as income. Hence employers would make a loss if the whole of the increased employment were to be devoted to satisfying the increased demand for immediate consumption. Thus, to justify any given amount of employment there must be an amount of current investment sufficient to absorb the excess of total output over what the community chooses to consume when employment is at the given level …" (Ibid, pp. 24-25)

We do not quote the rest of this paragraph, as it has more frequent instances of the well-known basic categories by Keynes ("propensity to consume", "inducement to invest", "marginal efficiency of capital") that we don't use in our study. They exist either in the form of some vague hypotheses or, in cases where they are presented as factual data, they do not materially differ from plain statistical data. In either case, they will likely be useful *for analytics*, especially for speculative market analysis ("propensity", "inducement" and "expectations" are all prominently featured there). However, in our view, they don't fit a fundamental theory. For example, the "marginal efficiency of capital" sounds quite academic, but it is clear anyway that entrepreneurs want to make more money than they spend. Using the "profit" category would be sufficient here, once we are talking about a fundamental theory. As for using terminology to describe the relationships in the financial markets of paper capitalism, a good deal of categories associated with this local "theory" would simply disappear with a transition to the PCM. The rest will be subordinated to the basic monetary categories that we use. Over time, of course, some new financial vocabulary that is typical for the new formation will be formed. This does not mean, however, that it would need to be implanted into theoretical economics.

One way or another, it is easy to grab the essence of the quoted passage, even if it is not easy to imagine why "… employers would make a loss if the whole of increased employment were to be devoted to satisfying the increased demand for immediate consumption" (Ibid, p. 25), especially given that Keynes's views on the "psychology of the community" were not flawless (we'll talk a bit about this in the next thesis). Still, you can see a faint resemblance of the described problem between our paragraph above marked with an asterisk and this quote from Keynes, including his appeal to a possible loss of profit at the firm. However, the explanations of the problem and therefore the directions of further research are radically different. What we have collapsed into the shaded box a few pages earlier is the central piece of Keynes's theory.

Actually, this box is all we need, as our explanation is based on technical features of money issuance under paper capitalism. There is no need to invoke psychology, mathematics or those notorious marginal quantities. Our technical explanation shows that stressing the need for sufficient levels of investment, like Keynes does in his theory, is overreaching in a sense (we'll clarify this sense in our *Note 1* below). Generally speaking, ***consumption growth in a market economy under the natural course of events will always jump-start investment demand***, but the opposite – as we saw in the box above – while being feasible, comes bundled with mandatory aberrations.

One of the reasons why Keynes did not attach due importance to the fact that the inverted model contained a fundamental contradiction was his fascination with the term "demand" at the expense of the term "supply".

We have mentioned briefly that the supply of money by the broad government has its particulars. In a strict classical model that will be driving our PCM, the money issuance (injection of new money through the allocation of budget funds with the subsequent use of purchase and sale, hire, and land rental deals) is being formed, strictly speaking, *above the macroeconomy*. Under the present formation that we are analysing (first and foremost, in the "wonderland" part), the injection of new money is based on credit deals, which puts money issuance and macroeconomy close together, up to their partial symbiosis. As we have mentioned in the box above, the *supply* of "new broad money" takes place with an accent on the *supply* of money for *investment* and this is fraught with insufficient supply of money from consumers precisely for this reason. *Here, substituting the italicised "supply" terms for "demand" would take us off course, as we won't be able to see the money issuance particulars.*

Two final notes are appropriate in this context.

Note 1. Speaking about the erroneous nature of Keynes's accent on the priority of investment, we unequivocally mean that the idea of stimulating the real sector of a market economy by government investment is erroneous for the classical economy under the PCM. As for paper capitalism, this idea hardly even passes the definition of an idea, as it simply reflects the priority of investment that is baked into the theoretical particulars of credit issuance of money.

Still, if this idea assumes the strengthening of this *preset* priority of *investment* by using manual management of the central bank's rates, namely by lowering them, this management would be more precisely classified as a tactical move within the framework of the existing model, i.e. the analytical framework. These moves – which, by the way, always have an ambiguous effect due to a violation of the natural sequence of factors (consumption → investment) – have to account, by default, for the theoretical particulars of the model. We keep bringing up these particulars throughout our study, but let's use an alternative, simplified narrative (as a short story used to explain our planetary economy to an "alien").

We should start our story with the statement that the Earth's economy is highly globalised (like a set of communicating vessels) and it has some global currencies. If there are some currencies more resilient to depreciation, then there are also some that are less resilient to it compared with a certain "normal" level – for instance, the level of any country in the future world economy under the PCM. If there is a lower interest rate, there must be a higher one. If there is a lower inflation rate, there must be a higher one. Finally, if there are countries with an elevated level of consumption, there must be some other countries with lower levels. So, with all due respect to Keynes, his theory does not describe the realities of the world economy, even with this oversimplified picture.

Note 2. The idea of stimulating consumption through government expenses is erroneous both for the PCM and for the near-classical ("regular") countries under paper capitalism (see the thesis "*Technological evolution: movement of investment money* ..."), but it is largely valid for the "wonderland" countries under the existing formation. Keynes deserves credit for it, even though he did not separate countries into two groups as we do.

At the root of the drawbacks of Keynes's theory is his excessive enthusiasm for psychology while studying the "inner workings" of *demand and supply branches*, instead of analysing the movement of property in deals ("intersection of branches") and from one deal to another. This is one of the reasons that instead of analysing systemic costs, the Keynesian theory focuses on the monetary and credit policy, which is expected to correct the negative consequences of the psychological particulars (expectations, propensity, etc.) of market participants. This policy is an important part of the exciting "up and down" analytical game, watched by the world for decades. No wonder that with Keynesian theoretical accents, this game may seem a perpetual one, despite the critical attitude towards it expressed by Keynes himself.

Psychology and rationality in theoretical economics. Notes for John M. Keynes's theory (continued).

Understanding the psychology of market participants is very important for a *practical economy*. Meticulous accounting for human psychology (motivation) is indispensable for negotiations, working inside a firm and for marketing promotions. The spectrum of motivational nuances is quite broad and diverse between industries and occupations. It is also constantly evolving along with technological and societal development, so there is no magic list where nothing can be *added*.

Theoretical analysis leads us to a thought that a reverse approach may be warranted, namely creating a list of basic sources of motivation (further referred to as basic motivators) for *Homo sapiens*, which cannot be *shortened*. The aspirations, created by these basic motivators, serve as an umbilical cord that connects theoretical economics to its mother science, biology.

A well-known aphorism by Friedrich Schiller goes: "Love and hunger rule the world". ***As applied to the economy, these are indeed two basic motivators forming the source of people's economic activities: the***

aspiration to increase their property (i.e. consumable property). It would not be sufficient to limit oneself to only these two motivators, for example, while managing a firm, but they are genetically imprinted by natural selection, and this is a decisive factor from a fundamental perspective. That is, reflections by *Homo sapiens* can, to a degree, correct the manifestations of basic motivators (for example, by filtering them through some moral or legal norms), but such reflections cannot cancel these motivators. In critical situations, the said basic instincts can totally command the brain. But if, when referring to "hunger" (hereafter, we will use the more general term "self-preservation instinct"), there are no problems with understanding, then the influence of "love" (or "reproduction instinct") on the desire to increment property requires clarification.[128]

Clearly, the children of those humans who did not care about the material well-being of their offspring died prematurely and their genetic lines were terminated. So, it's easy to assume that because of thousands of years of natural selection, we are all descendants of humans with an elevated sense of responsibility for their children. We can say that this maternal motivator is key when considering the influence of the reproduction instinct on the economic motivation of *Homo sapiens*, launching consistently all others.

In our basic theoretical constructs we are sufficiently quickly leaving the household proper, concentrating on the analysis of the macroeconomy and microeconomy instead. As a rule, households are present in this analysis only in the form of end points associated with consumption or accumulation. The internal workings of households are of little interest to theorists and this study is no exception. However, the household is the very cell from which we start to grow our fundamental relationships by pointing out the desire to property increment, which is naturally inherent in people. ***Further down (literally through the step), our analysis of the property increment leads us to the cost regulators that are directly or indirectly associated with major kinds of property increments (rent, wages, interest, profit).*** It is important to understand what this intermediate step is.

If we were to limit ourselves, at the fundamental level, to merely an indication of psychology (basic motivators), it would barely distinguish us

---

[128] I noticed that while reading this material, people subconsciously expect to see some supporting references – either statistics or opinions of other specialists. As for statistics, they are hardly available, as the forming of basic instincts dates back millennia. As for the opinions of other specialists (not economists), these are hardly decisive for reasoning about the *desire to increment property*.

humans from the "economies" of other inhabitants on the planet, whose instincts for self-preservation and reproduction also compel them to a compulsory and tireless incrementation of their (family) "property" (Schiller's aphorism is also literally true for our rather smaller brothers). The economy proper, i.e. the economy of *Homo sapiens*, is distinguished by the presence of a second "bud" on the economic "twig" growing from a biological tree, namely the ability to voluntarily alienate property. With the development of their intelligence, people realised that to materialise their desire to property increment, they can not only take away someone else's property (through war and, generally, violence) but also give up their property by exchanging it (an economy). Unlike striving for property *incrementation* originating from basic instincts, we owe our ability for the voluntary *alienation* of property to our highly organised brain. Thanks to this rational[129] behaviour in a practical economy, deals (and then **money**) come to exist. And here, speaking of theoretical economics, we formulate our basic definition of price through property alienation. With this definition, we introduce the certainty of exact equations into our calculations. First, we see exactly how the classification of types of property *incrementation* leads to the final and basic cost regulators, and then paves the way to calculated money issuance. We'll need no other clarifying interpretations of "rationality" at the fundamental level. Any intended clarifications will require further clarifications and reservations, and this would become a weak link. ***All rational economic behaviour that is important for us is based on the ability of*** **Homo sapiens** ***to voluntarily alienate property. Through the process of reasoning – "Is it more or less?" – it is leading us to the deals that form economic equations.***

Please note that without leaving the domain of human biology, we found through simple reasoning that people have **an aspiration to increment their property and an ability to alienate it**. Thus, we outlined the contours of the main theoretical building blocks of our study, namely **price definition and basic cost regulators**. Subsequently, everything

[129] Reflections of the dealmakers happen in the "more or less" corridor, as each one tries to get more in exchange for less. Comparable deals serve as universal guidelines to avoid major losses and stalemates caused by extraordinary demands. Reflections become radically easier once diverse kinds of property are compared to numbers (money). I do not see a particular reason here to dive deep into the laws of the universe. Be it reflections by the Cro-Magnons in their barter exchanges or the reasons why kids may trade their bicycle for that special postage stamp, let's leave it to the specialists to study. There is no apparent usefulness in these abstractions but some kind of ghost-like "value" may accidentally creep in.

else, including our case for the new formation, is a chain of sound logical reasoning.

Now, let's return to psychology, i.e. to the aspiration of people to increment their (consumable) property. This powerful biological "spike" in motivation is the ancestor of the entire economy. However, this primordial might does create problems, with the chief one being an overproduction crisis. Let's generally agree with Marx that the main driver of the overproduction crisis is the institution of private property in the economy (to paraphrase it using our terminology, we can clarify that in this case this driver is the aspiration of entrepreneurs to increment their property). Marx chose the option to dismantle this institution and therefore we won't have many intersections with his theory.

In our views on the main drivers of an overproduction crisis, we'll have more differences with Keynes, who *delved* into human psychology. Believing that a decrease in "aggregate demand" was a technical trigger for a crisis, the British economist put his main focus on the frugality of people. It is fair to say that frugality is a component of the aspiration to increment property ("a penny saved is a penny earned"), but this still shifts the accents. Keynes delved further into psychology, exploring people's (negative) expectations while looking for a reason for their increased frugality. In general, "expectations" seem to be the starting point of the logical reasoning in his *The General Theory* ... (expectations → investment volume → production volume → level of employment). Let's note that in this chain the accent is already shifting towards consumers of investment goods (means of production and working capital), whom Keynes is calling "investors". [130] Keynes believed that negative expectations, linked to decreases in consumer demand, provoked investors into an acute frugality. This causes investment and, further down the chain, employment to decrease. Thus, by stimulating employment through government expenditure, one can stimulate consumption and improve investor expectations.

The question is not whether this logic is erroneous (we purposely chose a version that does not cut the ear), but rather whether it can be considered fundamental. The selected set of psychological nuances that are *different from basic motivators* appears to be subtle enough to become a weak link.

[130] We'll be rarely using this term to avoid ambiguities, as "investors" can apply to buyers of investment goods, creditors and even buyers of securities on the speculative market, even given that the proceeds from their purchases do not get into the real economy.

In particular, Keynes's hypothesis (which he considered "the fundamental psychological law") regarding consumption lagging behind income brings about some serious questions. The observations by Simon Kuznets showed this lag exists but only in the short term, so we omitted this hypothesis while focusing on Keynes's main logic, in order not to obscure anything that looked important or plausible. Fundamental characteristics differ from plausible insight by the depth of their vision, or, using a construction analogy, the height of a building depends on the strength of its foundations. Like Marx before him, Keynes was constructing his theoretical "building". Both of them succeeded, albeit they left behind only temporary structures.

I believe there are three major theories in economics: one by Adam Smith, one by Marx and one by Keynes. As for our study, at the fundamental level – first and foremost, regarding its focus on the self-regulating market economy – it is more conservative than it may seem at first glance. This study, although it relies on the category of "formation", which was introduced by Marx, is ultimately a reconstruction of "the house that Smith built", albeit with large-scale alterations from bottom to top, using some "modern materials". We call a self-regulated market economy a "classical economy", avoiding the term "liberal" whenever possible to cut it out from an established context. This context, when using this term, consists of two main elements: the worldview one and the economic one.

The worldview aspect refers to the hypersensitive attitude to the systemic limitations of the principle that "I earn money the way I want to." Many people want to think that all systemic limitations for managing owners nowadays belong to the pages of history books. Psychologically, this is understandable, but these people would do better to read fantasy fiction – there, one can really find oneself on a backward and sparsely populated planet where one can do almost anything. From this viewpoint, slave ownership would be the most "liberal" formation in history.

From a purely economic ("technical") point of view, I am a liberal economist, i.e. a supporter of the self-regulated market economy protected from government regulation to the extent possible. However, the existing linkage of this term to capitalism is in the way of understanding the economic essence of the context of the term "liberal economy". Both models of capitalism are indeed important stages in the development of a market self-regulated economy but neither model is really this. This likely explains why in ordinary life this dry formulation (i.e. with a subconscious correlation with the modern model) is often accompanied by sarcasm and hostility. It is not difficult to see the main point of sarcasm. Having largely abandoned the production of goods in favour of a market economy, the government in a broad sense (including the central bank) de facto controls the same process through the credit system. And when the market economy, demonstrating a lack of self-regulation capacity, creeps into a crisis, state control over the entire financial sphere and, further, over the entire economy in general turns this "liberal" economy into an étatist one.

It's harder to figure out rational is popular dislike for liberal economists in near-classical countries, where applying their recipes in critical situations is often accompanied by the impoverishment of the population, up to the manifestation of "natural selection processes" in an everyday (cruel) understanding of these words. It is thought that the degree of moral responsibility of the liberal economists for these disasters is largely related to their inability (or unwillingness) to explain the essence of the modern ways of combining countries into a single global economy.

You can imagine the modern world economy in the form of a "butterfly", where the body is the "consuming" countries that issue global currencies ("wonderland") and the wings are the ordinary "supplier" countries. To fly up, such a butterfly must shake off extra costs from its wings, which is especially clear during a crisis. It is easier to understand why we start with the wings if you replace "extra costs" with "excess consumption". The reduction in consumption in "wonderland" countries will technically lead nowhere, as its function is exactly the opposite. That's why liberal economists offer austerity measures for the near-classical countries during a crisis, as there is no alternative way to keep the butterfly aloft (to simplify, the sooner "everything" falls relative to the dollar, the sooner the deflationary crisis will end). We are trying to get rid of this "liberal" context by using the term "classical economy" for our PCM.

In addition to my wishes for an honest explanation of the "butterfly" principle, I would like liberal economists to stop using the following "extra flexible" liberal question in science: "So, who's stopping you?" (In this case, who is preventing you from issuing your own global currency?) This "slamming" method is known from the age-old times (a bully hits a midget and asks a similar question). It has been used, and will continue to be used, in disputes and negotiations, but it does not prove anything by itself as situations may differ. It may be smarter and more appropriate – at least in the 21st century – to put it this way: "We have a global currency market, which *inevitably* leads to the emergence of elite currencies and certain insurmountable aberrations in the global economy. It's time to switch to a currency exchange system that *excludes* the emergence of any elite currencies." We'll talk more about this in Chapter 3, but it seems appropriate to mention the "butterfly" early and in general terms. Some important principles of its "body" were, to varying degrees of authenticity, described by Keynes. He himself may not have suggested this exchange system, as he was supporting the introduction of "bancor", a single global vehicle for settlements. Since we have already mentioned bancor, we should add that a single global currency in all its variations is a bad idea, but we'll talk about this too in Chapter 3.

Keynes demonstrated a remarkable accuracy in understanding the main points of the current practical situation. Particularly, his advice to FDR helped us design the new financial system as part of this study. Unlike Marx's theory, our conclusions on preventing the overproduction crises have some similarities with the findings of Keynes for one natural reason that in both cases we are talking about a market economy. However, this similarity is mainly limited to Keynes's proposal to use some elements of direct issuance of money.

"Pink-coloured glasses", or why the institution of private property provokes overproduction. Price forming in a practical economy. Final notes on John M. Keynes's theory.

"Pink-coloured glasses" are the motivational prerequisite for the appearance of excessive goods. They are one of the stages of striving for property increment, which is clearly manifested mainly among the entrepreneurs. There is a relevant urban legend that says when Joseph Kennedy heard reasoning about securities from a shoeshine person, he immediately decided to cash out; when shoeshiners start investing in the stock market, it is the best time to escape from it. Perhaps it is rather a legend than Kennedy's real, entire train of thought, as people like simple explanations of causal relationships, but this example still sounds good. From a psychological point of view, a situation with overproduction of goods is approximately the same as with the overselling of securities.

First, a person named Adam realised which particular widgets would sell well in the marketplace. Then, a John and a Michael saw his success and drew the correct conclusions from it. Other producers followed Adam, John and Michael, while the first three were also ramping up production. At some point, the market got saturated – generally, this is the end of the story. This is a psychological cause of overproduction at the microeconomic level, and it is the reason for the *ebb and flow* built into the institution of private property. Under capitalist varieties of the monetary system, this ebb and flow *lays the groundwork* for a long-term overproduction crisis. These "pink-coloured glasses" (to see how successful entrepreneurs make money and to make money oneself) have been around for many years and they are here to stay.

> By the way, as a former entrepreneur I'd like to say something cynical: the top prizes – gold, silver and bronze at local competitions and at the World Pragmatic Olympics – usually go to the first three entrants (Adam, John and Michael),[131] while the rest have to be content with an "honourable mention". At the same time, the economy as a whole derives most benefits from other, lesser-known followers. After the champions have skimmed their first-mover advantages, the followers are competing by lowering costs, increasing quality and introducing many small technological improvements. This second wave may well produce new market leaders, but in general, "the fight for precious metal" is much harder for followers than for pioneers. The difference is so striking that it cannot be explained solely by certain personal advantages of entrepreneurs (or by some higher considerations, like "abstract labour" or something similar). During these moments, one can feel the importance of plain old luck. For example, Steve Jobs had many traits of a talented entrepreneur and a phenomenal flair for the end product. However, even the shortest story about Jobs's career would not be complete without mentioning that when he was

[131] We mean those who were able to commercialise the project, not those who merely had a good idea. They are not always the same people – precise implementation and speed to market are advantageous.

still an ordinary young man from the Silicon Valley, his friend was someone named Steve Wozniak.

If we are to squeeze another practical conclusion from the example of Steve Jobs, it is simple: competition in sectors that do not require specialised technical or scientific skills from entrepreneurs is stronger than in most hi-tech sectors. In traditional industries, every entrepreneur who is minded to be a "techie" or a "humanitarian" can understand how things really work, and therefore competitors are numerous and competition is fierce. I witnessed how some of my entrepreneurial-minded friends were perplexed by competitive pressures when they found themselves in an "old city marketplace jammed with horse carts and peasants wielding their whips". Later, some of them surfaced in hi-tech industries and felt quite at home there. Thus, with a comparable level of entrepreneurial skills, someone's path to business would be less thorny and would pay back more if they have a specialised technical education matching the industry. It is clear that the economy becomes more specialised. For example, the simplest explanation of the economic obsolescence of socialism[132] is the impossibility of fully fledged centralised planning in a highly specialised economy, because

[132] We are talking about real socialism, which was quite competitive for its time (with total dominance of administrative control), and not the contrived socialist model (with its "self-governing worker collectives") that could be competitive only in the dreams of private property's opponents. Socialism was not a random twist of history, as it can be described theoretically, but it was not a mandatory formation. Socialism has one more "popular science", non-rigorous feature – there is no other formation the lifespan of which could be so easily described using our Rough History of "from tractors to computers". Without the advent of tractors, Bolshevik Russia would likely have perished in hunger rebellions due to the absence of private property in agriculture (which has remained a weak link in the Soviet economy even after the introduction of other farming machinery. Unlike in heavy industry, the natural diversity of farmland and uncertain weather conditions were poor companions to the centralised planning). Anyway, the country would have been defeated in World War II due to a lack of workers for industrial development. As for computers, they serve as a quintessential indicator of scientific and technological acceleration at the end of the 20th century – high technology is hard to imagine without the use of computers. Despite the chaotic character of historical turns that at times look like a chain of disconnected events, the Bolsheviks led by Vladimir Lenin picked the right time and place (Russia) to transition to socialism, while Mikhail Gorbachev and Boris Yeltsin, in turn, dismantled it in time. Though the return to capitalism has not brought (and will not bring) much relief for the Russian economy, stepping back to socialism would spell a quick economic death.

timely decisions should be made by knowledgeable people at the forefront of enterprises and not by bureaucrats in the capital, who only have a vague idea of industry-specific problems. These *responsible* local decisions (backed by the managers' personal property) will be made faster and with more precision in the economic system built upon private property. This will be most visible under the PCM.[133]

Whether you have a technical background or not, the following passage can be of use to anyone. Quite often, we cross paths with people who are no good at mental calculation. By no means does this suggest a low intellectual level. For instance, our calculus professor at university confessed to being one of these types and I have heard the same from other obviously very smart people. In business, however, being proficient in quick mental calculation is very beneficial. It is not shameful to use a calculator, but it may not be available, or it may not be a good idea to interrupt your counterpart. The life of an entrepreneur is largely about sharing information with other people and this information directly affects our decisions. It is important "to digitise" this information, turning it into costs, possible losses, sales volumes and sales prices, etc., to anticipate how all of this will change depending on certain conditions. Often, it is important that entrepreneurs do it in their heads so that the numbers are realistic. Different people may associate different numbers with the same "picture", not because they lack multiplication skills, but because they can assume different numbers for the "picture" or forget to account for something. By the end of the working day or week, people get tired, meetings become less productive, or your counterpart may speak too fast. Therefore, the greater the ability of our brain to turn information into numbers in an automated fashion, the better. Then, it is more likely that in the head of the manager there will be more complete and fundamentally important information. And it is less

---

[133] This reason also underlies the obligation for Russia to change its current course (as the existing model can be described as a mixture of state and oligarchic capitalism) towards a more market-driven one. The point is not that "the market will decide everything" (because each model has its own specific issues). The bottom line is that under the conditions of rapid development of the economy along the path of high specialisation, there is no strategic alternative to market self-regulation of interaction between responsible professionals. The "last Bolsheviks" came to this general understanding more than a quarter of a century ago and called off their state economy project, regardless of how hard this decision was for them.

likely we'll miss the elements that are crucial for understanding both the present and planned future situations. A good understanding is vital for sound decision-making.

Here, I invite the reader to consider skipping to the end of this shaded box, as the ensuing set of memories and impressions comes from "under the hide of an entrepreneur". It might be more difficult to read (these passages are mostly tied to pricing) and possibly less interesting.

Entry into a practical economy requires a precise approach (we might have bored the reader with our approach disclaimers). It's one thing to represent the firm in the form of numbers characterising the results of its activities (this is in the analytics domain). But it is another thing (and it is important for the theory) to present the basic rules by which property flows through a single firm, similarly to a city road map. True, there is a big difference in the "firm map", where the "main road" sign at intersections may change location (up to the appearance of new roads and disappearance of old ones), while intersections themselves often stand at the crossing of more than two roads or paths. At the same time, there is no chaos here, as each property flow is described in numbers. The focus here is not on the resulting indicators, as in analytics, but on the prices – those same primordial prices of the property that the firm operates. *Depending on prices* (directly or indirectly) and accounting for external factors (there are other "cities" on the map), the *signs for the main road (decision-making priorities)* may change. No matter how detailed statistics can be, it merely gives us a frozen picture – or more precisely, a ton of pictures, given that firms are very different from each other, and in trying to find the main traits there are many possible variations. It is much more difficult to discern the principles of property flows from these pictures than, say, for a football statistics fan to understand the intricacies of game strategy at the level of players and coaches. It is harder because the economy is more complex than football, as the game, in contrast to the workings of a firm, can be watched. The field will always be the same size with the same number of players who are all playing by the same unified set of rules, the violation of which will cause the game to stop immediately. Of course, one can play with the bookies, armed with football statistics. Likewise, one can play on the stock exchange after studying economic statistics, but statistics alone won't be enough to understand the principles of the market game. Personally, I am not aware of any other way to get in the know when discussing the flow of property during reproduction of goods, except for professional knowledge of the principles by which these streams change in firms. I would not take the liberty to say that it is necessary to be in the shoes of an entrepreneur (the world is not without smart people), but it is highly desirable to try to get into this hide, at least mentally. Conversely, focusing on the priority of statistics is a dead end (let's stress it only for the theory since the usefulness of statistics for analytics and business management, not to mention managing a national economy, is difficult to overestimate).

The following considerations (they will slowly unfold throughout this box) actually relate to price formation, but they will be strung on the axis of doubt (in the simple sense that we begin with them and finish with them). The doubt is about the need for extended logical chains that are common in theoretical economic literature. In these chains, authors typically add excursions to jurisprudence, sociology and other related disciplines, or digress to engineering problems, climate, politics, etc. Despite the fact that each link leaves little doubt of what an intelligent author wants to say, in general it creates a headache. Whenever a small problem leads to a headache, one can classify it as a theoretical "art house", an ivory tower or something similar, with all due respect to the author. This is not the logic of theoretical economics mainly because this is not *economic* logic. We surmise that economic logic, both theoretical and practical (if the latter is deficient, one has to part with money, making it a powerful learning experience), is designed in exactly the opposite manner. One starts with a headache and, through setting priorities and applying accents, gets to a set of *actions*.

At times, the complexity of the logical chain of reasoning is exaggerated in the practical economy as well (or else business would be the exclusive domain of high intellect types with no room for those stereotypical "New Russians" – they may be simple-minded and naive, but they know arithmetic well and can read other people to anticipate their actions in certain situations). With a disclaimer that an aphoristic style always contains some conventionality, we can say that those who can precisely plan just one move ("what happens if I do this?") can be entrepreneurs; if they can plan two moves, they can eventually build big businesses; and if they can plan three moves, there is no limit to their future in business. One easy-to-understand and appealing example is stock-market trading (up or down). However, if we want to stay in science and not accidentally cross to alchemy, here's a more correct two-move example from the real economy. First, as we said, "what happens if I do this?" i.e. how will prices change (for example, with a different production volume), and how will people react to it both inside and outside the firm? Correspondingly, the second step may be: "what are my actions in response to this reaction or absence thereof?" Reflections on the second question may lead to various options, ranging from correcting the initial step to expanding the strategic planning horizon. This will appear as a combination of decisive actions (looking risky to an outsider) and, vice versa, cautionary actions (at the moment when an outsider may believe it is a good time to hit the accelerator).

You may have the impression that we have jumped over to purely abstract thinking, reducing entrepreneurship to a sort of chess game. This is not exactly the case, so let's get to the root of it with the help of the famous expression, "Don't put off until tomorrow what you can do today." Many years ago, while thinking about my weird life, I realised that whenever I did something useful, I was guided by this simple motto. There are no universally applicable aphorisms and in this case the irony is lurking too ("haste makes waste"), but consistent application of the first one over time helps reduce the likelihood of the materialisation of the second one. As in any other job, there is a lot of routine in entrepreneurship and if you do something today, you'll have more time tomorrow. Also, before you do anything, you take time to think about it – and not in the rapid-play mode, but calmly. And when you follow this method, some small consequences (first and foremost, interactions with other people) clarify your reflections on the "moves" that we talked about in the last paragraph (they can even be modified with some degree of visibility, because "tomorrow's deadline" is not here yet). The most useful consequence is that your brain learns to function in a *timely planning* mode. When I promised in the Introduction to tell something new to each reader, I certainly did not mean this boring paragraph (try to read it to your child and maybe you might even notice the very moment when it flies right over their head). But I just had to say a few words about the vicissitudes of entrepreneurial work, as many do not even fathom the fine line that sometimes separates the "lucky" from the "failures". I often watched "race cars", calmly and without slowing down, bypass their competitors on a sudden turn while the rival drivers, tyres screeching, moan the timeless like the race itself, “Well, who knew?!”

Let’s return to pricing. It complicates the exercise of getting into “the entrepreneur’s hide”, which is quite useful for a researcher of fundamental economic laws. As we have already stated, *it is pricing that reveals if the accents were put correctly while analysing situations in a practical economy.*

One of the reasons for paying inadequate attention to pricing is that, as a rule, the spectrum of a firm’s activities and, accordingly, the areas for entrepreneurs to focus on are much wider. For example, there might be a developer in the firm who comes up, figuratively, with a radio, while everyone else is still using smoke signals, and this firm may command the whole market. Here’s a real example from the 1990s. While an “ordinary” post-Soviet entrepreneur is forced to borrow hard currency from petty usurers at 5 per cent a month, a “well-connected” one takes a half-billion-dollar loan at the symbolic interest rate at the commercial bank and buys entire industries. These extreme examples (we can think of some more) demonstrate that pricing by itself does not describe entrepreneurial activities. We’ll touch upon this topic in our thesis “*Excessive stratification* ...”, though it will look more like a discussion between the author and the readers rather than a narrative from “inside the entrepreneur’s hide”.

In the most successful firm I have ever managed, I tried several times to delegate pricing (at the top, initial level, not just within certain preset price bands) to the most astute workers. By the way, some of them have since made successful entrepreneurs themselves. Then, I stopped running these experiments, as they invariably ended up in either loss-causing mistakes or confessions that it was unexpectedly hard to line up the key factors into a simple-looking but sufficiently precise hierarchy. Even a talented worker needs experience, then pricing takes place intuitively. The problem is that nobody is eager to put an established business in danger for the sake of bringing up future entrepreneurs, to say nothing of future theoretical economists.

Moreover, the effectiveness of such an upbringing has natural limitations. To understand why, let’s recall the timeless Pavlovian dog: the entrepreneurs will develop better pronounced conditioned reflexes, as every decision they make, unlike those made even by some top-ranking hired workers, will be *fully* reflected in their property increment or loss. The italics in the previous sentence are not an educational moment ("so that they know their proper place"), but an arithmetic refinement. Reward or punishment for an employee, even when the scale is adjusted, will never fully reflect the real *ratio* and the real *significance* of their good or bad decisions, and therefore will *not* be properly reflected in the conditioned reflexes being formed.

Therefore, even if the reader agrees with the central role of pricing, here we can only make some important generalisations:

- The indication of general *pricing priority*[134] for entrepreneurial decision-making *in the competitive market*, be it long term or short term.
- The importance of defining, case by case, the key factors that influence pricing. With the accents set correctly, in most cases there is no need to calculate any mind-blowing combinations for many moves ahead. With incorrect accents, the firm starts to experience difficulties and then managers are often forced to scramble in order to remedy their own, often barely noticed, mistakes.

The truth is that I don't know how to lay out the pricing algorithm "from a clean sheet". Perhaps some marketing specialists know how to do it. As for mere mortals, they compare, for example, a new product with a similar one that was priced earlier and then try to see how the new situation differs from the one experienced before. On our quest for truth, the word "experienced" sends us not to a piece of paper with a mechanically calculated algorithm, but to the mysterious workings of our brain. By "uploading" a new situation to the brain, for example, I was moving (in simple cases, it happened faster than you will read this phrase in parentheses) some

[134] The word "priority" sounds harsh and I have been asked more than once if pricing is really more important than strategy, production volume, product line-up, worker qualifications, etc. Without pricing, everything listed here will be "dead". Thus, we are talking about the main thread connecting all other components and not about "the biggest building block".

mental slider along an imaginary supply price scale until the brain "told" me, "Here."[135]

As you may guess, in many relatively simple situations I trust my brain when building theoretical logic as well. Of course, in this case, no numbers, schemes or revelations appear, either in a dream or in reality. Mainly, there is a rather quick, "from the point of view" of my brain, pruning of versions that do not match a real situation.[136] An additional difficulty is that not all these versions are absolutely false: there are situations and situations. However, it is much easier to highlight the nuances distinguishing one situation from another when we already know these, even if only intuitively, and subsequently decipher (if necessary) and categorise. For alternative calculations (even by the best minds) performed without the primary "database", the multitude of factors to take into account can be unreasonably high.

The above paragraph has been leading us to the thought that multiple logical moves in theoretical economics are also naturally suspicious to me. At times, we have much more detailed discussions about some particular moments and they would, in turn, require some chains of logical reasoning (as a rule, these chains are short, but whenever we talk about some stubborn theoretical errors, the size of our narrative may explode). As for the constructive logic, it is relatively simple (any complexity of understanding is caused mainly by the influence of stereotypes). For example, note that in our thesis "*Psychology and rationality in theoretical economics ...*" there is some fundamental theoretical logic.

---

[135] We mean the new reference price. Volume discounts, etc. can be handled by the sales and marketing department.

[136] For example, you might have noticed that priority of demand in firms, despite the fact that we used it in the Introduction as one of the highlights of this study, does not play a major role in building the main theoretical model. This bodes well with the difference in theoretical importance of macroeconomic and microeconomic relationships in general. Understanding this priority helps to avoid misconceptions and, looking up all the cases where we revisited this priority, we can be sure it was used in this manner. You may also remember our refusal to use transaction, marginal and opportunity costs. These are the most obvious examples, but generally speaking, the book is mostly devoted to clarifying certain erroneous ideas. Not that intuitive understanding can replace reasoning in the final text, but that practical experience helps intuitively avoid many pitfalls while building some promising versions.

> However, we have enough fingers on one hand to enumerate its main postulates, from the ancient times to our PCM, as they do not exceed five. This must be the only example in our study – the example of *pivotal* logic of universal development laws of the *Homo sapiens*' economy, all the way from basic instincts to basic cost regulators – where we do apply multiple logical moves. In other cases, I see no reason for this complexity, as it creates weak links. There is nothing new in this, as since medieval times this principle has been known as Occam's razor.

Let's return to our main characters. The businesses of Adam, John and Michael have been growing. They open or buy new locations, use branding to strengthen their leading positions, issue stock and expand into new markets. However, there is a flip side of the coin, one that we have already touched upon and one of the key points of our study, namely the growth of coordination costs in a large firm. Under the financial system of capitalism, large firms can to some extent avoid the negative consequences of this growth or at least postpone their occurrence, since the existing financial system creates certain privileges for them. With the elimination of such privileges after the transition to the PCM, many such firms simply would not survive competition with more compact private firms *except in cases* where business expansion leads to significant technological advantages (to put it bluntly, when engineering solutions are prioritised and most often this can be observed in manufacturing). Overwhelmingly, large and especially large integrated firms are cumbersome with bloated costs (including credit liabilities) and bloated compensation funds while their products periodically fail quality standards.

Large (integrated) firms are very similar to socialist enterprises. They are de facto managed by hired management, the same as under socialism, and somewhere very high up there is Adam in the rank of a "minister" (more often, the whole "cabinet of ministers"). In most large integrated firms, there is no trace of that former private entrepreneur – frugal, knowledgeable about the production process, and not hesitant to punish the negligent and acknowledge and promote talented workers. Even if the owners of such large firms are willing to be constantly on the road, visiting numerous locations and plants, they still won't be able to get all the details to the desired depth. No analytical overview is a substitute for a personal, no-rush perception. Abstract, formalised information cannot replace the data perceived through human senses and processed by the brain almost subconsciously.

We have already discussed all this in detail and, as a theoretical generalisation due at this point, note that some uncertainty of coordination costs (for example, it's impossible to accentuate precisely) is akin to the uncertainty of "pink-coloured glasses" that are the root cause of the overproduction crisis. At the heart of both coordination costs and the crisis of overproduction lies *the desire to property increment*. Without this desire, without such a powerful spike of energy, living things would not have had any economy. The theory of Keynes is both complex and vulnerable because while concentrating on this "volcano of passions", he was also trying to describe both the eruption and its negative aftermath by using hard-to-formalise psychological categories.

Considering the large number of psychological assumptions, the theory of Keynes is markedly personal. It shows the master's touch to an extent beyond expectations (possibly due to my theoretical thinking brought up on Marx's logical reasoning, I appreciate depersonalised logic, regardless of my own desires and qualifications). Among the fields of intellectual effort, there is nothing more distant from art (as every piece has an imprint of the master's personality, even if history did not keep the master's name) than the fundamental laws of the universe. They do not belong to anyone. They can be understood but cannot be created.

How credit should work in the new financial system and why today's interest rates are not really market rates.

Let's see how money should be raised in the framework of the full action of the "invisible hand" of the market. Any firm applies to one of the private domestic banks and takes a collateralised loan at the market interest rate, denominated in national currency units. The loan is either repaid or refinanced at some rate, or the commercial bank keeps the collateral. Actually, that's all or almost all[137] – nothing but plain old

[137] One other option is selling the commercial bank's loan receivables but only as an intermediate step, after which everything is back to these three main outcomes. For example, the commercial bank is short on liquid assets, so it sells its loan receivables, i.e. the rights to the principal, interest and collateral (if required) to another bank. Here, it is important not to cross the watershed between the existing and new financial systems. It means that in the future only another domestic commercial bank, and not just any other firm (for instance, a special-purpose entity set up by the selling bank to go around the central bank's regulations) or an individual, will be able to buy the loan receivables. Also, this sale should not be accompanied by the issuance of any kind of security with a credit component. If

"conservatism". It is important that there are no other ways to raise capital. The only option is taking out a loan at a private domestic bank, only in the form of national currency and only at the market rate. The responsibility for the loan is very transparent: the borrower takes out a loan at the commercial bank against a collateral and both are liable by their respective property (unless there is a third-party guarantor in the deal). There is no need for other methods, lest we interfere with one basic cost regulator. However, in order to achieve this simplicity, the rights of property owners (firms, banks and the government) in the credit market would need to be limited.[138] To make it clear what rights we are talking about, let's see what other ways to raise money are used by firms today:

- Issuing securities
- Government (backed) loans
- Foreign credits
- Trade credits.

As a rule, these options assume lower effective interest rates compared with the rates offered by ordinary private banks, otherwise there would be no sizeable demand. In the case of higher interest rates, private banks would hesitate to loan the required amounts as they would not be comfortable with the borrower's risk level. In other words, all these

---

the buying commercial bank is not comfortable with the level of risk associated with the quality of receivables, it is welcome to use plain old insurance to hedge it. The only participants in the deal are the licensed commercial banks and, if required, licensed insurance companies. Their ranks will be limited (much fewer than "everyone who has money") and they will highly value their licenses.

[138] This does not mean that with the transition to the market interest rates, the said market participants will only face new restrictions. For example, at the same time domestic commercial banks will get a monopoly on making loans and the state (government) will get a monopoly on the new money. Thus, we are mainly talking about the regrouping of rights, explicit or implicit. As a result of these restrictions, "regular" firms will have more opportunities to compete with large integrated firms. There will be clear winners (the insurance firms) and losers (various financial companies, exchanges and individuals dealing with securities trading). The existing financial system resembles a house of cards, constantly falling apart due to rampant arbitration and motley credit channels, which the authorities are trying to shore up. The new financial system will be a rather solid house, backed up by the "invisible hand of the market", where many of today's financial services won't be required as they are harmful. The new house will be both solid and lightweight, as we are going to substantially lower the costs paid for financial services in the global economy. Still, this house needs a rigid frame, so the outlined restrictions are mandatory.

alternative methods are attractive to borrowers due to lower rates, a relaxed qualification threshold, or both at once. Formally, nothing prevents smaller companies from invoking these arcane procedures. In practice, lower-priced credit goes mainly to large property owners, which leads to further monopolisation (primarily of the sales channels). This trend would have been prevented by one fully fledged, working basic cost regulator, namely the market interest rate.

There is hardly a need to explain why borrowers benefit from lower interest rates and there is no blame on large firms for it. Managers simply have to procure resources at the lowest price possible, unless it is prohibited by law, and it is not their fault that a basic cost regulator is "broken" as a result. There is a need for political decisions to modernise the legal system as a whole. Let's discuss the related processes.

Excessive stratification resulting from property distribution at artificially low prices. Enrichment and competition.

The results of Russian privatisation at the end of the last century are common knowledge. The reform planners initially wanted to organise it "in a fair manner", having distributed the privatisation vouchers at no charge, in order to jump-start free-market relationships. The result was extreme stratification with the emergence of very large owners. I will give one more example from my personal business experience. Our firm, at the time engaged in agriculture and food processing, was going through a yearly ritual of sending applications for subsidised loans to a well-known commercial bank. Indeed, the government was allocating funds to stimulate farming development and the commercial bank was receiving these funds. However, we did not get any of these loans.

Note that no market participants experienced direct losses in either example. Those selling their vouchers were paid in cash and filling a stack of forms once a year was not a burden for our firm (at the same time, we did not have high hopes for subsidised credit anyway). However, at the level of the entire national economy (many other businesses were also applying for subsidised loans), what was planned did not correspond to the outcome, despite the vastly different scope of these examples. Here, we could have pointed a finger at law enforcement, given the large-scale fraud and other criminal offences during privatisation. Still, there is also an objective component, which is the subject of our consideration. Excessive stratification resulting from property distribution at artificially low prices appears to be a natural consequence and thus it cannot be entirely avoided, even with a high level of state control.

This applies to both free-market and administrative-planning models. In either case, this distribution of property is often accompanied by corruption. However, in the second case, this property is washed out to the black market, helping law enforcement track the illegal movement of property. Under the free-market model, the redistributed property is changing hands legally.

There is an additional technical difference. In the administrative-planning economy, the arrival of artificially cheapened property on the black market creates large owners (for that system), many of which would not have otherwise existed. In the market economy, "money comes to money", as existing large owners further enrich themselves.

We'll consider this additional enrichment in the free-market economy as "non-market and criminal", with a disclaimer that formally these situations look legal and there is only an implicit criminal component. Here, we won't even try to classify all the cases of non-market and criminal enrichment, leaving it to some experienced lawyers instead of economists. We are more interested in the economic details of the processes accompanying property distribution at artificially low prices.

Using arithmetic, it is easy to understand how entrepreneurs enrich themselves in this case. It is one thing to buy, say, resources at market prices and use these resources to add something to earn a profit, but it is quite another to get these resources at a discount. In the latter case, the profit is already contained in the price difference for resources and all it takes is not to lose this price advantage. The question is: why do some succeed doing it this way and some don't, given that everybody is seeking to buy (or lease) resources and pay less than competitors?

The fact is that the result of property distribution at a price lower than the market average has a weak correlation with the ability of beneficiaries for economic *management* proper. Most of such property will be distributed among people highly talented for property increment in general. There are indeed many entrepreneurs among them, but not only this sort of person. Someone can become rich even with a poor understanding of a market economy and by having, for example, political or legal talents instead, i.e. strong abilities in other methods of managing people. It is not always illegal, but in this case we talk mainly about corruption, when the ability to establish connections or use legal loopholes plays a paramount role. Unfortunately, the problem of corruption can only be solved by political methods.

A purely economic difficulty lies in the fact that cases of systemic property distribution that are most typical for capitalism, i.e. bypassing the market interest rate, do not have such an odious character with a noticeable criminal tint, like the two examples at the beginning of the thesis, where it is also impossible not to notice the role of the state. The indicative, albeit for some an unexpected, example of non-market enrichment without a criminal overtone is an IPO of securities. Both in everyday life and in economic literature, the issue of shares by a firm going public is commonly idealised. Someone interested in the economy can disdain derivatives, but at the same time treat the issue of shares like it were Caesar's wife – above suspicion. We'll talk more about this in our theses on securities, but for now let us return to the abilities of entrepreneurs.

The difference between the talents of a manager and an entrepreneur is understood in everyday life approximately as the difference between a talent for economic management and a talent for enrichment (in turn, we know that the decisive theoretical difference is lurking not in their talents but in their degree of responsibility). Distinguishing these abilities between entrepreneurs (and accordingly, between the firms they founded, even if the full correlation is diluted as firms grow) is hard and it may seem an impossible task. However, we have a good "road sign" to distinguish economic management from all other methods of enrichment. It is called *market competition*.

There is a wide spectrum of views on how the economy works but there are some things that all, or nearly all, economists agree upon. In this case, it is economic competition – the more intense it is, generally the better it is for the national economy. In passing, note that the known negative attitude of economists towards excessive stratification among property owners is also largely due to the fact that excessive polarisation of property indicates the lack of competition in a given national economy. One of the most important reasons for the lack of competition is corruption, which, as already noted, can be reduced only by using political methods.

It is easy to see that the more intense the competition, the *better* the quality of management in companies operating in competitive conditions, but conversely, the *weaker* the ability of each individual firm to increment its property. Simply put, the more crowded the marketplace, the more precise and energetic maneuvers are required and the lower the average piece of the “pie” that each participant gets. This pie does not grow at a rate high enough for everyone to be satisfied.

The ability of entrepreneurs for economic management is more important for the national economy (or for society, if you like) than their talents for self-enrichment in general, although the latter may be more important for the entrepreneurs themselves.

Every entrepreneur wants to wake up a monopolist, if only in some regions, if only in one goods’ group and if only for a limited time. So, entrepreneurs strive to ensure that the marketing phrase “Here and now is the best thing!” becomes a reality and buyers, with all the choices available to them, really first consider the goods offered by the entrepreneurs’ firms. In the real economy, without such a local (by place, industry and time) monopoly, you will not get rich. This conclusion, barely distinguishable from the outside, is an important incentive for entrepreneurs. In the conditions of a *competitive market* (later we’ll see whether additional clarification of the degree of competition is required here), there are three main tools: competing on price (lowering costs accordingly), product quality and offering novelty products. The incentive that we mentioned forcefully focuses the efforts of the producers on these tools. This is an important moment for civilisation’s development (as all three tools are tightly linked to technological progress) and for the competitiveness of the national economy.

Everything is logical and wonderful, but economists and modern public administrations, well aware of the continuing importance of the eternal aspirations of entrepreneurs to become champions, should realise that the desire of businesses to achieve a monopoly status must have the distinct shade of the pursuit of an unattainable carrot. If you let any firm fully enjoy their monopoly status, everything else turns less rosy.

We are already familiar with the coordination costs that are *inevitably* rising with business consolidation. This is especially true for the firms controlling a significant part of a market sector that in turn *inevitably* involves some degree of horizontal and vertical integration. With a mature state of the classical economy’s instruments, i.e. under our PCM model, coordination costs form a natural barrier for large firms to control the market by reducing their competitiveness.

This is the time to clarify that we meant precisely the PCM model when talking about costs, quality and novelty products as the three essential elements to achieve the desired local monopoly. In the existing formation, there is a fourth factor, which we started talking about in the thesis "*Division of labour and coordination of labour (conclusion) ...*". The expansion of business helped by money raised bypassing the market interest rate (for example, through an IPO) allows you to control a more significant part of the market. In the existing market, the visible deterioration of the firm's competitiveness may not occur. But *inevitably*, there will be a subtle accumulation of systemic costs in the entire national economy and in the global economy as well. The reason for this is precisely that there was no cutting of excessive costs at the lower level, i.e. in the competition between firms.

Trade credit.[139] Retail chains.

Even those sharing my views may doubt the suggestion to prohibit trade credit.[140] It is one thing to restrain "damned bankers and financial dealers", which is likely to be perceived rather favourably with the only difference being opinions on how exactly to do it and how far to go. But it is another thing completely to restrain producers of goods, whose lives are already "hard enough". The last case may seem fraught with some destructive consequences and technically impossible to do.

The prevalence of trade crediting in the modern economy is striking. A large mass of finished goods is being stored in warehouses before being shipped, gradually making its way to retail outlets and ending up on store shelves. Commercial banks are involved in providing loans for these operations but a trade credit loan – or, as it is called in everyday life, a deferred payment – is more prominently featured in settlements for

---

[139] Here, we would prefer to use "commodity credit" as an exact theoretical term, as it reflects the fact that commodities are used as credit. However, we use the established term "trade credit", given the narrow meaning of "commodity" as "raw material" in contemporary English.

[140] Back at the beginning of Chapter 1, thesis "*The multiplication of credit deals ...*", we clarified that "credit is money". At that point, you were unlikely to seek faults, classifying this statement from its context as something related solely to the banking system's technological particulars. However, looking for faults would be warranted, as under capitalism – then, we were talking about the existing banking system – not only money but also money surrogates and other basic types of property, like goods, can serve as credit. Conversely, under our PCM, the phrase "credit is money" is ultimately refined.

described deals within a microeconomy (as opposed to the deals at the junction of a microeconomy and households). One of the reasons is the dominance of large retail chains in the market for finished goods that puts manufacturers and wholesalers in front of a very simple choice: either they accept all conditions (deferred payment, "entry fee", retro bonuses, other marketing discounts), or their goods will not make it to the store shelves of these networks.

The dominance of large retail chains is not part of the beneficial development of the market economy but rather part of the consequence of the capitalist financial system's development. One of its main features is neglecting interest rates as one of the basic cost regulators. When retail chains assume the role of credit (or in this case, more precisely, deposit) institutions in relation to the rest (the difference to commercial banks being that retail chains do not offer to put any deposits while their suppliers are forced to extend trade credits to them), some aberrations arise. Retail chain costs are poorly regulated. Moreover, they spread over to trade counterparts. Let's briefly describe how competition works: the "invisible hand of the market" rewards manufacturers that produce the best products. At the same time, it limits or even removes others from the market. More precisely, this is how it should work if the legal system fully protects the "invisible hand of the market". The encouragement of large companies is typical of capitalism: the larger the horizontally integrated chain, the harder the terms it can dictate to its suppliers, and the larger the supplier, the easier it can handle these terms. Small businesses find it difficult to get into retail chains, no matter how good their product is. There is a substitution – the best product doesn't win the market but rather "money makes money". Of course, the goods displayed on the shelves of chain stores are also subject to competition, but this competition is not "organic" as it is formed by retail chains themselves.

If retail is monopolised by large chains, the *Perfectly* Competitive Market will never happen. If the sales of final goods are ruled by monopolies, they will tailor the rest of the market to fit themselves. This market will cut out a significant number of medium-sized producers, since they will not meet the requirements of the chains. However, large companies will be able to carry on since they personally deal with their monopoly retail partners. There is little choice, as at the retail store you can only buy what is on the shelves. So, this aggregate "sausage" (leftover goods) will be slowly fed to buyers. Of course, one can set up another bureaucratic squad that will determine how many retail locations hit a "monopoly threshold" and how many do not. However, a better solution is to leave this all to a basic cost regulator: the interest rate. In the end, owners have varying abilities for economic management. Where one owner can set up and manage a hundred competitive stores, another will not even have access to a couple.

When the principle of market interest rate is implemented under a PCM, it will put a barrier against the dominance of large retail chains. If you remember, in our new system only private banks will have the right to issue loans. This principle also removes trade credits from the practical economy. This means that chains will have to pay for deliveries of goods immediately (whether they will need to take a bank loan for this or not is less important).[141] If retail chains follow this principle, the goods will flow into their stores, otherwise they will not. A timely payment to a large extent breaks the link between the large merchants and suppliers of goods, shifting the focus from the creditworthiness of suppliers to the attractiveness of their goods to buyers. Retail chains will now be vitally interested in not going broke with a pile of stale items. In turn, the emphasis on representation of the shelved goods will shift between big suppliers and smaller companies in favour of the latter due to their textbook flexibility in considering actual demand from buyers. Note that we are talking about a gradual shift in focus as this new formation develops, and not about the total bankruptcy of large suppliers as they will still be of value to the chains.

Before we see what is going to change in the retail chains themselves, let's note what will not change. Fundamentally, the format of individual stores will not change, as supermarkets, i.e. large stores (we emphasise not networks but individual stores), will still be convenient for both customers and store owners. After the release of the previous book, I had to face the impression by even some seasoned economists that the author was calling for breaking plants into workshops or devolving from large supermarkets and shopping centres to stalls. Apparently, this was the case when I did not find the right balance between the succinct terminology and the actual volume of presentation.

---

[141] At the very beginning of Chapter 1, while talking about the payments made by using bank cards, we found out that at present in the combined credit and payment system, the gap between selling goods and getting paid may span several days. This is not a major problem for retailers, but they still effectively issue credit to buyers (more precisely, to the commercial banks participating in this chain). In the unified payment system, this gap will shrink to minutes, removing this technical problem altogether.

Of course, there was nothing like that in my thoughts. The sizes of both firms and individual enterprises are dictated by the level of technology and market requirements regarding the optimal cost level. This is how it is now and how it will remain. However, under the new formation, the influence of the "invisible hand of the market" (basic cost regulators) will be more pronounced. This will happen in the framework of further *personalisation* of responsibility for the costs created. With all that, we do not construct anything very sophisticated or artificial here. In this case, while talking about the retail chains, we merely bring the credit mechanism to its natural order. Any parties that need to borrow money (retail chains, in this case) obtain it *directly* at the licensed commercial banks at the market rate typical for a given sector of the national economy and bear *direct* responsibility for this credit. This minor reform in one given retail sector will cause a major landscape shift. We are not going to see the downsizing of single enterprises (i.e. shrinking supermarkets into "stalls" and manufacturing plants into "shops"), as their optimal size is determined largely by technological requirements. It is the large integrated companies that are going to shrink, as the excessive coordination costs intrinsic to them will be revealed.

After the transition to a PCM, the large retail chains – for example, those with *big box stores* – will have fewer stores on average, leading to an increase in the number of companies competing in the market. It is one of the simplest forecasts I have ever made. There is also a simple answer to the following question: Why would the chains, however small, remain at all? Why wouldn't they split into single stores or small firms? This is because they shrink to the level where the economies of scale from combining several stores will compensate the labour coordination costs that inevitably arise with managing large collectives of people working at different sites. That is, before the coordination costs decrease to an acceptable level, there will be a noticeable tendency to shrink a large business. By the way, here we do not have fundamental differences with Coase, except with the terminology used.

Not all trade credit deals happen within retail chains and here seller financing comes to mind. Machine building is an important part of the real economy but this does not excuse it for overproduction through bypassing market interest rates. I have witnessed plenty of cases where a firm is slowly going bankrupt upon having leased brand-new equipment (the lessee often has a false feeling that it is "nearly free"). This is especially dangerous for absentee owners who stay away from the production process.

Rest assured that the classical market economy has all the necessary mechanisms to help businesses obtain the equipment they need. A bank loans money to a firm looking to buy equipment, the firm pays the equipment supplier (actually paying less than in a traditional seller financing deal, as the seller is paid upfront) and makes instalment payments to the bank over the lease term. The commercial bank may deny the loan if the equipment deal is not considered worthwhile or reliable. It is likely that some commercial banks will naturally specialise (by forming a strong team of banking specialists in this area) in equipment-financing deals. Then, the potential lessee's reasoning will be backed up by the reasoning of the specialists at the commercial bank who have experience servicing these deals.

In the case of retail chains, a prohibition of trade credits will lead to the development of market mechanisms and lower costs, thanks to the easily understood de-monopolisation process. The benefit of prohibiting equipment-seller financing (with instalment purchase) is not so obvious. The theory is nice, but who would be worse off if we made an exception for equipment financing, allowing the equipment sellers to continue issuing trade credits? Even if some answers are not difficult to formulate, a comprehensive understanding can be achieved only at the level of systemic consequences for the national economy.

For instance, one possible answer goes as follows: violations of trade credit regulations will lead to (a) violation(s) related to going around the market interest rates; and (b) violation(s) of the payments discipline. Both will cause increased costs in the national economy. The situation may develop in the following (deliberately exaggerated) way. Today, there is a news broadcast about a commercial bank not extending credit to an enterprise, while equipment-seller financing is not allowed (hungry children, silent parents and an interview with an expert). Tomorrow, equipment-seller financing is allowed. The day after tomorrow, the national economy will experience a tremendous growth in pseudo-financing. In a system where what's allowed is clearly separated from what's prohibited, such as the credit and payment system under a PCM, the commercial banks and the central bank will manage credit and payments supervision functions naturally. As soon as legitimate loopholes appear (driven by the best intentions, of course), these functions would require the commercial banks to increase their costs substantially. However, this may not be entirely feasible despite the central bank's requirements.

The deals originated by one single firm *in the scope of national economies* transitioned to a PCM can be roughly presented with their relationship to the nearest node of the credit and payment system (see, for example, *Letters of credit* ... below). Of course, this system won't control the quality of the supplied goods, but it will maintain a high level of accountability by ensuring that *with cashless payment* the quantity shipped corresponds to the sum paid for it. Simply put, a firm will get paid upon having shipped the goods and vice versa. Over time (as some time will be required to learn and understand how the system works), this will allow firms to save money on deal protection (including legal documentation) and make their financial (first and foremost, credit), logistics and production planning easier.[142] With loopholes, the effect of these savings will be diminishing.

Trade credit (continued). Accounts receivable as the beginning of an overproduction crisis. Credit discipline as a mandatory condition for the Perfectly Competitive Market.

I'll tell a simple story that will help us find ourselves "inside" the economy and usher in some important conclusions.

Back in 2008, when most of the world was already in crisis, the Russian economy was doing relatively well. By the middle of the year, the public's perception of the surprising stability turned into euphoria, at least with a humorous shade of misunderstanding. Of course, not everyone shared this exuberant optimism. I periodically exchanged views with my fellow Moscow State University economics graduate Andrey Makogon. In the spring of that same year, he said he had developed a firm impression about the systemic deterioration of the economic situation, despite its perceived stability. By the end of the summer, he was more categorical ("this should start any moment now") and in September the decline did start. He based

[142] We can say it in a simple way, carefully using ethics terms – this will be the economy marked by trust (in deals). The lowest "mistrust costs" (expenses for lawyers, physical security, state control organs) will be in a hypothetical "economy of siblings". In the real world, the mistrust costs tend to be lower in small, ethnically/confessionally uniform countries. The high level of trust between people under socialism deserves a special mention. At times, there is an interesting combination of factors known, for example, as "Basque socialism" or "Scandinavian socialism". An elevated level of trust in the PCM economy will have, in our understanding, another (technical, rational) foundation.

his conclusions on the unusually persistent decline of sales, in terms of money and volume, at the firms of various sizes and industries. As an experienced banking specialist, Andrey observed this decline of many clients of the commercial bank where he worked.

In these cases, the economists rightfully say that firms see their credit ratings deteriorate, paving the way further to explain the reasons for bank problems due to the increase in the share of the non-performing loans. The deterioration in firms' ability to repay loans is often associated with problematic sales. The chain of causal relationships is as follows: problems with sales lead to the deterioration in a firms' ability to fulfil its loan (repayment) obligations. This deterioration harms creditors (commercial banks) and can snowball into imbalances in the entire financial system, causing problems even at previously stable firms and commercial banks. In this case, we follow Andrey by moving in the opposite direction, inside this chain of cause-and-effect relationships.

Here's another bridge leading to the bottom of the problem: with trade credits, the sales process is split between shipping goods to the buyer and a delayed payment.[143] On one hand, the firms do not extend trade credit to random counterparts, and thus they consider the goods "sold" once they have been shipped and proceed with preparing further shipments while counting on the funds booked as accounts receivable. On the other hand, receiving money from customers still remains the most important moment – if this takes too long, a firm may experience (potentially catastrophic) liquidity problems. As a result of this practice, the indicator of the level of accounts receivable is vitally important. Therefore, the unusual and persistent deterioration (increase) of this indicator at several companies in a modern economy dominated by trade credits enabled Andrey to predict the subsequent chain of events, up to and including the crisis.

In the end, we found nothing magical in Andrey's logic: accounts receivable → sales → borrowing ability of the companies → stability of the commercial banks → crisis. As for me, I failed to draw any

[143] A deal is considered completed once it is paid for. In lease deals, payment and delivery usually happen at different times (at least, in the real economy). Conversely, in the case of a purchase and sale deal, we subconsciously imagine some simultaneous bilateral movement of property, like it happens in an old marketplace. A trade crediting deal is a surrogate one, having features of both credit deals, and purchase and sale deals. With a high level of credit discipline under a PCM, all surrogate versions of the purchase and sale deal will be largely removed, as delivery and payment will happen as close to each other as possible.

fundamental conclusions from my first discussion with Andrey in the spring, even after having noted that his conjectures were important ("Yeah, here's another interesting piece of information, yet there is so much going on every day in the market and I am not so good with analytics to sort it all out"). Still, when – by the end of the summer after talking to Andrey – I had an epiphany and scrambled to warn my closest business allies about the coming "winter", they just shrugged. It is likely that this break in the knowledge-sharing chain was ubiquitous and it was too late to lock the stable door once the horse had bolted.

Besides Andrey's pronounced abilities to classify facts, note one simple moment. As he was always working with the same group of the bank's clients, he was alarmed by the increase in the accounts receivable indicator that could not be explained merely by management drawbacks at these respective firms. What we called a broken chain of knowledge sharing is related to the fact that Andrey sensed this information and did not receive it mechanically by, say, plugging numbers into a computer. It would have been more difficult for other people who had only formal knowledge of the commercial bank's clients. Of course, some of the input data could be formalised, but next time similar number patterns may be related to a different situation, or, conversely, the same outcome may ensue, though the preliminary information would be different. When the patterns do point to a crisis, the economy may be managed by a different generation that does not have personal experience with these observations.

Our example shows, in particular, why some commercial banks can be ahead of others understanding, or at least feeling, any forthcoming changes, as these banks receive compatible information from different sectors of the economy. However, the example will primarily be useful for us to demonstrate how the market interest rate will counter the development of overproduction crises under our new financial system.

From our example, it is clear that overproduction is slowly accumulating. It is also clearly visible that the split of the sales process due to the use of trade credits can obscure the onset of a crisis. The goods shipped are considered "sold" to some extent and firms (almost invariably) tend to treat any increases in accounts receivable as usual, temporary problems while carrying on with production. Production continues, as increased accounts receivable do not spell radical changes in the national economy. Thus, putting the brakes on production seems to be an unduly serious decision to make.

With the outright absence of trade credit, the retail firms (unless they are part of a vertically integrated structure, i.e. they belong to the goods producer in the scope of the *same* legal entity and trade only the goods *produced internally*) will have to pay immediately. This practice will help stop the accumulation of accounts receivable in the national economy right away. Nowadays, the stores tend to interpret any drop in demand as temporary, especially when they don't run much risk (as a rule, retail chains negotiate the right to return unsold goods to their suppliers). With trade credit outlawed, they either receive goods and pay immediately, or refuse to take deliveries because of decreased sales, which is also visible to their commercial bank. Following the production and distribution chain, this will lead to the situation where the market interest rate will begin to force *some* producers to curtail their output *regardless of their own wishes*, well ahead of any meaningful overproduction. Simply put, a working market interest rate will prevent the entire economy from plunging into the debt pit, normally caused by seemingly harmless and convenient trade crediting. There is also no serious reason to bestow equipment leasing with a privileged status. Without bank credit involved, it appears to be the same trade credit (i.e. goods supplied in exchange for instalment payments) as any other.

There may be a fear that the uncompromising action of our market interest rate will seriously complicate the appearance of new products on the market. There are more psychological fears here than real dangers and everything will be the opposite, at least under a developed PCM. We have already discussed this more than once (you might have missed it due to the lack of anchoring specifically for trading companies), but let's talk about it again. Fears arise from the imaginary situation where a merchant agrees to take novelty goods only if the producer assumes all marketing risks. Just a couple of theses above (in "*Excessive stratification ...*"), we touched upon how this actually works in a *highly competitive* market. It said, in particular, that no big money can be earned without securing a local monopoly in the real economy. Accordingly, companies are forced to focus on the "three pillars" of costs, quality and *new products*. All this also applies to competition between trading firms.

It would be naïve to think that in a highly competitive market one could offer the same goods day in and day out and "quietly wait for retirement". A lot can be achieved this way but not a desired local monopoly. Let's put in a disclaimer that it would also be naïve to think that under a developed PCM, wholesale purchasing *for a single store* would, on the contrary, turn into a speedy kaleidoscope. The stores would always treat new goods with caution, but this would largely apply to the goods of *new companies* that do not offer any fundamental technological novelties but represent an attempt to penetrate the market with a new trademark without corresponding "brainwashing" of potential buyers through massive advertising.[144] The expedited introduction of new goods will be driven by a noticeable increase in the number of trading companies in the market and not by constantly changing the nomenclature of goods offered by a single store.

We have already stated all the fundamental moments, but to wrap it up, here's an essentially technical note that may be helpful for a better understanding of economic processes. A closer look at the structural consequences of banishing trade credits suggests that besides the shrinking of retail chains and large producers, there will be some resuscitation of wholesale trading companies. Any fears that costs would go up as a result largely stem from the prejudice against trading in general ("easy money"). The truth is, wholesale trade has been a potent means of lowering macroeconomic costs forever. This is neither fair nor unfair; it is just the way it works.

Wholesale trading is agile, not burdened by serious capital investments or by the large number of employees that are mandatory for manufacturing and retail industries. When the latter experiences problems due to structural changes in the economy and the industry reacts intrinsically slowly to these changes, the wholesale traders will have an advantage. They can move quickly across the categories of goods, industries and

[144] Sure, advertising is indispensable for sales but in modern times it often gets too invasive. Initially, it was indeed necessary for the economy as a whole, due to the underdeveloped communications infrastructure and corresponding lack of knowledge about possible alternative choices among market participants. Nowadays, when the "grapevine" has been rapidly turning into a "mobile high-speed internet grapevine", massive advertising benefits primarily large marketers, advertising agencies and maybe the celebrities starring in commercials. For ordinary firms, it increasingly becomes a race of mutually increasing, excessive costs. For the national economy, the most unpleasant effect is the unnecessary distortion of market competition, leading to the monopolisation of industries. The competition of goods is being replaced by the principle that "money makes money", with an ever-increasing use of the communications infrastructure. I am almost certain that future generations will gradually cut down on consumption of advertising that cannot be easily tuned out (today, this applies mostly to outdoor advertising and television). It is easier said than done, and there is a quite a distance between realising that "free cheese is only in the mouse trap" and giving up "free" broadcasting.

regions. It is easier to calculate costs (compared with manufacturing) and there is not much in terms of mandatory overheads.

Once the transformation of large retail chains into more compact businesses is finished and the dust has settled, profits of wholesale traders will start to decrease due to various reasons, including the partial return of managing the bulk movement of goods to retail chains. As often happens in life, advantages also have their dark sides. For wholesale traders, this dark side is beneficial for the national economy. Their agility when entering and exiting various sectors coupled with easy-to-understand technological processes leads to extremely high competition. Any excess "fat" is being cut off faster than in other sectors, provided that large wholesale traders are not allowed to use legal loopholes and their connections to come up with a plausible excuse to stifle free competition. However, this disclaimer applies to any sector of the economy.

To be fair, let's note that with the wholesale traders being squeezed out right now, costs technically do decrease, though this is attributed to the development of computer technologies in the same period and cannot be credited to the retail chains and large producers who took full advantage of these new opportunities. Computer technologies have made not just a positive but also a truly revolutionary impact on accounting and logistics (we'll be using this term in its simplest meaning: the organisation and calculation of transportation and warehousing operations). To visualise the influence of logistics on technical cost reduction, let's imagine a picture of preparing a simplified (for a better understanding) trade deal in the future.

Pedro Gonzalez, a purchasing manager in a store located in Tierra del Fuego, launched a computer application searching for the goods he needed to procure[145] and found a small manufacturer in the Balkans. Without leaving his computer, Pedro contacted several logistics firms to find out when the goods could be delivered and how much it would cost, choosing the best possible offer. A logistics firm can use its own transport or contract with other carriers. It will also handle customs clearance. The

---

[145] We should mention "standardisation" at least once in this study. We have not touched upon it, as it is an element of the Rough History (i.e. resulting from actions of the engineers) and so it cannot be directly tied to the particulars of any formation. However, this element is very useful, as standardisation has been and always will be playing a serious role in technological costs savings. Here, the software enabling this search process is assumed to be working with standardised information prepared for potential buyers (alternatively, it needs to have some AI features).

goods ordered by this manager will share delivery routes with other goods, like we share planes and elevators with other people while travelling from our home to a hotel across the globe. In this case, there may be no need for large wholesale trading firms (and likewise no need for temporary structures such as electronic commodity markets which standardise information for their specific region or sector). Thus, Pedro may only need a commercial bank in addition to the logistics firm in this example. This does not mean that in the future there won't be wholesale firms, as there will always be a need for preliminary goods selection and timely delivery. However, these firms may gradually become less prominent. It is important for this to happen solely because of technological evolution. Conversely, today retail chains have displaced some wholesalers primarily due to their trade credit leverage and there is nothing positive in this outright displacement. Once wholesale trading shows signs of life again, this won't signify any progress by itself as there is nothing new in it. Our reasoning demonstrates that decreases in the size of retail chains will happen not only in a simple, "quantitative" way (say, we take a global chain of stores and divide it into ten smaller firms), but also with breaking out some functional areas, primarily into wholesale and logistics firms.

Besides, we saw once again what was meant under the organic increase of physical turnover in our new system. All these links will now work with each other as independent counterparts entering proper deals.

In general, while discussing the essence of changes caused by abolishing the dominance of large chains, besides the just-mentioned increase in physical turnover and therefore the amount of money in the economy,[146] there are some principal moments to consider:

---

[146] Let me remind you of some technical moments that were discussed earlier in the book but might have been forgotten or obscured by a lot of subsequent material. First, the amount of money required by the economy is most precisely determined by the volumes of physical and credit turnovers. Admittedly, this is not always easy to realise, especially when systematic deviations from a rigorous classical model are present. However, a theoretical tie between the amount of money to GDP, national income, gold, other kinds of national wealth, or something else will inevitably lead to obvious or hidden conceptual errors (for example, stereotypes, when particular cases are treated as being theoretically significant). Second, after the separation of the credit and payment systems, the amount of money will increase and its velocity will decrease. There is less money and higher velocity (credit chains) in the combined system, so in crises times when the credit chains break, the demand for money ramps up to the point where the supply of money as credit is insufficient and the government needs to pump more money

- When a buyer (in this case, a store) pays its supplier immediately, the price of this deal will naturally go down and the store's margin will increase. This reflects the fact that the store itself is now responsible for procuring credit for the deal.
- There is no fundamental change in the usual retailers' practice of earning most of their profits on some goods and merely "tolerating" other goods simply because they have to offer a wide and available selection. However, the reaction (price drop) for goods becoming stale will be more pronounced.
- The retail sector will still be dominated by chains consisting of large stores, as these are convenient for consumers. However, this sector will be very difficult to be monopolised by a few national chains.
- The logistics sector will have to be modified, causing a temporary increase in costs.
- The coordination costs in the retail sector will go down but the effect won't be visible outright, given the previous point.
- Increased competition will gradually but inevitably lead to a better quality of goods offered by retail chains (and as a result, better quality in the corresponding sectors of industry and agriculture).
- All marketing relationships between the stores and their suppliers will be likely included in the single price of a deal. Returning substandard goods assumes a payback, but in reality it does not happen often (you need to be careful about picking your goods and your suppliers), especially in cases where wholesalers have already made their selections. In case these or any other "strange" deals become habitual, the store may be fined or closed with its license revoked. (This may seem hard to understand from today's perspective, but our PCM is quite simple in its fundamental principles and any similar irregularities would become clearly visible over time.) It is unlikely that in addition to the deals' control, a developed PCM will also require regulations for anti-monopoly pricing, goods selection or the number of stores. Most of this "dirty work in the trenches" will be performed by the commercial banks. The latter, as we have already noted, won't have much choice – they will have to work with the real economy either closely or very closely.

---

into the economy, An excessive generalisation of these and other particulars of the combined system (for example, in Keynes's theory) may also lead to giving them a fundamental character while reasoning about the factors influencing the amount of money.

In general, a PCM allows the laws of a classical economy to refine some very simple logic to perfection. The monetary resources of a country are at a given level at a given moment (this is not the case under capitalism, but under a PCM this becomes obvious, due to the money issuance calculated within the national economy which is closed for foreign credit). Use of these resources happens (and must happen) only through the commercial banks, only with the personal responsibility of creditors and borrowers (or the co-signers of the latter), and only at the market interest rate. This is what the rational use of resources, plain and simple, looks like to me.

Among other things, it will lead to a visible increase in competition, namely the number of firms, which is beneficial for the economy. The most visible effect for the economy is the increase in the amount of money backed up by physical turnover.

The monetisation of trade credits will also contribute to the amount of money growth by increasing credit turnover. The more money that is servicing the economy for the given GDP level, the more (in general) money issuance there will be under the same level of GDP growth. In turn, this opportunity to increase money issuance without exerting undue inflationary pressure on the national economy will make it possible to either cut back taxes or finance a larger volume of government expenses, depending on the priorities chosen. Therefore, GDP will grow faster while using the same number of resources. Hopefully, you have been paying attention to all of our reasoning, starting with separating the credit and payment systems, so as to not consider this conclusion a mere trick.

Simply put, the gist of our reforms is not only to offer a way to avoid massive crises, but also to demonstrate an arithmetic gain from the consistently accumulated cost savings. The state budget is one of the places where this gain will be showing.

Letters of credit. The “marketplace”. Credit relationships between households. Illicit credit. Advance payments.

Letters of credit will play an important role in our new financial system. Here, we are talking about letters of credit in general (the exact form, be it revocable, irrevocable or some other, will be determined by the central bank), which are used to mitigate a lack of trust in deals. Writing a letter of credit in the new system will not have a mandatory tie to commercial banks. The market participants will be able to originate their own letters of credit using the payment system independent of commercial banks, possibly in some virtual "trust zone". Licensed law and insurance businesses, as well as logistics firms servicing the deal, will have access to it (although it is easy to suggest that logistics firms would not mind lingering in this "trust zone" permanently, albeit in a separate quarter of it – and why not?). The computer systems at the central bank will be *merely* recording the deal, opening the letter of credit after receiving an electronic notification about the receipt of goods from the buyer. We can also suggest cases where the commercial bank lending money to the buyer will want to have greater control over the use of loan proceeds and therefore would issue it in the form of a letter of credit to the seller. Thus, with insurance and logistics companies added, it would be a deal with three parties participating.

Letters of credit alleviate suspicions about both illicit credit in the form of prepayment and trade credit framed as deferred payment. The cheapest way to control credit discipline would be to have a law that a borrower may appropriate any illicit loan proceeds (be it trade or money) while the state guarantees protection for these borrowers. There won't be many volunteers to issue an illicit loan then. If someone wants to participate in credit operations, it would be easier to register a commercial bank and take advantage of the protection by the law than take chances breaking it. Such a rigorous law is better than an army of corrupt "overseers" and it will be known to be taken seriously after the first bankruptcies of those borrowers who promised the law-breaking creditors not to use it.

Active market participants will have to try it for themselves once the above-mentioned law is adopted. This journey will take less time if the government is proactive in warning market participants about the negative consequences of those "friendly loans" in advance and continues to do so thereafter, citing examples of actual illegal credit. The law enforcement will be sure to contribute too, zeroing in on professional "friendly creditors" but I won't elaborate on this here. Let me state my opinion that over time, it will simply be poor manners to ask anyone to loan any significant sums of money, regardless of societal standing.

Any fears that a country will be flooded with illicit black-market loans that would need to be subsequently extorted from borrowers appear to be overblown, at least some time after the law is adopted and the situation normalised. One should not exaggerate the risk appetite on the part of some imaginary "loan sharks" (ostensibly rich but ignorant and fearless at the same time) in a country where all commercial banks are in the business of making loans to the real economy. If an entrepreneur had no luck getting a bank loan, the chances of him/her returning an illegal loan are not 100 per cent at the outset. In addition, there is a lingering danger of illicit creditors falling under the scrutiny of law enforcement (credit security is one of the pillars of the new economy) plus the high probability that a borrower facing a problem returning the loan will ask the authorities to help using the above-mentioned law.

Let's return to the prepayment scenario. If prepayment (full, partial, revolver, etc.) is being made to confirm the serious intentions and solvency of the buyer under our PCM model, then all these variants fall entirely into the scope of letters of credit and then we just need to visit the "marketplace". If, conversely, the seller intends to use prepaid money to produce the goods for this contract, this will be classified as a money loan (under any financial system, the difference is only in legal terminology). In this case, under the PCM system the road leads to a commercial bank, as *only banks have the right to issue loans*.

At present, a simplified version of this scenario goes as follows: a "Big Firm" is issuing a loan (in the form of prepayment) to a "small producer" and waiting, for example, for the harvest time, hoping for the intended use of credit funds by the borrower (checking for the nature of this use creates perennial headaches for the lawyers and finance professionals, as there is no set algorithm for this). After the abolition of loans not issued by commercial banks, the scenario may look as follows: one participant of this planned forward deal contacts a bank in advance and involves the counterpart in these negotiations. The commercial bank then issues a loan to the producer of goods (in our example, agricultural produce) with the "Big Firm" *guaranteeing* the loan.

If the producer fulfils its commitment to supply goods, it pays back the loan to the commercial bank upon the goods having been paid for by the "Big Firm". In the case of a failure to supply goods (depending on the details of the guarantee), the "Big Firm" may, for instance, acquire a low-liquidity[147] collateral from the commercial bank at a pre-negotiated price.

[147] As a rule, low liquidity of collateral acquired following a deal gone awry in the real economy means that some help is needed from a firm specialised in this particular sector in order to get the money back. That firm should include the property (mainly goods, but in some cases, land) initially offered as collateral into the chain work of its operations performed by qualified employees. Quite often, this requires additional investment and an individual approach to the situation (collateral obtained from the real economy is often hard to manage but this risk is

Commercial banks will learn how to use this seemingly complex process to work with low-liquidity collateral (over time, some of these will be treated by the banks as more liquid), solving the chain of non-payments in the microeconomy as a technical driver of crises in the current formation.[148] Gradually, in the framework of the general credit system based *strictly* on a market interest rate, the economy will shift into this new reality.

Securities (theory). Particular moments of leasing land (L←M). Problems of stock compatibility with the theoretical framework of the PCM.

When we talk about the PCM being incompatible with securities, we mean only securities *trading* in the secondary market. For instance, the PCM will not be compromised by having private joint-stock companies without state participation. Concurrently, we also recommend the abandonment of preferred shares, as these securities assume guaranteed income essentially similar to interest income in credit deals.

Also note that securities have practically ceased to be "paper certificates" after their transition to an electronic form. Therefore, we'll include here not only traditional securities such as shares and bonds but also other financial instruments with unnaturally high *liquidity*.

Under our PCM model, paper currency and money in the electronic form (non-cash money) will cease to be the securities (which they are now, to an extent) issued by the central bank and will finally become money (means of circulation) in its pure form. This will happen as a result of the transition to the direct issuance of money facilitated by the division of credit and payment systems. Under gold capitalism, paper money was

---

justifiable, as for every one or two complex deals there may be ten highly profitable deals where the participants fulfil their contractual obligations). If a firm (in our example, the guarantor) can reasonably count on the positive bottom line even in complex deals, the commercial bank may face problems simply trying to liquidate the collateral. If the transaction does not have a qualified guarantor and the bank justifies either a collateral size increase or a higher interest rate through poor liquidity of the collateral, the small producer may not agree with this.

[148] In the simplest version of this chain, the creditor won't receive even a low-liquidity collateral. In our PCM, the mandatory participation of commercial banks in these deals eliminates the threat of non-payment chains while not posing any danger to the payment system. In addition, as commercial banks *inevitably* gain experience (under the PCM model, for the real and the credit sectors, there is no option but to work with each other), the number of bad loans will go down.

represented by IOUs issued by private banks. The subsequent centralisation of paper money production in the hands of the "broad government" has essentially cancelled its original IOU character, but formally, under paper capitalism, paper money is still presented as the central bank's IOUs, contributing to the confusion.[149]

The most important clarification for us is when we are talking about forbidding securities, we mean securities *with a credit component*. Generally, in the new formation, any securities diluting the influence of not only the market interest rate but also the remaining basic cost regulators are harmful. However, these securities are not widespread (and won't be so) due to particular features of the PCM model (for example, due to the simplicity of the currency exchange system). Eliminating them can be treated as a finishing touch, while for us it is important to focus on the fundamental distortions stemming from the use of securities with a credit component.

Bonds are the simplest example of these securities. This example is universally understood, unlike stocks where it is difficult to see both their credit component and the harm they cause to the economy. It is also not difficult to see the credit component in most derivative securities, despite all their sophisticated nature. Sometimes this leads to the principle of "if … then …". For instance, if using credit leverage is taken out of futures contracts, then "these won't be the futures anymore".

At the same time, using securities for trading precious metals and goods in general may remain (considering the system of currency exchanges that we are going to address in Chapter 3). The state has always regulated the trade of precious metals and will continue to regulate it with varying rigor, but this regulation does not stem directly from our theoretical constructs. Let's clarify that in this case under "securities" we don't mean anything but the rights to a certain quantity of metal stored in a vault, regardless of the ability to physically obtain the metal.

These were our general theoretical clarifications. Now, let's dive directly into the theory to sort out the origins of these clarifications and the abandonment of the securities market in general (once again, we mean only those designed for open trading and having a credit component).

---

[149] See thesis "*FAQ: The old central bank versus new central bank …*" in Chapter 4.

The main theoretical idea was expressed in the Introduction – securities with a credit component distort the process of forming the market interest rate as a basic cost regulator. Unlike the classical credit deal that *fixes* and *localises* the responsibilities of each party, raising money using securities dilutes the responsibilities of the borrower and gives creditors excessive influence on the economy through a convoluted and powerful secondary market. A distortion of the interest rate (as well as other basic cost regulators) causes systemic costs that cannot be eliminated by plain competition. These systemic costs contribute to monopolisation processes and periodic overproduction crises. A transition to the market interest rate won't save the economy from crises entirely, but it will make acute currency depreciation crises less frequent and eliminate the most severe deflationary crises and therefore their expansion throughout the world. Outside the crises times, the market interest rate will contribute to de-monopolisation, and promote an increase in competition with a corresponding self-regulation of costs in the national economy and, finally, more impressive growth compared with the existing formation. A mandatory element of all these effects is the abandonment of securities with a credit component.

Let's recall the four basic deals that are crucial for our study, first and foremost for the forming of basic cost regulators. When talking about these basic deals, there is presumably a psychological effect: against the background of many years of concentrating on "labour" ("value") and "production" ("microeconomy"), these alone may seem insufficient. These clichés would not disappear even in view of the authority of Keynes who has done so much work to shift theoretical accents to the macroeconomy. Keynes himself, aiming to introduce "employment" into fundamental categories, over and over again tried to discover that proverbial philosopher's stone: a unit of labour. Therefore, let's recall that exchanges, reflecting a high level of rationality, effectively set the economy of *Homo sapiens* apart from others at the *fundamental economic* level (improvements in the means of production are credited to the *natural* sciences). Price is formed exclusively in an exchange. Therefore, we can derive precise economic equations only from exchanges. It would be logical to suggest that our theoretical attention to the basic, most important types of exchanges (listed below) will help us to draw equally important conclusions:

Purchase and sale: $C \leftrightarrow M$,
Lease: $P \leftarrow M$,
$L \leftarrow M$,
$M_C \leftarrow M$.

As we have already noted, the demise of the slavery formation includes the abandonment of P↔M, the purchase and sale deal. In its theoretical purity, this deal is intrinsic to commodities, so let's formulate it in such a way that by abandoning slave ownership, we give up at the system level the commodity component that earlier applied to people.

This is the simplest way to represent our hypothesis that any further refinement of the economy is tied, among other things, to giving up the commodity component in credit operations, i.e. the securities with a credit component that facilitate *purchase and sale deals*.

Still, we have the L←M deal that requires substantial explanation due to the simple reason that land purchase and sale deals are in use and will continue to be in use in the future (and our PCM is not an exception).

An equivocal understanding of any phenomenon means that there exists an internal contradiction that requires a combination of fundamentally different solutions. This internal contradiction of land is most precisely shown through its "liquidity". We may note that a pair of liquidity components (transportability and reliability), in the case of land, take two extremely opposite positions.

Land (our planet's biosphere, suitable for life and the economic activities of people) is not reproducible. Assuming the priority of land for human life, it determines the ultimate *degree of reliability* of this type of property and therefore the high liquidity of land. We are talking about land's strategic reliability, ever more obvious with population growth and economic development. Over a short timeframe, the prices for various plots of land can fluctuate greatly, depending on their exact location and the time. At the same time, land has a *minimum possible degree of transportability*, which, under most conditions (not counting building dams, for example), can be safely considered as zero. This extremely low transportability of land is the factor that is potentially driving its low liquidity.

The non-reproducibility of land coupled with its priority importance for the human population's existence dictates mandatory restrictions for land property rights in order to safeguard it against monopolisation. The leasing deal is ideally suitable for this. With the lease deal, only money is alienated, while the property being leased (in this case, land) is not. That is, each managing owner receives land from the owner (in most modern cases, from the national community which realises these rights with the help of the state) to manage it as private property with certain restrictions, as nobody gets land as “regular” private property. To understand the limitations of the right to own land, the easiest way is to compare it with the right to goods as private property. With goods, we can (a) export them or (b) destroy them (or consume them entirely). Besides, as a rule, we do not pay taxes on goods after we purchase them, except for a few exceptions such as vehicle taxes and especially real estate taxes which are, to some extent, a hidden form of payment for the use of land. We won’t be able to perform actions (a) or (b) to land and, as a rule, there is a use tax.

Even if the landowner (the national community, or more precisely in legal terms, “the government”) does not exercise its right to terminate a land lease, it can regulate the amount of payment (i.e. rent, under which we mean the land tax). This tax is the only possible method – albeit with all the accompanying bureaucracy – to guarantee against monopolisation of land. We can be sure about this, based on our analysis of coordination costs. As land parcels accumulate in the hands of one managing owner, there will be a moment when these costs start growing. At some point, yet another tax increase (due to inflation or real estate development), either immediately or after an economic downturn, will force this managing owner to part with some of these land parcels. As we have already mentioned, this does not exclude any administrative, anti-monopoly regulation of land sales in cases where there are limited mineral deposits.

As for a “pure” purchase and sale deal (with complete private property alienation, like in the case of goods), it won’t prevent land monopolisation but on the contrary, promote it. Besides, it will contribute to runaway land price increases in high demand areas, hindering any change of ownership in favour of more efficient owners. This is the way it is happening when the land use (or real estate) tax is too small compared with the value of a parcel. Current owners can still afford to pay the tax, despite their low income. With the tax increase, these plots of land (or real estate) will more often be offered for sale at discounted prices, due to the dual effect of expanded supply and shrinking demand (not every owner will be ready to pay higher taxes).

Despite a theoretical (anti-monopoly) priority of the lease deal, land purchase and sale deals are actively used and will be used in the new formation. A complete ban on private landownership and therefore land purchase and sale deals, especially considering the non-reproducibility of land, would greatly increase the national economic costs of land circulation due to the legal red tape and corruption related to hidden sales of land by state employees.

Land by itself, as different from other basic types of resources, has uniquely low transportability that in principle leads to higher property transfer costs. As a result, the liquidity of this basic resource type is lower and its transfer to more efficient owners is more complicated. For example, compare the case of an entire business moving to a different location and settling there with the case of people coming in themselves looking for employment, or one of loan proceeds being deposited into your account with minimal additional costs. Generally, a purchase and sale deal greatly facilitates the transfer of property and liquidity of the latter compared with lease deals, as it does not require negotiating the rights of deal participants for the same property and accompanying control procedures for the safeguarding and return of the property after the lease is up.

We'll be calling the purchase and sale deal that assumes (explicitly or implicitly) its subordination to the lease deal a "service deal" and will write it down in the following way:

$R_{PL} \leftrightarrow M$, where R_{PL} is the right to the primary lease (the right to economic management).

These are the exact types of deals we close when we think that we are "buying land". Even if in legal terms it is reflected as "land purchase", we just buy the right to the primary lease. With civilisation's development on the same planet of a given size, this is more clearly visible. The purchase and sale of the right to the primary lease can be observed for another type of resource, namely people. However, it does not apply that often, with one exception known to me: for the "sale and trading of athletes". Of course, professional athletes are not slaves and hence the expression the "purchase and sale of the footballer Zlatan Ibrahimovic" is merely a shortened everyday phrase, akin to the "purchase and sale of land".

Let's sum up our reasoning on the land deals in the following chart:

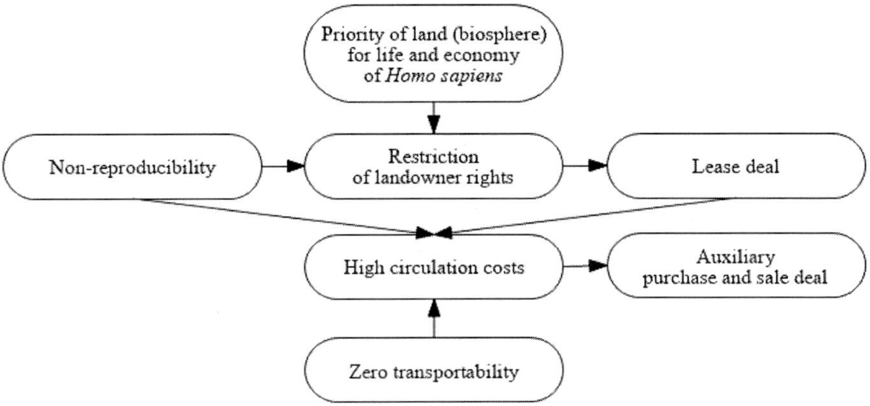

Fig. 2-2

To help explain where R_{PL} came from, let's introduce a simple formula that will also be useful when we talk about stocks:

$R_C = R_L + R_{PL}$, where R_C is the complete right of ownership, R_L is the legal right of ownership and R_{PL} is the right to the primary lease (the right to economic management).

The case of stocks is much more complex than that of bonds. At this point, let's offer some clarifications in two separate parts. First, we are going to point out the characteristics of a credit deal that are present at the issuance of a stock (and *in this form* they are absent when stocks are traded on the secondary market). In the second part, we'll be focusing on other distortions of a classical purchase and sale deal (tied to the non-classical high liquidity of the commodity and money surrogates). Conversely, these distortions are present on the secondary market and absent at the time of the IPO. This is not the last clarification regarding the incompatibility of stocks with the PCM (we'll continue talking about it in subsequent theses), but these are the most important points.

Strictly speaking and unlike a bond issue, a stock issue is not a trivial substitute for a credit deal. A purchase and sale deal is the source of the stock issue – the owner sells part of his/her firm.[150] That is why the vague phrase "raising money" is used in lieu of a precise "borrowing money"

[150] To save a few disclaimers, we are going to discuss the simplest case – *one* owner is selling a *minority* stake in his or her firm.

while talking about securities as a whole. It is still being used, *unlike a regular market purchase and sale deal with a mutual property alienation (where goods and money swap their respective owners)*. In the case of stocks, the money raised from an IPO by the owner is not the owner's absolute property (it belongs to the same firm that is the legal issuer of stock but with a partial change in the ownership structure). By the same token, the share of the firm determined by the stock purchased in an IPO is not the buyer's absolute property. This somewhat vague standing of the new shareholder of the firm (not "absolute" property) is easier to understand using the formula we have written above: $R_C = R_L + R_{PL}$. By purchasing (through buying IPO stock) a legal right to part of the firm, the buyer leaves the right to economic management of the firm in the seller's hands. In return, the buyer receives specific documents (shares that can be traded on the stock exchange) that not only confirm the buyer's legal rights R_L but also have some characteristics of collateral. As we have noted earlier, for someone buying openly traded shares, the essence of the deal lies precisely in this "collateral". Otherwise, one needs to have firm belief in their luck to count on striking gold from their share of the profits, having given one's money to strangers and not having any real leverage over the management of the business. Often, there is also no realistic picture about the company's performance, as published numbers give only partial and chronically late information. This explains, by the way, why private joint-stock firms, with shares essentially not meant for open trading, have a limited number of shareholders.

As a result, the issuance of stock has characteristics of both the purchase and sale deal and the credit deal. In this stock issue deal, the issuer has received the proceeds to manage but without the absolute right to this money, similar to ordinary credit. Meanwhile, the buyer trusted his/her money with other people to manage, in order to get paid. At the same time, the buyer may choose to get the money back (with a profit or loss, but usually at a profit as shares on average appreciate over time) by selling the shares to a third party. Given the massive volume and anonymous nature of trading on the secondary market, the actual return of the money invested into stocks happens unconditionally, like in credit deals. Conversely, had an entrepreneur decided to buy partial ownership or certain production assets of a firm in the real economy and subsequently sell it, it would be a regular purchase and sale deal. There is no trace of the unconditional return of the money invested but merely another deal. If there is an urgent need for cash, the seller would typically lose part of the property, even if the firm's finances have not deteriorated.

A mix of characteristics is typical for surrogate deals, and issuing stock is the most complex case of mingling purchase and sale deals with credit deals among all kinds of issuing securities, save for derivatives.

Let's return to some subtle moments. If our reasoning seemed a bit convoluted ("Well, the stocks do trade"), I can clarify where this may be coming from – specifically, from a lack of trust in our formula, $R_C = R_L + R_{PL}$. If we adopt this formula, it is easy to see that only R_L is being sold and it is changing owners, while R_{PL} remains with the original owner. This points to the mixed nature of the deals *regardless* of consent to add some collateral features to the shares being transferred (understandably, "collateral" here may offend the ear). To me, such an addition seems simply to be the most logical assumption, once we agree on this fact of mixed deals: since the money paid in exchange for shares is not divided into money as payment and money as credit, the transferred shares are not just goods being sold but also something else.

Now, let me try to explain the possible reasons for a lack of trust in our formula in the context of this discussion. It is easy to imagine R_L (as the initial stock offering assumes a change in ownership structure from the outset) but R_{PL} is more challenging. Hopefully, the following simple consideration helps to understand it better. Those who have R_{PL} (in the simplest case, the owners of the controlling stake) have the right to manage *the whole* firm, albeit they are restricted by the articles of incorporation. Examples include determination of (or major influence over) the strategic direction of the firm, selection of its business partners, developing relations and draft contracts with these partners, setting up the management structure (and the cost structure in general), and making decisions on the merits and type of new securities issues. The fact that the firm's management (especially with a widely distributed ownership) is reaping benefits from R_{PL} does not change the nature of this: on the contrary, it emphasises the realism and significance of R_{PL}.

Despite all our clarifications, the reader may still have doubts. Therefore, let's invoke a proof by contradiction by shifting the accent to the secondary market. A share meant for open trading is a commodity and a money surrogate (unless we want to add stocks as a separate, fifth kind to our four basic types of property of *Homo sapiens*). The commodity component stems from the purchase and sale deal, while the monetary component is due to the high liquidity of stocks and other financial instruments. If we deny the credit element in this monetary component, then only the payment element is left (as in a deal, money can be either credit or payment). We know of securities with a pure payment nature, namely cheques. Without denying the existence of a payment element in stocks, I believe that one needs to agree that stocks are closer to bonds than to cheques (especially if we remember about preferred shares that are, in turn, somewhere in the middle between bonds and common shares).

In our case, using these "clarifications" ("closer to this or that", "somewhere in the middle") is justifiable, as it reflects the nature of the surrogates in focus. To my mind, one can rather expect trivial logic while trying to draw exact boundaries (for example, using mathematical constructs). To show that "trivialisation" is not an abstract idea here, let's try to imagine our PCM model with a stock market in it. This is easier said than done (since a good deal of logic in this book would then become contradictory), so I am only going to point out one consequence of this hybrid model. We'll need to revisit the credit issuance of money that is driven, as we remember, by supply and demand (or more precisely, by market demand and administrative supply). We have to account for the surrogates' market while planning for the direct issuance of money, but accounting for commodity (physical) and credit turnovers are two fundamentally different things.[151] Given that we cannot draw a boundary between the commodity component and the monetary component of stocks, any estimate of the margin of error to be used in calculating money issuance seems to be not bold but rather reckless, due to the following reasons.

(The subtle moment.) One natural assumption while thinking about the reasons for fuzzy boundaries between the components of stocks is that *these boundaries may change depending on the specific situation*. In this case, we mean not only the changes stemming from the kind of typical deal (an IPO or transfer of shares to another owner on the secondary market) we focus on (these are easy to see). It is about the differences between specific cases inside typical deals (or between the groups of specific cases, but one way or another, these differences cannot be precisely calculated and thus should not be classified in detail). It is easier for me to come up with this assumption, as I already "know" about possible boundary shifts between components of a service deal that are unique examples of a "legitimate" surrogate (thesis "*FAQ: Services ...*" is

---

[151] We are talking about an order of magnitude difference. In the thesis "*Money alienation (payment) as a moment when property price is formed ...*", there is a detailed description about this difference, in the long technical footnote.

in Chapter 4, where the material is not hardwired to our main text), while the reader likely does not.

One way or another (at this point, we are not going to repeat the contents about services, though it would be beneficial to learn about this subject preliminarily), with a goal of transitioning to some "intermediate" PCM model that would include a stock trading market, we'll end up with three kinds of theoretically distinguishable aberrations that would prevent us from precisely calculating money issuance. The first one is the shadow turnover of cash. This problem is a temporary one and can be solved. Besides, accounting for this aberration is not complicated by the "mystique" of surrogates. The second one is services. A mix-up of purchase and sale deals with people-hiring deals cannot be solved and this has always left (in any formation), and will continue to leave, traces of inflationary effects *in some situations* (in our thesis on services we explain why it cannot be defined *theoretically* with more precision). If desired, this aberration can be estimated using, for example, statistical methods, as the hiring deal is simpler. *The second component (hiring deal proper), unlike the credit component of securities (credit deal), has nothing to do with forming the price of money.* Therefore, *a correction of money issuance will not be required*, as we'll be able to better understand what's happening and where inflation is coming from using simple analytical methods. Once we add the need to account for the securities turnover, we won't be able to understand what's going on and resuscitating the credit issuance of money is back on the agenda.

As our reasoning was taking place in the theoretically murky waters of surrogates, the readers likely had questions for the author. I would counter these with just one, "Do we really need all this?", meaning whether we need to keep the securities market, with its tangle of unsolvable problems.

Securities: weakening of the final cost regulator's effects.

All the valid reasoning that securities and public joint-stock companies once promoted the development of capitalism do not mean that they need to be used forever. Securities are nutritious "food" for this development, but it is too heavy for times of higher specialisation in an understanding of this world. This requires fine-tuning the economy to personal responsibility for decisions made and costs accrued. In olden times, eliminating unexplored places on the map and introducing rather simple machines (through building some capitalist "juggernauts") justified rough methods of accumulating capital by any means available. Nowadays, securities are increasingly linked not as much to the technological development of our civilisation but to the convenience of making money by large firms, banks, countries issuing the global currencies and a plethora of "observers" operating on the financial markets. What is convenient for some turns out to be a burden of high costs for others, due to the monopolisation processes facilitated by the use of securities, accompanied by chronic imbalances in the world economy.

These pain points have been exacerbated by the appearance of computer technologies that have given even more liquidity to assets trading on the stock market and moved this market even further away from the real economy, where production and sales processes are naturally conservative.

Giving up securities is as frightening as taking a pacifier from a baby who does not want to let it go. Indeed, certain inconveniences are possible but they are not as scary as they may seem. Meanwhile, there is no real danger in sight.

In our earlier thesis about trade credit, we went into detail over the bloating of retail chains that use free credit from their suppliers. Once the financial responsibility of borrowers is personified, the false nature of the perceived competitiveness of the chains becomes obvious. Likewise, absent the securities trading, there will be similar changes towards shrinking and bankruptcies of bloated publicly traded companies and other issuers of securities, with corresponding growth of small and medium enterprises. Consider this yet another forecast among the simplest ones I have ever made. Note that we do not put any single company and sector under the magnifying glass of fairness or lack thereof, but merely switch the economy towards a higher level of borrower responsibility driven by the market interest rate. All these changes will happen exclusively within the framework of market self-regulation and strict adherence to the classical credit principles.

Let's try to identify three main elements that will cause the firms that issue securities to shrink.

First, let's note two different situations with two different outcomes, namely a firm's manager raising funds in the securities market versus the same manager taking out a loan at a commercial bank. Even with commercial banks competing for customers, the manager may get less money at a higher interest rate this way, as the bank will evaluate the client's ability to pay back the loan in case the business goes bust. By raising funds in the securities market, large firms transition to another level of financing with less clearly defined responsibilities. This level allows them to successfully cover their coordination costs and further *increase their market share* while medium and small businesses, being less attractive for the stock market players, remain at the same classical level that assumes rigorous personal responsibility of their owners. With the transition to the strict classical PCM model, large firms will lose these opportunities.

Second, besides raising more funds with less defined responsibility through initial stock offerings, asset price increases become an even *more important* factor inspired by trading on the secondary market. There, entrepreneurs may count on much higher profits from selling their business (or part of it, but ultimately all). Interestingly, appreciated asset prices can be used *again* to raise even more funds – this applies primarily to the issuance of stocks. I noticed that while discussing the merits of stocks, economists often use the example of an important invention (technological leap) that would be difficult to implement without issuing stocks. I don't want to offend anyone, but this example looks more like an obsession than a reality. It is clear where this elegant example about the usefulness of stocks for the economy (or futures for farmers hedging their harvest) comes from. The truth is, implementing an invention is not a significant reason for issuing stocks but it sounds so convincing that it makes for a perfect example.[152] The "farmers" do not play a major role on the futures markets either. Further, we'll talk about issuing stocks as an alleged "must have" for implementing an invention. In general, if one is

[152] There might be a feeling that by removing an IPO altogether, we are going after technological progress. Simply put, if we apply this to say, Google, it would mean that if the firm's market capitalisation were not \$600 billion but merely \$60, there would be no search engine or other products by Google. Most likely, the only thing missing would be the clearly monopolistic flavour of this or another business on today's stock market (let's remember the cult slogan of the present financial system: money makes money). Correspondingly, the competition would be more intense on this market, which is generally a positive influence on both the quantity and quality of goods offered, e.g. often new ones and at lower prices. In your opinion, is there a link between periodic, high profile anti-monopoly investigations into the largest computer technology firms and the inflated (from a PCM viewpoint) price of their assets? Or can we suggest that said investigations would occur more often if this "monopolistic flavour" were not so attractive for some government agencies? To be fair, let's note that if the first question is rhetorical from a theoretical perspective, then the second one may be simply too emotional to warrant a theoretically precise answer.

interested in the real state of things, we have already mentioned the main motivation for entrepreneurs to issue stocks in the very first sentence of this paragraph.

A simple interpretation of this mechanism is as follows: by issuing stocks, we define a new level of demand for our firm, as though we have just defined a new level of demand for the goods we produce by discovering a certain new territory inhabited by people who are ready to purchase our products.[153] Whatever other selling points are claimed in the IPO process, be it an invention, trademark or sales volume, it is a technical and largely marketing question. After the transition to the PCM model (once the price rush accompanying this transition process settles – it is hard to say how long this might take), the market value of private joint-stock companies will drop (in other words, the stock prices will be more realistic) and they won't be able to borrow as much money as they did before.

The third reason is related to the second one, by simply explaining the mechanism of a stock price decrease. Once the minority shareholders in a firm notice that after the transition to the new system dividends become the only source of income, they may start disposing of their shares. It will become clear that not only entrepreneurs, but also all other shareholders are not quite ready to trust their money to the firms they do not have any real ways to control, hoping to receive some bona fide dividends.

The main reason driving decisions to buy publicly traded shares is their expected appreciation on the secondary market. People cannot be blamed for their desire to make money using any legal ways to do so. However, the development of the economy is seriously slowed down by the existence of this layer of fractional equity owners (if we are talking about shares) and debt owners (in the case of bonds). The efficiency of private management is driven not only by the profit "carrot" but also by the mandatory "stick" of possible negative profit. The negative profit of managing owners is the final market regulator for replacing poorly performing managers by firms and commercial banks (read: by the economic property of *Homo sapiens*). It is as effective as natural selection in general[154] and can be similarly painful. However, the effectiveness will

[153] The existence of the secondary market may also influence the projected stock price of a firm in cases where this business is of interest to the market. Such a firm can be privately sold at an elevated price with a possible IPO in mind.

[154] In developed human society, the natural selection features are limited to those in line with the development of civilisation. However, it would be illogical and short-sighted to ignore it in our context. The *Homo sapiens* population itself has

be obvious only if the replacement of a manager (who has raked up losses) happens in a *timely manner*. Otherwise, a firm's decline might go too far and subsequently restoring the firm's efficiency will be too expensive, which would make these underperforming businesses a drag on the national economy's competitiveness. The existence of a layer of fractional owners and creditors hinders the process of replacement of inefficient managing owners. Thanks to those poorly informed fractional investors, these managers can find ways to absorb the costs of substandard management, including those stemming from excessive expansion.

In the thesis on trade credit (the accounts receivable part), we talked about how costs accumulate in the national economy due to the chronic delay of the "invisible hand" reaction. Here, we also see the accumulation of costs due to the delayed reaction of market regulators. The underlying reason is identical: the ability to raise funds bypassing the market interest rate (more precisely, more money than a firm could have borrowed under a strictly classical credit system) allows a firm to maintain untrue competitiveness and continue to churn out products despite its high costs. Some independent outside observers (e.g. market analysts) may try stopping this process with their warnings but they won't be any more successful than a flock of birds trying to stop an elephant falling from a skyscraper (especially when the elephant is falling from an entirely different skyscraper).

In the new system, such firms are forced to reduce output when excessive costs are incurred because of the decrease in the amount of money raised, *whether they want it or not*. In both cases, such decisions will be made by the specialists of specific commercial banks and not by external observers.

Under the existing system, once the accumulation of costs in such a firm finally becomes obvious, the reaction of the observers may take the shape of a panicked collapse of the share price. If there are many such firms, this share price collapse might become akin to the fall of an asteroid on the national economy. The reaction of the securities market is not timely enough and is markedly harsh.

---

become a ruling species thanks to natural selection. This ruling species is still responsible for its own survival and that of life on Earth in general. Either picking capable professionals will follow the path of natural selection, or they will be appointed based on principles of personal and clan loyalty, simply as smart, easy-going people, or randomly. Options for applying the natural selection principle are not open everywhere, but we are lucky to have them available in the economy, i.e. the foundation of *Homo sapiens*' dominance on this planet.

We admit that with the abolishment of the securities market, observers and analysts might lose their source of information on firms and commercial banks. Honesty must be mutual, so therefore let's put in a disclaimer that, first, we are talking about large firms and commercial banks issuing securities (nowadays, outsiders know very little about medium and small firms, anyway), and second, the majority of such market observers and analysts either play on the market themselves, or prepare and sell this information to other players. Still, let's try to figure out whether reducing such publicly available information creates danger or just a minor inconvenience for the economy. But first (I think you will agree that this is more important), let's look at the situation not from the perspective of outside observers but from that of real stakeholders – will there be enough information for them in the absence of a securities market?

For example, if entrepreneurs want to borrow funds from a commercial bank, they will show and tell much more detail to the bank than can be learned from public reports, as the bank would require full disclosure and the entrepreneurs would need to build a trust relationship to secure better loan terms. Regarding the information about competitors (i.e. other firms in the industry), the firm's management is much better informed than any outside observer. The same applies to mergers and acquisitions with other firms in the industry. (Note that the word "acquisition" will not sound so ominous in the new system, due to the lack of securities and non-bank loans, and the corporate raiders will find their job *extremely* difficult as well.) This information trickles into a firm from buyers and manufacturers working in the industry, as well as from personal contacts between entrepreneurs, employees, competitors, government agencies, consulting companies, banks, etc. Some information also comes from analytical and market research conducted, for example, by former employees deciding to go it alone. But no matter what significance is given to the analysis of public reports in these studies, the use of the information contained in them is negligible for existing firms in the industry. Its value increases for entrepreneurs deciding whether to take their chances in another industry or at least seriously considering it. However, this value should not be exaggerated. Here's my own account of it.

I placed an ad and hired a specialist who was knowledgeable about sales in the industry that I wanted to enter. Gradually refining my questions to him, I drew the pattern representing the *movement* of products from manufacturers to the stores in the industry of interest to me. I also needed the characteristics and interaction patterns of the main market participants. Regretfully, when I had already hired a second specialist for data verification and started pondering options to work with the stores, the engineering studies conducted at my request concluded with a verdict of the impossibility of any radical improvement in the technological characteristics of products that I wanted to start selling. So, I had not gained anything, apart from the satisfaction from having finished a market study on my own. It was more rewarding than some purchased analytical industry research material that contained very little relevant information. I did not need a "general" story about the industry with technical data attached, but a practical guide for a narrow industry segment with points of interest to me (you might have noticed that I was looking for those points in the movement of property – simply put, certain money labels on the map of movement of goods in the industry). It is worth adding one finishing touch. The purchased analytical study relied mostly on non-public data, as this industry was not of much interest to the securities market; that is, such information will always be available on the market, regardless of securities market trading.

As a little sidetrack, note that in the case described there was no relationship between the fate of the invention and, from a distant perspective, my firm going public in the case of a technological breakthrough success. Going public would have mainly affected *how much I would earn*. Sure, this single case is not indicative, as there are more large-scale projects that require raising significant funds. However, the difference between a public and a private business is *usually* not in the fate of technological improvements, which are important for society, but whether the entrepreneur earns, roughly speaking, $100 million or, due to the rise in the share price of the firm, $1 billion. I have long been surprised by such sentiment towards the size of the estate of some individual, albeit talented, people against the background of neglecting the economy as a whole.

Returning to the flow of information in the new system, note also that the state (government and central bank) will learn everything that it needs to know, first, from the unified payment system (it's logical to assume that the central bank will know "everything" and the government will only know some things to the extent permitted by law). Second, there will be information from the financial statements of the entrepreneur (here, of course, on the contrary, the government will have priority). Considering that deals in the new financial system will be much safer to settle using non-cash funds to avoid ambiguities and suspicions of illegal lending, the information coming from the payment system will be immeasurably more complete compared with what can be obtained from the commercial banks now.

As for the commercial banks themselves, having lost control of the payment system as a whole, they will still know as much about their borrowers as they see fit, requesting financial accounting or some other data from them. Let's not forget that in the new credit system, only commercial banks will be able to lend money, so we can safely assume that it will be difficult to avoid abiding by these requirements in general. Nothing prevents us from developing special access for the creditor bank to view the borrower's accounts in the payment system. Again, commercial banks have, and will have, channels to receive information from third parties similar to the channels used by the firms.

In other words, no significant dangers are visible to the economy in the absence of information, which is nowadays directly or indirectly produced by the securities market. However, if the state deems it necessary, it can oblige businesses to either provide regular reports on their activities with a certain frequency and detail, or publish some aggregated information from the payment system and the tax authorities, for example. Let's recall that the regularity and completeness of public disclosure by securities issuers are not "born on the market" by themselves but are controlled from above, by state and non-governmental organisations, so that these publicly available reports are not merely advertising.

I cannot predict exactly what the reports intended for publishing will look like or what the depth of coverage of firms and commercial banks will be, and whether there will only be official data from the payment system and tax authorities. It can be assumed that in the absence of market-traded securities, two main factors working in opposite directions will be taken into account. The more that the state considers such an ancient entrepreneurial instinct as "my business is my secret", the more comfortable entrepreneurs will feel. But on the other hand, with broader coverage of businesses and more regularly published reports, there will be more of those willing to at least take a look at the features of this particular market. And, as we know, once the keen eye of a potential buyer turns onto your product, it is considered partially sold. Under the "sale of a product", here we refer to the influx of direct investments into a national economy. Let's sum up the above: the main purpose of publicly available reports will remain the same as it is now, i.e. advertising for potential investors. Some national economies will need more of it and some will need less.

Let's say a few words about one more inconvenience of abandoning securities with a credit component, namely the impossibility of using them as collateral. This decrease in available collateral options will require more thorough and complex work with physical collateral, including goods in transit and in warehouses. These inconveniences are undoubted, but at the same time they should not be exaggerated to spell real dangers. First, this collateral is used mostly by the commercial banks, other financial market players and large firms. For most of the real economy companies, nothing would fundamentally change in this regard. In other words, it's not so much a problem of the lack of liquid instruments but a problem of lost opportunity to make money on the market for securities with a credit component that can also be used as collateral. This is one popular way to earn money in the financial market – lend money to one actor (for example, the state) and then borrow (for example, the same amount) from someone else, securing the loan by the debt obligations (securities) of the first actor. Even if a firm from the real economy is engaged in these activities, then it's still all about diversification.

Second, neither this nor any other features of the new financial system will lead to an increase in the average interest rate. In fact, the rate will decrease after the *complete* transition to the PCM. We'll discuss this in more detail in the thesis "*FAQ: The shrinking of money stock and the interest rate.*" Now, we just note that one assumption is hardly deserving detailed attention, namely that a shift to calculating physical collateral for *large businesses* would make a banker's work too laborious to be attractive, resulting in lower competition in lending. Based on a simple argument of an increased supply of loans to the real economy, we can say that once private banks enjoy an exclusive right to lend money with a concurrent diminishing of the current financial markets and their proposed alternatives, the situation is more likely to be the opposite.

Note also that the "average interest rate" in today's world economy is akin to the "average temperature in a hospital", since interest rates are artificially low in the countries issuing global currencies and high in the peripheral countries. Therefore, after the complete transition to the PCM, the rates would increase in the former and decrease in the latter.

Securities: increasing cyclical development swings. Futures contracts.

The securities market is not merely slowing down economic growth by introducing extra costs into the economy but weakening the effects of market competition to control costs in general. It promotes the ragged nature of capitalist economic development. It increases the cyclic amplitude of the expansions and recessions that are inherent to capitalism.

Economic expansion takes longer than it should, for the same reason that an artificially low interest rate indulges a false sense of well-being for borrowers. However, securities give extra support for this false sense of prosperity. First, issuing securities curtails some natural market mechanisms designed to keep this pumped-up economic growth in check. There are no market players who would, without reservations, guard the economy from the irrational use of money resources. Commercial (credit) banks, those natural "guardians" of the market, not only stay away from this task but to some extent also switch sides. Securities comprise a substantial share of commercial banks' assets, so the banks are interested in their appreciation, like all other securities holders.

The term "guardian" as it applies to commercial banks possibly requires additional clarifications. The goal of both firms and banks is profit. With all that, producing goods is a socially important mission of firms, as reflected in the occupations of their employees. Likewise, commercial banks are engaged in lending by hiring specialists in this sphere. One mandatory specialised function of commercial banks is collateral management. The task of taking a small portion of our civilisation's economic property away from the former owner who did not manage it properly, cleansing it from accumulated debts and handing it over to a new managing owner is an important part of the banks' designation. If one wants to be perceived as a kind soul, they should not consider a banking career.

The idea of making money in the securities markets is not at all foreign to highly educated people. To an extent, this sustains favourable reasoning for the merits of these markets. Everyone might have heard, for example, about the "use of futures contracts for hedging risks of the real economy". Some specialised websites may tell you that without the futures market the economy is in danger of returning to a subsistence economy. Let's try to check if this is the case. Looking ahead, we'll see that the usefulness of futures for the economy is exaggerated, as well as that futures are in fact harmful.

Speaking about exaggerated usefulness, we mean that, first, not all the inputs and supplies of interest to the real economy (raw materials, parts, equipment, real estate and contracts) are traded on the futures market. Second, price changes, for example, of raw material contracts traded on the exchange do not matter much for a lot of firms. Either they don't use a lot of the material or their processing cycle is quite deep.

In other words, there is no life-and-death dependency on the futures market among many real economy firms. For instance, in my own management practice I had no need to use futures contracts. It may be a little uneasy that, unlike those "hedging farmers", the businesses I ran did not rise above that humble "subsistence economy" stage, though they were indeed among the largest in their respective sub-sectors. Still, my soothing assumption is that from this perspective, most hi-tech firms are indeed "stuck in the past" (like me), as they rarely depend on raw materials traded on the futures exchanges.

Nevertheless, there are some real economy firms that indeed actively use futures contracts. The example of airlines, which are hedging against rising fuel prices, looks convincing enough. However, let's look at this situation from a higher vantage point. Imagine that futures trading technologies have developed to the degree that all firms on this planet who care a lot about fuel prices have bought the respective contracts. At some point, fuel prices substantially increase and every market participant has their potential loss compensated. Did the costs in the global economy decrease as well? Not at all, but they increased to, say, reflect new higher costs of oil extraction (of course, if these costs were not covered by the inhabitants of another planet who had made the unfortunate mistake of deciding to open short positions on the oil futures market on Earth). With new higher prices, everyone buys fuel at a higher price. What really happened was the redistribution of money *on another market*. Meanwhile, the firms for which fuel prices are critical will sooner or later raise their own prices.

We may need to clarify the feeling that in this made-up situation the "damned speculators" lost, whereas the firms in the real economy won. The fuel price increased but it could well drop – that's what happened, for example, in 2014 when many well-known airlines (including Delta, Lufthansa and Aeroflot) lost millions of dollars due to their unfortunate hedging. In the real betting world, only the "house" wins – those who set up and service the trading process – as well as the specialists skilfully using both legal and secretly obtained information. One can always "buy something, pay for it in full and forget about it" on the spot market without relying on credit. Futures contracts require constant professional attention and associated skills. The aggregate player will always lose and the "real economy" firms are part of this aggregate player. They are forced to engage in activities that are totally foreign to them.

The high volatility stems from the particulars of paper capitalism, including trading of those same futures contracts. Moreover, some market swings could have possibly been avoided under the strictly classical economy. The characteristic rise of oil and gold prices in the early 21st century was provoked by the introduction of the second global currency (the euro) and to some degree by futures trading (we'll talk about these later). The real harmful side of futures contracts is bestowing price volatility, which is critical for the real economy, on the traditional material assets.

To sum it up:

- Securities with a credit component distort the market interest rate and decrease the responsibility of managers for the costs incurred.
- An excessive secondary market liquidity of securities (the latter should, in theory, reflect actual economic property and processes) contributes to their higher prices compared with their underlying prototypes. The main sources of this excessive liquidity are the use of purchase and sale deals in credit relationships, and the anonymous (secondary) market. Another factor contributing to the increasingly excessive liquidity of securities is their materialisation on paper and later in electronic form by analogy with money.
- Rising securities prices create additional (on top of the already happened non-market rate fundraising) opportunities to raise money. By itself and by suppressing the "ordinary" firms on the market, this enables extra consumption on the part of market specialists, securities owners, employees of the firms issuing securities and people who live in the countries issuing global currencies (the latter case means additional demand for securities denominated in those currencies). This consumption[155] contributes

[155] Due to the complexity of material in this book, let me remind you of a few moments. (1) The people in question are not "evil", as this book is not about "the good and the evil" in general (even though similar interpretations are inevitable thanks to the author's intention to explain certain relationships in the simplest way possible) but rather about "how this all works". (2) Since the people in question do not consume money proper, the resulting downstream chains touch upon people of many different occupations, so with the formation change there will be inevitable problems, which, for the lack of a theoretical possibility to describe the transition period, were outlined in our dragon tale above. (3) Counting on the "dragons" (see

to the world economy's costs, slowing down its development and triggering the process of monopolisation, among other things.

- Excessive liquidity and inflated prices cause a high volatility of securities (especially on the securities markets denominated in peripheral currencies). As a result, this increases instability in the real economy ("the tail wagging the dog"). Hedging on the futures market is largely provoked by the securities market itself. Strategically, this volatility appears in the accelerated appreciation of securities at a time of economic expansion, with costs also growing out of proportion (a rapid rise in the securities market contributes not only to elevated consumption by its beneficiaries but also to excessive consumption in the economy as a whole). Meanwhile, basic cost regulators, still underdeveloped under capitalism, manage these growing costs solely by crisis-like purging (local currency depreciation crises in peripheral countries and a global deflationary crisis). It is easy to notice that during this radical cost purging, the securities market is indeed the place where excessive costs accumulate, as the securities prices fall most visibly. However, this fall does not bring about any rapid relief from a deflationary crisis. Worse, it tightens the problem knot even further, as securities are an important link in collateral procedures and credit chains. The already convoluted credit system of paper capitalism turns into a major headache after a landslide depreciation of "convenient assets".

Securities: the artificial nature of high liquidity compared with the liquidity of physical assets.

It makes sense to talk a little more about the high liquidity of securities in the secondary market. This liquidity is in stark contrast with the purchase and sale of entire businesses or parts thereof in the real economy. For illustration, imagine that there is no secondary market and you face the task of buying an entire firm or some parts of it to manage (or participate in managing this acquisition). Of course, there are some cases where entrepreneurs want to enter an unfamiliar sector where everything looks

---

our thesis "Reduction of systemic costs"), even if their consumption ostensibly "creates jobs", is an obsolete model of the world economy. (4) This can only be seen by abandoning the theoretical emphasis on the "aggregate demand" that mixes theory and analytics (Keynes's theory). (5) Throughout this study, as we mentioned in the Introduction, we have discussed the main economic mechanisms with an emphasis on "macroeconomic costs", i.e. the national economy's costs.

rosy to them and so they tend to rush things. As a rule, these buyers demonstrate professionalism and a good knack for business in excess of what a seller would want to see. These purchase and sale deals do happen in the real economy but, first, they take a lot longer and, second, the prices on average are markedly lower[156] than if the deal assumed the purchase and sale of stocks. The exaggeration of share prices on the market is largely related to the shorter time to get deals closed, i.e. it is related to the greater liquidity. Typically, out of a pair of identical doors leading to uncertainty, we would choose the one that we could exit from faster. If we were to lower the liquidity by, say, restricting the sales of shares[157] in a three-year period following the purchase, there would be less demand for the shares and their price would go down. Strictly speaking, the exaggeration of share prices on the market is caused by the large number of parties who want to purchase shares (as you remember, we compared a firm going public with the discovery of a "new territory inhabited by buyers"). The massive character of this demand is caused by the high liquidity of securities trading. As we have explained before, the restructuring of publicly traded firms into private joint-stock companies would cause a landslide decrease in the number of potential buyers, triggering much lower business valuations.

Lower business prices will facilitate the transition to more efficient (for instance, younger) entrepreneurs, including the transition of single enterprises which are part of integrated businesses into more compact, independent firms. However, the gist of lower business prices is the world economy getting rid of extra *costs*, i.e. excessive consumption by securities issuers, securities holders, securities market operators and indirect beneficiaries. One can forever argue to what extent the securities market is useful under capitalism but it is not needed for PCM. Those few inconveniences experienced by all players along the learning curve are worth neither the amount of goods consumed by the securities market participants nor the distortions of the classical economy that are induced by this market.

---

[156] Two details are important here. The first one is that we are talking about "average" pricing (single deals can be expensive at any time) and for the second one, you need to imagine that there is no secondary market at all. As we have noted before, in order to calculate the market price of a private business today, some methods compare it to publicly traded peers.

[157] Everything we say here about stocks liquidity is valid for bonds as well, with a few small caveats. For example, if the money invested in the 30-year US Treasuries could be returned only upon maturity, there would be much fewer buyers today.

These distortions stemming from high liquidity are most visible during a crisis-related fall of the securities markets. At any rate, with the cyclical development of capitalism, once an overproduction crisis hits, the prices fall for industrial real estate, equipment and information infrastructure of firms. [158] But when, on top of that, the economy is getting rid of exaggerated business and credit valuations on the securities market, this fall takes on a grotesque character. True, there is not much laughing in this grotesque, as the falling prices crush the entire financial system of the world economy. Despite the virtual character of their prices put together under systematically exaggerated valuations, the securities are organically woven into the system of bank and state assets. Thus, the financial system, thrown out of balance by the hit of yet another cyclical "asteroid", not only complicates the clean-up of the real economy from excessive costs but also adversely impacts its day-to-day activities.

Let's rephrase the last sentence: instead of healing the real economy, the existing financial system exacerbates its misery. Conversely, ***the financial system of the PCM will not only service the creation and movement of goods and other types of property in the real economy, but also promote its healing*** by applying preventive measures, and it will even rapidly restore the vitality of it, which is the most important aspect for people.

In the formational development of the economy, like in life generally, there is hardly a situation where all the characteristics of a bygone era are worse than those of the new period. Certain inconveniences related to the abandonment of the market for securities with a credit component will always be felt. It is also quite possible that, over time, some modern books will be perceived with a degree of nostalgia for the old times, like we perceive *Gone with the Wind* or *The Cherry Orchard* today. We either give up the past and move forward, or we don't give it up and stay where we are, as no alternative combination is possible.

---

[158] The information infrastructure of a firm consists of its management structure (current internal system regulating production and distribution of information) plus the firm's image (accumulated external information layer). This lenient definition is not too important for our study, but to demonstrate that it is not a made-up one, we need a brief explanation. In the real economy, a buyer can (a) buy the entire firm and subsequently either use all thus purchased information infrastructure or replace part of it as needed; or (b) lease and use any given part of this information infrastructure (for example, by associating with the firm's image through franchising or by simply luring over the whole management team).

Preview of Chapter 3.

The essential part of Chapter 3 is a complete liberation of the fourth basic cost regulator that we are going to call the cross-price of a national currency, or simply, cross-price. If the interest rate is the price of a national currency expressed in monetary terms when we are dealing with money as credit, then the cross-price is the price of a national currency expressed in monetary terms when we are dealing with money as payment. It is easy to notice that the price of money as payment can form only in purchase and sale deals (a bilateral exchange). The only case of a purchase and sale deal when this price is expressed in monetary terms is a currency exchange deal, where a certain sum in national currency units is being exchanged for a certain sum in foreign currency. As there are multiple foreign currencies, there are many cross-prices.

The market forming of a cross-price puts the final touch on destroying deflationary cyclical crises by the “invisible hand of the market”. By this time, the main job has already been done by the market interest rate. Let’s recall the sequence of key events that have made it so efficient:

- The transition of a three-layer payment system into a two-layer one;
- New money entering the economy without credit liabilities, through calculated money issuance;
- National borders closing for trespassing by credit in either direction;
- There are equal lending conditions for all firms (the state and non-licensed creditors are removed from the credit market; the market for securities with a credit component and one for trade credit are forbidden).

These measures have concurrently laid the ground for the “liberation” of a market cross-price. The market interest rate safeguards the national economy from excessive viability of unnecessary costs and therefore from creating multiple bubbles. However, the national economy can still lose, for instance, competitive fights in the market for tradable goods. In this case, the fourth basic regulator kicks in, as the national currency is depreciated by the market. Currency depreciation is a sort of “market punishment” for the inhabitants of a country where the national economy has excessive costs, as it lowers the consumption of imported goods and services, both inside the country and while travelling abroad. Still, this “punishment” gives them another chance literally overnight, as it instantly lowers the cost of domestic goods compared with imports and thus increases their competitiveness. In other words, the fourth basic cost regulator instantly cuts excessive consumption, shifting the national ratio of investment (microeconomy) divided by consumption (households) to a more or less acceptable level, i.e. in favour of investment.[159] Let's repeat that excessive consumption is cut not by a state regulator (government or central bank) but by a *market* control. Having achieved the market interest rate operating at full capacity, we can proceed to emphasise the next step: currency depreciation deals a death blow to deflationary crises.

It may seem that we have had a smooth sailing from the beginning of the main text. We have turned the established financial system upside down by easily changing the functions of the central bank and direction of money flows, liquidating entire sectors, and finally, building a computer-assisted, ultramodern configuration of the financial system. In the end, having reached the last "room", we discover the most conservative mechanism there. This was the case with the third regulator, when we got quick and effective cost reduction in single firms using a simple and well-known deal between an entrepreneur and a banker. This will be the case with the fourth basic regulator, when in our quest for the truth we get to something we have known all along – the mechanism of national currency depreciation on the foreign exchange market – that has been hidden in that remote "room". This mechanism can quickly and efficiently[160] lower the

[159] Here, investment and consumption are "general" categories. Despite the material nature of all expenses that are easy to calculate and classify at the individual business level, investment and consumption cannot be basic categories, as there is no simple and feasible algorithm to calculate them *at the national economy level*. The System of National Accounts (SNA) appears to be a by-product of periodically changing agreements rather than an example of the methodical application of a theoretical algorithm. This situation is not helped much by dividing the macroeconomy into sectors that are more oriented either towards households or microeconomic consumption. For instance, the same products may be used for both household and business consumption. We are not just talking about telephone sets, chairs or staples. For example, cement used in residential construction cannot be directly classified as capital investment, even if the SNA treats it this way.

[160] In the countries where the national economy is organised around exporting raw materials ("we sell raw materials and buy manufactured goods"), restoring efficiency after a price increase for the equipment's spare parts will take time under any formation. This is a normal process. Everything should be paid for and our PCM will not be an exception. However, the normalcy of this process will be obvious only under PCM, when it won't be exacerbated by the Dutch disease (at least, not in today's form) and there will be no other "burdens" of the existing

costs in the entire national economy. Everything that we are doing in both cases is simply demolishing barricades made of old furniture, removing cobwebs without remorse and cleaning up the gears from accumulated debris. Then, we oil the gears and restart both mechanisms to run at their designed capacity. Even before that, we have changed the office layout, including getting rid of the people who tried to manually perform the tasks earlier reserved for the mechanisms. We also laid *new communication lines* to make it known that mechanisms are back at work in the whole house. We have long understood that those mechanisms exist and we have known how important they are, albeit intuitively (the "invisible hand of the market"). We also did not know exactly how they worked, or thought that we knew, by taking for granted any manifestations of their activity, both useful and harmful.

For example, under the existing system, the phrase "currency depreciation deals a death blow to deflationary crises" is perceived as nothing but words. The depreciation of a single regular currency in crisis will not achieve much for a given national economy. First, this would not be the only nation experiencing problems. Second, the households of the main ultimate buyer on planet Earth, the US, due to the oversized development of consumer credit during the last crisis, have already consumed enough products for "a few years ahead". Unfortunately, there are no other inhabited planets where devaluation against their respective currencies can help and where potential buyers can fly from to help quickly deal with a deflationary crisis in the world economy.

In the new formation, actions of the fourth basic cost regulator will be fully fledged. If we imagine the entire collection of national currencies as a set of white piano keys, then these keys would be pressed (currency depreciation scenario) or released either one by one, or in some simple "chords", but for sure they would not be all pressed at the same time. However, for the fourth basic regulator to work, we need to undergo one

---

financial system, manifested in the wild swings of raw material prices, exchange rates and clearly manufactured (from the PCM perspective) overproduction crises. From a theoretical viewpoint, the opposite process does not appear to be normal ("we sell manufactured goods while we buy raw materials, *and nothing else*"), observed in countries having the so-called "island mentality", with Japan being a prime example. We will not go deep into this complex topic, instead just noting the work of a "useful bad boy" naturally performed by imports, competitively cleansing the national economy of excessive costs. The situation cannot always be remediated by the "artificial" efforts of monetary authorities, and it is rarely possible without accompanying side effects and distortions.

more floor-plan rearrangement in our financial house, namely at its floor where the dollar and (to a lesser extent) the euro rule nowadays. Our new system of national currency interrelationships will look like a daisy. ***The petals (national monetary systems having equal rights) have a common central hub where currency exchange takes place.*** The "petals" are totally isolated (no foreign currency is allowed to circulate within the national borders), while the central hub, having limited physical "outlets" (in some extraterritorial zones, like at the airports before crossing a national border), is mostly virtual as it is implemented in the computer systems of a unified currency exchange. Strictly speaking, the *need for computers* for the transition to these national currency units having equal rights lies in the fact that without computers it is almost impossible to imagine the currency exchange counters that would stock all global currencies (as the costs would be prohibitive). And if this is impossible to implement, global currencies will inevitably materialise. We don't welcome these. Even if we leave the distortions alone, which they introduce into the rational use of our planet's resources, it is simply hard to imagine that the pinnacle of our economic civilisation is represented by a system that has the core competency of being able to sell nicely decorated paper to other nations.

CHAPTER 3.

CROSS-PRICE

Imagine that we have just landed at a foreign airport and the financial system of the Perfectly Competitive Market is already mature. Having cleared passport control (the national border before passing the customs), we come up to one of the cash machines installed on the way.[161] It is hard to make a mistake, as they are all labelled identically in every airport in countries that have transitioned to the PCM – "The Planetary Exchange" (the name is provisional).

The Planetary Exchange is neither a global nor monopolistic seller of foreign currencies. Moreover, it is not a merchant at all. In our case, the Exchange sets up worldwide currency trading, being sort of an "electronic errand boy". Our "electronic errand boy" runs across the entire electronic customs "city" of the planet and credits your bank "card"[162] (which, as you may remember, is the one issued by our national central bank) with a requested sum of local currency bought at the currently best available rate. When leaving the country, there is no need to look for the cash machines once more. As soon as we clear the exit control, the border guard sends a signal and our "electronic errand boy" performs the reverse operation. Any remaining local currency is converted back to our national units. Our potential losses (let's remember that we are talking about a *developed* financial system under the PCM) will be much lower compared with what we typically pay today for making card purchases and getting cash abroad. The "electronic errand boy" commissions will be a tiny fraction of these

[161] I cannot see how this might work with "remote" access to a cash machine, at any rate, because of the boundaries of this area at the airport in our example. Maybe someone can suggest a way.

[162] I don't know what the cards will look like in the future and whether there will even be any cards, but for now let's use their traditional representation. We used quotation marks around the word "card" because, strictly speaking, the money is credited to your temporary account, which is automatically opened at a local central bank.

and just enough to finance the operations of the Planetary Exchange itself. With these negligible fees, anyone entering a foreign country would not hesitate to get enough local currency.

If we want to buy something abroad for personal or business use while being in our home country, we can use the same card, either at any central bank's cash machine or online. Then, the Planetary Exchange's "electronic errand boy" would perform similar operations, with the only difference being that the foreign currency purchased to fulfil our order will be credited to the seller's account at its national central bank (for the seller, this currency will be national) while we receive the goods. Neither buyer nor seller possess the foreign currency during this whole deal (thus, unlike the situation we have described at the airport, the possibility of remote access does not create any significant issues).

This is all we need to describe the general principle on which our system operates. Of course, there are some important details, so we are going to address these in the following theses. It should also be noted that only practitioners will be able to clarify full technical details while working on the blueprints for the new system.

The participants in the deals.

The main participants in foreign currency exchanges are firms, organisations (including governmental bodies) and individuals based either in their home country or in extraterritorial zones who conduct import and export operations, as well as the licensed banks servicing them.

The need for bank participation will vary. For example, it will be small during the daytime servicing of foreign currency deals between two adjacent countries with a high volume of cross-border trade. In other words, bank commissions will be minimal in locations with an intensive bilateral movement of goods and services. Nowadays, this happens as well, but not for all currencies and not for all parties participating in trade. In the new system, after a certain degree of development, the competition in the foreign exchange market will become close to perfect, without the degree of conditionality that we put into the words "Perfectly Competitive Market".

National domiciles of the deal's participants.

It is important that all market participants are distinguished by their national identities, i.e. the country of registration for banks, firms and organisations, and the country of permanent residency for individuals. If the country of registration for the legal entity poses no questions, the determination and subsequent corrections of the country of permanent residence for individuals requires certain innovations. The simplest version may look like this: adolescents open their personal accounts at the central bank and get their bank cards[163] concurrently with their national identity documents. All the required account security features are also set (PIN-only or more advanced security, including fingerprints, iris scans or some other biometric characteristic required when using the card at store tills or at a cashpoint). If the national identity document changes, all relevant personal data is automatically shared with the central bank. In cases where we decide to change our country of permanent residence, the authorities of the new home country issue a new central bank's card. As soon as this new card is issued, the authorities order the local central bank to fund it using the balance of the temporary "foreign visitor" account and automatically send a notice to the old home country's central bank. That bank transfers our money out to be exchanged by the "electronic errand boy" into the new country's currency. Afterwards, the funds are credited to our new account in the new country of residency. The old card and any old accounts become defunct.

Corporate cards. A foreign affiliate business in the new formation.

Corporate cards are valid only within the customs borders of the country of registration. Of course, we can use them to pay for foreign purchases made from within our country, but if there is a need to send a home country employee on a business trip abroad, the required sum will need to be transferred to that employee's card. In cases where a managing owner develops commercial interests in a foreign nation, an affiliate firm can be opened abroad.

---

[163] In a version easiest to understand, a person may only need one account and therefore only one card, as in our new system the entire payment system is maintained by the central bank. Further, we'll refer to this "card" in the singular. Conceivably, the number of personal cards is limited only by the processing capacity of computers.

Comments: The foreign affiliate business that we have just mentioned will be a plain, autonomous business for that foreign nation. In particular, it won't be able to use any hidden or open loans from other firms, including its parent entity (especially those from the parent entity, since in our case it would be a foreign business). We assume that the only channel for financing this affiliate by the parent firm will be through paid-in capital (the reverse process of taking the profits back to the home country will surely be legitimate). If additions to the paid-in capital happen too often or serve as a disguise for other deals, these operations may be subject to fees.

These control measures will be aimed primarily against any possible currency speculation, in a broad sense, under which I mean not only the Forex market gambling proper but also a desire to keep certain amounts of cash temporarily in a more stable currency. No doubt, we cannot point out all possible loopholes before a practical realisation of our plan and there will surely be constant attempts to come up with new tricks. However, in the end, currency speculation won't play a significant role.

This is because, first, the financial system of the PCM is a very simple construct, with clearly defined boundaries between its different segments. Any difficulties that a reader of this text may experience stem solely from its novel character.

Second, currency speculators won't have natural allies among the countries. With my understanding of a need to explain this in a simple yet non-rigorous way, I may suggest the following: today, money is more important than goods, while in our new formation, the opposite will be true. Here's a more rigorous but imperfect explanation: under paper capitalism, the "export competitiveness" of money is strategically more important than the export competitiveness of goods, while under the PCM it is the opposite. Under the existing system, the leading role is played by the global currencies that enjoy higher demand not directly related to the competitiveness of the goods produced by the issuing countries. Under our new system, such unrelated demand would only have an adverse effect on the economy of a given country, because the strict reason for additional money issuance is an increase in physical and credit turnover, while an increase in foreign currency turnover is not a reason for it. This national currency will gain, due to a higher demand for it and without a respective increased issuance of money, lowering the competitiveness of national businesses.

The "electronic errand boy" and currency exchange banks. Multi-currency deals.

The transparency of the currency exchange system within our worldwide "electronic city", including its unequivocal anti-speculative purpose, can be attained by these regulations (or at least similar ones):

- The licensed banks have special accounts set up at the Planetary Exchange, with the number of these accounts being limited to the number of currencies being exchanged in the scope of the PCM.
- The banks have unrestricted control only over a single account – the one used to store their national currency. They may freely move funds into and out of this account. The direction of the money movement is quite simple, as the account of this bank at the central bank only serves as either the destination (with funds coming from the exchange) or the sender (with funds entering the exchange).
- Any other money movements, including movement of foreign currency, happen solely in the process of currency exchange deals, set up exclusively by the "electronic errand boy".

This means that only the "electronic errand boy" may credit the banks' foreign currency accounts, for example, having sold roubles on behalf of a Russian bank. In this operation, the foreign currency automatically goes to the open exchange market (as there are no other methods), so the bank puts the price in roubles (or it is ready to sell at market prices) for this foreign currency. Let's assume that a Russian firm needs to pay a foreign supplier. The firm pays in roubles, while the "electronic errand boy" documents the deal between the firm and this Russian bank (the bank sells foreign currency and the firms buys it). Right away, the "electronic errand boy" transfers the sum in foreign currency to the supplier and credits roubles to the bank's account. This mechanism also works for multi-currency deals when the "electronic errand boy", for example, performs a currency round robin – from the importer A to bank B, then foreign currency from bank B to bank C, then foreign currency from bank C to the foreign trade partner of A.

The possibility of multi-currency deals will significantly reduce the costs of the deals' participants. Thus, a bank would not need to worry about carrying all the planetary currencies "just in case". Consequently, banks would not need to include higher margins for operations with these rare currencies in order to compensate their carrying costs.

The last important assumption (from the bulleted points above) means that no two deals' participants may strike a separate currency exchange agreement, as all deals are settled exclusively by the "electronic errand boy" in open trades. And if you have paid attention, in all our examples of foreign currency deals there is always a counterpart that is external to the exchange. That is, we have no deals where banks (i.e. their special accounts set up to enable the Planetary Exchange) are the only participants. Our "electronic errand boy" will perform a foreign currency exchange operation only if it is initiated by a central bank account holder. Due to the importance of this rule, let's reiterate: no bank can initiate an exchange deal on its own. If a bank needs to purchase any goods (e.g. computer equipment) abroad, it will follow the rules set for other "mere mortals", i.e. through the "electronic errand boy".

Cash.

Here, we are back to a "feudalism" of sorts but the landowning formation has nothing to do with it. We are talking about the relics inherited from the now defunct formations superimposed on our PCM.

Even today metal coins are relics; they do not serve the purpose of determining and comparing monetary value by measuring the relative value of metal, and they are too expensive to be used merely as "numbers". While the cost to print paper money is many times less than its nominal value, the cost to manufacture metal coins cannot boast any savings. This is especially true for small-change coins made of cheap metals and even for collectibles made of precious metals. Being less susceptible to wear and tear than banknotes, coins seriously complicate the automation of cash circulation. They are largely a nuisance that can sometimes be dismissed.

After the transition to the PCM, paper money will become a pronounced anachronism, too. The problem is that paper money will pose a danger towards the true independence of currency "petals", making it hard to maintain the prohibition of foreign currency circulation within a country. As you may have noticed, the discipline of non-cash money circulation is attained using simple methods, without separation of people into "good" versus "bad" groups, or into law-abiding citizens versus criminals. This simplicity stems from a high level of centralisation that can be achieved only for non-cash money circulation. All payment terminals inside the "petals" belong to the national central bank, while money is traded at the international currency exchange by our "electronic errand boy". Conversely, the circulation of paper money is radically decentralised, as it can be simply pocketed and carried by individuals anywhere they choose to.

The centralisation of money printing was a mandatory condition for the fully fledged development of paper capitalism. The development of our PCM model requires the centralised control of money circulation but paper money acts as an impediment here. With all that, only well-developed and highly urbanised nations will be able to stop using paper currency at some point in the foreseeable future. The good news is that the centralised production of paper money is an absolute must, while centralised control over its movement is required only to preserve the well-defined boundaries of our "daisy" model. The circulation of paper money inside a national economy surely impacts the efficiency of fiscal and other controls. Besides, there will be costs required to create a system to manage cashiering operations for any large sums of cash under our new payment system. However, these assumptions do not pose a "to be or not to be" dilemma. The bad news is that violations of either the centralised production of paper money (counterfeiting) or the required centralisation of paper money circulation (use of foreign currency inside a country) should be treated as criminal offences.

Keeping funds in foreign currency as part of its circulation. Diminishing the currency depreciation effect.

The mere opportunity to store foreign currency promotes the demand for it. Besides, the presence of foreign currency on hand mitigates the desired effect of currency depreciation, i.e. cost reduction (let us recall that currency depreciation in the new financial system is the main stage of inflation from costs). Therefore, to achieve the desired level of a national economy's competitiveness, a national currency would need deeper depreciation compared with the necessary level of currency depreciation under a mature PCM.

Let's talk about the diminishing of the currency depreciation effect in more detail. First, let's focus on the differences in the mechanism of currency depreciation under different formations. Under our PCM model, it will work within a mechanism of simple competition among goods and services. If demand for the currency of a given nation goes down on the international currency exchange, this means that demand for goods produced in this country is now lower as well (this also includes demand represented by foreign tourism, when visitors come from abroad and purchase locally produced goods). Under the new financial system, one can expect that the cross-price's fluctuations will be smooth. The possibility of panic would be minimal compared with the existing state of things, where individuals, firms and banks rush to get rid of a cheapening currency and buy a more stable one. Let me remind you that corporate cards are not meant to buy foreign currency and that there are no currency deals between the banks. Moreover, the banks have to offer all foreign currency for sale the moment they receive it and only the holders of personal cards may buy foreign currency, and only when they travel abroad.

In the current system, peripheral currency rates need government regulation (meaning regulation by the broad government). Otherwise, any cyclical or local crisis, or simply some massive movement of speculative funds coupled with panic in the population, can trigger a currency depreciation so profound that both foreign and national investors will shy away from this national economy. Besides, the economies of most countries are woven into the international credit system, whose sources are directly or indirectly tied to the money issuance centres of global currencies. After currency depreciation, the ability to pay back loans taken in foreign currency is sharply reduced.

In the context of globalisation of credit, the low resilience of banks in peripheral countries becomes a critical issue when currency depreciation happens. Let's recall that due to the mix-up of credit and payment systems under capitalism, the monetary base is relatively small. As a result, the uninterrupted credit operation of banks is a mandatory condition to ensure that the entire credit and payment system works. Meanwhile, a significant part of banks' liabilities is represented by loans received in foreign currencies (typically, in global currencies). While the national currency is resilient, this approach pays off due to the difference in interest rates. With a currency depreciation, red lights show up throughout the banking system, as the net assets of banks may now decrease to a critical level. This reduction will occur either due to direct losses of a bank (if the bank had taken a long position in the national currency against foreign-currency-denominated liabilities, i.e. the bank borrowed in "dollars" and issued loans in "roubles"), or due to the creation of reserve provisions for bad loans issued in foreign currency (in "dollars") but the borrowers struggle to repay these loans in full due to currency depreciation. Therefore, large and small barriers spring up throughout the entire credit and payment system, preventing the flow of money into the real economy.

With devaluation, reducing the price of money (expressed in property; alternatively, it is called "purchasing power") acts as a punishment for the inhabitants of the country. However, it is an effective and useful punishment that increases demand for domestic goods. This usefulness lies mainly in its simplicity of implementation and speed, as costs in the entire national economy are all falling at one point compared with the costs in competing countries. After currency depreciation, prices for domestic goods denominated in the national currency do not grow as much as prices for imported goods, which thus provides domestic goods with a clear advantage in price competition.

Of course, one phrase cannot explain all the various changes in the market that will begin after its participants analyse what has happened. The scale of these changes in each case will depend heavily on the type of formation, industry, region, nature of the deal, depth of currency depreciation and many other factors, up to a specific type of product. However, the direction of these changes will be set because the cost of domestic goods denominated in foreign currencies after currency depreciation will decrease. The cost of goods reflects all the payments made by the manufacturer during production and delivery to a point of sale. All this money is received as income by the people connected within the firms, or through the firms or the state. *This income is depreciated after currency depreciation (punishment), which in fact reduces costs and restores competitiveness.* If keeping funds in foreign currency is allowed, this punishment does not affect the income that was previously transferred into this currency. This makes currency depreciation insufficient, i.e. its "arithmetic" effect is not properly reflected in the economy. Previously earned income stored in foreign currency did not decrease but in fact increased if expressed in national currency. This relative increase in savings by itself provokes an increase in prices for goods.

Note that the situation of keeping savings in foreign currency that we have just described will not completely reflect the picture of households' well-being. The poorest who have little or no savings and entrepreneurs who do not export their goods will lose more from currency depreciation than others. Even though these entrepreneurs may be wealthy, most of their wealth is usually invested in business. Assets of non-exporters at each point in time consist mainly of goods with prices tied to the local currency ("rouble") and "roubles" proper. Less affected groups include the middle class and all kinds of renters. The latter are not relevant for our analysis, and a substantial part of the middle class is represented by middle and top managers. Reduction of salaries versus savings expressed in terms of foreign currency to some degree demotivates these workers. This may be expressed in a subconscious change of attitude towards work or in a conscious mindset: "For this kind of compensation, I'd better stay out of work and look for opportunities." As a result, in many companies the quality of management either deteriorates or the costs to pay managers increase to keep this quality sufficient.

Such a "strike" does not mean that such managers are "irresponsible citizens". In their place, I and any another person might well do the same. We just observe a local deflationary effect: if one has some savings, it can be more profitable to use these than to work.

Deflation from costs.

Deflation (during a deflationary crisis) lowers the costs in a national economy but this process is slow and painful. During the last crisis in Europe it even got its own nickname, "internal devaluation", although deflation and devaluation are two opposite processes. Where devaluation lowers salaries automatically, for instance, this does not happen with deflation. A deflationary cost reduction is accompanied by layoffs, hired labour losing their qualifications, entrepreneurs going broke and production facilities declining. These unpleasant effects have always existed and will always exist in a market economy due to competition, but a very important sense of proportion is missing from the existing capitalist economy.

In its pure form, the deflationary effect, like deflation (from costs) itself in its classical meaning, is forever lost in the era of the gold standard. Back then, the "pink-coloured glasses" that we discussed in Chapter 2, encouraged by banks' primary lending with issuing notes (these banknotes were the paper money proper) led the economy into an overproduction crisis. Bank failures followed the bankruptcies of the goods producers, so banknotes lost their reliability. Thus, the amount of money in the economy shrank, with a natural backstop represented by gold and silver.[164] The overproduction of goods that started while there was still a lot of money available only got worse with this shrinkage. Simply put, the price of

[164] We may say that under gold capitalism, these precious metals were the "high-powered money". Under paper capitalism, this function got transferred to the monetary base represented by paper money, as opposed to the part of "money stock" represented by bank liabilities. Under our PCM model, as we have stated, due to the separation between credit and payment systems, bank liabilities will be entirely deprived of their payment function. There will remain just money.

money expressed in goods went up while the price of goods expressed in money fell. Entrepreneurs might have faced the fact that after selling their goods they had less money than they had spent on production, and not because they lost to competitors – the latter found themselves in a similar predicament. The situation was totally the opposite with the money owners, as the price of money expressed in goods increased and it made more sense to not rush to part with money. Entrepreneurs would have been glad to get out of this vicious circle, but an exit from the economy's real sector is next to impossible during a deflationary crisis, barring a possible chain of fortunate events. Nobody is eager to offer acceptable prices for non-monetary assets. As a rule, freezing production is not an option either, as without sales, one's fixed costs will likely cause a ruin.[165]

Under paper capitalism, it is more difficult to see this simply defined deflation (money appreciation relative to goods), as the value of gold

---

[165] The naturally conservative nature of these processes, radically different from the high liquidity of stocks trading on an exchange, saves the market economy from inevitable nationalisation. We just don't think about it, but if the opposite were true and anyone could exit the real economy in the manner similar to stocks, by a mouse click, we would all likely live under some kind of socialism. Then, during a deflationary crisis intrinsic to capitalism, there would be no danger of the civilisation diving into a hungry chaos due to a freeze in the economy. Maybe it would not be a chaos but instead a sort of "hungry capitalism" would ensue had we chosen to return to the pure gold standard suggested by the Austrian School. This would be a chronic overproduction crisis interweaved with hungry protests (where the entrepreneurs refuse to lower prices below cost, at the same time as offering lower pay to, or simply laying off, workers in order to reconcile their costs with a notable appreciation of money compared with goods). Keynes, to my mind, did not exaggerate when he called the gold standard a barbarous relic. In case you sympathise with this perennial technological idea by the Austrian School, I would advise you to pay attention to the fact that the fourth basic regulator, being discussed in this chapter, either would not work or would destroy the gold standard. Currency depreciation is not possible either in cases where every national currency is tied to gold and every country has enough gold to back up their money, or, in cases where there is not enough gold, the gold standard goes up in smoke. Good old capitalism, the funeral of which I hope to witness, apparently has more common sense compared to an economy based on a pure gold standard. Not long ago, we experienced as a civilisation the real (soft) gold standard, when bankers issued their own paper money (promissory notes, for example) in varying proportion to the amount of gold in their possession. At the same time, with this easy-to-understand fallacy of returning to the gold standard, I would bet my whole net worth against a crumpled ten rouble note (counting on easy money) that even if the Austrian School finally gives up this idea, similar retro "innovations" would still spring up periodically.

money is out of reach for paper money due to the natural shortage of material to manufacture the former. The functions of gold money have been partially inherited by the global currencies, with the main difference being that compared with gold money, one can print "as many dollars as you want". Thus, under a global deflationary crisis we have a mix of both the traditional appreciation of "high-powered money" (just money) relative to the part of "money stock" represented by bank liabilities, and the appreciation of global currencies relative to other currencies. From the perspective of the latter, they experience depreciation. One has to look at the context when trying to understand whether an ordinary currency is undergoing depreciation or a global currency is undergoing deflation.

Let's return to our example with the classical depreciation of currency. In the first iteration we pointed out that the effect of currency depreciation is a decrease in the prices of domestic goods (prices expressed in a foreign currency) compared with the prices of foreign goods. Then, we took a deeper look and pointed out that this decrease is caused by a relative decrease in production costs for domestic goods. Production costs, like any costs in general, reflect consumption, i.e. the income of people. Subsequently, we split this income into consumption and saving, and I tried to show that the effectiveness of currency depreciation is determined not only by a relative decrease in wages but also by a relative decrease in savings.

Now, let me offer a simple generalisation that unites wages and savings. Through currency depreciation, the "invisible hand of the market" (*under the PCM,*[166] currency depreciation will be an entirely market phenomenon) cuts excessive consumption by a country's population. The root cause of a crisis is excessive consumption, so until this consumption is sufficiently lowered, the crisis will not be over.

Gold under paper capitalism.

Centralised money printing marks the onset of paper capitalism. It greatly increased the reliability of paper money and in the end allowed it to replace coins made of precious metals. The latter were quite expensive in terms of production and circulation. However, the above statement on reliability is valid only for money proper and not for "money stock" (see the very first thesis, "*Money and money stock ...*"). This difference clearly

[166] This reasoning about the mechanism of currency depreciation is correct for a classical or (largely) near-classical national economy but it cannot be applied to "wonderland" countries.

manifested itself during the Great Depression, when clients could not get their money previously deposited in the banks that failed. We can draw a parallel: under gold capitalism, paper money (bank notes) formed some "layer of unreliability" around precious metal money, while nowadays such a layer around money is represented by the remainder of "money stock". Both layers are united by the fact that they are bank liabilities.

As a little digression, let's point out a well-known fact that in recent years, depositor fears have greatly subsided due to governments guaranteeing to compensate, to some extent, their losses stemming from bank failures. From the PCM model's inner logic perspective, these guarantees are populist measures. First, not all deposits are guaranteed in the case of mass bank failures. Second, the people who trusted their money to the banks in order to make a profit should understand all the risks involved, as money does not multiply automatically.[167] In particular, there will always be those who lose in credit operations. However, none of the capitalist formations are purely market ones, so under the given circumstances this fits very well: in the case of a bank run, the viability of the entire payment system, facilitated by the banks, is at stake. Under the PCM system, the money kept in all current accounts will be fully protected from massive bank failures, even though there may be no apparent reasons for them.[168]

Reformatting the structures of "broad money" under paper capitalism was not limited by forming these two new layers. In the middle of the last century, the US dollar stood out from the number of other paper currencies, as recorded in the Bretton Woods Agreement of 1944. Initially, it did not look like something fundamentally new, since throughout the entire economic history currencies of some countries were distinguished. Besides, as in the case of the US dollar, it was always somehow related to the reliability provided by the precious metals. However, with the refusal of the US to exchange the dollar for gold in 1971, there was a fundamentally new element created – a genuine global currency intrinsic to paper capitalism.

---

[167] In my first book, *A Strictly Classical Economy*, published back in 2007, I cited a well-known example. If, at the dawn of the Common Era, someone deposited one aureus (a quarter-ounce Roman gold coin) in a bank at 3 per cent interest and 2000 years later some grateful descendants remembered this odd generosity, the coin with all the accrued interest (1.03 to the power of 2000) would have turned into a gold bullion weighing $3.78*10^{20}$ tons, or the equivalent of five moons.

[168] There is even less reason for the central bank's failure, as it won't be involved in any credit deals, including those with the central banks of other nations.

As a result of abandoning the "gold standard", the main functions of gold in the monetary system transferred to the global currency. After the centralisation of paper money production strengthened its reliability, the most important function of the global currency was its use in foreign trade in lieu of gold. To complete the picture, let's add that due to the super-resilience of global currencies they largely replaced gold as a means of treasure. In addition, high net-worth owners invested in the government bonds of the countries issuing global currencies. Accounting for the interest income, these holdings were for a time more attractive than gold.

Let's finish this preamble and get to the point. Since the year 2000, the prices of gold and other precious metals used for centuries as a safe investment hedge against inflation have been rising consistently. Taking into account a substantial drop in gold prices in 2012–2015, one could probably call this a "bubble". Still, for the purpose of our study we better depart from this terminology bearing a stock exchange connotation. The term "bubble" reflects a danger of losses stemming from a sudden drop in listed prices or, like market analysts say, from exceeding an "equilibrium (or fair) price".

We have already discussed this last term. It does not make sense to lash out on the everyday use of a term that briefly describes some centre of price fluctuation due to the continuous interaction of supply and demand if everyone puts the same sense into it (or more precisely, almost the same, because as soon as we touch upon a specific situation and "put different thinkers in separate rooms", they may offer different perspectives on the technical analysis of this particular situation).

As for the "bubbles", despite the simplicity of the name – unlike the near-scientific sounding "equilibrium price" and the fact that not all fears turn into bursting "bubbles" – it's hard to argue against that they do really happen. However, "bubbles" can be referring either to some local speculative surge in an isolated industry, or to a feverish growth phase preceding a cyclical overproduction crisis in the global economy. For us, these are fundamentally different cases. Thanks to its scale and theoretical significance, the described appreciation and depreciation of gold deserves special attention when talking about paper capitalism.

The emphasis here is as follows. The appreciation and depreciation of gold at the beginning of this century constitutes a reaction of the financial system of modern capitalism to the birth of another global currency with a level of influence comparable with the dollar. It is specifically about the emphasis, since other factors influence gold price fluctuations as well, but this emphasis unambiguously appears to us as the main one. Due to the existence of many centres of economic policy, the euro – the currency of the community of economies that are powerful in aggregate albeit inflexible – established itself in the market just at the turn of the century. From that moment on, there have been doubts about both the exclusivity and indispensability of the dollar.

With all that, the dollar is still the number one global currency, i.e. the preferred currency used to settle international trade. For as long as this is the case, the dollar will be held in high esteem by the holders of ordinary currencies. Therefore, the above-mentioned doubts about the indispensability of the dollar do not materially change these feelings. However, they were reflected in the depreciation of the dollar (and other currencies, concurrently) relative to gold (as well as platinum, silver, oil and other exchange-traded commodities).

Let's digress a bit to decipher the "doubts" by outlining the main functions performed by a global currency. Note that the well-known use of dollars, euros and securities denominated in these currencies as a savings vehicle (for instance, for state reserves) stems from these functions.

The first function is settling international trade. The second one is facilitating international credit turnover. These two functions are directly related to purchase and sale deals, as well as pure credit deals. The third known function, which is specific to the existing financial system, may appear a bit more complicated. The most popular securities (including derivatives) are denominated in global currencies. We won't have great difficulty with the theoretical understanding of this function, as we have already gone over the surrogate mix of credit deals, and purchase and sale deals represented by securities.

The high liquidity of global currencies is naturally reflected in the elevated liquidity of these securities. Of course, the fact of issuing securities that are denominated in dollars is not a panacea for a firm. However, other corporate securities are often dumped simply because the currency of denomination appears to be unstable. Global currencies, on the contrary, are super-resilient by definition.

As a result, US government securities enjoy the highest liquidity as a safe haven, due to the US being the issuer of the number one global currency. Still, every investor understands that the value of their holdings will be preserved only in the case where the dollar remains a global currency. Otherwise, they would get back some greatly depreciated dollars. Doubts about the indispensability of the dollar as a global currency, as viewed through a simple practical lens of actions by financial market participants, primarily translate to fears for the redemption of funds invested in the US Treasuries. Therefore, commodities as alternative safe havens, and first of all, gold, showed price gains.

With the onset of the crisis, doubts about the viability of global currencies have only increased and gold has gained even more. Note one important moment which is that when the crisis unfolded, the price of gold did not fall. The price increase for gold is undoubtedly linked to the phases of a cyclical crisis, but this link is not direct and is rather influenced by the perception of a role for the euro. Following the crisis's onset, the scale of the harm threatening the euro area was not immediately clear. Over time, it became obvious that the fate of the dollar and euro could take fundamentally different turns. Where the US was able to take care of the dollar's reliability, restore economic growth using the stimulus measures and supply the world economy with dollars all at the same time, the euro area was forced to concentrate mainly on the euro's survival.

The crisis uncovered one problem related to the introduction of the second global currency. For the world economy, the costs of having the second locomotive of consumption represented by the population of the euro area turned out to be too high. Let's stress that "the crisis uncovered one problem related to the introduction of the second global currency" and not, as it may have ostensibly seemed, that the crisis began as Europeans started to consume too much. Concurrent with increased consumption by countries issuing global currencies, consumption also increased in the rest of the world. For instance, it went up markedly in the nations exporting raw materials, following major commodity price increases.

Taking into account the transition of most people in the euro area into consumers of *accumulated* issuance income (we'll give some terminology clarifications shortly), our "butterfly" would have to shed more costs in the near-classical economies to continue flying after the crisis ended, as compared with the situation before the introduction of the euro.[169] One

[169] It is hard to say whether the Deutsche Mark (DM) would have become a second fully fledged global currency, absent the euro, taking into account the economic problems of Germany's reunification and how exactly the situation unfolded. However, what happened, happened, i.e. the transition of a large number of nations with an amorphous management centre into the ranks of consumers of the world's

possible chain of future events is that decreasing costs in "the rest of the world" economies due to tightening Federal Reserve policies may shrink the size of the "wonderland". If this does not happen, we believe that the world economy would still be impacted by excessive consumption while waiting for yet another technological "miracle".

The term "issuance income" *is organic to the PCM model.* It is easy to calculate and to represent correctly: here's the level achieved by the national economy "yesterday" and here's the new money issued "today" (i.e. the issuance income), with the latter in the simplest case being equal to the "one day" increase of both physical and credit turnover. In the existing model, this income cannot be calculated correctly due to the credit issuance of money and the securities market. As a consequence, this income is difficult to understand, especially in the "wonderland" nations, where the national currency plays the role of a global currency. There, both issuance income and GDP appear as an accumulated transition from the "negative" to the "positive". We have discussed this in the Chapter 1 thesis "*Physical turnover expressed in monetary terms and global currencies ...*". Since we have already gone over detailed discussions about credit and securities in Chapter 2, let me offer a simplified scenario of contrasting near-classical and "wonderland" economic systems.

One entrepreneur appeals to the government in a "regular" nation, "My securities have all turned to junk, I have enormous debt and no bank will extend me credit, so I cannot even afford the payroll. If I

---

issuance income. This transition constituted a certain leap and was different from a situation where Germany would keep beefing up its economic muscle and gradually, under some competitive pressure, increase the share of the DM on the currency market to the present share of the euro. The actual leap was not towards a more advanced economy but to a new perception in people's minds (Germany is just a country, while a combined Europe represents the largest economy in the world). From the perspective of classical economic laws (let's call this perspective "technical" here), this combination of European nations has *deteriorated* their economies due to the subdued effect of the fourth basic cost regulator. One should not think that the notorious examples of regional protectionism that followed the highly publicised removal of trade barriers constitute the real reasons for unification (just by looking at the shelves of some French supermarket chains, one can see, without having the complete picture available, the protective measures that have been negotiated for domestic producers by the French European officials). As we have already noted while talking about the issuance of stocks, the real motivation of issuers can be quite different from its advertised packaging.

am able to continue my business, everyone would win, including myself, my employees and you, the government." And the government answers, "Sorry we can't help. We have crushing debt here as well, a negative balance of payments, the national currency has lost value and so nobody will lend to us at a reasonable rate. Maybe you could lend us some money? What did you say? You have no money either? Take it easy, go for massage therapy – they say services are cheap now ..."

But the same dire situation with debts for both sides in a "wonderland" economy plays differently. The state has a "golden" magic wand represented by a super-resilient national currency that is capable of turning anything into "gold", including junk securities and expensive services. People still have jobs, government securities (which will never be paid back at comparable prices) are still considered the most reliable investments and no investors vanish.

If we consider the issuance income in a country that issues a global currency in the same way we would do for the PCM model, our attention would automatically focus on the magnitude of money issuance. I would argue that issuance income in this case exceeds money issuance proper, so it would be fitting to talk about *accumulated* issuance income. This would become obvious once such a country returns to the level playing field of competing producers of goods. For the ensuing drop in state income (as well as the income of business and workers), it would be logical to conclude that the total resulting losses are close to the global currency issuance income lost in the process.

The creation of a single global currency by Western nations.

This scenario is *unlikely* to be practical, but it would be useful to talk about certain theoretical features in this regard.

Here are the initial considerations, which are the same as we had at the end of the last thesis. As a world economic leader (in other words, as a country whose well-being directly depends upon the world economic growth rate and corresponding increase in international turnover of commodities, credit and securities), the US must help reduce costs in the global economy when it's necessary. This involves a tight credit policy in order to promote a deflationary cost reduction. Let's clarify that it will be deflationary from the perspective of the US only. For the rest of the world, it will appear as, conversely, property depreciation against the dollar (thus, for currencies other than the dollar, it will mean their devaluation). As we have already stated in the thesis "*The partial direct issuance of money ...*", among the measures to mitigate the latest crisis, the soft (Keynesian in nature) policy in terms of cost reduction was started too early. The period similar to that in the 1920s and 1930s (at that time, leading to the Great Depression but allowing the reduction of costs) was missed. Nevertheless, future events may lead to a situation where the geopolitical allies of the US will undergo a similar cost-reduction cycle. Accordingly, the euro may then be discredited as a global currency. To soften this possible blow for the geopolitical allies of the US (or those whom they do not want to have as adversaries), they may want to create a certain unified (transatlantic or transpacific) economy.

Depending on the degree of this economic unification, there are two main options available: "a customs union plus" or just "a union". The "plus" qualifier refers to all sorts of additional clauses to the customs union in the form of a standardisation of rules for businesses, banks and government regulators throughout this new association of countries. The alternative ("union") option means the additional introduction of a single currency. The first option is quite realistic, despite the inevitable and unpleasant consequences (for market self-regulation of national economies) of a touching unity of international bureaucracy in their fight against bureaucratisation. However, it is not very interesting for our theoretical discussion.

As for the union option, this project to unify the collection of the world's issuance income by people of Western countries is meaningless in terms of resolving the fundamental issues of paper capitalism. But against the background of this idea (here, we will leave out the idea of the Western union, due to its low probability), we can dwell on the problems related to the creation of such a mega-currency.

The idea of a supranational currency, like the gold standard or communism, will apparently always live in some hot heads. A reasonable reaction to all these three ideas is "hopefully it will never happen". Generally, there are two options for introducing a supranational currency.

The first one, which is quite realistic, is that while preserving their political independence, all countries of the world completely abandon their currencies by launching, say, "UNency" instead. This is fundamentally possible, as vividly proved by the euro-area countries. The main problem – for which this option, in my opinion, should be immediately excluded from consideration – is that in this case we refuse one of the four basic cost regulators, namely the cross-price. In other words, we move to an economy always prone to deflation and poor countries would not have any other cost reduction options besides slow deflationary impoverishment, as happened in Greece. Moreover, we cannot even fully imagine the depth and frequency of such impoverishment, accompanied by workers losing their skills. Under modern capitalism, the fourth regulator still occasionally works, even in the form of catastrophic national currency collapses. In addition, there will be nobody to help outsiders on the same scale that Europe (having the profits from the issue of the global currency) helped Greece.

A lack of flexibility and ability of the national economy to self-heal rapidly are the inevitable consequences of abandoning the fourth regulator. The negative effects may seem to be enough of a price of the right to issue a global currency in the euro area. However, it's safe to say that after the transition to the PCM model, most European countries will return to their national currencies, while preserving certain elements of economic integration. Once there are no global currencies, there is no valid reason to either bail out the laggards or continue living in a slowly deteriorating economy where people do not have well-paid jobs.

The second option is to introduce a single global currency (close to the idea of the bancor that was proposed by Keynes) with the sole function to facilitate international settlements. This idea may exist, albeit only in the form of purely speculative and mutually incompatible initiatives. By the way, a prototype of the bancor has existed since 1969, when the IMF created Special Drawing Rights (SDR). A seemingly sophisticated name is well balanced by the wretched existence of this account's unit.

The problem with the bancor idea is that there is no mechanism acceptable to the "invisible hand of the market" that would help create (when and how much?) and distribute (to whom and how much?) such an immense property as world money, without running into some large-scale problems. Such questions arise because there must be an owner defined for this new money from the very beginning. For example, now it is the central bank and under the PCM it will be the government. One can, of course, try out various compilations of gold capitalism, paper capitalism and PCM, but armed with the simple principle of Occam's razor, I may politely ask:

What for? If we are going to limit the circulation of "UNency" only by international settlements, we get the same "daisy" as the PCM. There will be inevitable bans on currency crossing national borders, with just one odd element, namely the entire international currency. And it won't be just one unit, but a beast locked in an unreliable cage that will encroach on national basic cost regulators and require extremely bureaucratic control over the distribution of this new world money to prevent the emergence of gigantic imbalances.

How the famous "decay of capitalism" might happen.

The birth of the euro has shrunk the safety margin of paper capitalism. If a third global currency appears, this tendency will become even clearer. In this situation, the main hope of the beneficiaries of the existing financial system is to wait for the next technological breakthrough. This would enable an increased issuance of global currencies, boost the securities markets and overshadow the shortcomings of the system with the optimism of an economic recovery.

If the wait is delayed, the best option for capitalism (and the worst for the speedy transition to the PCM, as it gives back to capitalism a certain margin of safety) is the destruction of one global currency by the other, with a sharp decrease in the number of consumers of the world's issuance income. The more graceful (albeit more complicated) scenario would be a reduction of the euro area stemming from the exclusion of some laggard national economies. If the euro area copes with problems without a significant loss of members or even staying intact, it is possible to expect it to go through some stagnant manoeuvring while waiting for the next technological breakthrough.

A real godsend for the world economy would be to replace both existing global currencies, the dollar and the euro. I think, in this case, people in the US and Europe would not want to give up a single day's worth of their national issuance income. This reincarnation of the elves as gnomes obviously would not suit them, meaning that they would likely advocate transition to a PCM. However, this option looks much more remote than others.

In the current situation, the political elites of the US and Europe will most likely delay (or just keep silent about) a possible transition until some countries of the world produce political leaders who no longer want to put up with the neo-colonial division of the world that is slowing the development of the global economy. It is also quite possible that any leaders who initiate the transition of their countries to the PCM model will appear on both sides of the "divider".

CHAPTER 4.

FREQUENTLY ASKED QUESTIONS

(AND OTHER APPENDICES)

FAQ: Can you explain the gist of modern capitalism's problems in plain English?

Problem #1: **Too little money in the economy**

This problem, characteristic of both capitalist formations, appeared along with the development of industrial production, which allowed for a pace of economic growth never seen before. In an economy without enough money, credit and money surrogates (i.e. securities) proliferate. At first glance, they help solve the problem of facilitating economic growth, but their unbridled proliferation creates fundamental aberrations. If the problem of an inadequate increase in available gold has been well understood since a long time ago, the problem of not having enough money under paper capitalism can only be seen when comparing the latter with the PCM monetary system. At a closer look, it is clear that the existing monetary system does not handle its task of facilitating economic growth to the extent possible given today's level of technological progress.

Problem #2: **The inequality of national currencies**

Global currencies also started to emerge under gold capitalism but they became fully fledged once the gold standard was abandoned and the paper money of the world's most developed nation, the US, replaced gold in servicing international trade. This created certain non-classical interconnections, quite visible to the naked eye. However, theoretical studies have failed to reflect these major aberrations and, correspondingly, the way they hinder the development of the world economy.

Only with the emergence of modern computing technologies can both problems have their possible solutions.

FAQ: The old central bank versus new central bank. Illustration of the existing three-tier payment system and the two-tier payment system under the PCM.

1. The main characteristic difference of the central bank under the PCM will be that its operations related to *issuing* and *transferring* money will no longer need to be accounted for on its balance sheet.[170] This will apply not only to the central bank, as upon transition to the PCM model, all money transfers in the economy will no longer need to be reflected on bank balances. Simply put (here, I am about to make a bold statement), the whole economy will get rid of the excessive influence of bank balances. In the existing formation, this influence weakens only when cash is used for settlements. The circulation of cash, due to its simple nature and precise identification of currency units, enables and even demands for much simpler accounting based on a "receipts and expenses" principle. The abandonment of cash under the PCM appears to be natural, due to the simple reason that non-cash money, in terms of its simplicity and precise identification, will be no different from actual banknotes and coins.

The significance of bank balances for accounting economic activity under the PCM will decrease, due to shrinkage of the financial system in general and banks' exclusive rights to issue loans in particular, as well as due to certain fundamental simplifications inside the banking system proper. Above all, for the first time in history, banks won't have anything to do with the transfer of money, as the payment system will be taken away from them.

Moreover, there won't even be a hint of their participation in the money issuance. Again, for the first time in history, all kinds of "multipliers", the effect of which a bank balance helps to align to a common denominator, will disappear. The most visible effect of the multiplier, as the multiplier of money proper, arose from the parallel circulation of paper and gold money, as banks issued more paper money than their gold holdings.

---

[170] There will remain a function of controlling the commercial banks, with the latter still using their balance sheets to account for their relations with creditors and clients. Use of the term "bank" (in the phrase "central bank") will still be justified, for this sole reason.

Gradually, everything became more complicated. Various "instruments" that we have patiently sorted out in this study (with incessant terminological clarifications) gained more influence. Now, we will not complicate the narrative and will just list their main types as sources of "multipliers" (prudently trying not to casually clarify where or how the multiplication of money ends and the multiplication of certain assets or liabilities begins) – balances in bank accounts, i.e. non-cash money of the payment system (in our PCM model, we got rid of the "multipliers" thanks to the split into credit and payment systems); foreign currency ("electronic errand boy") and securities with a credit component (banned).

As a result of our transformations, banking will become much more unified (raise "small change" from many and loan these collected money resources to a few). However, the commercial banks themselves will still use the bank balance, as the accounting of credit deals will remain the main reason for using it by banks. The division into liabilities (what we owe) and assets (what we have and what we are owed) to some extent reflects the theoretical essence of the credit deal, i.e. a unilateral rejection of property. However, it is helpful to combine awareness of the importance of a bank balance for accounting activities of commercial banks with an understanding of one unpleasant side effect, namely that the bank balance shifts the emphasis in the reflection of economic events. Therefore, it would be a fundamental mistake to allow too much space in the PCM for the bank balance, instead of simple cash accounting based on the principle of "receipts and expenses".

Here is the difference. The latter principle first transmits the very essence of the deal: which property is being transferred to whom. For example, we gave our partner some apples and got money in return (C↔M). Now, our partner has the apples (which are still called apples) and we have the money; it is all quite clear. Conversely, there is a speculative division into assets and liabilities on the bank balance sheet that immediately complicates the perception of the deal. This stems from the specifics of a credit transaction, namely the unilateral property alienation that we have mentioned, and one unique feature of the basic credit deal: there is one and the same kind of property (from either a physical or sensual point of view) on both sides of the deal. There is no inscription on the money whether it is credit or not, and therefore using different terms for the money depending on a particular operation appears to be more justified. Yes, the features of a credit deal require the use of specific terms but the latter imply further difficulties, like a proverbial Chekhov's "shotgun hanging on the wall". Note also that for a borrower who is not going into the money-lending business, there is no need for this complex distinction. Having received a loan, a borrower would use the proceeds like any other money (paying regard to the terms of the principal and interest payments).

The significance of the second difference, which we are going to address here, is more pronounced. Although there is no criminal in sight (not counting the gold standard), the proverbial "shotgun hanging on the wall" occasionally goes off by itself. The point is that, unlike the cash method of accounting for the "receipts and expenses" which more accurately conveys the essence of a deal as an event (it happened and ended; something happened to us and we reflected it – and this is true for all deals, including credit), bank balances show the "continuity of the universe" (nothing appears from nowhere or suddenly disappears). It sounds sober, given that banks strive to account for every penny. If a bank does crank up complexity, its customers are shielded from it.

Certain fundamental difficulties are experienced not by commercial banks nor by their customers, but by the central bank under the existing formation. The central bank tries building the "assets–liabilities" paradigm into a coherent theoretical scheme to use it as guidance for managing the national economy. Meanwhile, distorted records of the deals (there are no such theoretical economic categories as "assets" and "liabilities", as these are merely accounting terms) are hindering this guidance, or, more specifically, impeding the display of money issuance as a process of manufacturing new money. Using the "receipts and expenses" accounting method, we simply record, for example, a new-born calf. By applying the bank balance principles, the "birth" of new money (i.e. as the economic common sense suggests, the newly emerged assets) must be balanced by a corresponding record in liabilities. However, the opposite takes place as new money is recorded as liabilities, counterbalanced by purported assets of the central bank. Banks practised this technique back in the times of the gold standard, by issuing paper money (bank notes) backed by their gold holdings. This practice reflected the economic reality of the situation, as banks committed to exchange the notes back to gold on demand. However, upon abandonment of the gold standard, once centrally issued money-as-numbers occupy the top place in the hierarchy, its representation as bank notes is erroneous. (By the way, this representation goes contrary to one of the principles of constructing a bank balance, which is a priority of economic essence over form.) Therefore, the "liabilities of the central bank" appear to be, to put it simply, a fake. The central bank has nothing valuable to offer in exchange for bank notes, besides other notes (possibly in a different denomination).

Here, it would be fair to make an important note that the credit issuance of money performed by central banks under paper capitalism is vicious in principle. The central banks issue new money as if they own it, although this new money is earned by the entire national economy (which is nevertheless forced to borrow it). The attempt to mitigate this distortion of economic sense by reflecting the new money as central bank liabilities appears to be a clumsy manoeuvre that in turn causes new distortions. It makes no sense to argue for changes under the existing financial system (I see no original malicious intent in this at all). The central banks do what they can, while the bank balance appears to be indispensable. But one should not wonder why, in that part of our study that deals with money movement, we do not have much consideration for the way central banks offer to name certain parts of their balances.

2. Illustration of the three-tier payment system, using an example with two banks (B_1 and B_2; see Fig. 4-1). Each commercial bank has two clients. The bank's correspondent accounts at the central bank are depicted as BA and the client accounts are depicted as CA. The movement of *non-cash* funds is represented by a solid bold connector. Money issuance (as a decision to manufacture new money) is indicated by the dashed line. The triangles drawn in dash-dotted lines reflect the movement of "clearing money" within the banks. The bottom two-sided arrow sides points to settlements inside the bank; the one-sided arrow sides point to the clearing of payments between the clients of different banks that are using correspondent accounts. Unlike the former, the latter payments partially require the "usual" movement of funds between BA_1 and BA_2. Apart from the funds' movement depicted by dashed and dash-dotted lines, any other supplementary information (orders, accounting, invoices) is not drawn on the chart. Hence, it may not look like some other illustrations.

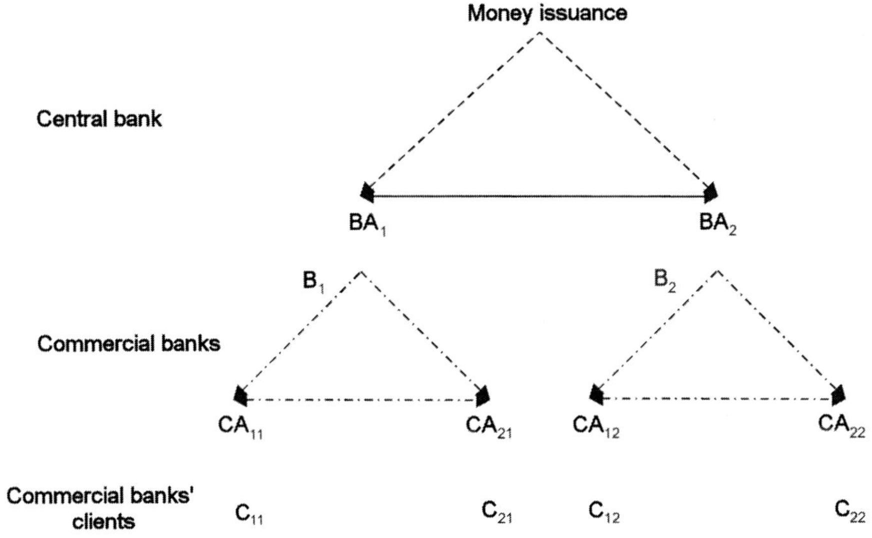

Fig. 4-1

3. Illustration of the two-tier payment system, using an example with two clients of the central bank (with the added issuance income that goes to the government):

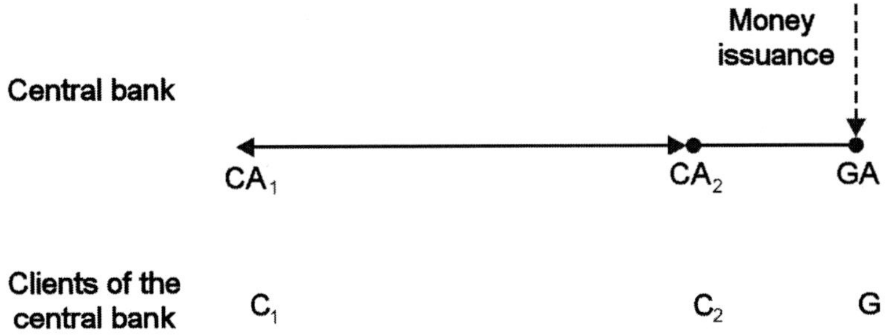

Fig. 4-2

These illustrations omit the following:

- Movement of cash (paper money). If we were to draw additional arrows showing this movement between any two economic agents, this would surely enliven both illustrations, especially the first one. However, if I properly understand how illustrations are to be used, they should facilitate but not complicate the learning. Meanwhile, the movement of paper money does not change the gist of either illustration.
- Cross-border movement of money. We'll just note a fundamental difference of the PCM financial system, namely our "electronic errand boy".
- Details on how the loans are issued. These details stem largely from the features of the payment system.

FAQ: The shrinking of money stock and the interest rate.

From the beginning of Chapter 1 where we started modelling the monetary system of our PCM, we set out to move the payment system away from the commercial banks. As a result, part of the "money stock" (current accounts that were reflected as bank liabilities) morphed into full-bodied money (see the thesis "*Money and money stock* ..."). One might have the suspicion that this decrease in commercial banks' liabilities will shrink the "money stock" and, as a result, will push the interest rate upwards.

At the time of the introduction of the new payment system, a technical reduction of "money stock" will indeed happen (we'll talk details later). Until the banking system changes to a new pattern, it can indeed *briefly* push the interest rate up. But it looks like (we will talk about this later, too) the said effect can be "treated" by the central bank without any problems. There may be more problems while transforming the retail sector, due to the prohibition of deferred payments. There will be a peak demand for loans from the retailers and getting over it will take time.

Going forward, I think that the *world-average* interest rate will be even lower than now and for certain it won't be noticeably higher. There are several reasons for this:

First, the amount of *money* in the economy will increase significantly, compared with the current financial system. This is a fundamental point for analysing interest rates, unlike the value of the "money stock" that consists mainly of commercial banks' liabilities. But here are some subtle moments: this difference is hard to notice through an abstract comparison of static images. It is better to reason in terms of an imaginary chain: "An increase in the amount of money due to the separation of credit and payment systems → increase in the amount of money due to an increase in the volume of money issuance" (we will discuss this reasoning separately). The difference discussed here would have been very visible in times of deflationary crises. With the onset of hard times under paper capitalism, the "invisible hand" of the classical economy can't reach the *money* tied up in credit chains, while the gigantic volume of "money stock" can only offer a little help. With the PCM, there is much more money in the economy. Where previously under paper capitalism there would be a crisis with a spiked demand for credit and the concurrent collapse of surrogate assets, under the PCM model the impact will be limited to a "light disturbance".

Second, the demand for credit will decrease due to major shrinking of the financial sector. Meanwhile, the supply will increase for this same reason, as part of the savings that people used for financial transactions would go to the commercial banks and part may be invested in new businesses (this part of the money will go into the real economy without credit obligations). The counterargument that the supply of foreign loans will decrease due to the closing of credit frontiers has every right to exist but acknowledging it requires some caveats. When we talk about closing the credit frontiers, let's not forget that nobody offered to shut the borders for direct investment. Accordingly (earlier in the same paragraph we also indicated this in parentheses), there is every reason to hope for an increase in these cross-border investments. But the most important thing to consider is that under the PCM, the interest rates won't be so much all over the place to the extent that is inherent under paper capitalism. Nowadays, the existence of the global currencies – directly or indirectly – predetermines the presence of both non-classical low rates and non-classical inflated rates. This factor determines both the direction and volume of cross-border lending. It may be difficult to reconcile all these arguments and counterarguments in a single bottom line, but from my point of view, the very first phrase of this paragraph is crucial.

Third, new money will flow into the economy without the interest attached.

Fourth, there will be no reserves required.

Fifth, the demand for loans in the *mature* PCM system will decrease due to an increased credit self-discipline of retail stores and networks. Many producers run up high debts now, which directly stems from the fact that they *are forced* to extend supplier credit to trading companies. These demands for delayed payment originate in the retail sector – i.e. for producers, these terms are *others'* decisions. Regardless of their ability to conduct business and the attractiveness of their products, manufacturers are doomed to keep knocking on creditors' doors. It does not even occur to anyone that with reasonable ways of doing business, one can prosper without borrowing and even afford funds for reasonable expansion.

Yes, under the new financial system, the credit burden will fall on the retail trading business but their decisions will be *unforced*. They will determine the speed at which to expand. That is why we are talking about "self-discipline". Now, here's a word about discipline proper. The selection of goods, for which one has to pay immediately, will become vital for retail business. Stores are the last stop in the movement of goods that either need to be sold or will have to be "thrown out" (one can still send some for recycling, which is often a close alternative). Commercial banks will also understand this situation by treating their loan decisions for retail businesses very carefully. Bulk procurement technologies (which trigger massive demand for loans down the chain) will begin, to some extent, to give way to the personal participation of entrepreneurs and their best specialists (including, as they say, natural-born traders) in the selection of goods. At the same time, we must accept as a given that both the mental and technological restructuring of the industry as a whole will take time and compromise. Until the retail makeover is completed, the demand for credit will indeed *increase*. A revolution – even an economic one – has never been an easy accomplishment.

Now, let's discuss some of the details, starting with reducing the "money stock" at the time of separating out the payment system, as mentioned at the beginning of the thesis. All this will be much clearer if we immediately disregard cash. During the transition to our new system, there won't be any significant changes with regard to paper money. Considering also that in the new system there will be no trading of securities, we will delete these from our reasoning (talk about momentary technical consequences of their elimination is entirely about the transition period, which cannot be described theoretically). We will only have the obligations of banks remaining to their depositors about the return (or safekeeping) of their money, reflected in bank liabilities. Now, we can get rid of the term "money stock" without much hassle because the negative subconscious impact of this term appears to be insignificant. In reality, this impact can be plain destructive, since money proper (remember, we are only talking about non-cash money) in the existing system is reflected in commercial banks' assets and these are not functionally or quantitatively identical to liabilities. Let's also recall that bank liabilities in the existing system can be combined for simplicity into two groups: term deposits and demand deposits. We have agreed to call the latter "current accounts", without segregating their owners into individuals or legal entities. In the process of separating the credit and payment systems, we transfer current accounts to the central bank. We mean this technical moment when talking about "a decrease in money stock and an increase in the monetary base". In reality, one can talk about the complete disappearance of the "money stock" *as a category*, since *term deposits will not be used in any way in the payment system*. There will be just the records of credit liabilities of commercial banks and nothing else.

By the way, here we should not be confused by terminological discrepancies between traditional notions and those that we have worked out while analysing the movement of money from the very beginning of Chapter 1. For example, the accounts of business entities (except commercial banks) in Russia's Central Bank are now treated as money stock. This reflects exactly the fact that the accounts of these entities are difficult to classify as "monetary base" (which is even more difficult than classifying them as "money stock"). It does not pay to search for anything deeper than a forced choice here. This rule is based on a comparison of the terms "monetary base" and "money stock", when the semantic difference between "stock" and "base" becomes a natural key factor. Here, "base" is understood as the source of the creation of "broad money" by the commercial banks under the existing mixed credit and payment system, while non-bank "business entities" are assumed to be engaged in some other activities. We are not interested in the subtleties of the word "base" (as well as the word "stock"). Most likely, after the separation of credit and payment systems, the word "base" will simply die out or will be replaced, but the fundamental word "monetary" will remain. While in the term "monetary base" the first word is appropriate with a few reservations, the "money stock" has a very distant relation to money. It is a fancy mixture of money proper with stereotypes, liabilities, mirages and surrogates. This rough term may fit into the alphabet soup of the financial system of paper capitalism, but our conversation with an emphasis on the new formation requires more rigorous terminology in principal moments.

Returning to the topic of this thesis, note that we should neither underestimate nor exaggerate the technical difficulties of transferring current accounts into the monetary base. The main problem is clear:

- From the point of view of the central bank, at hour X, the balances in the transferred current accounts will double. The central bank "takes away" liabilities from commercial banks (the accounts mentioned), i.e. banks' liabilities to their depositors, places them in its monetary base and thereby converts them into money. Commercial banks' assets will temporarily remain at their disposal and the extra money will be returned by the banks to specially designated accounts at the central bank. Later, the central bank will take out a big eraser and void them.

A less significant problem is as follows:

- Some of the demand deposits are interest bearing. The main solution algorithm is simple as well: commercial banks will have to add any accumulated interest directly to the transferred current accounts of depositors in the unified payment system controlled by the central bank.

Now, let's consider one moment that is relevant to a local increase in the lending rate in the new financial system immediately after the transition. The amount of "money in general" (including the mirages of clearing money) that was used in deals for some period will be comparable to the amount of new money (full-bodied domestic money, given the slowdown of its velocity) used over the same time immediately after the transition. From the perspective of the "residents of the lower floor" for whom that old "mirage money" does not fundamentally differ from the regular domestic money, and the money turnover period is "not highlighted" on money either, the amount of money in the economy immediately after the transition will remain the same.

To put it more precisely, it will remain almost the same, as there is a small and temporary reservation. If it is not considered, it can cause an unpleasant chain reaction. The thing is that credit turnover will decrease, as the central bank has just pulled all current accounts, i.e. the old payment system, from the commercial banks. If left unattended, this will raise the interest rate and therefore will deal a blow to physical turnover.

However, this problem looks scary only at a first glance. With a full understanding of it, the central bank, as already mentioned, will not require an early repayment of loans issued by commercial banks using funds from the payment system. Moreover, the central bank may roll over these loans to the interest-free ones, gradually pulling them from the banks, until "the theory will prove itself".

Let's remember how the theory will work and why the money issuance will increase (this is the chain we specified above, in the "*first*" clause):

- There will be an increase in physical turnover due to reflection in the monetary base of payments in the current system, taking place between customers of a single commercial bank (*immediately*).
- There will be an increase in physical turnover due to reflection in the monetary base of all payments now moving between customers of any two banks and reflected in the total balance between them (*immediately*).
- There will be an increase in physical turnover due to the increase in the number of businesses (due to the shrinking of large integrated companies) with a corresponding increase in payments between them (*gradually*).

Note. The first two bullet points comprise the main "magic" of the unified payment system. I'll try to explain why I used this word. Granted, the new payment system will increase reliability, accelerate payments, reduce costs, allow a departure from the credit issuance of money provoking deflation crises and ditch the "evil bank multiplier" together with required reserves. It will make managing the national economy more transparent and it will be a decisive step towards getting rid of paper money. Finally, it will also help reduce taxes. We have analysed all these effects step by step but for all their significance, none of them looked like "magic" but only a step of a hard journey. The first two clauses create a feeling that "money is being made out of thin air" (*immediately*) and at the heart of this process is a sharp decrease in the velocity of money (i.e. monetary base). Ding! One of our old stereotypes has just fallen apart. It was possibly a bigger surprise for me. For years prior, I had been "running around with bags of money" to make sure that this money was not sitting idle. Conversely, under our new payment system, a central bank's view on money velocity is rather calm, compared with the entrepreneurial rat races ("no worries, why run?"). At a closer look, the components of this attitude appear to be relatively simple – the races "at the lower levels" continue as before, and the issuance income did not come from thin air but rather was taken away from the commercial banks together with the payment system. Finally, "the magic source" is explained (money is just numbers, and no matter how long they sit idle on the hard drives of the central bank's data centre and how much is stored there, the cost is negligible).

Let's point out a clause related to the increase in credit turnover and therefore to the increase of money issuance:

- The monetisation of trade credits (*over time*).

One immediate counterargument tells us about an elevated demand for credit from retailers immediately after the prohibition of trade credits. We have been listing all these clauses as driven by the following logic: increase in the amount of money → increase in the supply of credit → lower interest rates. Meanwhile, monetisation only compensates a part of the elevated demand for credit. Unlike physical turnover, the growth of which allows for an increase in money issuance by the same amount, the increase in credit turnover, as shown by price definition, allows a money issuance increase only in the amount of interest payments (see the thesis "*Forming the price of money in a credit deal.* ..." in Chapter 1). Meanwhile, we have already addressed this counterargument *separately* from the monetisation of trade credits (above, in "*Fifth*, the demand for loans ...") and did not see interest rate increases *in the long term*. As restructuring retail businesses would take some time, the feverish demand for loans on their part seems to be realistic and therefore it may take a while before lower interest rates materialise.

Now, let's point out one more clause with a slightly different undertone:

- Lower taxes.

Note that unlike the previous clauses, a tax decrease won't lead to more money being available in the national economy as a whole. However, it will contribute to having more money in the market sector as a lighter fiscal burden means less need for borrowing.

This undertone arises due to the reason that the monetary system of the PCM is optimal, as compared with any previous system. It is indeed close to perfection, for one obvious reason: **money is just a number**. For the current thesis, this undertone manifests itself as *the importance of the interest rate under the PCM model is not as overwhelming as it is now*. Under paper capitalism, lending (starting from credit issuance of money) fits into every production process, permeating through literally the entire economy. Under the PCM model, the emphasis bends towards the optional nature of credit. Borrowing is required mainly for accelerated growth of a firm (understandably, this does not apply to commercial banks).

FAQ: Full-reserve banking.

The difficulties of creating a unified payment system may lead us to think about one well-known option – voiced by many economists and especially actively by contributors to the Austrian School – collectively known as "full-reserve banking". On the back of some strange proposals by the Austrian School (elimination of the central bank, transition to private currency and quite a shocking thought of moving back to the gold standard), mandating a full-reserve ratio for demand deposits looks like a good idea once we consider it separately from the rest and also not as a dogma but as a starting point for reflections.

We will consider full-reserve banking *only within the scope of our new financial system* (we'll call it "System 100") as a replacement for one of its nodes, namely a unified central bank payment system.[171] This means above all that there are no demand deposits (current accounts) at all. This alleviates many problems (the most obvious one being that commercial banks need to make interest payments while it is impossible to use this money) and, strictly speaking, makes the term "full-reserve banking" conditional. Rather, it becomes a tribute to the original idea. For example, in "System 100" there are no required reserves at all. Each commercial bank has two types of correspondent accounts in the central bank: one for the credit system and the other for the payment system.

Thus, term deposits and the commercial bank's own capital are reflected on the "credit" account, and this money is not regulated, including reserve requirements, by the central bank. At any rate, banks are free to use this money to offer loans. Proponents of "System 100" are not worried about the multiplier because if this money travels to another commercial bank, it is first recorded on a correspondent account of the second type that banks have opened at the central bank.

All current accounts are reflected on this (payment) correspondent account. The money on these accounts can only be used upon instruction from account owners. Therefore, "endless" credit chains break, as a commercial bank now cannot use the funds from the payment system to

[171] This option was offered to me by Andrey Makogon. Frankly, we were not particularly interested in how this system would behave under capitalism, so we did not discuss it in detail.

offer loans (thereby benefiting from rates lower than the primary lending rate). The mechanism of central bank interaction with a commercial bank here is closer to how a correspondent account is used and not how the reserve requirement works (settlements for required reserves between a commercial bank and the central bank happen, say, once a month, while settlements to facilitate payments via a correspondent account happen at least daily).

"System 100" leaves the payment system to the commercial banks but they lose their ability to create "endless" credit chains using the money from this system. These measures will decrease the multiplier and the notorious "money stock" by initiating expansion of the monetary base. The main problem is that "mirages" arising from the mix of credit and payment systems would not disappear. We'll end up robbing ourselves.[172]

Our logic is as follows: the price of money[173] is formed in both purchase and sale deals, and credit deals. In this case, we are interested in the purchase and sale deals (physical turnover expressed in monetary terms). Having counted an increase in this turnover (besides "documented" deals, an increase in any cash deals not run through cash registers should also be evaluated), the central bank includes it in the money issuance projections. However, its decision to issue additional national currency would be justified only by an increase in the deals where this currency is used. Conversely, an increase in the deals where commercial banks use only the records in their accounts without invoking the monetary base does not fully justify the additional issuance of national currency. Therefore, at any moment, a (justified) money issuance in "System 100" will be smaller than the money issuance in our new financial system, where the separation of credit and payment systems is one of its fundamental principles. If we ever want to issue the same amount of money in "System 100" as we do in the fully fledged, new financial system, we'll run into issuance-induced inflation – the economy does not need all this new currency as commercial banks create their own money. As this always remains true, the monetary

[172] See theses "*A continuation of the game ...*" and "*Physical turnover and large integrated firms ...*". Let me remind you that we have shown how commercial banks create their own (clearing) money in the combined credit and payment system: a bank is able to settle payments between its own clients without using the monetary base, i.e. regular domestic money. Several banks that open correspondent accounts with each other can do the same. Meanwhile, "System 100" is still a version of a combined credit and payment system.

[173] See thesis "*Forming the price of money in a credit deal. ...*".

base can accommodate less money with the full-reserve banking compared with the split credit and payment systems.

I don't know whether this economic model would be better compared with traditional capitalism but it will definitely be worse compared with the fully fledged economy of the PCM. The national economy would grow slower with "System 100", due to the limited issuance of money going entirely to cover government expenses. Neither you nor I, taken one by one, will rush to build infrastructure or save the country from a climate crisis, regardless of how perfect and competitive the formation is. If we want to maintain a high level of government spending, we'll need to raise taxes.

Another characteristic of "System 100" will be a higher average interest rate, resulting in the uneven development of the national economy. At the same economy level, there will be about the same amount of money available to use for payments under "System 100" as under our new financial system (the monetary base plus clearing money at commercial banks). However, with "System 100" there will be less money available to be used as credit, as we have eliminated the ability of the banks to manufacture "credit money", so only the monetary base can be used for lending. The situation is almost the same in the fully fledged financial system of the PCM, although with "System 100" the monetary base will be substantially smaller. Accordingly, here we have one more factor within "System 100" (the higher average *market* interest rate) contributing to the weakening of the national economy. This necessitates a more frequent depreciation of the national currency and, as a result, an even higher average interest rate.[174]

Yet another problem with "System 100" is its high cost for national society compared with a separated system. Even if it is hardly noticeable

---

[174] If you are confused by the statement that a higher interest rate would cause more frequent currency depreciation, remember that we are talking about the "System 100" as an option for the new financial system and the word "market" has been italicised in the previous sentence as a reminder. Under the existing financial system, the average rate depends on the rate set by the central bank to control the money issuance volume and thus the reverse logic (an administrative increase in the central bank's rate will lead to a decrease in the amount of money entering the economy as a result of credit issuance and, consequently, to strengthening of the national currency) is more familiar. By the way, the second part of the logical reasoning (that instability of national currency leads to an increase in the average lending rate) will not materially change.

at the transition stage, after some years it will be as obvious as the higher cost of sticking with human telephone exchange operators versus automatic exchanges. The costs will be further exacerbated by a more complex central bank control over the commercial banks to make sure that they play by the rules (for instance, to make sure they don't use the funds in the second correspondent account without the owner's approval).

Let's summarise it. A mixed credit and payment system with a 100-per cent reserve requirement will cost more for the national society, while the national economy will generally develop slower and often balance on the brink of crisis situations. These pronounced drawbacks will seal the fate of such a national economy once it competes with economies adopting the fully fledged financial system of the PCM.

FAQ: How will budding entrepreneurs raise money, given the strict credit discipline of the PCM?

For budding entrepreneurs, the only way to raise money is to find a guarantor. If you have no cash, do not embark on gambling. There is hardly anything new in this logic and it does not only apply to the newbie entrepreneurs. It is one of the two main components of a simple prediction that monopolistic retail trading chains will shrink dramatically. They simply won't find enough money to pay for all the goods they order (the other component is labour coordination costs – they won't be able to manage price forming accurately and precisely).

One should not try to hand-hold any budding entrepreneurs, as in a kindergarten. This would not be good for them nor for the national economy. The fifth basic regulator (negative profit) works precisely because entrepreneurs are afraid to lose *their own* money. They should learn how to swim themselves, beginning with earning their initial capital or finding business partners who have capital and are willing to share risks with a talented professional (but maybe not right away). These partners may need to exercise rigorous control, once their money is at stake. There is a key difference between someone who has been granted "nobody's" funds (for example, bureaucrats), and a person who sees and understands it all and has a vested interest in a successful outcome, starting with choosing this particular junior partner. This has been and will need to be the case – any aspiring entrepreneurs should pass their initiation rite (i.e. to find capital) without any outside help.

It is possible to earn the initial capital while either making a career at a large business, or while working in trading. The first option has the advantage that one can learn about technology and gain know-how along the way, and have enough money to spend. The second option is preferred for learning the fine moments of commerce and in cases where things turn out right, as an opportunity to earn some really good money. I have some deep knowledge of the first option, as I observed it in the businesses I ran. As well as seeking partnerships, I used the second option myself. I cannot say much about the distant third option ("swipe something valuable"). (However squeamish we all may feel about this last option, it does exist.)

The common thinking goes like this. There is a young entrepreneur with a (no doubt, genial) idea, who needs help. Over time, we'll have modern businesses and new jobs will be created. I can name at least three reasons for this common thinking. We have started this thesis with arguments against helping "from above" aspiring candidates turn into entrepreneurs (the first reason). The second one is the worshiping of securities. We have discussed this in detail in Chapter 2. The third reason is that the figures of an inventor and of an entrepreneur are being subconsciously merged into a mystical creature of such enormous power, and so we should simply forget this boring nonsense about costs. Possibly under the influence of well-known examples from history of the industrial revolution in Britain and, later, of industrial development in the US, the commonness and the effects of this amalgamation may be somewhat exaggerated. Since those times, there has been a noticeable push towards further specialisation of professional activities.

This is how it happens, from my personal observations. Most of the entrepreneurs I have known (including pure "technologist" types) trace their beginnings to trading. Subsequently, most of them turn to manufacturing operations.

Of course, these are merely my own personal observations that do not cover all possible options, but there are two understandable reasons that help explain them. The first one is that small trading operations do not require a large amount of initial capital. The second one is that to make money, one should receive more for their output than they spend on the input (whether we are talking just about the goods intended for resale or about the components to manufacture some other goods). Without a solid trading knowledge, an entrepreneur will keep making mistakes regarding pricing and these will hurt over time.

Nowadays, the retail market is increasingly dominated by large trading companies (and therefore, the industries are increasingly dominated by large manufacturers, including transnational businesses, but we are not going to repeatedly address the entire nexus of problems). If someone wants to increase the number of active entrepreneurs (budding entrepreneurs may be too inexperienced to own supermarkets, but as we have stated at the end of our thesis "*Trade credit. Retail Chains.*", the entire trading sector will be freed from the grip of large retail chains), they should think about those who have already *cleared* the thorny path of the entrepreneurial initiation but at some point ran into monopolies and since then cannot find a sensible use for their *existing* capital. To put it better, they should think about a rigorously market-driven interest rate and this would take care of it all.

Finally, let's try to express the essence of this thesis in the simplest question-and-answer format:

"Who is the culprit behind the distortions in the natural cycle of grooming new entrepreneurs under modern capitalism?"

"The retail chains are."

Appendix: Marginal cost. The priority of sales (demand over supply) in the market microeconomy.

The term "margin" may have a lot of similarities with a mathematical "limit". Indeed, if students diligently follow the calculations laid out by a mathematician economist, they would gradually find themselves in a world where any marginal quantities are replaced by derivative functions. However, attempts to project "marginal quantities" onto the work of real businesses inadvertently show the artificial nature of parallels with calculus. Moreover, at a closer glance and leaving the calculus aside, it turns out that the entire concept of marginal quantities needs some other emphasis, at the very least. Once we put the right emphasis on it, there is a lingering doubt regarding the existence of these categories. Hopefully, our readers will experience doubts as well. As for me personally, I consider this to be a mixture of some contrived categories and plain statistical data that is somehow considered to be extremely important.

The main body of critique is in the second section. There, we are periodically peeking inside a regular firm to check how the assumed marginal quantities may match some plain reproduction processes that the assumed categories are supposed to describe. Meanwhile, let's make ourselves more familiar with the law of diminishing returns that is used in economic literature when talking about marginal quantities.

The law of diminishing returns.

Let's open the *Economics* textbook by Campbell R. McConnell, Stanley L. Brue and Sean M. Flynn. The law of diminishing returns is meant to demonstrate a decrease in productivity when "… a variable resource (say, labour) is added to a fixed resource (say, capital or land) …"[175] Most of the textbook examples come from manufacturing, where the number of hired workers is growing, and due to the constant number of machine tools, starting at a certain point each new hired worker produces less and less. However, to demonstrate the universal character of the law, the authors start with an example of a farmer cultivating his plot of land (an immutable, fixed resource). The farmer weeds the field daily but cannot achieve a radical yield increase. According to the textbook, daily work in the field is an increase in the usage of a variable resource. Still, if we add "a bit more economics" to this example and use the monetary category of "variable cost", then, unlike in the manufacturing example, I do not see a necessary cost increase. In this example, one farmer, who is simultaneously an owner, keeps working. For the analogy to be correct, we would need to have one worker (who is also an owner) in the manufacturing example.

The analogy will be clearer if we, as in the industrial example, increase the number of employees who cultivate this plot of land. Then, upon eliminating a mismatch in monetary categories and returning to the in-kind accounting categories, we will actually see a decrease in output from one employee. True, a look at the nature of the "fixed resource" used makes an analogy between the two examples very remote. Let's see what happens if we take a step aside to look at the output from the use of fixed assets in these examples. It is easy to do, as we are talking about different basic resources.

In working the plot of land, we'll witness a certain process of a decreasing return. However, it will be a decrease not in the absolute return, as in the industrial example, but in a diminishing rate of yield increase. Simply speaking, we are talking about the well-known law of diminishing soil fertility, when adding variable costs leads to an increase in yield from a given plot in absolute terms, but the rate of this increase is going down. Let's explain right away that in the first sentence of this paragraph, in the

[175] McConnell, Brue and Flynn, 2018, p. 183-186.

industrial example, the indication of a decrease in return in absolute terms was not a slip of the tongue. Machine tools, like all products and unlike land, are subject to wear and tear while being operated (we spoke about this in the Introduction). Therefore, in the industrial example, the return from a machine will decrease at some point, regardless of the number of employees or a pause in production, whereas in agriculture it may increase due to a pause related to crop rotation.

Thus, in one case, the absolute return from fixed investment increases and in the other case, it decreases. If this contradiction is not removed (at least, the accounting department would not agree with this), it is mitigated by indicating that the law of diminishing returns has a short span. But is there a need for such a law (which claims to be a fundamental one) that nullifies the simple understanding that land, which is primarily self-healing, is basically a different kind of property compared with a machine that just wears out? And is it worth it, from the outset, to employ some time-horizon tricks (short term versus long term) just to find some common features for these two kinds of property? If this seems valid so far, we'll see the notorious "short-term" approach as obscuring the logic when we dive into the "marginal cost" (at some point, it turns out that the "short term" has been "temporarily" left out). Looking ahead, it's proper accounting for the time factor that will clearly indicate the artificiality of theoretical constructions around the "marginal cost" category. We'll get to this later, but for now, we have no plans to come up with some other universal law in lieu of the law of diminishing returns. Pointing to the appearance of significant inconsistencies at the level of basic resources in the seemingly helpful analogy, let's just leave out the farmer example and move on to the industrial one because it appears to be central in this textbook.

As previously mentioned, the decreasing output of one employee ("marginal returns") is explained using the example when workers gradually outnumber the machine tools. As this example is deliberately simple, apparently to indicate its universal nature, it seems that workers are quite simply wandering around. Accordingly, at the initial stage, the output is growing because at first there are fewer workers than machines and the installed machines are waiting for the workers to arrive. If you consider that the number of machines in this example is constant, there is nothing to formally argue about. However, this unpretentious logical exercise isn't a stronger candidate to become a law than a child's riddle about some sticks and jackdaws. (If one jackdaw perches on each stick, we lack one stick, and if there are two jackdaws perching on each stick, then one stick is extra. How many jackdaws and how many sticks are there?)

Since the law of diminishing returns is boringly simple, once deprived of its phraseological "advanced economics" decorations, let's take the opportunity to talk about some equally easy to understand but more important market interconnections. The thing is, in the law of diminishing returns, one main category is marginal returns (output, i.e. the amount of product manufactured by the last worker we added), which goes down at some point.

We are going to talk about "marginal quantities" later, when we address marginal cost, but for now let's note that "output" possibly may be perceived as some kind of average of the production volume and the sales volume, with an implicit assumption that whatever is being produced is also being sold. Accounting for both is important for business operations, but in a market economy, the accent on sales is fundamentally more important for the mere existence of a firm. One can spend a lifetime calculating the production costs and achieve remarkably low projections, but if the goods do not sell, the firm incurs losses. And if the goods take too long to sell, the chronically negative cash flow (the difference between cash receipts and expenses) will drain the blood out of the firm (in case you buy into the argument that money facilitating commodities' circulation is indeed the "blood" of the economy). If, however, we are to choose one or the other for our theoretical and practical analysis of business activities in a competitive market, it would be more accurate to emphasise the importance of the sales volume.

The total amount of goods and services available for consumption is really important for a national society. However, consumers (acting through the government, directly or indirectly authorised by them) want to be sure that these goods and services are offered at the best available cost and quality. Therefore, the output goes through the crucible of competition between producers and natural economic selection takes place. As a result, each individual business is driven by the *priority of sales*. Here, it would be fitting to consider one barely noticeable corollary that the priority of sales within a firm seriously hinders the efforts to formalise microeconomic processes.

Maximising output and minimising costs are, to some extent, tasks that can be formalised; there is a caveat, though. An opportunity to explore these functions within a firm relies primarily on the fact that decisions aimed at maximising output and managing costs are made internally by the manager(s) of the firm who is authorised to confirm these decisions by spending the budget. Conversely, decisions to purchase goods offered by this firm are made by someone from outside and, for them, these are also decisions on spending their money. Here, management decisions are important to the well-being of the company, but to apply some formal functions within the company is extremely difficult. As we have already mentioned, the most important decisions are driven from the outside. Even if we point to an order backlog as some universal solution (and orders are also not always paid as agreed upon), these orders usually cover only a small portion of output in a competitive economy.

True, a deal happens by the will of two parties, and it is quite pleasing and productive to investigate the macroeconomy as a grand total of all deals measured in clear units: money. But as soon as we step inside the microeconomy, where *deals are prepared*, we find ourselves in a world of uncertain outcomes. It is very important to rely on clearly defined accents. One of these accents in a market economy is a mantra for practitioners: it is easier to buy than to sell, since giving up your money is pretty easy but it is hard to get someone else's money.

On the contrary, in the economy of the now defunct "developed socialism", the shortage of goods was a main driving force. Therefore, it made sense that the Soviet economists have done a lot to formalise the maximisation of output and minimisation of costs with extensive use of mathematics. The process was made much easier by an *administrative setting of prices*. Ultimately, it has once again been confirmed on a global scale that the priority of sales (mandatory for a managing owner) works better to maximise output, minimise costs and achieve a higher quality of goods within the national economy. It is this change of priorities when moving from socialism to a market economy that has rendered the significant body of knowledge developed by Soviet economic mathematicians largely unclaimed.

Marginal cost.

When talking about microeconomic relationships, we often try to visualise them in our mind and I am no exception to this. But as soon as it comes to "marginal quantities", I find myself in some sort of vacuum. Logically, it seems to be about my past work and about the business decisions attributed to me, but I can neither picture myself in the situations described, nor imagine the situation proper. It is also hard to grasp the gist of the "marginal cost" category – as soon as you try to identify it in the real economy, it slips from your hands like a bar of soap. No one can know everything and in general these "margins" do not bother me very much (I just ignore them). Before taking on the task of costs' systematisation, I considered it a waste spending time on them.

Let me remind you that "Marginal cost (MC) is the extra, or additional, cost of producing one more unit of output".[176] As already clear from the topic sentence, we will gradually pull off the veil of "advanced science" that is obscuring the system of marginal categories. We'll choose the simplest tactics for it, and look at marginal cost and the related processes from the point of view of an observer located inside an actual firm. Of course, not all theoretical processes can be seen from within a business. However, if a theoretical algorithm claims to explain the nature of some real processes inside a firm and at the same time it contradicts them, then there is a choice: either modify the firm's activities or drop their theoretical interpretation. In our case, as we are going to see later, it is just impossible to fundamentally change business activities to fit the theory that we are discussing.

Further in this thesis, we'll see how the supposed connections between marginal cost and real economic processes are falling apart. Some questions may arise – why has this all been around for so long, and why does it seem plausible enough to be included in textbooks? There are three probable reasons for that. The first component is historical, i.e. the authority of famous economists of the past, such as Alfred Marshall and Ronald Coase. Marshall introduced the "equilibrium price" and offered the famous triad "marginal utility – marginal cost – equilibrium price". This "marginal utility" did not particularly inspire confidence compared with the other two and, later, Coase dismissed "marginal utility" as a far-fetched category[177] (it's hard to disagree with him, but I just need to add that the other two are not much better). However, Coase began to actively use "marginal costs" to justify the existence of "transaction costs".

The second component is the abundance of mathematics, which often has a hypnotic effect on readers, akin to a boa constrictor hypnotising a rabbit whose brain simply turns off at this uneasy moment. Meanwhile, mathematicians are known to be able to model just about anything but they will start reworking this model immediately (unless they consider

---

[176] Ibid, p. 189.
[177] Coase, 1990, p. 2.

themselves authorities in the other science) once it is refuted by the experimental data. In this thesis, we'll provide some straightforward verification of basic assumptions of the theory of marginal quantities against some real-life scenarios.

The third component of ultimate interest to us is methodological. The system of these categories is a largely encapsulated system, or, in philosophical terms, a noumenon. Its remoteness from the actual economy is to some extent obscured by the frequent use of special terms (these are terms related not only to "marginal" but also, for example, to the "additional unit").[178] Any words, even those with little or no initial meaning and when frequently repeated in various combinations with common concepts, begin to sound increasingly important. But the main opportunity for the vitality of such remoteness provides the use of *in-kind* categories with the concurrent creation of a separate, small world.

Such constructs are very vulnerable to testing by common units of measure, i.e. money (we are talking about fully fledged testing, not about some isolated references with an immediate transition to the "safe haven" of mathematics). This can be seen from our earlier paragraph about the law of diminishing returns. If you remember, as soon as we introduced the term "variable cost" instead of a murky "application of variable resource", the example of a farmer required some rework. Accordingly, such constructs are wary of being included in the analysis of deals, because the main economic role of money is precisely its use in deals. So, we'll do just that, gradually changing the language of our discussion to use terminology more suitable for actual business practice. In particular, we'll be using "goods" in lieu of "products", as the proverbial "additional unit" is clearly meant to be sold by the firm producing it (the costs are calculated for this). Here, we do not steal anything from the marginal quantities theory, as from a physical turnover perspective, goods and products are essentially the same.

Despite the simplicity of the textbook definition ("marginal cost is the extra, or additional, cost of producing one more unit of output"), here we are immediately dragged into a sort of "catch me if you can" game. On one hand, marginal cost is nothing but the cost of producing an exact ("one more") unit. On the other hand, the vague character of this definition

---

[178] For some, it may be a little surprising that "additional unit of output" and "marginal product" are two separate categories. Our analysis is mainly about "marginal cost" and "additional unit of output". We also mention "marginal product" infrequently.

allows us to assume that the cost of goods that have already been produced simply changes because of that additional unit. Then, in the second case, while talking about unit costs (including that same additional unit) we already mean average cost. Meanwhile, the whole "practical gist" of marginal cost (let's stress, *whole*) is contained in the declaration that by analysing it, a manager is allegedly capable of making a decision that is impossible to make based on the analysis of average cost. Therefore, we have the right to declare a version of the definition in which marginal cost is the cost of producing the given unit.

Our rights aside, this ambiguity, coupled with the hidden appearance of average cost, is not a drawback of this textbook's definition; it is a contradiction built into the category itself. We assumed that we "got rid of" average cost in the preceding paragraph but we'll definitely encounter it in the next one. This is easier to illustrate with some examples.

Those who have visited African marketplaces may remember clearings between some baobab trees that were filled with a variety of souvenirs, including some artfully crafted, tall, wooden figurines. Let's imagine a woodcarver who found a suitable piece of wood, carved out a figurine, sold it at the marketplace either to a visitor or to a middleman, and then went back for more raw material, etc. On one hand, this situation is not a good example of the marginal quantities theory – there are neither additional workers being hired, nor additional figurines produced in a given period. On the other hand, here we are able to calculate the cost to produce that mysterious "additional unit" and, *then*, according to the "theory", to make a decision.

In an average modern firm, we cannot arrange all the goods being produced in a certain order on an imaginary "assembly line", attaching a label to each unit with the cost specific to that unit. We'll have to operate with the average cost, as nearly everything we buy in stores today is produced *in batches*. However, this is not all yet. The production itself often takes place at different locations (for example, on different assembly lines) and parts are sourced from different suppliers, with frequent overlap between batches of different parts and batches of finished goods, often in disparate accounting periods. The further we walk away from the woodcarver example, the clearer is our understanding that in reality, we can operate only in terms of average cost (here and throughout this thesis, it does not matter much if these are average variable costs or average total costs, but “average” is the keyword).[179]

This ambiguity of the marginal cost definition reflects the exact type of embarrassment that attentive economists must experience once they try to overlay theoretical assumptions on realities. In lieu of any “marginal cost”, there is indeed average cost in these realities and the woodcarver’s scale is unlikely to support the scope of the marginal quantities theory’s claims. On one hand, the textbook authors indicate that “average-cost figures do not provide this information”. Under “information”, the authors mean the same “practical gist” that we spoke about; “Marginal costs are costs the firm can control directly and immediately. Specifically, MC designates all the cost incurred in producing the last unit of output. Thus, it also designates the cost that can be ‘saved’ by not producing that last unit.”[180]

On the other hand, even a cursory dive into the world of actual firms reveals that in the vast majority of cases, “marginal cost” cannot be calculated other than by using some sort of average cost.

Generally speaking, we can send “marginal cost” into the trash bin for this reason alone. Everything is painfully simple, but the reader may still have certain subconscious doubts as we dismiss the work of many economists using just a couple of observations. Thus, let’s continue our reasoning.

The second ambiguity lies in tying marginal cost to *variable* cost. Note that there is no link in the marginal cost definition (for example, in the same textbook, there is a formula below the quote that points directly to total cost). However, the link surfaces later in a seemingly logical manner. We’ll put this logic to the test a bit later, but I guess that I have a simpler explanation. Without this link, the marginal cost theory would die on the spot, as accounting for fixed costs immediately sends us into calculating the average cost. Then, even those students who only remember “depreciation” from the whole fixed costs curriculum may doubt the existence of marginal cost.

The logical link between marginal cost and variable cost is formulated in this simple way: marginal cost does not depend on fixed cost, as the latter remains constant in the process of making that additional unit of goods (or

---

[179] In one of the companies I managed at the turn of the century, there was a database and software developed to track the costs for each good as it was being produced. However, it was still the average (and only estimated) cost.
[180] McConnell, Brue and Flynn, 2018, p. 189.

"product", as in the original text). This sounds plausible and I would also partially agree with it from a practical viewpoint. At one of my companies, some 50 million units, split into hundreds of commodity groups, were produced each year. Since I handled all sales, and thus any price changes, cost changes and any associated production volumes, I would have trouble saying that I always accounted for fixed cost changes, as well. On the other hand, I would not agree if someone pressed me to say that I have "never accounted for these changes". Moreover, it can be argued that if certain managers set a goal to scrupulously calculate marginal cost, as suggested by adherents of the theory that we are discussing, they would necessarily need to take into account the changes in fixed costs for some *time period*. The reason is that with a production increase *over a certain period*, we will face the technological need to increase fixed costs at some point and rather sooner than later (in large companies, almost daily). There are a lot of diverse fixed costs (not only figuratively speaking, investments in machine tools once in 20 years, but also hiring more office employees or changing salaries, for example, for janitors).[181] Fixed cost generally differs from variable cost in one aspect: it is impossible to increase it exactly by the amount necessary for the production of one unit of output. Therefore, to increase production, fixed costs often need to be increased with further room to grow and for some associated overspending.

---

[181] In management accounting, unlike tax accounting, the situation is complicated by the fact that it is not always clear how to classify expenses as either fixed or variable. There are many products (the simplest example being paper clips but often the situation is more complex), the consumption of which seems more like using working capital in production, from an in-kind point of view. However, from a production-cost-accounting perspective, expenses for these products seem more like fixed ones. Of course, this detail is not always important and in some easy-to-manage companies one can basically trust the usual accounting principles. But in one of my companies where I had to plunge into all the "niceties" of matrix reporting, this problem (within the scope of a more general problem of allocating the fixed costs among different units) was looming large, as the decentralisation of profit accounting automatically triggered the decentralising of cost calculations. Here, it was necessary to understand that with the "decentralisation of profit accounting" in a large firm (none of these look alike), we were dealing not with some abstract cost centres but with specific employees who were keenly interested in the objectivity of the distribution of profits and, accordingly, the allocation of costs. For the sake of accuracy, I would add that this situation took place over 15 years ago when computer hardware and software, as well as communications infrastructure, were not as developed as they are today. Perhaps nowadays these problems can be solved more easily.

You probably have noticed that in the previous paragraph there were two italics, both related to the time factor. Intriguingly, in the respected economics textbook that we constantly refer to, specifically in the thesis "Marginal Cost", there is no indication of a time factor, neither in the text nor in the attached charts. The authors only give the name of the section where this thesis is located, "Short-Run Production Costs". Generally speaking, the theory of marginal quantities takes into account the relationship of production processes over time with negligence, akin to the ensign from that old army joke about a sergeant who sets the task of digging a trench as "dig from the fence until lunch". The reasoning is mainly limited to pointing out the short-term time span. Closer to the end of this thesis, we will see how this negligence in considering the time factor leads to ridiculous outcomes. For now, let's clarify the words in italics used in reasoning about fixed costs in the previous paragraph.

If there is no time frame specified at all, then nothing prevents us from assuming, for example, that the increase in production is accounted for cumulatively regardless of time. That is, the situation in which we produce 100 units in January and then only one unit in February, with monthly fixed costs allocated to this one unit, is not contradictory. But if I suddenly used this example as an argument to prove the fallacy of the assumption about the immutable nature of fixed costs, I would likely be ridiculed because of this obviously far-fetched example. To make sure that discussion takes place in an atmosphere of mutual respect, we have pointed out the time factor. As soon as we did it, it was easy to see that an increase in production volume over a period will surely mean the need to change the fixed cost per unit of output.

The conclusion here is that rigorous treatment of marginal cost as variable cost is possible only when we abstract from fixed cost at the definition level. One can either ignore them or declare them constant, and there is a difference. The first option casts doubt on the fundamental nature of the theory, so with the help of a qualifier trick called "short term" the second option is typically chosen. This approach has a flaw, which we'll see as soon as we face the necessity to consider changes in fixed costs while looking into real business cases. Each time when we see detailed graphs of "marginal costs", this apparently means that a very clever someone has identified and removed from the graphs all fixed cost changes because they are "insignificant". It is appropriate to recall here that the whole theoretical gist of "marginal costs" is based on the hypothesis that only by thinking about them an entrepreneur is able to calculate the correct pricing. Maybe our lone woodcarver has such a happy opportunity. Meanwhile, the main scourge of real modern firms, as we have already mentioned more than once, starting from the introduction of labour coordination costs, is precisely the struggle to control the growing fixed costs. These are just the "creeping" costs that are either impossible or extremely difficult to account for in the cost of certain types of goods. With accurate and impartial analysis, a clear understanding of this problem will be ready, even before we leave that purported "short term", so, as trusted researchers, we'll be forced to account for average cost right away.

It should be noted that despite this rather long reasoning, doubt about the possibility of treating marginal cost as variable cost is only one side of the problem. As we have already mentioned, the simple reasoning that products in a modern economy are typically produced in batches, and that components are purchased in batches, shows the artificial nature of marginal cost applied to the real economy more clearly. For our critique of marginal cost, the principle of cost breakdown (i.e. splitting these into fixed or variable costs) is not as important as the principle of using average cost. The latter principle is opposed to calculating costs to produce a particular unit of output, which is tempting to use in the formalisation of economic processes but does not fit well with economic realities. Perhaps it was not so noticeable in the times of Alfred Marshall, but it is clearly visible when one takes a closer look at the modern economy.

Like any thorough researcher, we would not even accept a truce: for example, let's agree that in certain situations, marginal cost equals average variable cost. If we first calculate the former and then the latter, and then we compare them, this algorithm is correct. If we are not able to correctly calculate the former (i.e. marginal cost) and just equate it to what we can indeed calculate (i.e. average cost), and thereby implicitly endow the former with the right to exist, this approach seems to be quite sly.

Nobody is trying to endow average cost with some magical properties, nor to say anything about using these to develop a scientific algorithm for making management decisions. The thing is, purported marginal cost also does not lend itself to any particular "direct and immediate control". Suppose we decided for a while to leave out our arguments about the batches. Suppose we agreed to downplay the importance of decoding the exact location of marginal cost, whether it is hidden in the "last unit of output" or in the "additional" one.[182] Even in this case, we still need to

[182] Often, estimated cost is also considered marginal cost. However, when we look at the invariably attached chart depicting marginal cost, we feel that we are in an

make one more big assumption in an attempt to resuscitate marginal cost. Whenever we talk about a unit of output, we will assume a single batch of homogeneous product units (say, 1000 units). Under "homogeneous" we mean not only identical output units but also the same exact cost of all purchased components, including raw materials, energy, wages, loans and other leased property for every batch. Achieving this uniformity is conceivably quite difficult. Under "marginal cost of an output unit" we actually mean the cost of a single batch of identical goods (we'll refer to it as the "CSBIG"). This approach could build a bridge, albeit temporary, between marginal cost and reality. Personally, I have not dealt with these batches produced over a long time. Although it is quite possible that some technological process assumes their existence, as a rule we will deal with fractional output quantities. We will produce these batches in ideal conditions, one batch after another, which in all likelihood excludes the case of several production lines. I can hardly imagine a complete ongoing synchronisation, both in terms of time and costs, of technologically *independent* production lines, except in the case of a rare coincidence. At the very least, we'll have to run separate calculations for each line. If any of the conditions listed are not met, this brings us from the world of the "near-average" CSBIG into the ordinary world of average cost and, there, as marginal cost theories warn, we immediately lose the declared benefits of control over the situation.

Note that according to our assumptions about the scale coefficients, both the "last unit" and the "additional unit" refer to an entire batch of 1000 products. True, now it is even harder to meet the condition of the marginal cost algorithm that the fixed cost is constant, as neither the financial director nor the chief engineer will be happy when we begin to casually adjust the accounting of the firm's activities to some "1000-piece" batches. They would probably think that the manager had gone crazy. Thankfully, we are approaching the end of our walk in the world of economic mirages.

So, we have spent a lot of time discussing this idealised picture to provide at least some possibility of calculating marginal cost in the form of the CSBIG. As soon as we are ready to proceed further, we run into a ridiculously simple technical inability to apply these calculations. First, when a batch of goods is produced and we need to start making the next batch, the cost calculation for the previous batch can be completed only

---

absurd situation, since by default it is clear that the chart is using the actually incurred costs.

when a buyer has already prepaid for it. Even if this is the case, we can still think about accounting for shipping costs, but the main factor here is market unpredictability. After coming off the production line, the goods begin their journey to the consumer and it is much more unpredictable in terms of final costs than more standardised manufacturing processes. In a competitive market, we may not know when and where our products will be sold and, accordingly, what the actual final cost will be. If our products are stuck at a warehouse due to slow demand, we may run up additional costs to the extent of cardinally changing our plans for future production. According to the marginal cost algorithm, we must know these costs at the moment we start producing that "additional unit" but in reality we can't know it. This is the mirage that marginal theory feeds upon. A reliance on average cost calculations does not account for any possible market fluctuations either, but nobody endows average cost with magical properties.

Second, there is another funny and simple-to-understand reason. Typically, a firm begins to order components well ahead of production. There is no "last" or "last but one" unit in production yet, but a manager must decide whether to start production of a batch of goods *several months before* it is prescribed by the marginal theory. The manager has no time machine to know the marginal cost and it would be extremely odd to discuss any "cost savings" when the production line is idle.

In general, this is the end of the story that we concluded with the unsophisticated use of the time factor. I see no sense in the "marginal cost" category, as it can be used in the way it is declared only in some isolated, insignificant cases. Whenever the use of this category is expected in discussing actual economic processes, some flavours of average cost are used instead. The latter are either calculated post factum or estimated with a necessary margin of error intrinsic to average cost in general. The entire reason for marginal cost has been its declared timeliness and precise calculation. To put it simply, this category exists not in a real economy but in an imaginary one, inevitably leading to distortions in the understanding of real processes, regardless of any promised mathematical enlightenment.

I believe that marginal quantities can be split (without any remainder) into the unnecessary and plain silly. The first group comprises such statistical indicators as marginal efficiency of capital and marginal propensity to save (as mentioned in our discussion about Keynes's theory). These are quite realistic but not required to explain the fundamental economic links. They also add complexity and distort these links, making them weaker. The second group comprises outright fantastic categories (marginal utility) and barely realistic ones, such as marginal cost, marginal revenue and marginal product. Having analysed "marginal cost" in detail, we won't dwell on the others. If desired, the readers can take on this task. Just imagine yourself as an entrepreneur and apply a couple of simple considerations: priority of demand (which is hard to formalise, as we remember) and priority of monetary categories to the most natural actions of a manufacturer acting in real-*time* conditions. This will resemble our analysis of marginal cost, though one should be ready to add some new, albeit unsophisticated, considerations.

For example, "marginal revenue" (additional revenue derived from the sale of an additional item), unlike marginal cost, does not conflict with the priority of microeconomic demand, but this will be the only good news for the supporters of this category. Next come the same unsolvable problems that manifested themselves in our analysis of marginal cost:

1. Similarly, when looking at the actual production process in a modern business, in the overwhelming majority of cases there are no "additional" or some other "units" but there are batches (the size of which also vary), which throws us into studying the average quantities.
2. Similarly, the time factor (a manager makes purchasing decisions for raw materials and components, and also starts producing subsequent batches, without waiting for the current batch to be sold) makes it really *impossible* to obtain the data that, in theory, are the basis of those impressive formulas and graphs. That is, the time factor requires (if we, of course, talk about a scientist and not a charlatan who, say, imagines production processes at the level of observation of a lone carver of wooden sculptures or something else in an equally primitive manner) that these formulas and graphs reflect the assumed revenue and cost. Apparently, *assumptions* are poorly aligned with the *fundamentals*; therefore, in the graphs and formulas we do not see such clear indications. Even if one of the supporters of marginal categories honestly indicates, in a footnote under the graphs and formulas, that they are based on expected values because of the inability to obtain actual data. (There is still a crucial contradiction with #1 above, as in reality we can only estimate the *average* quantities. One hopes that some would agree, while looking at Keynes's theory, that the underlying data can be not factual but assumed.)

To summarise it, we have removed the fantasies from the small area of common sense. An entrepreneur is really thinking about future production based on assumptions about average cost and revenue. Having more accuracy would be desirable, of course, but it is what it is. The desire of scientists to help the entrepreneur by distilling mathematically precise cost and revenue indicators is understandable and rational, but everything is good in moderation. When there is no common sense, these calculated indicators help only the scientists themselves (say, to obtain their degrees), while everyone else is only confused by these mathematically sanctioned lies. Moreover, taking into account the size of the "tumour" that has grown in theoretical literature, it creates confusion at the system level, forming false fundamental relationships in the minds of students as future theorists (as though the alleged precision of marginal categories existed in the real economy). Relaxed assumptions are permissible in analytics. For example, an economist believes that *in certain cases* an observational error is not crucial, but from a theoretical point of view, a total mismatch between actual algorithms used by managers and their "theoretical" reflections must put an end to attempts to present the latter as anything fundamental. It is the introduction of the theoretically false foundations of economics into young minds that is the biggest nuisance, and not the scientific degrees and prizes obtained through the study of marginal categories (as mistakes are an essential part of searching for truth).

Therefore, I have a better solution, in line with my earlier suggestion to the readers, which is to reflect on other marginal categories. In the early 1990s, when I was just out of college and studying the basics of entrepreneurship, I became the victim of a "protection" racket (details are not that important). I asked for advice from a colleague at a friendly small business who was quite shrewd in those elements of the practical economy that do not make it into the textbooks. He listened to me and recommended to forget about it, meaning that any action on my part could result in major mistakes. He was actually right, as I followed his advice after some deliberation and the situation was resolved. This case is remarkable, as in similar situations one is usually expected to undertake some urgent actions.

My best advice regarding marginal quantities is to forget about them. However, there is a little caveat for students: they must remember that they are preparing themselves to work in one of the most pragmatic spheres of human knowledge and skills. Therefore, it pays to get a good grade first, if the "marginal" categories happen to be included in the curriculum. Then, forget them for good.

FAQ: Services, "post-industrial society", information, opportunity cost.

A service is a lease of goods (means of production) in the scope of a purchase and sale deal (C↔M) in the microeconomy, macroeconomy, or financial or state-owned firms. Within the household sector, what is commonly called a service (for instance, hiring a servant) is essentially a hiring deal, though the use of the "service" term is not a crucial error. In general, a service is a result of mixing the purchase and sale of goods (their alienation, including wear and tear of the means of production) and hiring. The fact that after purchasing a service the consumer does not receive any material objects (goods) stems from the hiring deal component. It is easier to observe the mix of the deals where we, as consumers, visualise both the staff (whom we convey our requests to) and the means of production (that we use) – for example, at a hair salon or inside a passenger aircraft. As Captain Obvious would add, we give orders and use something to the extent the service firm allows us.

The main difficulty in understanding the service category (and it tends to be quite slippery when we attempt to nail it) stems from the mix of basic deals. First of all, we are faced with the fact that the surrogate nature of the deal makes it next to impossible to visually demonstrate its features. Therefore, the very speculative nature of these features inevitably leads to a variety of opinions on the subject. Let me indicate the most important features of services from my own point of view:

1. It has already been noted that unlike the production of goods, which is concentrated in a microeconomy, the provision of services and hiring deals permeate all sectors.

2. A feature that is more difficult to understand is the ongoing increase in the importance of means of production, driven by ***technological evolution***.

The reason for the increased complexity is that in-kind and price categories may change a situation in different directions when it comes down to the provision of services. Here, we need to take into account one subtle moment, which was not in scope before we started talking about services. At the stage of forming the list of basic types of property, in-kind categories have a priority. This specified priority is preserved while considering a single basic deal. It is easy to notice, as the right side of all deals consists of money as payment. However, the difference between deals is the basic types of property on the left side. Thanks to the universal measure on the right, we have the opportunity to correctly channel our reasoning with the help of price categories when entering the "open space" of the economy, where interactions of various property types happen. True, service is a surrogate but it is a base surrogate, if you will, and one can only acknowledge its existence.

The ever-increasing importance of means of production *from an in-kind point of view* shifts the theoretical equilibrium within a service from a hiring deal to the purchase and sale of goods. This evolution of service, where engineers who communicate with entrepreneurs are constantly coming up with novelties, contributes to excessive theoretical activity. If we do not assume that *a lack of theoretical equilibrium has been already embedded in the essence of the service as a surrogate*, then the appearance of novelty services may provoke an observer to think that something new has appeared, from a theoretical point of view ("This is a completely different economy!"). It is quite possible that, when scrutinised under a microscope, this new deal has really appeared (as a previously unseen version of mixing two basic deals) but it fits into the theoretical framework when thinking about services as surrogates.

By the way (and this also relates to the subject of the next paragraph), the evolution of services affects the above-mentioned placement of services (as noted in Feature 1 above – "…the provision of services and hiring deals permeate all sectors") in the national economy. Following technological evolution, services are increasingly leaving the household and going into the microeconomy. Accordingly, we are increasingly not hiring people but paying a firm. Today, if we approach a proverbial kid in the street and offer him a coin for running an errand for us, most likely we'll be left without a service (and the kid will have something to post on social media).

The situation is further complicated by price categories. Lately, it is easy to notice the *increase in the share of services* in GDP, especially in developed economies. In the depths of sociology, this brings to life the concept of the "post-industrial society", which is a by-product of dividing the economic development of our civilisation into pre-industrial, industrial and post-industrial epochs.[183]

---

[183] We are not going to talk about the merits of using this tradition in sociology (it is entirely up to sociologists) but rather about the correctness of porting it over to theoretical economics.

However, the point here is that in the modern economy, the expanded reproduction of goods is handled by machines, while all the money belongs to people[184] and they distribute it among themselves (as machines do not receive "wages"). Since the main channel of money distribution between the property owners of the planet (*Homo sapiens*) is the deal of hiring, which in the case of a service is "built into" the left side of the basic commodity deal, the share of services reflected in GDP is growing. If you teach machines, which can already handle formalised information processing better than people (this has decisively influenced the production of goods), to process the information that so far only a human brain is able to, then machines can think (much) better than people and will be able to replace people in the provision of services. It will lead to the hiring deal, including services, being replaced with the ordinary purchase and sale deal of the AI-enabled machines. The share of services will decrease, as the share of agriculture and industry did before (we do not think, for example, that an air conditioner or a fan provide a service while cooling a room).[185] The actual importance of certain sectors,

---

[184] We began introducing basic categories with the definition of "property". This may also be interpreted in a way that, by our accent on "property", we have removed (human) labour from the top categories. This category has been ruling theoretical economics from its early days, often taking on the form of a "sacred ritual" (not in the economy, but in its theoretical reflection). This was most pronounced in the 18th and 19th centuries, when it was believed that human labour created "value". In the 20th century, this topic was expanded, as Keynes introduced "employment" and subsequently the "post-industrial society" appeared. The latter concept clearly lags behind "employment", to say nothing of "value", in its theoretical significance, but nevertheless it is an echo of this entire history.

[185] I am really not inclined to think that this "smart servant" idyll will last long (the difference between a year and a few decades does not affect the essence of it), as the planet's ownership will change in favour of those who are smarter. In other words, a fundamental correction of "property" definition will take place. The *Homo sapiens*' civilisation will face irreversible consequences, in cases where this change of ownership causes a shift of planetary power. The probability of this is high, unless people can, in some cases, agree on certain limits to civil rights and also consciously delay the appearance of AI until a time when they have a clear idea of what could guarantee their independence. For example, I would outlaw any work to develop robot emotions, starting tomorrow. We have touched upon the role of emotions in the work of the human brain in the Introduction while talking about forming an entrepreneur's conditional reflexes in the form of a certain "emotional punch card" that the brain of entrepreneurs (and not only them, I believe) "reads" from when making decisions. As an additional note to demonstrate the difference in relative importance of the "property" and "labour" categories: anything that happens to "human labour" after we lose our independence will not

industries and other elements of the economy, and relationships between them, does not simply map out the distribution of money.[186] This requires more subtle tuning than can be achieved by pointing out "pre-industrial", "industrial" and "post-industrial" phases.

I am not the only one concerned with this vulgarisation of economic mechanisms. Ha-Joon Chang, a Korean economist working at Cambridge University, expressed his scepticism about our allegedly "post-industrial" era as Thing #9 in his book *23 Things They Don't Tell You About Capitalism* (Penguin Books, 2010). We can also add that we do not live in some "post-agricultural" era either, though the number of people employed in agriculture has decreased even more dramatically. The introduction and improvement of machines, which is the exclusive domain of the machine building industry, is behind the current situation in both cases, whether we are talking about people attrition from agriculture or growth of the service sector which prompted the concept of "post-industrial era". Hardly any government of a sizeable country will be crazy enough to voluntarily give up the development of agriculture or industry. One additional important fact is that competitive pressure from low-wage countries is much tougher in the trade of agricultural and industrial goods than in the provision of services with poor transportability. If they are making cheaper goods in a distant Asian province, then thanks to merchants, we'll see these in our neighbourhood store. Conversely, if haircuts are half price in a nearby town (not to mention at a hairdresser's in the Asian province), we may not learn about it in our lifetime. If we do find out, we may not go there just for a haircut, since we have to spend money and time to travel.

In addition to technological evolution, the growth in the share of services in developed countries is influenced by particular traits of the existing formation. This is most easily understood when looking at the hypertrophied volume of financial services – under the PCM, it will undergo a sharp reduction.

The share of traditional services will also shrink due to the disappearance of global currencies. In near-classical countries, the prices of services are

matter much for the new owners of the planet. Except for the zoologists, there is no interest in the apes' labour (and by the way, we do not suffer because we are not "real apes").

[186] There is no theoretical contradiction here. If you remember, at the beginning of Chapter 1 we noted that money is a means of circulation and not a "measure of value".

still closely related to the international competitiveness of domestic goods and are the first to decline (if prices are expressed in a foreign currency) in the case of deterioration of this competitiveness accompanied by currency depreciation. Conversely, in "wonderland" countries, due to the non-classical resilience of global currencies, the prices for non-transportable services are largely protected from international competition. Besides, these prices are also influenced by a higher level of public social spending, which these countries can afford.

Our reasoning behind the link between services and currency depreciation finally leads us to a particular universal feature of services that explains why services "do not behave" in theoretical analysis.

3. Recording a service in the form of a deal C↔M, despite the surrogate nature of the service itself, is correct in terms of price categories, as the price of money in the hiring deal is not formed (zero is zero). However, this record does not reflect the in-kind features of the deal. Therefore, when these features are reflected in prices generated in the practical economy, we *have to* explain the resulting disturbances using in-kind categories. Meanwhile, our options are limited here.

For example, from a theoretical point of view we cannot correctly connect particular features of a service with such price categories as inflation or currency depreciation. The conclusion that prices of many services show reduced stability during currency depreciation can be drawn from a simple observation that once their fortunes deteriorate, people give up what they can do without. Here, services occupy the top positions on the list. We can, for example, deny ourselves a visit to a restaurant, while we cannot refrain from food in general. Or, at some point we might start thinking that visiting the fitness centre will have to be replaced with a workout at home. In other words, in our reasoning on currency depreciation, we assume an in-kind feature of services that a consumer, as they say, gets nothing "material" in return, i.e. a consumer does not receive any goods (or receives them as a small addition to the service[187]).

I won't take the liberty of deducing any general relationship between currency depreciation, inflation in general and services. Having pointed out the characteristic behaviour of the consumers under a currency

---

[187] I definitely do not consider the process of purchasing and selling goods that happens inside a trading business (including retail stores and marketplaces) as a service. Here, we may also recall the confusing division of the economy into some "spheres" (we attribute trading to the microeconomy).

depreciation scenario, I will prudently stop here. It is just not my job, or at any rate, I do not see how it can be done. Highlighting relationships that consider a multitude of nuances that depend on a specific situation (when dealing with a mixture of pricing and in-kind categories, this cannot be avoided) is done by economic *analysts*. At the same time, as we have observed above, it is useful not to exaggerate the in-kind variety of services. It is much less advisable to exaggerate their theoretical, i.e. fundamental, significance. For the economy and for people, goods are more important than services. Regardless of how much they cost, the latter only facilitate production of the former.

One can specify one more, slightly mysterious, problem. We are talking about information, or rather about the *theoretical* value bestowed on it. There are no special theoretical problems (information has always been around) if we correctly perform two successive separations. First, you need to cut off the elements of Rough History (that is, the technological evolution of devices related to the production and dissemination of information) and then further divide the information into the part that we need for decision-making and the part intended for sale. The first part should not be "materialised" (i.e. turned into some fundamental concepts) into theoretical categories (we'll go over an example of such "materialisation" at the end of this thesis). The second part is delivered either in the form of goods (newspaper, book, manual for a refrigerator, etc), or in the form of services, for public or private consumption.

On to the promised example of "materialisation" of reasoning.

In line with our research, we can easily state that all costs are formed as payments made by a firm. This is the method that has been practiced for cost accounting by all businesses across the world, although, for example, for management compensation, when payment is tied to sales or profits, the owners or the board of directors often use the opportunity cost (most often, this is due to reasoning about "what would happen if the owners withdrew their share of liquid funds from the business and used the proceeds to invest elsewhere?"). These calculations are an internal matter for a firm. It affects the assessment of management efficiency and the internal distribution of profits, but not the actual costs incurred by the firm. If the owners indeed loaned cash out while the firm had to borrow funds to compensate it, that would be a different story. The result could really be around the same but it could also be quite different, starting with the fact that one firm relying on self-financing, and another one using borrowed capital, may show varying degrees of stability. Also, note that the above-described situation of alternative investments by the owner is not a fail-safe scenario either, because it would work only in a "general case". The "general case" described here and the transfer of money to someone are two different things.

We have described only a certain typical situation. There are always additional inputs that will change the perception of "fairness" of the situation for one party or another in a practical economy. This only emphasises the conditional nature of opportunity cost as opposed to the actual cost incurred, and this difference is fundamentally important for theoretical economics *as a science*. For example, an entrepreneur keeps thinking about possible options, all the while relying on the arithmetic of estimated costs. Still, I see no reason to treat this *analytical* thinking as a *theoretical* category, even considering the usefulness of economists and students being aware of the interrelationships considered when planning a business.

Generally speaking, not all observations should be classified as within the theoretical economics domain only because an attempt has been made to structure them, whether we talk about single categories or entire studies (such as, for example, the Modigliani–Miller theorem, or the job-market signalling model by Michael Spence). Theoretical economics is too rigid to explain analytical relationships and the latter do not have the proper depth of generalisations, including alleged ones. Any fine analytics is here to stay. For example, the theory of Coase, despite its errors, will remain part of theoretical economics. More precisely, it will remain part of economics history, since "transaction costs" (as well as "marginal cost") are purely products of the mind. At the same time, opportunity cost has a right to exist (unlike "transaction" and "marginal" costs, it cannot be reduced to some category that more accurately describes economic events, i.e. opportunity cost has intrinsic, albeit imaginary, robustness) but only in the world of analytics.

FAQ: Transition to the PCM.

As we have noted already, the transition to the PCM cannot be described theoretically. We had an opportunity to get this partially confirmed earlier in this chapter when we were modelling the impact on interest rates of the transfer of the payment system out of commercial banks. As a result, this is how the following reasoning should be treated. The work of theoreticians is most needed at the stage of studying the final state of a system. With the onset of actual design work, the bulk of it will be handled by practitioners such as lawyers, mathematicians, programmers, analysts, bankers and other finance professionals. I presume they will be assigned to certain sectors (the central bank, commercial banks, currency exchange, etc.) with a central management hub facilitating the information exchange and coordination (including contacts with the specialists from other countries engaged in similar work). Theoreticians may still be required to evaluate the results in progress and how they correspond to the transition strategy.

The level of qualification of the specialists, especially those in top management, is hard to overestimate. Ideally, these people should be decisively "modern", well versed in both finance and details of software programming. The technological difficulty of modelling our new formation will be largely determined by the problems of creating a national payment system and the "electronic errand boy". This will take both time and money. To estimate the transition timeframe, one needs to put effort into creating these two pillars as guidance.

However, the main burden will fall on the head of state, or government, and the whole political advisory team, given the revolutionary character of the situation, the degree of responsibility to fellow citizens and the clearly complicated work that lies ahead on the foreign policy front.

In this thesis, we'll also review any possible actions by the state in a broad sense (including the central bank), say, one year after the unified payment system is created (the beginning of the transition proper). We'll call the moment when this (arbitrary) one-year period ends the "transition".

Unless the top political brass wants to see that the preliminary conclusions have been worked out by a team of scientists and specialists, and only then give the green light to the transition, it does not make much sense to prepare it "under wraps". Besides, isolationism will be harmful for the technology developers, in any case. Also, understanding the need for the transition by society may turn out to be a decisive factor, given the complexity of transformations and the fact that revolutions can hardly be kind to everyone. As a result, the national economy will become crucially better, while the real economy will be the largest beneficiary of the transition to our PCM model. As for private creditors, portfolio investors and financial speculators,[188] they would have to look for new jobs and

[188] There is not much to say about commodity exchanges from our theoretical logic perspective. There will be no more trading of securities with a credit component, and all international trading – for instance, in metals – will be facilitated by the

think about how to save their investments. Not everyone will be lucky there.

Even if the top political management decides on a shroud of secrecy, it would be technically possible only for the first step, namely transferring the current accounts of bank clients into the unified payment system at the central bank. As we have noted already, from a technological standpoint this is a complex manoeuvre, but as soon as it is over, the real sector of the economy as a whole won't be threatened any further,[189] as I will try to demonstrate over the course of the following reasoning. Even if some significant property redistribution takes place over the course of the transition, as typically happens with a change in economic models, the payment system will be saved from under the wreckage of those commercial banks that have not been conservative enough in their activities. The transition can be characterised by varied levels of impact, ranging from the total destruction of unnecessary costs by the basic cost regulators, with a full understanding that the real economy is shielded, to the "soft" incorporation of all property owners into the new system. The only caveat is that any "softness" also has limits.

To give enough time to act for those property owners with tight connections to the old financial system, they will be warned that after the transition, claims by illegitimate creditors won't be enforceable, with few exceptions. Any public joint-stock companies will be transformed to the private joint-stock model. Given that only domestic commercial banks can be legitimate creditors in the new formation, it is easy to predict a price drop for credit assets belonging to any entities that are not licensed domestic banks. After the transition, any liabilities owed to commercial banks will be treated by law as ordinary bank credits, regardless of their origin. The magnitude of the price drop will be deeper if these liabilities are not backed up by some physical collateral. With such a profound event as a change of the financial system itself, any collateral made up from assets intrinsic to this financial system can be very unreliable. On the other hand, having made the first step (the transition assumes redistribution and loss of property by the creditors, including those caused by borrowers

---

"electronic errand boy" and with mandatory shipment to the buyer's country using a letter of credit. We can guess that trading in precious metals will still be tightly controlled by the government (especially during the transition period) and that legitimate trading in gold bullion certificates will take place.

[189] Here, as elsewhere in this study, I am leaving out any talk about corruption. I consider it obvious that, first, theoretical economics is not intended to solve this issue and, second, weak state discipline and revolution are not compatible.

going into bankruptcy), the state should adhere to the next one (handover of the collateral to creditors, including foreign ones). The state should create legal mechanisms for this collateral settlement. Given the extraordinary nature of this situation, those mechanisms should be highly efficient to allow for the quick resolution of any problems arising. For instance, debt obligations may be settled through a partial secession of ownership rights by the borrowers (by converting corporate bonds into equity).

At the same time, the state should understand that a "soft transition" scenario is fraught with peril for the borrowers from both the banking and real sectors of the economy, due to a potentially lengthy and expensive litigation with an uncertain outcome. The state legislature should proactively plan for the most typical scenarios. For example, it may declare null and void any force majeure clauses of loan contracts where creditors have the right to demand an immediate and unconditional return of the borrowed funds.

Let's sum it up. While leaving some decision-making time for illegitimate creditors and while creating the legal mechanisms to keep borrowers responsible for their liabilities, the state should make it known that it will not allow any illegitimate credit operations ("in a broad sense") under the new formation. Either some of these operations are deemed legitimate at the time of transition, or they become illegitimate then. Any possible exceptions need to be clearly described and registered, with each individual loan contract and securities[190] issue cancelled in due course.

With the credit "monopoly" enjoyed by commercial banks under the new system, one can foresee a wave of new bank registrations immediately before and after the transition. I would be hard pressed to predict the reaction of the central bank, but most likely these will be treated

[190] For instance, I don't think that all corporate bonds will become illegitimate at once with the transition. It is easy to assume that immediately after the transition is announced, the issuance of any new bonds will be prohibited. However, it is possible that, for instance, some short-term bonds issued before the transition can "live on" to maturity. That is, the state generally will not practice a hard approach to the securities issued by firms in the real economy, provided it feels sure that this policy does not threaten to resuscitate the old securities market. At the same time, trade credits may be extended only for some simple leasing contracts. There should be ample time between the onset of the transition and the transition proper to cancel, for instance, regular contracts for goods' procurement by retail chains, in case they include deferred payment clauses.

favourably, given the problems likely to be faced by many of the existing banks. The more commercial banks that are ready to take on the functions of a legitimate creditor in the existing credit contracts, the softer the transition period will be. The new legal mechanism may provide for the easier transfer of creditor functions to another entity, while the borrower's consent for such a transfer may not be required, in cases where there are no changes in the payment schedule or other conditions.

All the above spells potential losses for foreign creditors of any kind, so it is important that they have enough time to evaluate this situation. The national orientation of all market participants in the new system must be considered. Under the mature PCM, this will mean that any operations with offshore businesses will become illegitimate. A business may exist either here or there, but not in two countries at the same time.

It is important to eliminate any ambiguities in the national affiliation of a borrower, so that all holders of its debt understand their possible actions. Other nations must be given a warning that upon the transition, all creditor claims of their residents, commercial banks and firms to legal entities of this country will become null and void unless they register their loan contracts at the designated national registry (for instance, one subordinated to the central bank). These contracts will become the systemic exceptions and, as such, they should be treated as a closely defined set, subject to centralised control. They are unlikely to include loan contracts originating after the transition starts, as this time will likely mark the watershed of legitimacy.[191]

The registration of any complex contracts, besides those with a clearly defined schedule of payments, may trigger a registrar's requirement to simplify the contract terms. For example, I would not recommend registering contracts that assume a floating interest rate depending on exchange rates, due to the possible catastrophic consequences for one of the parties. In this case, either (a) both the creditor and the borrower would close the deal before the transition, or (b) their contractual obligations would be considered void after the transition.

---

[191] A common consideration for the transition is as follows. The more precisely that government regulators work to exclude backdated contracts, the fewer problems will be faced by law-abiding firms, commercial banks and the state itself under the new formation. Possibly, this provision could be included as a separate line item, accompanied by measures intended to decrease the probability of circumventing the law, making investigation effective and punishment (including for the accomplices among bureaucrats) impressive.

Let's note the importance of government's responsibility for its own debts, as differences among the nations may cause radical differences in the transition architecture.

It pays to begin at the end – that is, from a possible government default. This is not critical for the Russian government, for example, but it practically cannot be avoided by the US or possibly the euro area nations if the latter get stuck in the seemingly attractive business of issuing a global currency. Even if the US does not formally refuse to honour its Treasuries liabilities and simply prints more dollars to pay the debts, and thus step over the traditional ways of financing the budget deficit, no current bond holders would get back funds comparable in their purchasing power to the money they had initially invested into the US debt. The default will still happen, albeit in a hidden form. I would boldly recommend that the US, first, does not delay the transition and, second, chooses to openly recognise this default de jure as opposed to the hidden default. As we are going to see shortly, neither option is beneficial to Russia, unlike the alternative option when my country chooses to make the leap forward and start the transition, coordinating its actions with its allies (here, we are talking about a limited and temporary version of an economic alliance, as it is quite difficult to predict which countries will want to pioneer the transfer to the PCM model).

Once we have made the fundamental conclusion that we need this new formation, it is important to understand that the costs associated with the separation of the world economy into two systems will be higher compared with the scenario of a simultaneous transition to the PCM.

What follows are purely arithmetic considerations. The hidden default will exacerbate the dollar devaluation to a catastrophic state, hurting all people and businesses with dollar holdings. The alternative (de jure) default will affect only the US Treasuries holders. This alternative default will also cause major devaluation, though a temporary opposite effect is technically possible. It will stem from a spiked demand for dollars on the part of sellers of credit default swaps guaranteeing the US Treasuries. The devaluation will happen, as the default will mean the dollar abdicates as the global currency and goes back home. This devaluation, characterised by a sharp drop in the price of Treasuries (expressed in dollars and foreign currencies, to say nothing of gold) *will happen anyway once the US announces its transition plans*, since in the PCM, all national currencies need to be contained within their respective national economies. Thus, a default de jure will oddly support the dollar, as this will mean that a hidden default will not flood the economy *with even more dollars*.

There is a counterargument, assuming the US would only gradually mint additional dollars to cover the outstanding debt. However, this will happen anyway, so some structural considerations step in. I confess that I lack imagination about how this may happen under the PCM for many years in a row. All my current reasoning has the technical assumption that the US will declare a transition to the new formation. This default (it is safe to expect a chain of defaults in other countries on the heels of the US default) will destroy a serious portion of assets in the global financial system. From the PCM perspective, these assets represent entirely fictitious capital, so this "particular tail" would be cut off at once, to prevent its rotting.

Let's skip any attempts to present a realistic picture and assume a complete "apocalypse" for simplification: all surrogate assets of paper capitalism have been burned in the inferno of intersecting defaults, leaving only money and commodities. Had the payment system been transferred to the central bank (we assumed preparations for this could be done secretly), all the horrors of this "apocalypse" would be concentrated in three major areas. There will be a one-time drop in consumption due to the disruption of economic ties (it takes time to restore them), a change in the line-up of large property owners (largely banks) and a colourful description of it all in the mass media.

I once heard a remarkable phrase in a movie: often, people expire not because of a critical situation but rather from the shame of being in this situation. Once, I managed not to take to heart the bankruptcy of my own business but witnessed other people's reactions to the same. (Under my calm stance I mean only the realisation of the outcome, as the uncertainty period is quite nerve-wracking by itself.) In the current financial system, this phrase would not apply, as one can expect a prolonged crisis to follow the depreciation of assets, for the reasons we have described earlier. Conversely, in our transition scenario there will be an upward push shortly after a crash landing of the financial assets and global currencies.

I don't think this reasoning will inspire Americans to immediately escape from their consumer paradise. We are simply trying to understand how the situation may generally play out depending on the behaviour of major world economies. Now, let's go, in the most general terms, over the options for the development of the situation depending on the states involved. Let's consider a more favourable option for Russia, as an example, if my country, along with other peripheral capitalist countries, begins the transition and countries issuing global currencies do not support it. Strictly speaking, this option is valid even without Russia.

Let's see what happens in the market of obligations to foreign creditors in the case when Russia, either along with its allies or without them, launches a transition which is not supported by the US or the euro area. One essential difference of this option from the coordinated transition is that Russia will have a "cushion" to pay off its liabilities in the form of foreign reserves in the Central Bank. When announcing preparations for the transition, Russia may announce some options to use these reserves for the early repayment of foreign debts incurred earlier by its domestic companies of the real economy and banks. After the transition, Russia will not need these reserves anyway, neither in a legal nor economic sense, considering the inevitable fall in the value of the reserves after the partial transition of the world economy to the PCM.

Not all peripheral countries that opted for the transition will have such a financial "cushion". It is easy to assume that the bulk of expenses for developing technology to power the main elements of the new financial system will be bankrolled by the richest of these countries. Still, individual states having little or no reserves may experience problems with the repayment of their debts, either state or corporate.

In addition, if the US and the euro area countries actively participate in the transition or even initiate the transition proper, Russia would lose a significant part of the "cushion". There are two important considerations here. First, there is hardly a need to fear the transition of domestic companies and banks into the hands of foreign owners, because with the PCM, special attention will be given to the national identity of businesses and banks regardless of their owners' domicile. Second, these problems should not be exaggerated for the simple reason that after the announcement of the transition plans, debts denominated in global currencies will become easier to service due to the inevitable fall in the dollar and the euro. Of course, we can expect a significant fall only when a major part of the world economy gives up paper capitalism.

Let's return to the general scenario. In private joint-stock companies, it is important to prevent the occurrence of the hidden circulation of shares and, at the same time, stimulate the concentration of management in private owners. For example, stocks purchased after the transition may remain restricted for five years, and not only from selling but also from alienation by any alternative means, including the use of shares as collateral. We are talking here about the registered shares, i.e. those with specific, known ownership. There is no point in forbidding decisions, voted for by all shareholders, regarding selling part of the firm with a corresponding decrease in all shares or a decision made by management within its authority, to use the firm's property as collateral.

Generally speaking, firms with a large number of minority shareholders are difficult to manage (it is possible that certain states would opt to stimulate a decrease in the number of shareholders inherited from the old formation, sometime after the transition). In the medium to long term, such companies deprived of funds originating from the non-classical growth in asset prices (caused by trading shares in the secondary market) will start to lose to their competitors.

Under the PCM model, the "invisible hand" will naturally identify the competitive advantages of more agile private management and even demand this management, given the high level of competition. However, this is an evolutionary process. Besides, each industry may have its own technological criteria driving the level of integration. Therefore, two trends will develop. On one hand, small shareholders, having lost gambling opportunities at the exchange, can be expected to quit. On the other hand, purchasing an ownership share in a business will remain one of the legitimate ways to invest money. I cannot predict how exactly this will be reflected in stock prices during the *transition period.*

Also, I don't think that during the transition, one needs to have severe restrictions for investors fleeing to gold. It is better to have one big bubble that will deflate or even burst later, with varying degrees of abstraction from the real economy (these processes are relatively easy to control), than many local bubbles associated with the real sector that may form during the initial panic. These bubbles will come anyway, but a large golden "lightning rod", well understood by investors, will cushion the main blow.

Further, let's discuss one problem arising when the world economy is split into two parts, namely paper capitalism and PCM. We are talking here about foreign trade gateways between the two systems and considering the full functional readiness of the "electronic errand boy" at the moment of transition, for certainty.

The countries that have decided to switch to the PCM model will work on technology and prepare these gateways even before the transition begins.

The rest of the world will be gradually connected to the gateways after the transition is announced. Participation in the united international currency exchange (we call it "Planetary Exchange") will not be limited to the countries that have switched to the new financial system. Commercial banks of other countries (we will call them "third-party" in this thesis) may also participate in the currency exchange, with the understandable condition that they abide by all of its requirements. These requirements will, to some degree, consider the peculiarities of currency regulation in the capitalist countries. I suppose that moving funds to and from the Planetary Exchange by third-party commercial banks can be facilitated by their correspondent accounts with the national central bank (not a requirement of the new exchange), but this channel will have multi-currency capabilities (with the exception of the currencies of the PCM countries). As a result, the "electronic errand boy" will require third-party banks to sell (using a mandatory auction) only the PCM currencies on the exchange. I believe these commercial banks will themselves decide whether to trade other currencies.

The same one-way multi-currency trading will be allowed for clients from other countries. The bank issuing a card does not have to be a member of the new exchange (these things are not related). It is easy to assume that immediately after the announcement of the transition, the Planetary Exchange will try to negotiate an agreement with the existing payment systems, to be able to service third-party commercial banks. In other words, the channels used to move money by third-party banks participating in currency trading on the Planetary Exchange, and the channels used by the customers of the Planetary Exchange from third-party countries, should not be confused. Tourists coming to and returning from third-party countries will need to use bank cards. If third-party banknotes have electronic tags to be detected by customs, this will greatly simplify currency controls for all nations. It can be expected that such tags on the banknotes of the PCM countries will be included ahead of transition.

We can add that the installation and testing of the "electronic errand boy", including installation of terminals and connecting prospective participants from the PCM countries, will likely be carried out even before the announcement of the beginning of the transition, concurrently with the installation and testing of unified national payment systems. The time remaining before the transition will be mainly spent on legal coordination and connecting third-party commercial banks and legacy payment systems to the gateway. As the legal framework takes into account the peculiarities of the “liberal” currency regulations of third-party countries, this coordination will mainly be a notification. And if the connections of third-party gateway members are tested to the turnkey grade, it is quite possible to finish it within a year.

I do not think that the cost of channelling individual deals through the gateway will be materially different from the cost to settle trades within the new exchange, thanks to the “electronic errand boy” being capable of multi-currency deals (as we discussed earlier). It will cause a serious decrease in the need for global currencies required for use in foreign trade between third-party countries and the PCM countries. Many importers convert their national currency to a global currency solely in order to pay their foreign suppliers and with the help of the gateway it becomes optional. The attractiveness of global currencies will be further reduced by their depreciation at the declared onset of the transition (albeit depending on the share of the global economy opting for the transition).

Technically, that is it, since we went over the details of the new exchange earlier. Now, let’s talk about what can be provisionally called technical issues. During the transition period, all foreign currency held in the accounts of a single unified payment system must be either transferred outside the PCM countries or converted into national currencies. Generally speaking, these are two sides of the same coin, since those who buy foreign currency will also have to transfer it out of the country. There is also a third case leading to the same outcome. Foreign paper bills will also be ultimately sent overseas. Only (and here we are faced with the “curse” of paper money in the new formation) if someone neglects to sell foreign currency from their account in the new payment system in due course, the “electronic errand boy” can sell it automatically later (unconditionally). As for the foreign cash remaining on hand, it can be a basis for criminal prosecution and confiscation.

Nevertheless, it is difficult to predict in detail how the legal regulation of the “great exodus” will actually proceed. Here, we can point out one common moment that all three cases represent the precursors for devaluation of the dollar, demonstrating how this may happen in practice. Therefore, it is not worth impeding the natural processes by imposing restrictions on the withdrawal of foreign currency during the transition period. This is no longer capitalism and the number one rule is that foreign currency has no place in the national economy. If any limits are imposed, foreign currency owners, of whom most are residents of the country, may lose more than residents of other countries. The awkward character of such restrictions will not add to social stability, which will be needed in such a historically difficult moment. In addition, restrictions on the withdrawal of foreign currency during the transition period can push people to keep it illegally, bringing harm to the PCM economy.

Alternatively, the state can offer to buy foreign currency (with any currency holder free to opt in or out of this offer during the transition period), with a detailed plan for using it, for example, to create a "cushion" in the settlements with foreign lenders.

Having discussed some technical and procedural moments, we'll now touch upon the main problem from a theoretical point of view. The main complexity for the concurrent existence of two systems is the fundamental unpredictability of money issuance in the capitalist system, in contrast with the calculated issuance of money under the PCM. This latter issuance of money is clearly associated with the cornerstone theoretical definition, which is the price definition. Were the money issuance under capitalism orderly, as in the new system, the formations of other countries would not matter to the PCM countries. Such an issuance of money is almost impossible under capitalism due to the instability of its monetary system.[192] This financial "anarchy" seeping through the gateways will, in one way or another, affect the financial system of the PCM. That is why, from the entire global economic perspective, it is best to see the US and the euro area nations among the first to opt for the transition. Most likely, it will mean that nearly all the leading nations will simultaneously begin their transition to the new formation. At the same time, this transition should not be postponed due to some parties not being ready or due to the dramatised fears of having two parallel financial systems. These can be mitigated by erecting appropriate customs barriers to separate various industries of the two systems. Conversely, the introduction of an impervious "iron curtain", in my opinion, can stem only from some acute political confrontation.

Sure, there will be difficulties, but one should not fear any catastrophic shocks, provided that the transition has been planned thoughtfully. It is very important to set priority protection against systemic shocks for the real economy, albeit without sacrificing any key principles. For example, it is safe to assume the in-depth attention of the developers of a new credit

---

[192] If we set out to improve capitalism (for instance, to have orderly money issuance) by adopting the definition of price linked to property alienation, it will in turn theoretically "grow" the entire PCM model.

system to the forms of guarantee by third parties, designed here to replace prepayment as a form of loan (see thesis "*Letters of credit ...*" in Chapter 2). The main difficulty for the developers of these forms consists in assuring their transparency. If this requirement has not been met, the guarantee itself may morph into a loophole for sinking all good plans, including the intention to stop the practice of trade credit received by retailers.

FAQ: Where did the "demand for money" go?

Reasoning on this topic will overlap with the arguments outlined in the text box about the money supply (in the thesis "*Technological evolution: movement of investment money ...*" in Chapter 2).

The first point to note is that despite the importance of supply and demand, they are not amenable to *scientific* analysis. Actually, this is the main complexity of *theoretical* economics.

The second point is that I attach a different meaning to the concept of "demand for money" compared with the popular one. In economic literature, the demand for money is understood as the amount of money that people want to hold (a.k.a. liquidity preference). The subtle point of the situation is that in this case we are not talking about a deal but rather about a holding (despite the byzantine umbrella expression of "want to hold", with more lengthy reflections on the traditionally understood "demand for money" we inevitably find ourselves on the "holding" side). Yes, everything that people hold they once received as a result of certain deals but these are different things. From my point of view, this is not "demand for money" but one of the options for the analysis of *savings*.

Given the diversity and intertwining of the forms that "demand for money" takes in the existing financial system, we can say that in the PCM model, the "mystery" of extensive reasoning about the demand for money is largely dead. With a separation of the credit and payment systems, coupled with the direct issuance of money, the demand for money is localised using simple, yet strict, methods. Let's remember two points of such localisation, given the dual nature of money in transactions (money as a loan and money as a payment):

- The third basic cost regulator: demand for commercial banks' loans is followed (together with the offer of credit) by genuine market interest rates. Here, it pays to mention that the supply of loans is formed based on banks' demand for primary loans (and, of course, the corresponding supply), with the forming of the market interest rate for primary lending.

- The fourth basic cost regulator: demand for domestic money by foreigners on the inter-currency exchange, followed (together with offering money to be exchanged for a foreign currency) by the market cross-price.

FAQ: The quantity theory of money (and monetarism as its extension).

At times, people treated my work as the quantity theory of money and me as a monetarist. Of course, I am not offended by any "charges" of being close to this theory. The quantity theory of money has been a tangible contribution to the development of economics in general and my own thoughts in particular. However, upon closer inspection, a significant difference, up to a radical mismatch, is revealed.

For example, my approach to the velocity of money or to "money stock" is significantly or even fundamentally different from that of the adherents of this theory and, in fact, it immediately separates this study from the quantity theory of money.

I will not solely emphasise the details. For example, the fact that the value of "money stock" is higher under capitalism than under the PCM, or that the velocity of money is vastly different, can be confusing. Nevertheless, we'll remember one assumption that naturally fits this situation: the quantity theory of money and monetarism (no matter how accurate their conclusions appear) are historically limited to classical and paper capitalism, respectively.

By itself, the way that the quantity theory of money is formulated (the amount of money in circulation determines the purchasing power of money and the price of goods) is another example of tunnel vision. This is regardless of whether it is a crude quantity theory stating that prices grow in proportion to the increase in the amount of money ("money stock"), or rather a sophisticated quantity theory, including monetarism proper, stating that price growth lags behind "money stock" growth. Not that the originally promoted idea is wrong; it is just too narrow. A change in the amount of money will evidently affect prices, especially if we mean final prices, i.e. nominal prices, as we do in our book. However, the study of these changes is not fundamental enough. This may be difficult to see in the scope of both capitalist formations, but it is very noticeable when considering the PCM model.

In the thesis "*Inflation and deflation*" in Chapter 1, we said that of the four main types of inflation and deflation intrinsic to capitalism, only inflation from costs will remain at the system level in the new financial system. Meanwhile, the quantity theory of money does not explain the origin of inflation from costs. Let's recall the essence of this type of inflation. A decline in competitiveness of domestic goods without any meaningful change in the amount of money in the economy leads to a fall in the cross-price of the national currency, which in turn changes both the prices of goods and the price of money expressed in goods. The core postulate of the quantity theory of money has no explanation for this because it does not account for the influence of the prices of goods (expressed in foreign currencies) on the price of money (the cross-price of the national currency), which then affects both the price of money (the price of national currency expressed in goods) and the price of goods (expressed in domestic money).

First, while searching for the root of the problems, I put a logical emphasis on final prices (in particular, both inflation and deflation represent changes in final prices). Second, from my point of view, goods are more important than money. Under the PCM, initially it is the change in various commodity prices (including the change in prices affecting the cost of goods) that affects the price of money and the amount of it in circulation. This cause-and-effect link is exactly the *opposite* to the logic of the core thesis of the quantity theory of money in general and monetarism in particular. At any rate, they do not allow for ambiguity in what comes first.

At the same time, it is undeniable that under capitalism (mostly under paper capitalism) the amount of money in the economy changes quite chaotically and strongly depends on subjective decisions. These changes seriously affect the processes in the real economy. Therefore, formulating the question about the effect of the amount of money on the economy under capitalism was important enough to be considered by the proponents of the quantity theory. In the new financial system, the main problems investigated in the framework of this theory are solved by using calculated direct issuance of money. Let me remind you that this money issuance is calculated on the basis of growth of physical turnover and credit turnover, and its volume is easy to compute (taking into account the velocity of money, although its value in the new monetary system will be diminished due to a significant increase in the amount of money). As in the previous thesis on the demand for money, one can say that the "mystery" is dead.

Let's summarise it. The direct issuance of money makes recommendations provided by the quantity theory of money in general and monetarism in particular largely unnecessary, with the adoption of the PCM.[193]

We could have stopped right here. As a small detail, it may seem that there is a similarity in the calculated direct issuance of money with the recipe offered by Milton Friedman, the founder of monetarism, to increase "money stock" by 2 to 5 per cent a year. We can try the mental exercise of combining monetarism with the PCM and substitute "money stock" in Friedman's recipe for money. Then, we are very likely to face issuance deflation, which by its negative effect is very close to the chronic deflation that a transition to the pure gold standard would cause. This 2 to 5 per cent annual increase in the amount of money roughly corresponds to the GDP growth (for clarity of reasoning, we can even afford to leave out a completely natural assumption that due to the sharply reduced systemic costs in the new formation, the GDP would grow faster). It can be stated with reasonable confidence that the total increase in physical and credit turnover, which has real influence over the amount of money in the economy, is usually greater than the GDP increase (see the theses on physical turnover in Chapter 1).

We are talking about the required amount of new money so confidently because the definition of price used in this study is simple and practical. It determines the final prices that form the living tissue of the real economy, while that same "equilibrium price", with all due respect for the long history of its formulation, is quite a speculative category (as something that reflects "value").

It is even less likely that one can catch the similarity with monetarism when considering the role of the state. Monetarism assumes an active

[193] To some extent, this will affect other theories developed to describe the existing formation. It is simply inevitable regardless of how good those theories are and how accurately this research describes the PCM. This is the traditional way (for example, Keynes pointing out the shortcomings of the conventional classical school). Economic theories, to a degree, are tied to the formation that these theories may not directly shout "final and eternal" but imply it nevertheless. In turn, I see no reason to doubt the "eternal nature" of the PCM, barring major changes in the very species of *Homo sapiens*, its status as a property owner or its habitat (the planet Earth).

monetary policy by the state, which is quite understandable in the existing formation, i.e. paper capitalism. In the new financial system, after the third and fourth basic regulators are turned on at the designed capacity, the role of the state is sharply reduced. The state will be completely separated from lending (the third regulator) and will not be able to accumulate foreign currency (the fourth regulator). Even the stalwart supporters of reducing the role of the state might feel uneasy with these plans. This is how a person dreaming about being closer to nature while sitting in front of the computer may feel when someone suddenly opens a door with a rainforest behind it and says, "Go!" It makes no sense to "traditionally" fear a radical reduction of the role of the state. In the PCM, that "rainforest behind the closed door" will be under the comprehensive control of the "invisible hand of the market".

CONCLUSION

Here is a brief description of the new financial system – the financial system of the seventh economic formation.

Imagine that there are no traditional plastic bank cards with the imprinted name of a payment system (like Visa or Mastercard) or the name of the commercial bank that issued the card. In the whole of country N (inside its customs borders), there is only one legally accepted card type with the imprint of "Central Bank N".[194] The payment system is owned by the central bank, which maintains payment accounts for all economic agents, including individuals and corporations (as well as commercial banks) without discrimination.

In the new system, we simultaneously move the payment system out of commercial banks and the credit system out of the central bank (and the state, in a broad sense). The central bank (unless there is a specially designated regulator) continues to exercise control over the lending activities of the commercial banks, but at the same time, it is not engaged in lending. The latter is the exclusive domain of private domestic commercial banks, while the issuance income goes to the state budget. Let's recall the link to the payment system: whenever a bank borrows money (as with any other loans, these must be accounted exclusively as term deposits), these funds are reflected, as they are now, in a correspondent account with the central bank (provided that the bank did not keep these loan proceeds in cash). Every time the commercial bank lends money in the new system, it immediately transfers these funds from its current account at the central bank to the borrower's current account at the central bank (or dispenses it as cash).

The world monetary system resembles a daisy, where the petals (i.e. independent national monetary systems) converge at the common

[194] This is simplified for easier understanding. For example, foreign tourists will still use their cards issued by their nation's central bank, but the funds they use to pay using their card at the moment will still be located at the Central Bank N. See Chapter 3 for details.

exterritorial centre. While the petals are quite visible as their shape coincides with the customs border of each nation, the centre is largely a virtual world. All currency traders of the world (licensed banks) work exclusively within this centre, while currency exchange is facilitated by the "electronic errand boy" of this Planetary Exchange. This system services currency exchange operations with or without the participation of the licensed banks, but these operations must be initiated exclusively by the account owners whose accounts are located outside the exchange. All the currencies in the world are equal and independent, and no currency is legal tender outside its national borders. All businesses in the world are registered in their respective countries, and all their payments and receipts can only use the respective national currency. While travelling abroad, an individual can only use the currency of the country where they travel to. Upon leaving this country, any remaining money is automatically converted into the national currency of the country that the traveller has chosen for their residence. All these exchange operations are also facilitated by the "electronic errand boy".

Now, let's try to picture what will be different from the current financial system.

The monetary base will grow, while such a vague category as "money stock" will lose its importance. This will result in a sharp increase in the money available in the national economy, with a corresponding drop in velocity (we are talking only about the velocity within the national economy, as the situation will not radically change for businesses, commercial banks or individuals). We did not aim to slow down the money circulation but tried to eliminate the credit chains ("credit money") arising under paper capitalism from the high velocity of money in the banking payment system. There will be no issues arising from slowing down the circulation of money in the computers of the central bank.

Concurrently, we get away from an artificially low interest rate caused by the low primary lending rate, as commercial banks use payment system funds for lending. Along with eliminating the credit chains, it will serve as a pronounced crisis deterrent, lowering the chances of a currency depreciation crisis and contributing to the prevention of a deflation crisis.

Note the substantial increase in money issuance due to the large, new monetary base. Since the money issuance proceeds are managed by the government (its volume is calculated by the central bank), it allows for either lowering of taxes or increasing capital investment in infrastructure projects. The direct nature of money issuance in the new system is also beneficial. New money enters the market economy, i.e. banks and businesses, “from below” (from depositors and buyers) and not “from above” (from the government through the banks) as in the existing formation. Households “voting with their purses” appears to be a more convincing market factor, which is directly related to the mitigation of economic distortions (overproduction) at critical turns and to the self-reliance of market competition in general.

Unlike under paper capitalism, with direct issuance new money from the government directly enters the economy without any credit load (obligations). This represents an important distinction between the capitalist economy and the classical liberal economy of the Perfectly Competitive Market. On one hand, we are finally giving a wholesome market character to the interest rate. As a result, we can rely on it (meaning the anti-crisis potential and precision of market-driven competition in general). On the other hand, we take away the broad government’s ability to enter credit relationships with any other player and thus hedging it (or more precisely, us) from unnecessary losses. The credit business is no less complicated than any other. In every formation, credit deals by the government were treated as a given, even more so in the existing formation, where everyone can lend to everyone else. Now, we have a chance to get rid of these government credit deals. Instead, the government can use money issuance, customs duties, taxes, rent and gold reserves for a rainy day, plus a separate line item for the retirement funds of people who opted to trust the government with these funds. Also, the government can regulate public expenses, with the government’s greater independence from legislature (this is inevitable with calculated money issuance requiring a quick reaction). All this will exist on the background of a much simpler economic system, due to its well-developed mechanisms of market self-regulation and, therefore, ease of control by the broad government. It is better to see the government facing some bumps while getting used to the new formation than forever tolerate the bureaucratic fascination with credit operations.

The new formation will definitely not be the most comfortable place for very large firms that now dominate most industries due to the particular nature of the financial system that allows these firms to bypass the market interest rate and (or) dilute the responsibility for prudent use of financial resources. Once that state, foreign and trade credit is prohibited, and especially after the circulation of commodity and credit surrogates (securities with a credit component) is outlawed, large firms will start losing to better managed private competitors, provided that either vertical or horizontal integration does not give them some purely technological advantages. In some sectors, this effect will be immediate, and in others it may take time and may not be outright visible. But at any rate, the scientific and technological progress in the entire national economy will be gravitating towards more compact businesses.

By the way, this is the key reason to abandon socialism. The ever-increasing specialisation in scientific research requires an equally consistent specialisation in technological progress. The latter, unlike fundamental research, should be happening within private business, as it is mandatory to be checked for feasibility by the real-world costs. As a result, a deeply specialised economy requires taking timely and *responsible* decisions *locally*, translating this into the need for private management due to the inefficiency of central planning. This requirement only becomes stronger over time. All this does not denigrate the achievements of the Soviet economy and especially those purposeful Bolshevik efforts at a time when the pace of the natural economic development of Russia was dangerously slow. However, the times have since changed. Nowadays, the "left-wing march" is becoming a very dangerous path for the economic development of Russia.

The institution of securities with a credit component (including derivatives) – which becomes obsolete in the PCM – only seems to be contemporary now because of computer technologies. The latter cardinally improve managing money and *money surrogates* by accelerating both their velocity and the analysis of fast-changing situations for decision-making. Liquidation of the most speculative trading (exchange trading of strategic commodities will remain, albeit without the use of credit leverage) will help stabilise the financial system and the entire world economy. Without this liquidation, it is impossible to avoid global crises. Also, after stopping the issuance and circulation of securities with a credit component, the world economy will trim excessive costs arising from securities trading income that is channelled by its recipients to the consumption of goods and services. In the existing model, obtaining this income appears to be a complex system of relationships between individuals, commercial banks and the state. It can be argued to what extent these relationships are valuable for paper capitalism, but the PCM will do without them. Current beneficiaries of securities-related income will have to focus on the economic activities that will be in demand under the new formation.

Generally, the removal of excessive costs by applying the full force of basic cost regulators is the foundation of the transition to the PCM. Over the course of this study, we focused on the numerous potential cost savings that together will contribute to meaningful economic growth. The latter means, among other things, accelerated consumption, so it may seem odd that a decrease in costs (excessive consumption) is the underlying reason for growth. This paradox is easy to decipher if we start our reasoning by removing unnecessary work. To illustrate it, imagine some workers digging a hole in the ground while others throw dirt back into this hole. The net result is zero, but everyone gets paid (and therefore, their share of the economic benefits). Now, project this onto the complex system of the world economy and dress some workers in expensive suits. It is important that the lack of purpose and harmful effects of this work can be revealed *only* under a more advanced economic model. When this model is implemented, everyone (including the redundant workers themselves) can understand that, for the same compensation, workers should be engaged in some other new activities and these should bring about additional goods.

The refusal to emphasise a stimulation of consumption, which contributes to the accelerated economic development (with respective growth in consumption), may seem an extension of this same imaginary paradox. The emphasis on stimulating consumption, which may seem a borderline madness on a planet with limited resources, seems to be quite rational under paper capitalism (in the "wonderland" countries and at times in some other developed nations). However, if this emphasis seems to be rational in one particular model, this merely indicates the irrationality of the model.

Dropping the priority of consumption is organically linked to the elimination of the global currency institution once the transition to the "daisy" exchange is completed. An important result of this process will be the end of global deflationary crises. Local deflation is possible under the PCM only in rare situations, like government blunders or a combination of big events (say, climate or military problems). Another rare scenario is nations with an "island mentality" (showing traditionally weak demand for imported goods, which in turn limits market depreciation of currency). As for a global deflationary crisis, I cannot imagine any valid reason for it, barring perhaps some apocalyptic scenarios with civilisation thrown back.

Dropping the institution of global currencies under the PCM will mitigate the most striking differences between the nations, not only in the level of consumption but also in the interest rates and traditional inflation (money depreciation relative to goods). The Dutch disease in its current stagflation mode will disappear. Countries with a high share of exports will still face problems caused by the appreciation of their national currencies, while countries exporting raw materials will experience some "reduced GDP monetisation" (money issuance will be lower) compared with the economies exporting manufactured goods. However, mandatory inflation will disappear if money issuance calculations are performed correctly.

Another important result of the transition to the "daisy" exchange will be the fully fledged fourth basic cost regulator, the cross-price. It puts the final touches on the market self-regulation of both national economies and the world economy. Here, we mean, first of all, a mechanism for *gradual* (compared with the situation as it is today) but effective cost (inflation *from* costs) pruning by currency depreciation. In addition, states are taken out of the business of currency trading. This becomes possible not only thanks to the way the "daisy" is set up but also to the measures that we take to make the third basic cost regulator (the interest rate) work to its full potential.

A few final words.

The monetary system of our Perfectly Competitive Market will be nearly perfect indeed. It is simple and inexpensive to maintain. It is rich and generous, as there is a lot of full-bodied money at the onset and money issuance is generous, too. It is stable and caring, as it will not provoke crises but prevent them. It is democratic due to its technological foundation, and it will not separate nations into "exclusive" and second class. It is also democratic due to its simplicity. If today's financial system is well understood only by Mr. Nobody, the future system will be easy to learn by anybody who has a little spare time.

The system is humane due to its simplicity. As we discussed in the thesis about Rough History, it seems that, thanks to the everlasting curiosity of nerds, future developments will not be limited to small unfortunate happenings like cryptocurrencies. Very soon, humankind will face an existential fight against AI creations and will need to preserve its independence. This independence will be more assured if humankind does not need AI to make its monetary system work. Unlike the present massive and murky financial system, where some 80 per cent of decisions in its trading sector are already being made by robots, people will only need "good old computers" to operate the PCM financial system. As a result, the task will taper to making an efficient barrier with an easily visible inscription: “Thank you, we better manage it ourselves”.

GLOSSARY

basic cost regulators The prices formed by the exchange of money as payment for basic types of property (except for goods): wages, rent, interest rate, cross-price. To simplify the text, the definition is used in this non-rigorous way (this becomes more visible when pointing out that the price of credit is the interest, not the interest rate). Strictly speaking, basic cost regulators are per unit values of these prices, namely the price of leasing one worker for a unit of time, the price of leasing one square unit of land for a unit of time, the price of borrowing one unit of money for a unit of time, and the price of selling one unit of money when buying foreign currency.

basic deals Purchase and sale deals (deals with bilateral property alienation, typical for commodities and services), C↔M, and three leasing deals (deals with unilateral property alienation – money as payment – typical for basic resources), P←M, L←M and M_C←M.

basic resources of the national economy Outside of deals, these are people, land and money that is not being used as payment; in the deals, these are people, land and money as credit. The strict version of this definition is valid solely for the PCM. At present, money can be used as a resource outside the national economy, as well. In addition, various types of securities are widely used.

basic types of property Goods (commodities in deals), people, land and money.

capital A term with no theoretical need after breaking down property into the four basic types.

capitalism A misfit but established term. In the Rough History, capitalism was the time of the industrial revolution, when engineering achievements made many, if not all, elements of the economy literally go faster. From a theoretical perspective, capitalism is an epoch of the accelerated development of credit relationships, which not only allowed entrepreneurs to keep up with the industrial revolution but in turn also stimulated engineers' activities for accelerating operations and increasing their volume. With the invention of computers, "credit acceleration" of the economy became, first and foremost, an accelerated development of the financial sector, which is supported by people working in the real economy. The term *capitalism* itself does not reflect any of these features. *Credit formation* (based either on the gold standard or the centralised issuance of paper money) would likely be a better term. For simplicity, it is possible to accentuate gold capitalism as a "credit-industrial formation", with the understanding that it is rather equivocal: some may be putting emphasis on the word "industrial" (either willingly or by virtue of misunderstanding) than a mere indication of the onset of the industrial revolution. Other variations are possible as well, depending on the desired degree of brevity.

category A generalised notion (a basic category is an extremely important generalised notion). I was taught that category is a more general notion (with regards to economics, the accent was on relationships or processes understood in general). Thirty years later, I consider using the extremely general philosophical categories in economic science as a doubtful luxury. Theoretical economics, due to particularities of the study subject (the practical economy), give us an opportunity to rely on categories that assume a generalised but uniform, and even identical, understanding by experimentation (see *materialism of categories*).

central bank Unlike commercial banks, the shift of accents in the central bank's activities while transitioning to the Perfectly Competitive Market will be towards the decrease of credit functions (up to the function of a non-market regulator). As for carrying out monetary functions (in the PCM financial system, monetary and credit policy won't be synonyms any more), on one hand, they will visibly shrink with regard to money issuance, and on the other, they will greatly increase due to the new functional operator of the unified payment system. See *credit and payment system*.

classical economy (a.k.a. liberal economy, a.k.a. Perfectly Competitive Market economy) The economy based on market self-regulation with the minimal possible state participation. Our use of this term differs from the traditional one, where the term "classical" is related not to the type of practical economy organisation, but to the early period (late 18th century to the early 19th century) of theoretical economics development, influenced by Adam Smith's understanding of the liberal economy based on the labour theory of value.

commercial banks The financial institutions that will undergo the most profound changes in the transition to the PCM. These changes can be briefly described as the transformation of a credit and payment institution into a strictly credit one. See also: c*entral bank* and *credit and payment system.*

costs Money-measured expenses calculated for the payments actually made. In the end, costs represent human consumption (all the money belongs to the people). It is the most important and complex category for both the theoretical and practical economies.

credit issuance of money Credits issued by the central bank within the reverse issuance of money under paper capitalism.

credit and payment system Under the PCM, this system will be divided into two credit and payment systems. The circulation of money as credit will be a domain for the private domestic banks, which will enjoy an exclusive right to lend money, while the central bank will retain its control functions. The circulation of money as payment will take place in the scope of the unified payment system, which will be managed exclusively by the central bank and used by commercial banks without discrimination. Given the direction and depth of these transformations, we use the "separation of the systems" notion in this book, though from a technical perspective, a complete separation will not happen, as the non-cash circulation of money as credit will take place in the scope of the payment system.

cross-price The price of a currency expressed in the currency of another country. The term does not fundamentally differ from cross-rate, yet it is more accurate from a theoretical point of view. "Price" is the essence of the term, without an overt or hidden implication that it is a currency rate relative to one of the elite currencies. For example, in the PCM, all currencies are equal.

daisy A virtual representation, reflecting the relationship between the national currencies under the PCM. It consists of peer-national "petals" with an exchange ("electronic errand boy") at the centre. The circulation of foreign currency inside the customs borders of any country is prohibited, while international payments are settled by the exchange.

deal Exchange. Not all agreements are deals in the strict sense – for instance, cartel agreements regarding common price policies between the firms (we take an agreement example most closely matching prices that are formed in deals). These agreements may be implicit or explicit, and they may have meaning for other firms, state regulators or analytics, but they are beyond the scope of a theoretical study (as there is no unit of measure or any rigorous foundation to classify these). Also, there is no apparent interest in studying these agreements (oral or written, say, in letters of intent). As they are essentially preparatory stages for deals, these agreements are not always kept and their final versions are reflected in the deals.

deflation from costs The decrease in costs, which is intrinsic to both capitalist systems, either in the national or world economy. It has a long-term character due to the absence of the devaluation of gold (under gold capitalism) or global currencies (under paper capitalism).

direct issuance of money Money issuance with a more natural entrance into a market economy. The state injects new money into the economy without any credit liabilities for recipients. New money enters the firms from the buyers (households or state infrastructure companies) and the commercial banks from depositors (mainly households), with a market interest rate for primary lending. This type of money issuance may lead to inflation; therefore, our PCM model provides for the calculated direct issuance of money (calculations of changes in physical turnover and indicators of credit turnover, based on money price definition). This lowers the probability, but does not guarantee the absence, of national inflationary (devaluation) crises.

Dutch disease The stagflation of exporter nations, where national currencies do not happen to be the global currencies. It is substantially more visible in countries with low levels of physical turnover (dominance of raw material exports). This is the only kind of stagflation that we address in the book.

economy (same as ***practical economy***) Reproduction of consumable property, sufficient for the expanded reproduction of the human population. It includes supplemental sectors (first and foremost, banks). From the outside, the economy looks like the movement of property.

electronic errand boy Multi-currency exchange under the PCM, allowing the global economy to function without any dominant (world) currencies and forming a robust fourth basic cost regulator (cross-price).

feudalism (serfdom) The name adopted in this book to denote the early stage of the landowning formation, the hallmark of which was the combination of (a) the full right of large owners to land (with the rent in favour of the state either absent or having a nominal character) and (b) personal or land dependence of residents on the owner of the land as remnants of the slave-owning formation.

final cost regulator Negative profit of a managing owner.

firms The real sector of the economy, immediately engaged in producing goods and services. Strictly speaking, it includes both the microeconomy and some branches of macroeconomy, though in this book it is used implicitly as a synonym for microeconomy. Our main theoretical relationships by default are studied using the examples of private (non-governmental) firms and banks operating in the competitive market.

formation One of the seven main stages of the *Homo sapiens* civilisation's economic development: primitive formation, slave ownership, landowning, classical (gold) capitalism, "paper" capitalism, socialism, Perfectly Competitive Market (PCM).

inflation Money depreciation relative to property or foreign currencies.

inflation from costs The depreciation of money (rapid devaluation of currency with subsequent slow, partial depreciation relative to goods), due to high costs for domestic companies and the corresponding decrease in competitiveness of domestic goods.

"invisible hand of the market" (free interpretation of the well-known phrase) Interaction between supply and demand, with cost regulators (final and basic) being a "visible" component of it.

labour coordination costs The costs arising from increased management complexity following the expansion of a firm (bank, organisation).

latifundism Shorthand for the late stage of a landowning formation based on the full right of large-scale owners to predominantly agricultural land (with the rent in favour of the state either absent or having a nominal character) without remnants of the slave-owning formation which were inherent in *feudalism (serfdom)*. The term is conditional due to the vague nature of the landowning formation in general and the term "latifundium" in particular. Large latifundia existed in ancient Rome and still exist elsewhere.

macroeconomy All deals in the national economy (not including barter deals where money is not used). Macroeconomic specifics of some sectors – banks, transportation (including storage services) and communications – are not accentuated in the book, though it is not difficult to notice their particular features. The mainstream, traditional meaning of "macroeconomics" (as the name of a science or a scientific branch) is not used in this book. The difference between our definition and the second traditional meaning of "macroeconomics" (close to the "national economy" term) is not accentuated in the book for easier understanding.

managing owner A person who has the right (or delegates this right) to close deals on his own behalf or on behalf of his (fully or partially owned) legal entity, for the transfer (with alienation or not) of his property (or property owned by the legal entity). The managing owners are liable with their own property (in the scope clarified by the legal system) for the outcome of the management (direct or delegated to other owners and hired workers) of the property owned or leased by the legal entity. The "deal" is the keyword in this lengthy definition (there are no other phrases in the book with so many clarifying clauses in parentheses). This word is also assumed in the second part of the definition, as the measure of responsibility (the bottom line, either positive or negative) is being calculated as the net sum of all the deals. Another, no less important, clarification is that the first part of the definition (closing the deals) is wider. If in the second part (responsibility for management) we are talking only about legal entities, the first part also includes the individuals – either the managing owners who lease themselves out (their talent) or the retail buyers. The references to the future hired workers and retail buyers are the most important ones (other types are also possible; for example, those connected to the elements of the shadow economy, which do not always overlap with the activities of the legal entities), as both represent the most numerous cohorts of managing owners, showing up at the points of interaction of households with the rest of the economy. However, first, these interactions are localised – simply put, at either the beginning or end of the events we focus on (hired workers show up after a legal entity is formed and the advent of buyers points to the final stage in the main purpose of the economy, i.e. delivery of consumable property to households). Second, despite their mass character, these interactions are functionally weak. Most of this study (say, 99.9 per cent) takes place outside of the immediate closing of a hiring deal between two managing owners, with one of them shedding this role, in the scope of the legal entity's activity described here. As for the retail buyers, despite the importance of demand in general, their functional participation in deals is usually reduced to the "silent negotiations", i.e. expression of their attitude towards, for example, the price, through willingness, or lack thereof, to close the deal. After that, retailers may (or may not) correct the prices based on the reaction from potential buyers. So, whenever the term "managing owner" is used, we are talking about entrepreneurs (as a rule), or possibly about private bankers.

materialism of categories (solely an economic definition, see *category* and *property*) Consistent understanding of categories by people, either perceptive or numeric. The ability to be calculated is mandatory for basic categories (mandatory "in general", as it is possible to point out a concrete kind of property where only a theoretical calculation of its quantity is possible).

microeconomy All firms; one of the reproductive blocks. The traditional notion (as the name of a science or a scientific branch) is not used in this book. See *firms* and *macroeconomy.*

monetary base in the PCM financial system Cash and client deposits on current accounts at the central bank. Other parts of the monetary base in a broad sense – reserves, banks' deposits in the central bank and bonds issued by the central bank – will naturally become extinct in the new financial system. The term "base" will likely be replaced by some other term.

money Valuable numbers, used within the national economy as a means of circulation. It has a dual nature in deals, acting either as payment or as credit. Money is a basic type of property, distinguishing the economy of *Homo sapiens* from the economic activities of other inhabitants of the planet. This definition is given within the scope of the classical economy model, as in the general case, instead of the national economy, some territory should be indicated.

money stock in the PCM financial system A less significant indicator, which is likely to disappear as commercial banks' liabilities in the new financial system are separated from the payment system, so their grouping in one category with money will offend the ear.

national economy The economy of a country, including macroeconomy and the main reproductive blocks, i.e. microeconomy, households and government. It is best suited for theoretical studies targeting the macroeconomy.

physical turnover (expressed in monetary terms) The sum of purchase and sale deals for a certain period of time (for example, in a national economy). This category, traditionally underestimated from a theoretical perspective, is invaluable for calculating money issuance under the PCM (along with credit turnover indicators).

price (of property A) Property B that is transferred and alienated in exchange for A in this deal. In turn, the price of property B is property A, provided that the latter is transferred and alienated. Only the deals where property B is "money as payment" can be studied theoretically, thanks to the identically perceived price category (see *materialism of categories*).

property Everything that belongs to *Homo sapiens*, privately or collectively (by default).

property alienation (an act of *voluntary* alienation of someone's *own* property) A rational action by a man, distinguishing the economy of *Homo sapiens* from the economic activities of other inhabitants of the planet. It is a mandatory stage leading to deals, prices and later, money.

property increment (1) The amount of property increment; (2) (the act of increasing one's *own* property) human actions based on perceptive instincts, the main ones being self-preservation and procreation, intrinsic to all inhabitants of the planet. Perceptual instincts are the main economic motivators. At the same time, they are the primary reason for excessive costs in general and they are especially pronounced during times preceding crises.

reverse issuance of money The money issuance of reverse rotation (when "new in a broad sense" money is entering the commercial banks and firms "from above"). Under paper capitalism, it comprises the credit issuance of new money by the central bank and the creation of credit chains by commercial banks (creation of "credit money"). The reverse issuance of money may lead to deflation and, due to the existence of global currencies, to global deflation crises, at the same time without providing a remedy for local devaluation crises.

service The lease of goods (means of production) in the scope of a purchase and sale deal, C↔M, in the microeconomy, macroeconomy, and financial and state-owned firms. It is a result of mixing the lease (hiring) of people with the purchase and sale of goods (their alienation, including the means of production's wear and tear). With technological evolution, the accent is shifting from the first deal to the second one.

stagflation The depreciation of money relative to goods without due depreciation of the national currency against foreign currencies.

systemic costs The same as macroeconomic or national costs. They split into management (analytical) and theoretical costs. Among the latter, we distinguish the formational costs (those accentuated in this study) from the crisis costs.

theoretical economics The science of studying the economy taken out of households. The only social science with a strong theoretical basis, i.e. internal fundamental relationships.

BIBLIOGRAPHY

1. Chang, Ha-Joon. *23 Things They Don't Tell You About Capitalism.* – London: Penguin Books, 2011. – 286 p.
2. Coase, Ronald H. *The Firm, the Market, and the Law.* – Chicago: The Univ. of Chicago Press, 1990. – 218 p.
3. Commons, John R. *Legal Foundations of Capitalism.* – New Brunswick, New Jersey: Transaction Publishers, 1995. – 394 p.
4. Fisher, Irving. "The Debt-Deflation Theory of Great Depressions". *Econometrica*, Vol. 1, No. 4 (Oct., 1933), pp. 337-357.
5. Friedman, Milton; Schwartz, Anna J. *A Monetary History of the United States, 1867–1960.* – Princeton: Princeton Univ. Press, 1971. – 860 p.
6. Huerta de Soto, Jesús. Money, Bank Credit, and Economic Cycles / Translated from the Spanish. – 3rd English ed. – Auburn, Alabama: Ludwig von Mises Institute, 2012. – 881 p.
7. Keynes, John Maynard. *The General Theory of Employment, Interest, and Money.* – London: Palgrave Macmillan, 2018. – 404 p.
8. Leontief, Wassily. *Essays in Economics: theories, theorizing, facts, and policies.* – New Brunswick, New Jersey and Oxford: Transaction Books, 1985. – 411 p.
9. Marshall, Alfred. *Principles of Economics.* – 8th ed. – Basingstoke: Palgrave Macmillan, 2013. – 731 p.
10. Marx, Karl. *Capital: A Critique of Political Economy* / Translated from the German. – London: Penguin Books, 1992. – Vol. 1-3.
11. McConnell, Campbell R.; Brue, Stanley L.; Flynn, Sean M. *Economics: Principles, Problems, and Policies.* – 21st. ed. – New York: McGraw-Hill Education, 2018. – 875 p.
12. Mishkin, Frederic S. *The Economics of Money, Banking, and Financial Markets.* – 11th ed.; Global ed. – Boston: Pearson, 2015. – 724 p.
13. Ricardo, David. *The Principles of Political Economy and Taxation.* – Mineola, New York: Dover Publications, 2004. – 320 p.
14. Roubini, Nouriel; Mihm, Stephen. *Crisis Economics: A Crash Course in the Future of Finance.* – Updated ed. – New York: Penguin Books, 2011. – 359 p.

15. Rothbard, Murray N. *A History of Money and Banking in the United States: the Colonial Era to World War II.* – Auburn, Alabama: Ludwig von Mises Institute, 2005. – 510 p.
16. Samuelson, Paul A.; Nordhaus, William D. *Economics*. – 19th ed. – Boston: McGraw-Hill/Irwin, 2010. – 715 p.
17. Smith, Adam. *An Inquiry into the Nature and Causes of the Wealth of Nations*: A selected edition. – Oxford: Oxford Univ. Press, 1998. – 618 p.
18. Голод, Игорь. *Новая финансовая система*. – Москва: Экономика, 2012. – 237 с. [Golod, Igor *The New Financial System* – Moscow, Economica, 2012. – 237 p.]
19. Голод, Игорь. *Строгая классическая экономика*. – Москва: Экономистъ, 2007. – 128 с. [Golod, Igor *The Rigorous Classical Economics* – Moscow, Economist, 2007. – 128 p.]
20. Капелюшников, Ростислав. *Теория трансакционных издержек* [Kapelyushnikov, Rostislav. *The Theory of Transaction Costs*]. URL: http://www.libertarium.ru/10623.

INDEX